KU-825-969

THE YEARBOOK

The Yearbook of
OBSTETRICS
and
GYNAECOLOGY

Volume 10

Edited by
David Sturdee, Karl Oláh, David Purdie and
Declan Keane

RCOG Press

ISBN 1 900364 72 7

Published by the **RCOG Press** at the
Royal College of Obstetricians and Gynaecologists
27 Sussex Place, Regent's Park
London NW1 4RG
Registered Charity No. 213280

RCOG Press Editor: Sophie Leighton
Cover designed by Geoffrey Wadsley
Typeset by FiSH Books, London

Contents

List of contributors

Asif Ahmed
Professor of Reproductive Physiology
Department of Reproductive and Vascular
Biology
S111 West Wing Extension
The Medical School
University of Birmingham
Edgbaston
Birmingham B15 2TT

John Bidmead MRCOG
Consultant Urogynaecologist
King's College Medical Hospital School
Denmark Hill
London SE5 8RX

Eve Blair
Research Officer to Western Australian
Cerebral Palsy Register
Centre for Child Health
TVW Telethon Institute for Child Health
PO Box 855
West Perth
Western Australia 6872

Jan Brockie
Menopause Nurse Specialist
Menopause Office
Women's Centre
John Radcliffe Hospital
Oxford OX3 9DU

Michael Brudenell FRCOG
The Barn
Station Road
Hever
Kent TN8 7ER

Linda Cardozo FRCOG
Professor of Urogynaecology
King's College Hospital
Denmark Hill
London SE5 9LS

Carl Chow MRCOG
Clinical Research Fellow
Women's Health Department
Jenner Building
Whittington Hospital
Highgate Hill
London N19 5NF

Amanda M Cotter MRCOG
University of Miami
Department of Obstetrics and Gynaecology
PO Box 016960
Miami
Florida 33101
USA

Sarah Creighton FRCOG
Consultant in Gynaecology
The Portland Hospital for Women and
Children
209 Great Portland Street
London W1N 6AH

Sean F Daly MRCOG
Master
The Coombe Women's Hospital
Dolphin's Barn
Dublin 8
Ireland

Neelima Deshpande MRCOG
Specialist Registrar
Department of Obstetrics and Gynaecology
Royal Wolverhampton Hospitals NHS Trust
Wolverhampton WV10 0QP

John Dewhurst FRCOG
21 Jacks Lane
Harefield
Middlesex UB9 6HE

James Dornan FRCOG
Reader
Department of Obstetrics and Gynaecology
Queen's University
Royal Maternity Hospital
Grosvenor Road
Belfast BT12 6BJ

James Drife FRCOG
Professor of Obstetrics and Gynaecology
Department of Obstetrics and Gynaecology
The General Infirmary at Leeds
Clarendon Wing
Belmont Grove
Leeds
Yorkshire LS2 9NS

Sean Duffy FRCOG
Consultant in Women's Services
Department of Obstetrics and Gynaecology
St James's University Hospital
Beckett Street
Leeds
Yorkshire LS9 7TF

Frank P Edenborough
Consultant in Respiratory Medicine
Northern General Hospital
Herries Road
Sheffield S5 7AU

Roy G Farquharson FRCOG
Consultant
Women's Hospital
Crown Street
Liverpool
Merseyside L8 7SS

Philippa Greenfield
Clinical Research Fellow
Department of Obstetrics and Gynaecology
Imperial College Faculty of Medicine
Northwick Park and St Mark's Hospitals
Watford Road
Harrow
Middlesex HA1 3UJ

Katie M Groom
Clinical Research Fellow
Institute of Reproductive and Developmental
Biology
Imperial College School of Medicine
Hammersmith Hospital Campus
London W12 0NN

John Guillebaud FRCOG
Medical Director
Margaret Pyke Centre
73 Charlotte Street
London W1P 1LB

Peter Hewett DRCOG
32 Hardy Avenue
Weymouth
Dorset DT4 0RJ

Paul Hilton FRCOG
Consultant Gynaecologist and Subspecialist in
Urogynaecology
Royal Victoria Infirmary
Leazes Wing
Queen Victoria Road
Newcastle-upon-Tyne
Tyne and Wear NE1 4LP

Kristina Hofberg
Specialist Registrar in Psychiatry
South Staffordshire Healthcare NHS Trust HQ
Corporation Street
Stafford ST16 3AG

Nigel Holland MRCOG
Consultant Obstetrician and Gynaecologist
Warrington Hospital
Lovely Lane
Warrington
Cheshire WA5 1QG

Graham R V Hughes
Consultant in Rheumatology
The Rayne Institute
St Thomas's Hospital
Lambeth Palace Road
London SE1 7EH

Rhona Hughes MRCOG
Consultant
Department of Obstetrics and Gynaecology
Edinburgh Royal Infirmary
1 Lauriston Place
Edinburgh EH3 9YW

Munther A Khamashta
Senior Lecturer/Consultant Physician
Lupus Unit
The Rayne Institute
St Thomas's Hospital
Lambeth Palace Road
London SE1 7EH

Charles R Kingsland MRCOG
Clinical Director
Reproductive Medicine Unit
Liverpool Women's Hospital
Crown Street
Liverpool
Merseyside L8 7SS

Ronald F Lamont FRCOG
Consultant in Obstetrics and Gynaecology
Department of Obstetrics and Gynaecology
Imperial College Faculty of Medicine
Northwick Park and St Mark's Hospitals
Watford Road
Harrow
Middlesex HA1 3UJ

Adrian Lower MRCOG
Consultant
St Bartholomew's Hospital
West Smithfield
London EC1A 7BE

William E Mackenzie FRCOG
Consultant in Obstetrics and Gynaecology
Princess of Wales Women's Unit
Birmingham Heartlands Hospital
Bordesley Green East
Birmingham B9 5SS

Paul McGurgan MRCOG
Specialist Registrar in Obstetrics and
Gynaecology
Merit Centre
Bradford Royal Infirmary
Duckworth Lane
Bradford BD9 6RJ

Albert Mifsud
Consultant in Microbiology
The Royal Hospitals NHS Trust
The Royal London Hospital
Whitechapel
London E1 1BB

Michael Milligan FRCOG
Director
Department of Obstetrics and Gynaecology
Kent and Canterbury Hospital
Ethelbert Road
Canterbury
Kent CT1 3NG

Catherine Nelson-Piercy
Consultant Obstetric Physician
Directorate Office (9th Floor)
New Guy's Home
Guy's Hospital
London SE1 9RT

Peter O' Donovan FRCOG
Consultant
Bradford Royal Infirmary
Duckworth Lane
Bradford BD9 6RJ

Julia Palmer MRCOG
Specialist Registrar
Solihull Hospital
Lode Lane
Solihull B91 2JL

Nicholas Panay MRCOG
Consultant
Fertility Centre
Queen Charlotte's Hospital
Du Cane Road
London W12 0HS

Sara Paterson-Brown MRCOG
Consultant
Department of Obstetrics and Gynaecology
Queen Charlotte's Hospital
Du Cane Road
London W12 0HS

Charles H Rodeck FRCOG
Consultant in Obstetrics and Gynaecology
Department of Obstetrics and Gynaecology
University College Hospitals NHS Trust
UCL Medical School
86–96 Chenies Mews
London WC1E 6HX

Guillermo Ruiz-Irastorza
Consultant Physician
Service of Internal Medicine
Hospital De Cruces
48905 Bizkaia
Spain

Michael Savvas FRCOG
King's College Hospital Medical School
Denmark Hill
London SE5 8RX

Albert Singer FRCOG
Consultant in Obstetrics and Gynaecology
The Whittington Hospital NHS Trust
St Mary's Wing
Highgate Hill
London N19 5NF

Fiona Stanley
Professor
Western Australian Research Institute for
Child Health
PO Box 855
West Perth WA 6872

Angus JM Thomson MRCOG
Specialist Registrar
Whiston Hospital
Warrington Road
Whiston
Preston
Merseyside L35 5DR

Joanne Topping MRCOG
Consultant
Liverpool Maternity Hospital
Oxford Street
Liverpool, Merseyside L7 8BW

Derek J Tuffnell FRCOG
Consultant Obstetrician and Gynaecologist
Bradford Royal Infirmary
Duckworth Lane
Bradford BD9 6RJ

An Vanthuyne
Research Sister
Department of Sexual Medicine
Hawthorn House
Heartlands Hospital
Bordesley Green East
Birmingham B9 5SS

Rajesh Varma MRCOG
Consultant in Obstetrics and Gynaecology
Department of Obstetrics and Gynaecology
Basildon Hospital
Nether Mayne
Basildon SS16 5NL

Andrew D Weeks MRCOG
Lecturer in Obstetrics
Department of Obstetrics and Gynaecology
Makerere University
PO Box 7072
Kampala
Uganda

David J White
Consultant in Genitourinary Medicine
Department of Sexual Medicine
Hawthorn House
Heartlands Hospital
Bordesley Green East
Birmingham B9 5SS

Nicholas J Wood MRCOG
Specialist Registrar in Obstetrics and
Gynaecology
Bradford Royal Infirmary
Duckworth Lane
Bradford BD9 6RJ

Foreword

This volume vividly demonstrates the extraordinary variety and broad expanse of our specialty of obstetrics and gynaecology, which keeps those of us directly involved constantly stimulated and must amaze our less fortunate colleagues in other medical disciplines. The 33 invited chapters, including six eponymous College lectures, range from before the start of life (with 'forgettable contraception') through to the aetiology of cerebral palsy. The end of pregnancy is covered by details of royal births; then there is the relatively new problem of tokophobia, with which our psychiatrist colleagues are providing useful support, and the topic of anti-oxytocic tocolytic agents, and – what is an increasing problem in antenatal clinics and, undoubtedly, a factor in the rising incidence of caesarean section – patients' demand for caesarean section.

Surgical topics include the advantages of vaginal over abdominal hysterectomy, surgery for intersex, urogynaecology updates and postoperative adhesions. There are also four chapters on aspects of the endometrium, probably a tissue that presents more problems for the gynaecologist than any other, including microwave ablation for preventing menorrhagia and the risk of cancer in women taking hormone replacement therapy (HRT). Other endocrinological aspects are covered in chapters on the non-reproductive actions of oestrogens, problems of hormone implants, the management of hirsutism and the expanding multi-million dollar market for alternative medicine for HRT and there are updates on some of the infections that are relevant to our speciality such as vulvovaginal candidiasis and the role of human papillomavirus in cervical cancer.

Once again, we are very grateful to all the contributors for the consistently high standard of these chapters. I am sure that this volume, the first with colour plates, maintains the tradition of high-quality updates and reviews on the topical aspects of obstetrics and gynaecology, and will once more be a must-read for all those wishing to keep abreast of current practice in obstetrics and gynaecology.

David Sturdee
Publications Officer, 1999–2002

1

Royal births

John Dewhurst

Based on the Christmas Lecture for young people given on 20 December 1977 at the Royal College of Obstetricians and Gynaecologists.

The history of England has been influenced to a considerable extent by the reproductive performance of some of our queens and, in one striking case, by that of a princess who was heir to the throne.

MARY OF MODENA

In 1660 Charles II was restored to the throne of England. Two years later he married Catherine of Braganza and there was every expectation that there would soon be heirs to the throne who would secure the Stuart dynasty for generations to come. But it did not happen in this way. Catherine had no children; her only two pregnancies ended in miscarriage. The heir to the throne was James, Duke of York, brother of the king. He had married a commoner, Anne Hyde, who bore him six children: four boys, who died young, and two girls, Mary, later joint sovereign with her husband William of Orange, and Anne, later Queen Anne.

James, Duke of York, had strong Catholic leanings and later became a Catholic. In a country that was predominantly Protestant there was little enthusiasm for a Catholic monarch but, providing James did not have a son, the Protestant succession was secured, since his daughters had been brought up under strict Protestant principles. But in 1671 Anne Hyde died and, two years later, James remarried, choosing for his wife a devout Italian Catholic, Mary of Modena. If she were to bear a son, that boy would, eventually, become king.

The efforts of Mary, now Duchess of York, to give her husband the son he wanted were sad in the extreme. The outcomes of her first eight pregnancies are shown in Table 1.

Then, in 1685, the year following Mary's miscarriage in her eighth pregnancy, Charles II died and James became king. The country had a Catholic monarch, but there was little sign that the queen would bear a son to continue a Catholic dynasty. Indeed, after her last miscarriage Mary

Table 1 *Outcomes of the pregnancies of Mary, Duchess of York, married in 1673*

Year	Outcome
1674 (March)	Miscarriage
1675 (January)	Daughter, died 3 October
1675 (October)	Miscarriage
1676 (August)	Daughter, died 1681
1677 (November)	Son, died 12 December
1682 (August)	Daughter, died October
1683	Miscarriage
1684	Miscarriage

was far from well and three years passed without her becoming pregnant again; Protestant England began to feel that the chance of a Catholic heir was receding. Then, in 1687, the queen went to Bath to take the waters and quickly became pregnant.[1] But so fortuitous did this pregnancy seem that many doubted its reality. It was felt that she would pad out her clothes in a semblance of a pregnancy and that, when the time for her supposed delivery came, a newborn male child would be smuggled into the birth chamber, perhaps in a warming pan. Sceptics who had any right at all to be a witness to the birth were determined to be there.

The queen's labour began in St James's Palace between 7 a.m. and 8 a.m. on 10 June 1688. This was Trinity Sunday and many of those who had intended to be present at the delivery were at their devotions. Gradually, word of what was happening reached them and they began to make their way to the palace. Among those who were finally present were the midwife and a nurse, several Ladies of the Bedchamber, the Lord Chancellor, the Queen Dowager, members of the Privy Council and so many others that when the child was born 67 people were present in the room.[2] Mary asked James to cover her face with his periwig!

The child was a healthy boy and he was, without doubt, born to the queen. What the Protestant country had feared was now a reality that could not be allowed to take root.

Messages were sent to William of Orange, the champion of Protestantism in Europe, and he landed with a small force in Torbay on 5 November 1688. There were many desertions from James's army and he and his wife and son were obliged to flee to France. A successful royal birth had ended the Stuart dynasty.

QUEEN ANNE

William and Mary became joint sovereigns in 1678, but Mary had no children to carry on the line. She had become pregnant early in 1678 but she miscarried in the third month. Later that year she believed herself to be pregnant again, but when term was reached and there was no sign of labour she was obliged to admit that there had been no pregnancy; she had in fact been the victim of a pseudocyesis. Mary died childless in 1694 and, when William died in 1702, it was his sister-in-law, Anne, who acceded to the throne.

Few women can have had such a dramatic and unsuccessful childbearing history as Anne. In 1683 she had married George, Prince of Denmark, who was the progenitor of her numerous pregnancies, but was remarkable for little else. He suffered badly from asthma, which led one of the wags, John, Lord Mulgrave, to comment that 'George was forced to breathe hard lest he be taken for dead and removed for burial'. The king said, 'I have tried him drunk and I have tried him sober but there is nothing in him'.[3] But there was enough in him to make his wife pregnant many times: what Prince Consort could be expected to do more? The actual number of Anne's pregnancies while she was Princess of Denmark has been variously stated by different authorities. Bishop Burnet, writing in 1875 about her son, William, Duke of Gloucester, remarked that he was the only remaining child of seventeen that the Princess had borne, some to the full time, the rest before it. On the other hand, an anonymous publication in 1738 gave the number as only six. Another writer, Hopkinson, suggested in 1934 that Anne had had, perhaps, 10 or 11 pregnancies in all but Green, in 1974, agreed that the original number of 17 was correct. His record of the pregnancies and their outcomes appears in Table 2. His record must be examined in more detail.

Anne's first pregnancy ended on 12 May 1684 with a stillborn daughter, thought to have been due to a fall from a horse. This may, of course, have been true, although trauma of this kind is not a common cause of stillbirth. On 2 June 1685, a live daughter was born and christened Mary. Another daughter, christened Anne Sophia, was born on 12 May 1686 but, tragically, both girls died during February 1687 of an acute infection, possibly smallpox, which they caught from their

Table 2 *Queen Anne's pregnancies*

Date	Outcome
1684, 12 May	Stillborn daughter
1685, 2 June	Mary (died 8 February 1687)
1686, 12 May	Anne Sophia (died 2 February 1687)
1687, between 20 January and 4 February	Miscarriage
1687, October	Miscarriage (male)
1688, 16 April	Miscarriage
1689, 24 July	William Duke of Gloucester (died 30 July 1700)
1690, 14 October	Mary (two months premature, lived two hours)
1692, 17 April	George (born at Syon, lived a few minutes)
1693, 23 March	Miscarriage (female)
1694, 21 January	Miscarriage
1696, 18 February	Miscarriage (female)
1696, 20 September	Double miscarriage
1697, 25 March	Miscarriage
1697, December	Miscarriage
1698, 15 September	Miscarriage (male)
1700, 25 January	Miscarriage (male)

father. Shortly afterwards, Anne miscarried. Her fifth pregnancy is an important one from the viewpoint of determining the cause of her reproductive failure. Green simply records it as 'a miscarriage (male)', but it must be pointed out that the phrase 'miscarriage' in Anne's time did not mean what it means now. We use the term to mean a pregnancy coming to an end before the child is viable but in the 17th century the term simply meant a pregnancy that had not resulted in a live child although the pregnancy had ended much later than viability. The important point about the outcome of Anne's fifth pregnancy is that the sex of the child was known. Moreover, the child is said to have been dead in the womb for a month before being born. We will see the same thing happening again in later pregnancies. Anne miscarried in her sixth pregnancy on 16 April 1688 and no more details of the event are known.

The seventh pregnancy was the only one after Anne Sophia to result in a live child. William Duke of Gloucester was born at Hampton Court on 24 July 1689; he was to live 11 years before his death from scarlet fever on 30 July 1700.

Pregnancy number eight resulted in the birth of a premature daughter who lived only two hours and the ninth ended in the birth of a son, George, who died shortly after he was baptised. No further live children were born to Princess Anne. All her remaining pregnancies ended in what have been described as miscarriages, although in five of them the sex of the child was known and in the fourteenth pregnancy in March 1697 twin embryos were recognised. It is important to an understanding of the cause of Anne's reproductive failure to note that James Vernon, the Secretary of State, reported in a letter that a surgeon had opened the body of the child, had found it free from deformity and had judged it to have been dead for eight to ten days. The last child was reported by Vernon to have been dead for a month before birth. So, in Table 3 we see a modification of Table 2 expressed in modern terms.

It is unfortunate that we do not know more details of Anne's health and of her pregnancies. With the meagre information we do have, several doctors, over the years, have attempted to explain her reproductive failure, although some explanations, such as syphilis and contracted pelvis, can be ignored since there is no evidence whatever to support them.[3] Since on several occasions a child of known sex was expelled from the uterus after viability but before term, prematurity alone might be thought of as an explanation. So too might cervical incompetence, which classically allows the

Table 3 *Queen Anne's pregnancies in modern terms*

Year	Outcome
1684	Stillborn daughter
1685	Mary (died 8 February 1687)
1686	Anne Sophia (died 2 February 1687)
1687 (between 20 January and 2 February)	Miscarriage
1687 (October)	Fetal death *in utero*
1688	Miscarriage
1689	William Duke of Gloucester (died 30 July 1700)
1690	Mary (two months premature lived two hours)
1692	George (lived a few minutes)
1693	Fetal death *in utero* (female)
1694	Miscarriage
1696 February	Fetal death *in utero* (female)
1696 September	Miscarriage of twin embryos
1697	Miscarriage
1697	Miscarriage
1698	Fetal death *in utero* (male)
1700	Fetal death *in utero*

child to be expelled many weeks before term. When we remember, however, that certainly on three occasions (her fifth, 16th and 17th pregnancies) and probably more, the child had been dead within the uterus for some time before birth we see a different picture entirely. Anne's babies did not die from being born too soon but because they could not be sustained in the uterus to term.

In considering which conditions might have this effect, we think of diabetes, repeated placental insufficiency, rhesus incompatibility with a heterozygous husband and systemic lupus erythematosus, all of which could give rise to fetal deaths *in utero* in this way. None of these conditions would have been recognisable in Anne's time and we have insufficient evidence on which to speculate now.

Anne's reproductive failure had a profound effect on the course of our history. When the Duke of Gloucester died in 1700 and Anne lost her last child it became necessary for Parliament to decide who the heir should be if, as now seemed overwhelmingly likely, she died without issue. The Act of Settlement, which was passed in 1701, declared that the crown would pass to the heirs of Elizabeth, daughter of James the First and, briefly, Queen of Bohemia. The Hanoverians were about to become our sovereigns.

PRINCESS CHARLOTTE

The death in childbirth of Princess Charlotte in 1817 was a tragedy of the first order. To understand the full import of this catastrophe we need to go back several years and to consider briefly the childbearing history of her grandmother, Queen Charlotte, and the activities of her children.

Charlotte of Mecklenburg-Strelitz had married King George III on 8 September 1761. If the principal duty of a queen is to provide heirs to the throne, Charlotte was spectacularly successful. She gave birth to 15 children, nine boys and six girls, some of whom we will meet again (Table 4). Remarkably for the 18th century, 13 of the children lived to be adults, only two dying young: Octavius, aged four years and Alfred, aged two years. The queen had found childbearing extraordinarily simple. So quick, for example, was her eleventh confinement that she said, 'I was taken ill and delivered within 15 minutes'.[3]

Producing heirs to the throne might have been easy for the queen but not for her children. The

Table 4 *Children of Queen Charlotte*

Year of birth	Name
1762	George, Prince of Wales; later Prince Regent
1763	Frederick, Duke of York
1765	William, Duke of Clarence
1766	Charlotte Augusta Matilda
1767	Edward, Duke of Kent
1768	Augusta Sophia
1770	Elizabeth
1771	Ernest Augustus, Duke of Cumberland
1773	Augustus Frederick, Duke of Sussex
1774	Adolphus Frederick, Duke of Cambridge
1776	Mary
1777	Sophia
1779	Octavius (died aged four years)
1780	Alfred (died aged two years)
1783	Amelia (died aged 27 years)

Prince of Wales had contracted a clandestine marriage with a catholic lady, Maria Fitzherbert, but the union had been without the king's consent and the affair was kept secret. Outwardly, the prince remained unmarried and he seemed unwilling to embark on matrimony. The Duke of York was married but childless and the Duke of Clarence unmarried but anything but childless since he eventually produced ten little FitzClarences by his consort, Mrs Jordan. The Duke of Cumberland, who was most unpopular throughout the country, did marry but his wife had only one child who was stillborn. The Duke of Sussex had ruled himself out of the succession by marrying without the king's consent, so contravening the Royal Marriage Act. The Dukes of Kent and Cambridge were unmarried. The daughters were no more successful in bearing heirs. In due course, Charlotte Augusta gave birth to one stillborn child. Augusta Sophia remained unmarried and Elizabeth and Mary, although married, were also childless. Sophia was unmarried, although rumour had credited her with an illegitimate child. Amelia died when she was 27 years old.

So by 1795 there was still no legitimate heir to the throne. It was in that year that the Prince of Wales, who had, by his profligate lifestyle, amassed debts of half a million pounds, was obliged to agree to marry in order to persuade Parliament to provide some money.

His choice of a wife was extraordinary in the extreme. She was Caroline of Brunswick, unattractive physically, slovenly in manners and behaviour and, some said, unwashed. On seeing her for the first time, the prince staggered back and said to his equerry, 'Harris, I feel faint, give me brandy', and he spent only 15 minutes in her presence.[3] Their marriage was, in every sense but the production of their daughter, Charlotte, a disaster. Indeed, it seems possible that they cohabited only once, since the prince, on his wedding night, was so drunk that he collapsed on the floor in front of the fireplace in the bedroom, and only on the following morning was he able to summon sufficient strength to climb into bed and consummate the marriage. They lived apart thereafter.

Their child, Charlotte, the sole heir to the throne, was the darling of the populace, personifying, as she did, youth, beauty and vivacity, in sharp contrast to the antics of her uncles. As she approached marriageable age, it became important that a suitable husband be found for her and that they should produce heirs. An attempt was made to marry her to the Prince of Orange, but she disliked him intensely. Moreover, her eye had fallen on Prince Leopold of Saxe-Coburg and the couple were married on the second of May 1816. It seemed to be a love match that so caught the public imagination that bride and groom were hailed by ecstatic crowds wherever they went. The future of the monarchy rested with them.

Charlotte became pregnant towards the end of January 1817. We do not know the precise date of her last menstrual period but this seems likely to have been between the 9th and the 12th of that month. Three doctors were, in one way or another, to be involved in the princess's labour. They were Sir Richard Croft, Matthew Baillie and John Sims. Croft and Baillie had close links, since they were married to the twin daughters of Thomas Denman who was the leading figure in British obstetrics towards the end of the 18th and the beginning of the 19th century. Croft had inherited a large obstetric practice from his father-in-law, Thomas Denman, and he rigidly adhered to what Denman had taught and practised a quarter of a century earlier. Since Denman's approach was ultra-conservative, this was to have a profound effect on Croft's management of Charlotte's labour. Baillie had initially made his reputation in morbid anatomy but he later developed a large clinical practice as a physician.

The third doctor was, in the words of Sir Eardley Holland,[4] who brilliantly analysed the events of the princess's labour, the mystery man of the three. Although described as a botanist and physician, it appeared that it was mainly as the former that he was especially notable. There is nothing to suggest that he had any particular obstetric knowledge.

In the choice of Sir Richard as her obstetrician, Charlotte was far less fortunate than her grandmother had been. Queen Charlotte had had the services of Dr William Hunter for 14 of her 15 children. Hunter was beyond doubt a leading figure in the field but Croft, although the possessor of a large fashionable practice, was not. It seems likely that he had become notable simply through his father-in-law's influence and that he was not equal to the immense problem that the princess's labour was to present to him.

The facts about the princess's labour were established and thoroughly analysed by Sir Eardley Holland[4] in 1951 and they were based on a series of documents found in Ware, Hertfordshire, where the descendants of Croft were living. The more important ones were published in full by Professor Franco Crainz, formerly Professor of Obstetrics and Gynaecology in Rome, in 1977.[5] From these we learn that labour began at 7 p.m. on Monday 3 November when the membranes ruptured. According to Croft this was 42 weeks and one day since the last period. Pains were rather ineffective so Croft made a vaginal examination at 11 p.m. and found the cervix dilated little more than 2 cm – a halfpenny – in his words. At around 3.00 a.m. Charlotte vomited and Croft, feeling that this might expedite the course of labour, sent for the Officers of State and Doctor Baillie. They would have a long time to wait. Indifferent pains continued but some progress was made. By 6 p.m. Croft could feel only a small amount of cervix and by 9 p.m. the cervix was fully dilated. The first stage of labour had lasted 26 hours which, in those days, was not inordinately long.

During the next 10–12 hours we know only that contractions remained indifferent. Then, by 12 noon on Wednesday, 5 November, Charlotte began to pass a dark green material *per vaginam*, suggesting that the child might be dead. It is extremely interesting to learn, now, that Sir Richard Croft had no means of knowing whether this was so or not. The fetal heart sounds had not been heard in England in 1818; they were reported for the first time in Geneva the following year.[3] By 3 p.m., the head was down on the perineum and at 9 p.m. a large male child was born that had evidently been dead for some hours.

The third stage of labour was to prove fatal for the princess. Sir Richard realised that the uterus was acting irregularly and that the placenta was retained. He consulted Sims, who was still attempting to resuscitate the dead child, and Baillie, both of whom agreed that the placenta should be removed manually. There had not been external bleeding yet but Croft described how, when he introduced his hand, there was some blood loss; he also encountered a ring of uterine muscle contraction, although he was able to insert three fingers past this area and then his whole hand. Some two-thirds of the placenta was still adherent and this was separated. There was more bleeding during the manual removal. Croft then left the placenta lying in the vagina, which was the practice at the time but, when the princess complained of discomfort from its presence, he removed it and more blood loss occurred. It is not easy to form a reliable estimate of the amount of blood that had been lost during these manoeuvres. Direct palpation of the uterus through the abdominal wall was hampered by a bandage, which had been applied in accordance with the practice of the time, but Croft commented that, as well as he could determine, by feeling through this bandage, the uterus seemed contracted.

At first Charlotte seemed reasonably well, with a pulse rate of less than a hundred, although Croft's comment that she 'talked cheerfully' seems unusual since she had just been delivered of a dead son. By 11.45 a.m., however, she was not so well and she was complaining of nausea and singing noises in her head. She had already been given mild nourishment 'frequently' and now she was given more. By 12.45 a.m. she was extremely restless and was experiencing difficulty in breathing. Her pulse became rapid, feeble and irregular. Cordials, nourishment and antispasmodic opiates had no effect and she died at 2.30 a.m.

At a postmortem examination, the uterus contained a considerable quantity of coagulated blood and extended as high as the navel; the hourglass contraction was still present. The stomach contained nearly three pints of liquid, suggesting that Charlotte had drunk quite a lot of fluid in the frequent nourishments she had been given after delivery. The heart and lungs showed no fault. To what, then, are we to attribute Charlotte's death? Several possibilities have been suggested. These are:

• bleeding during and after the third stage of labour

• a tear or rupture of the uterus

• an inversion of the uterus

• a pulmonary embolus

• an amniotic fluid embolus.

The postmortem examination rules out several of these. The uterus was not ruptured or injured in any way. It was not inverted. No evidence of a blood embolus was found. An amniotic embolus remains a possibility, since the condition was not recognised at the time.

I strongly incline to the view that Sir Eardley Holland[8] expressed. 'It seems hardly possible', he wrote, 'to doubt that Charlotte died from postpartum haemorrhage'.

Bleeding had occurred before the placenta was removed, during its removal and when it was taken out of the vagina. There was bleeding into the uterine cavity later, which was disclosed at the postmortem examination. Moreover, the gradual decline in the princess's condition after delivery is much more in keeping with bleeding as the cause of death than, for example, an embolus. It is also important to bear in mind the condition of the princess before labour. It seems possible that the diet prescribed by Sir Richard might have left her hungry; bleedings had also been undertaken on several occasions and we should bear in mind that iron supplements were not administered in those days. A degree of anaemia could well have existed, on top of which the blood loss during and after the third stage proved fatal.

Could the catastrophe have been prevented? 'Almost certainly', is the answer. The use of forceps after the princess had been in the second stage of labour for six to eight hours or even sooner would have left her less exhausted and in a better condition to withstand any bleeding during the third stage. It also could well have saved the life of the child. Croft's extremely conservative approach can surely be criticised and it must have contributed to the extreme exhaustion of the princess after a second stage of labour lasting 24 hours.

Sir Eardley Holland called the event a triple obstetric tragedy. Not only were the lives of the mother and child lost but, three months afterwards, Sir Richard Croft shot himself while conducting another confinement. Mother, child and obstetrician all died.

AN HEIR TO THE THRONE

Not for 23 years had an heir to the throne been born but, following the death of the Princess Charlotte, two were born within 29 hours of each other and a third two months later. The desperate need for an heir meant that the three unmarried dukes, the uncles of Charlotte, began searching for wives. Not without some difficulty, all were eventually successful.

The Duke of Clarence, the eldest son of the three, married Adelaide of Saxe-Meiningen, the Duke of Kent married a widow, Mary, Dowager Princess of Leiningen, who had already proved her fertility by giving birth to two children. The Duke of Cambridge married Augusta of Hesse Cassel. All were to become pregnant quickly. The Duchess of Cambridge was the first to give birth. She was delivered behind locked doors in Hanover in the presence of the Duke of Clarence at 1.30 a.m. on Friday, 26 March 1819. The child was a boy, whose sex was established 'by actual inspection'. He was christened George and he was, at that time, the heir to the throne. The presence of the Duke of Clarence at the birth is, in one sense, strange since the Duchess of Clarence, who was also in Hanover, was far from well with a severe upper respiratory infection. This evidently precipitated premature labour and the duchess gave birth at 32 weeks of pregnancy to a daughter at 6.30 a.m. on 27 March. The child was christened Charlotte Augusta Louisa. She was heir to the throne, however, for only a few hours, dying at 1.30 p.m. the same day. George was restored as the heir.

He was not to be heir for long. The Duchess of Kent was also pregnant and she had elected to return to England to have her child. There, at 4.15 a.m. on 24 May 1919, she gave birth to Victoria who, as the child of the elder son, superseded George. The Duke and Duchess of Clarence, however, were still hoping for a child and, if they were to be successful, that child would become the heir. The Duchess became pregnant in the summer of 1819 and, perhaps unwisely, decided to come to England for her confinement; she miscarried around three months later while in Calais. Undeterred, the Clarences kept trying and the Duchess became pregnant again in 1820. All seemed to be going well until, once more, when she was 34 weeks pregnant, premature labour threatened. Everything that could be done in those days was done. The knockers of all the doors were muffled and straw was put down to deaden the sound of carriage wheels, but to no avail. At 5.20 p.m. on 10 December a daughter was born who was christened Elizabeth. Sadly, on 1 March 1821 she was suddenly taken ill and died in convulsions on 3 March.

All was not quite over. The Duchess of Clarence's last pregnancy ended in the birth of very premature twins on 8 April 1822 who did not survive. The Duke wrote an ineffably sad letter to his elder brother, now King George IV, to inform him of the tragic event. Thereafter there were several reports of pregnancies but none was confirmed.

The Duchess of Clarence's reproductive failure had left the succession to Victoria.

References

1   Oman C. *Mary of Modena*. London: Hodder & Stoughton; 1962.

2   Strickland A. *Lives of the Queens of England from the Norman Conquest. Volume 4*. London: George Bell & Sons; 1877.

3   Dewhurst J. *Royal Confinements*. London: Weidenfeld & Nicholson; 1980.

4   Holland E. The Princess Charlotte of Wales: a triple obstetric tragedy. *J Obstet Gynaecol Br Emp* 1951:58.

5   Crainz F. *Obstetric Tragedy*. London: Heinemann; 1977.

2

The myometrial response to gonadotrophin-releasing hormone agonists

Andrew D Weeks

Based on the William Blair-Bell Memorial Lecture given on 9 November 2000 at the Royal College of Obstetricians and Gynaecologists.

INTRODUCTION

Oestrogen was discovered in 1923 when Allen and Doisy[1] demonstrated that uterine hyperaemia could be caused by injecting bovine follicular fluid into castrated rats. Nestled between an article on the benefits of egg yolk as a treatment for rickets and another on the method for the prevention of mortality from urinary retention is their description of the effect of follicular fluid on the rat uterus: 'injection of this extract into spayed animals … produces typical estrual oedema, growth and hypersecretion of the genital tract'.

It had been known for many years before this that the ovaries produced substances that interacted with the uterus. In 1872, Lawson Tait performed the first successful oophorectomy, in order to 'arrest menstrual haemorrhage due to uterine myoma'.[2] He found that removal of the ovaries led to uterine atrophy and stopped menstrual haemorrhage. Despite a mortality rate of 38% in his original series, the operation caught on and gained widespread popularity. It was clear that there were considerable benefits to arresting ovarian function in the management of menstrual disorders. It was not until 100 years later, however, that an interruption of ovarian function could be achieved medically and reversibly by gonadotrophin-releasing hormone (GnRH) agonists.

This chapter describes the effect of GnRH agonists on the human myometrium and its vasculature. A detailed understanding of their effects is important for those prescribing GnRH agonists. However, the studies also shed light on the pathological changes that occur at the menopause and the roles that oestrogen and progesterone play in the process.

GONADOTROPHIN-RELEASING HORMONE AGONISTS

The way in which GnRH agonists affect the production of follicle-stimulating hormone (FSH) and luteinising hormone (LH) are well-known. The potency of GnRH agonists is about 100 times that of endogenous GnRH and they bind tightly to the GnRH receptors on the gonadotrophs in the anterior pituitary.[3] Initially this stimulates the production of FSH and LH. However, the fact that the stimulation is continuous rather than pulsatile (as it is with the naturally occurring GnRH) means that the receptor has no chance to regenerate following stimulation. This regeneration is vital for the continued stimulation of the gonadotrophs. Thus, after about three days, the production of FSH and LH falls. Ovarian oestrogen production therefore also decreases, reaching

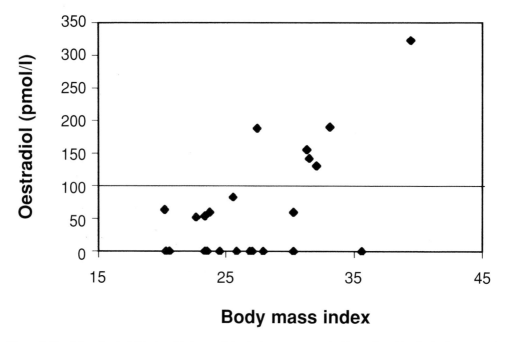

Figure 1 *Correlation of oestradiol levels and body mass index in those women treated with gonadotrophin-releasing hormone agonist for eight weeks*

postmenopausal levels after a mean of 20 days.[4] The ovary, however, is not the only source of the body's oestrogen and, during GnRH agonist treatment, oestrogen continues to be produced from other sources, especially adipose tissue. Here, testosterone and androstenedione are converted by aromatase to oestradiol and oestrone respectively. Thus, the final level of circulating oestrogens is dependent not only on the effectiveness of the GnRH agonist in reducing FSH and LH levels but also on the woman's body habitus. Although the amount of oestrogen produced from this source is usually relatively small, it may become important when the ovaries stop functioning, irrespective of whether this is natural or artificially induced. Figure 1 shows the relationship between the body mass index (BMI) and the serum sex steroid levels of 23 women at the end of eight weeks of treatment with GnRH agonists.[5] The oestradiol levels correlate with the women's BMI ($r = 0.64$). In contrast, the levels of serum progesterone are independent of adiposity (Figure 2). This diversity in response to GnRH agonist treatment can be used to assess the relative importance of oestradiol and progesterone in the uterine changes (see below).

Oestrogen and progesterone are not the only hormones affected by GnRH agonist therapy. Ovarian suppression also leads to a decrease in circulating testosterone levels while leaving the sex hormone-binding globulin levels unchanged.[6] This is the basis of using GnRH agonists in the treatment of resistant hirsutism. The suppression of testosterone may be the basis for the beneficial effect that GnRH agonists have on the serum lipid profile because, in contrast to the natural menopause, treatment with GnRH agonists results in a rise in high-density lipid levels, while leaving the low-density lipid and cholesterol levels unchanged.[7] It is important to recognise this difference when using the effect of GnRH agonists on the vasculature as a model for the natural menopause.

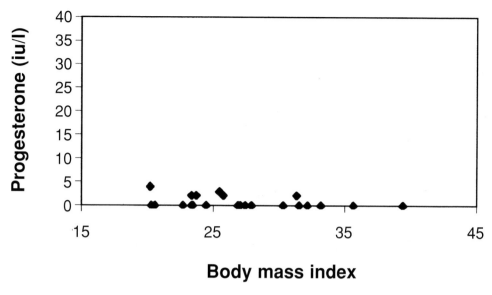

Figure 2 *Correlation of progesterone levels and body mass index in those women treated with gonadotrophin-releasing hormone agonist for eight weeks*

GnRH may also be produced outside the pituitary gland. It is also produced in small amounts by a number of other tissues throughout the body, including the uterus and ovaries, where it acts via local GnRH receptors in an autocrine fashion.[8] The function of GnRH within these tissues is not known exactly, but appears to be to 'fine tune' the effect of sex steroids. In the ovary, for instance, GnRH has an inhibitory effect on sex steroid production.[8] In myometrial tissue cultures, however, *in vitro* treatment with GnRH agonists blocks the proliferative effect of oestradiol and progesterone.[9] Some of the effects that we see with GnRH agonist treatment in humans, therefore, could also be a result of a direct effect of the GnRH agonist on the target organ. The effect is likely to be minimal, however, because the tissue concentrations required to achieve these effects are much higher than those achieved in clinical practice.

The effect of GnRH agonists on uterine volume

Most of the assumptions about the effects of GnRH agonists on the uterus are derived either from population studies where the uterus is assessed before and after the menopause or from studies on the effect of GnRH agonists on the fibroid uterus. These studies suggest that both fibroid and myometrial volumes are decreased by about 35% by the onset of the menopause, irrespective of whether this is natural or medical.[10,11]

The change in uterine volume that occurs when a non-fibroid uterus is treated with a GnRH agonist is similar to that for a fibroid uterus. In a double-blind randomised trial, the Leeds 'Pro-Hyst' Study, 51 women awaiting hysterectomy for menorrhagia were studied.[13] None had fibroids over 2.5 cm diameter on ultrasound and all had normal endometrial histology. Participants were randomly allocated to receive leuprorelin acetate depot 3.75 mg subcuticularly for eight weeks or placebo in a double-blind fashion. The women were examined by transvaginal ultrasound at trial

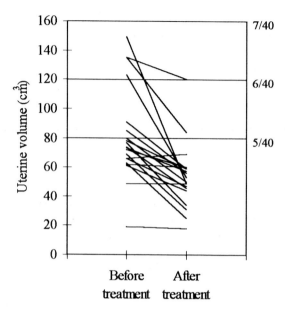

Figure 3 *Change in uterine volume in women treated with a gonadotrophin-releasing hormone agonist for eight weeks; the transverse lines represent the corresponding uterine gestational sizes assessed ultrasonographically by Goldstein[48]; figure reproduced from Weeks et al.[12] with permission from Mosby Inc.*

entry and after eight weeks to assess the uterine volume and uterine artery pulsatility index. All women underwent hysterectomy at the end of eight weeks and the myometrium and its vasculature were studied histologically and biochemically. The differences between the study and control groups were used to assess the effect of the GnRH agonist. We found that treatment with a GnRH agonist for eight weeks reduced uterine volume by 34%, while there was no change in those treated with placebo (Figure 3).[12]

MECHANISM OF UTERINE SHRINKAGE

Histological changes

The underlying morphological changes that result in the reduction in uterine volume have not previously been studied in human uteri. As part of the Pro-Hyst study, histological changes in the myometrium were assessed.[14] To assess the tissue morphology, a computerised morphometric analyser was used, while two pathologists independently examined histological sections to identify pathological changes. They examined full-thickness myometrial blocks stained with haematoxylin and eosin and graded histological features as absent, mild or pronounced. The morphological analysis was conducted on areas of tightly packed myometrium in which the myocytes were sectioned transversely using the See-Scan® computerised morphometry system (Cambridge, UK). This system gives values for the total area of the nuclei in a given area. If the cells within this area are counted manually, then figures can be obtained for cell density, the mean area of each cell and the mean area of each set of nuclei. The results of the morphometric analysis can be seen in Table 1. There was a significant increase in myocyte density. Assuming minimal stroma between the cells, the results also suggest that the myocytes significantly decreased their cytoplasmic area. The mean

Table 1 *Morphological analysis of the myocytes in women treated with gonadotrophin-releasing hormone agonist or placebo for eight weeks*

	GnRH agonist ($n = 18$)	Placebo ($n = 16$)	Significance (t-test)
Cell density (cells/mm^2)	6648.0	5054.0	$P < 0.001$
Mean cell area (μm^2)	150.0	198.0	$P < 0.001$
Mean area of the nucleus (μm^2)	17.4	15.0	$P = 0.45$

difference in cell area is about 24%. If this is compared with the ultrasonographically measured uterine shrinkage of the same uteri (a subset of the total Pro–Hyst sample), the figures are similar. The cell area differed by 24%, while the uterine volumes differed by 28%. It would appear therefore that a decrease in cytoplasmic area was the major factor in decreasing the uterine volume.

The histological analysis suggests that a reduction in the stromal oedema is also important (Table 2). Stromal oedema (Figure 4 – Plate 1) was prominent in many of the myometrial sections and, while it was also seen in those treated with GnRH agonists, it was significantly less common. Hyalinisation, the deposit of proteinous material in the stroma, was also significantly more frequent in the GnRH agonist group. This is usually seen where there is vascular damage and leakage of plasma proteins into the surrounding stroma (see section below on changes in the myometrial vasculature).

The role of progesterone

Previous studies on the fibroid uterus suggest that the decrease in uterine volume occurs predominantly as a result of a reduction in circulating progesterone levels. Carr *et al.*[15] used magnetic resonance imaging (MRI) to study the effect of GnRH agonist therapy on 16 women with fibroid uteri in a crossover trial. He found that add-back with medroxyprogesterone acetate 20 mg daily for the first 12 weeks (protocol A) delayed the decrease in uterine volume until after the progesterone was withdrawn, while in those without add-back (protocol B) the decrease was immediate (Figure 5). When the fibroid and myometrial volumes were differentiated using MRI, the percentage decrease in fibroid tissue and the myometrium were found to be similar. Similar results have been obtained from studies using the progesterone inhibitor mifepristone. These also show a decrease in fibroid volume of about 35%, despite having had no effect on oestrogen levels.[16]

Table 2 *Histological features in the uteri treated with gonadotrophin-releasing hormone agonist or placebo for eight weeks; each feature scored 0 (absent), 1 (present, but not pronounced) or 2 (pronounced); the mean score of all specimens is shown*

	GnRH-a ($n = 18$)	Placebo ($n = 16$)	Significance (t-test)
Oedema	0.75	1.41	$P < 0.05$
Fibrosis	1.33	1.00	$P = 0.16$
Hyalinisation	0.19	0.00	$P < 0.05$
Inflammatory change	0.17	0.19	$P = 0.09$

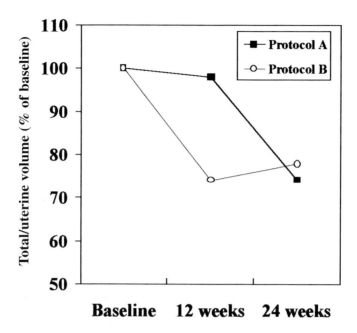

Figure 5 *The uterine volume of women treated with gonadotrophin-releasing hormone (GnRH) agonist from the crossover trial by Carr et al.[15]; all women started GnRH agonist therapy at time 0: women in protocol A used add-back with medroxyprogesterone acetate 20 mg daily for the first 12 weeks of the study while those in protocol B only started it after 12 weeks; figure adapted with permission from the Endocrinological Society*

As part of the Pro-Hyst study, we attempted to ascertain whether the reduction in progesterone levels was also responsible for the decrease in uterine volume in women without fibroids. We examined a subgroup of the women treated with GnRH agonists who had high body mass indices. These 'non-responders' had high oestradiol levels but low progesterone levels (see Figures 1 and 2). When compared with the women who had low levels of both progesterone and oestrogen (the 'responders') there was no statistically significant difference (Figure 6). The mean fall in uterine volume in those with oestradiol levels below 100 pmol/l after treatment was 33% while, in those whose oestradiol remained normal, the mean reduction was similar (22%).[5] Although with such small groups it is difficult to be conclusive, this supports the hypothesis that, as with fibroids, the decrease in myometrial volume is due to the withdrawal of progesterone rather than oestrogen.

Changes at the molecular level

The mechanism for the cellular atrophy that occurs when progesterone is withdrawn is not fully understood. The classical way in which sex steroids cause cellular growth is by increasing the cellular production of specific enzymes. This is achieved by increasing the rate of DNA transcription. After entering a cell and binding to a receptor in the cytoplasm, it attaches to a cellular response unit on the DNA. This is located upstream from the gene to be stimulated, and initiates transcription − the conversion of DNA into RNA − which is the start of the protein-building process. By initiating the production of key enzymes, the overall metabolism of the cell can be increased. In the same way, the removal of progesterone slows their production and thus the cell metabolism.

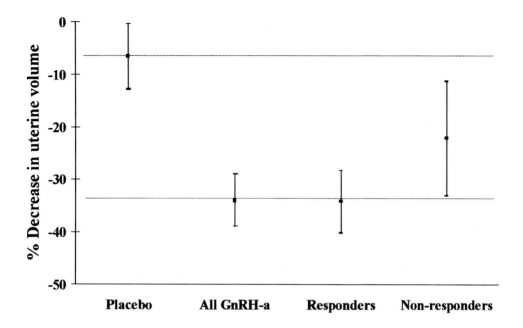

Figure 6 *The change in uterine volume (% ± SEM) among subgroups in the Pro-Hyst trial; the 'responders' are those treated with gonadotrophin-releasing hormone agonist whose oestradiol level was below 100 pmol/l at eight weeks; in contrast, the oestradiol levels of the 'non-responders' remained over 100 pmol/l*

It may not be the change in progesterone levels alone that affects myocyte size. A number of growth factors that affect myocyte growth have been found to be altered by GnRH agonist therapy. Myometrium contains high levels of epidermal growth factor and platelet-derived growth factors. Both have been found to be downregulated by GnRH agonist therapy, as have the levels of insulin-like growth factors I and II and transforming growth factor beta-1 (TGFb1).[17,18]

Apoptosis is a further mechanism through which GnRH agonists might exert their effect on uterine volume. Although little research has been conducted into this, a role for apoptosis seems unlikely, as the morphological studies outlined above demonstrate that decreases in uterine volume can be accounted for almost completely by the decrease in cell volume. In the Pro-Hyst study, the mean difference in cell area between women treated with placebo or GnRH agonists was 24%. Put into three dimensions, a 24% decrease in cell area represents a decrease in cell volume of 34% (assuming a spherical cell). This is identical to the decrease in uterine volume demonstrated on ultrasound. It is therefore unlikely that there was any change in the total number of myocytes in these women as a result of GnRH agonist therapy.

A final way in which progesterone may change the uterine volume is by an effect on the myometrial stroma. The histological studies conducted thus far were unable to measure directly the volume of the myometrial stroma and there are few studies that have examined the effect of GnRH agonists on the stroma at a cellular level. One of the few studies comes from a group in Boston, who compared the levels of collagen type I and II and fibronectin messenger RNA in explant tissue cultures from GnRH agonist-treated and untreated myometrium.[19] They chose these for study because they are the best candidates for substances likely to be affected by GnRH agonist therapy. However, they found no difference; further studies are awaited.

THE EFFECT OF GONADOTROPHIN-RELEASING HORMONE AGONISTS ON THE UTERINE VASCULATURE

As with those on uterine volume, most studies on the vasculature of the human uterus (Figure 7) have either been of the fibroid uterus or have been cross-sectional studies in which the uterine artery Doppler waveforms have been compared in groups of pre- and postmenopausal women. In the Pro-Hyst study we conducted longitudinal studies to explore the effect of GnRH agonist therapy on the non-fibroid uterus, and compared the vascular histology of women treated with GnRH agonist and placebo.

When women were treated with placebo, there was no significant change in uterine artery pulsatility index.[12] In those randomised to receive GnRH agonists, however, there was an overall increase in pulsatility index of 20%. While the change is similar to that seen in fibroid uteri,[20] its magnitude is far smaller than the immediate 50–75% decrease in pulsatility index that is seen in postmenopausal women treated with oestrogen.[21,22] This is a consistent finding throughout all previous studies and suggests that while oestrogen can stimulate immediate vasodilatation, its withdrawal causes only a slow change in arterial resistance. In women passing through the menopause this can take many years.[23] This indicates that the change is either secondary to some morphological change or that it occurs as a result of genomic change. Morphological changes that are under genomic control return only slowly to their natural levels once the stimulus is withdrawn. This is because the change in cellular protein concentrations occur as a result of spontaneous denaturation of the proteins, a process that may take some time.

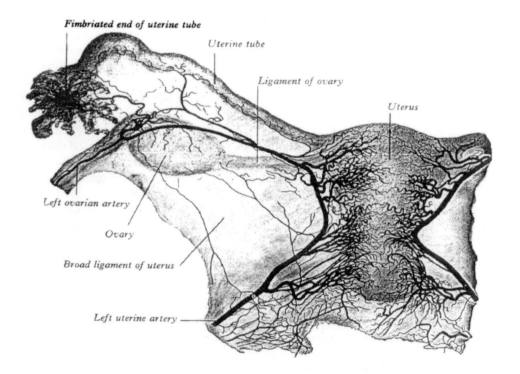

Figure 7 *The uterine vasculature; reproduced from Gray's Anatomy with permission from Churchill Livingstone*

THE MECHANISM OF INCREASING VASCULAR RESISTANCE

Oestrogen or progesterone?

Arteries throughout the body are notoriously sensitive to oestrogen both *in vivo* and *in vitro* and the uterine vasculature is no exception. Postmenopausal women treated with oestrogen, for example, have an almost immediate rise in uterine blood flow of about 50%.[21] This effect occurs far more rapidly than myometrial hypertrophy, suggesting that it is due to a direct effect on the vessels. If oestrogen causes vasodilatation, it would be logical to conclude that its withdrawal is responsible for the increase in pulsatility index seen when the fibroid uterus is treated with GnRH agonists. However, if a fibroid uterus is treated with a progesterone antagonist, then, surprisingly, the uterine artery pulsatility index increases despite the fact that the oestradiol levels remain unchanged.[16] This increase in pulsatility index occurs alongside a decrease in uterine volume and is of about the same magnitude as that seen in women treated with GnRH agonists. This suggests that the increase in intrauterine vascular resistance with GnRH agonist treatment in women with fibroids may not be due simply to the withdrawal of oestrogen-mediated vasodilatation. It could be a direct effect of progesterone on the vessels, but there is no evidence from either animal or human studies that progesterone has any vasodilating effect on arteries. It is more likely that the change in pulsatility index that comes about with progesterone withdrawal occurs as a result of a decrease in total uterine vascularity related to fibroid atrophy (see below).

The relative importance of progesterone and oestrogen in changing the vascular resistance were also explored as part of the Pro-Hyst trial. As we have seen, those treated with placebo had no change in uterine artery pulsatility index while those treated with GnRH agonists showed a 20% increase. However, if those treated with GnRH agonists are divided into 'responders' and 'non-responders' on the basis of their oestrogen levels at the end of eight weeks, an interesting pattern emerges. Figure 8 shows the percentage change (SEM) of uterine artery pulsatility index of those treated with placebo, those treated with GnRH agonists, those who 'responded' and those whose oestradiol levels remained above 100 pmol/l (the 'non-responders'). Although the numbers in this sub-group analysis are small, it is clear that, in contrast to the responders, the non-responders show no change at all in pulsatility index. This suggests that, in this group of women without fibroids, a drop in oestrogen is a prerequisite for a change in uterine vascular resistance. This is in contrast to the studies conducted on fibroid uteri discussed above. The difference could occur because of the high vascularity of fibroids. This would mean that when treated with mifepristone, the decreasing fibroid volume has a disproportionate effect on the uterine artery pulsatility index, disguising the fact that the more subtle oestrogen-mediated change in the myometrial vascularity is absent. In the non-fibroid uterus, by contrast, the overall tissue vascularity is less and the change in volume alone is insufficient to produce significant changes in the uterine artery pulsatility index. The situation will be made clearer with the publication of Doppler studies that assess the effect of mifepristone on the non-fibroid uterus.

Change in vascularity or vasoconstriction?

To explore whether the rise in vascular resistance was due to arterial vasoconstriction or whether there was also a change in myometrial vascularity, slides of myometrium stained with factor VIII antibody were studied. Factor VIII clotting factor is found exclusively in the vascular endothelium and immunohistochemistry conducted using antibodies to factor VIII demonstrates the vascular endothelium with high levels of sensitivity and specificity.[24] Figure 9 (Plate 1) shows a section of myometrium stained with factor VIII antibody. The number of vessels in a given area, as well as the amount of vascular endothelium in that area, can be evaluated using computerised morphometry.

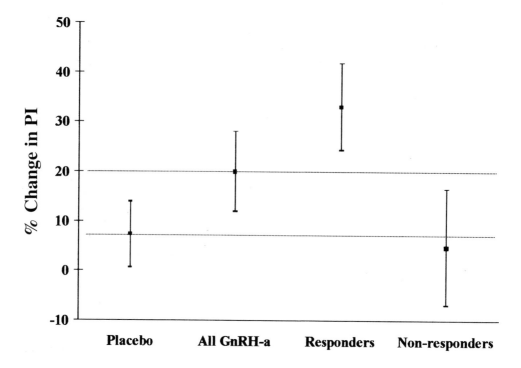

Figure 8 *The change of uterine artery pulsatility index (PI) (% ± SEM) of subgroups in the Pro-Hyst trial; the 'responders' are those treated with gonadotrophin-releasing hormone agonist whose oestradiol level was below 100 pmol/l at eight weeks; in contrast, the oestradiol levels of the 'non-responders' remained over 100 pmol/l*

The myometrial vascularity was significantly less in those treated with GnRH agonists (Table 3). As this reduces the number of vessels in the myometrium available for the blood to flow through, the uterine artery pulsatility index increases. The decrease in vascularity can be partly attributed to the absence of the angiogenic effect of oestrogen and partly to the capillary atrophy that occurs following a decrease in blood supply.[25]

Although we were unable to assess the effect of GnRH agonist therapy on the vessel diameters, there is considerable *in vivo* and *in vitro* evidence that oestrogen is a powerful vasodilator (see below). It is therefore likely that vasoconstriction also contributes to the increase in uterine artery pulsatility index with GnRH agonist therapy.

Table 3 *Vessel density and size measured on factor VIII stained sections from women treated with gonadotrophin-releasing hormone agonist or placebo for eight weeks*

	GnRH agonist (n = 18)	Placebo (n = 16)	Significance (t-test)
Vessel density (vessels/100 myocytes)	0.880	1.230	$P < 0.001$
Mean vessel circumference (mm)	0.001	0.001	$P = 0.65$
Mean lumen diameter (<mu>m)	0.220	0.220	$P = 0.65$

In summary, treatment with GnRH agonists results in an increase in uterine artery pulsatility index. In women without fibroids, this effect appears to be mediated through oestrogen, probably through a combination of arterial vasoconstriction and a decrease in myometrial vascularity. In women with fibroids, a reduction in progesterone alone is enough to increase vascular resistance, probably through its effect on fibroid volume.

GONADOTROPHIN-RELEASING HORMONE AGONISTS AND MYOMETRIAL NITRIC OXIDE PRODUCTION

In animal models, the administration of oestrogen results in massive uterine vasodilatation with corresponding increases in uterine blood flow.[26] Further studies have shown a delay of around 30 minutes before the uterine blood flow increases.[27] This delay is not because genomic change is taking place;[28] rather, it is likely to occur because oestrogen is acting through an intermediary product.[26] Numerous agonists and antagonists of uterine blood flow have been studied in the search for this intermediary. Changes in the endothelial production of nitric oxide, prostacyclin, vascular endothelial growth factor and endothelin-1 have all been linked with oestrogen withdrawal.[29–31] It is also known that oestrogen withdrawal sensitises arteries to the vasoconstricting effects of noradrenalin, hypoxia and angiotensin II, and can affect Ca^{2+} mobilisation and fluxes leading to further vasoconstriction.[32] There are clearly many vasoactive mediators of oestrogen, but the most important of these appears to be nitric oxide.

Nitric oxide is a powerful vasodilator that is produced from the amino acid, arginine, by nitric oxide synthase (NOS). NOS occurs in three forms and all are present in the uterus.[33,34] In the vascular endothelium, endothelial NOS (eNOS) is regulated by cellular calcium levels and is responsible for vasodilatation. In the nervous system, NOS is present in the form of neuronal NOS (nNOS) and acts as a neurotransmitter and smooth muscle relaxant. It also acts as a vasodilator when released from the nerve endings that innervate the adventitia of arteries. The third type of NOS is inducible NOS (iNOS). This is not regulated by calcium levels, but is switched on as part of inflammatory reactions.

There is good evidence that nitric oxide is responsible for mediating oestrogen's vasodilating effects within the uterus. In sheep, Van Buren et al.[35] demonstrated that infusing NOS inhibitors into uterine arteries prevented oestrogen–induced vasodilatation. Jovanovic et al.[36] and Azuma et al.[37] have since separately confirmed these findings as part of in vitro studies on human uterine arteries. The way in which this happens, however, is not clear. Tschugguel et al.[38] studied tissue cultures of human uterine myocytes and endothelial cells and concluded that increases in endothelial eNOS played no role in the regulation of uterine blood flow. They found that oestrogen receptors were present in the myocytes (but not the vascular tissue), while endothelial eNOS messenger RNA was present in the vascular tissue but not the myocytes. Incubation of both cell types with 17β-oestradiol did not increase the expression of eNOS messenger RNA. If eNOS is not responsible, then could the nitric oxide output be increased through a change in nNOS?

The myometrial samples from the Pro-Hyst study were studied in order to discover whether NOS activity was reduced in women treated with GnRH agonists. This was assessed by two separate techniques. The citrulline assay allowed a qualitative and functional assessment of NOS activity, although it is unable to distinguish nNOS from eNOS. These were distinguished in a separate experiment using Western blotting. The results of our experiments showed that while there was no change in the levels of eNOS or iNOS, the levels of nNOS were significantly lower in the GnRH agonist-treated tissue.[39] So, although in many tissues eNOS is the primary vasodilator and mediates the vasodilating actions of oestrogen, in the myometrium nNOS may be more responsive to changes in oestrogen levels.

ARTERIAL PATHOLOGY DUE TO GONADOTROPHIN-RELEASING HORMONE AGONIST THERAPY

It has been suggested that the reduction in circulating oestrogen that occurs at the time of the menopause accelerates the atherosclerotic process. As part of the Pro-Hyst study, pro-atherosclerotic effects of GnRH agonists on the uterine vasculature were examined. The arcuate arteries were chosen for the morphological studies as they were undamaged in all uteri (in contrast to the uterine arteries), and the histological section could be standardised by taking a full thickness section cut from the midpoint of each uterine fundus. The sections were stained with the Elastin van Geison stain, which allows clear identification of the internal and external elastic laminae. These laminae separate the vessel wall into the tunica adventitia, the tunica media (which contains all the smooth muscle) and the tunica intima (Figure 10). The 'See-Scan' morphometry system, the image (such as that shown) may be captured and the internal and external elastic laminae traced. From these measurements, the total vessel area, the area of the lumen and the smooth muscle area (tunica media) can all be calculated.

Table 4 shows the changes in arterial morphology. The major difference between the study and control groups was in the proportion of the vessel made up of smooth muscle area. Those treated with GnRH agonists appear to have undergone smooth muscle atrophy of the tunica media, despite the treatment having lasted only eight weeks. This is similar to the change that occurs in the uterine arteries following the menopause[40] and in coronary vessels in the early stages of atherosclerotic disease.[41] Oestrogen deficiency and atherosclerosis also cause smooth muscle proliferation in the intima of coronary vessels,[32] although in the Pro-Hyst study the difference between the groups did not reach statistical significance.

The changes seen in the uterine vessels following GnRH agonist therapy are unlikely to be restricted to the uterine vasculature; the coronary arteries of the trial participants were probably affected in the same way. Evidence for this comes from autopsy studies, which show a strong

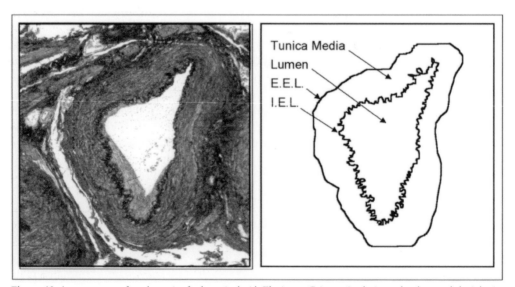

Figure 10 *An arcuate artery from the uterine fundus stained with Elastin van Geison stain; the internal and external elastic laminae (IEL and EEL) are clearly identified, separating the vessel wall into the tunica adventitia (outside the EEL), the tunica media (containing smooth muscle) and the tunica intima (between the IEL and the lumen); the diagram on the right shows the image obtained after scanning with the See-Scan© computerised morphology system; the operator traces around the IEL and EEL and then the computer calculates the area within each line*

Table 4 *Morphological analysis of the arcuate arteries of women treated for eight weeks with either gonadotrophin-releasing hormone agonist or placebo*

	GnRH agonist (n = 18)	Placebo (n = 16)	Significance (t-test)
Mean area within external elastic lamina (mm²)	0.28	0.38	$P = 0.060$
Mean area within internal elastic lamina (mm²)	0.10	0.10	$P = 0.910$
Mean diameter of measured vessels (μm)	493.00	547.00	$P = 0.220$
Tunica media as % of external elastic lamina area (mean)	65.00	72.00	$P = 0.01$

correlation between the degree of atherosclerotic change in the two sites.[42] Maybe this is not too surprising in that both are hollow, muscular contractile organs with a well-developed blood supply. This may help to explain a case report that implicated the use of GnRH agonists in the exacerbation of ischaemic heart disease.[43]

The association between the histological changes seen in the uterus and the heart may allow a woman's risk of ischaemic heart disease to be predicted at the time of hysterectomy. A small case–control study has suggested that women who die from heart attacks are more likely than controls to have had atherosclerotic change in their arcuate arteries at the time of hysterectomy, even if performed many years before.[44] Although further studies are needed, a detailed examination of the uterine vasculature following hysterectomy may prove to be a good predictor of impending ischaemic heart disease, prompting interventional strategies.

The most striking feature in the histological changes as viewed by the pathologists is the increase in perivascular fibrosis seen in the GnRH agonist-treated group (Table 5). Perivascular fibrosis and hyalinisation of the vessel are often seen together and are indicative of the leakage of proteins into the vessel wall following vascular degeneration. The same effect is seen in hypertensive disease.[45] These findings fit with the decrease in vascularity on the Factor VIII antibody stained slides. Both represent a breakdown of vascular integrity. Similar findings have been seen in studies of the fibroid uterus where GnRH agonist treatment is found to increase the amount of intimal and medial fibrosis.[46] The arteries of the postmenopausal uterus have also been seen to have degenerative changes with hyalinisation, fibrosis, reduplication of the internal elastic lamina and calcification.[47]

No difference was observed in the lumen area between the study and control groups. This is not surprising, as the process of arterial clamping during hysterectomy would disrupt the normal

Table 5 *Vascular pathology in uteri treated for eight weeks with gonadotrophin-releasing hormone agonist or placebo; each feature scored 0 (absent), 1 (present, but not pronounced) or 2 (pronounced); the mean score of all specimens is shown*

	GnRH-a (n = 18)	Placebo (n = 16)	Significance (t-test)
Perivascular fibrosis	1.72	1.09	$P < 0.05$
Myxoid change	0.06	0.09	$P = 0.53$
Hyalinisation	1.00	0.41	$P = 0.08$
Intimal thickening	0.78	0.50	$P = 0.22$
Medial thickening	0.97	0.60	$P = 0.12$

vascular tone and obliterate any subtle change that had been present as a result of hormonal variation.

CONCLUSIONS

When treated with GnRH agonists, the uterus decreases in volume, an effect that is due to a decrease in the myocyte cytoplasm and a reduction in the amount of stromal oedema. This effect is probably due to the reduction in progesterone levels.

The effect of GnRH agonist treatment on the uterine vasculature is to increase the vascular resistance. This is due to the decrease in circulating oestrogen, which leads to a decrease in myometrial vascularity and vasoconstriction; the latter may be mediated by reductions in neuronal NOS activity. On a microscopic level, there is a reduction in capillary vascularity of the myometrium and evidence of vascular damage. The smooth muscle of the tunica media undergoes atrophy, an effect associated with the development of atherosclerosis. This is likely to be due to the withdrawal of oestrogen, an effect that may be mediated by a reduction in neuronal NOS activity.

Acknowledgements

In conducting this work I have received help and support from numerous individuals, especially Mr Sean Duffy, my supervisor at St James's Hospital, Leeds, and Professor James Walker. The nitric oxide research was conducted in collaboration with Dr Jorge Figueroa and Dr Angela Massmann at Wake Forest University, North Carolina. The pathological assessments were conducted in collaboration with Dr Nafisa Wilkinson and Dr Deep Arora from the Department of Pathology at St James's Hospital, Leeds. The Pro-Hyst clinical trial was supported by a departmental grant from Wyeth Laboratories.

References

1   Allen E, Doisy EA. An ovarian hormone. Preliminary report on its location, extraction and partial purification, and action in test animals. *JAMA* 1923;81:819–21.

2   Jordan J. Pioneers in obstetrics and gynaecology. 5: Lawson Tait. *The Diplomate* 1996;3:228–32.

3   Filicori M, Flamigni C, Cognigni G, Dellai P, Arnone R, Falbo A, Capelli M. Comparison of the suppressive capacity of different depot gonadotrophin-releasing hormone analogs in women. *J Clin Endocrinol Metab* 1993;77:130–33.

4   Ron-El R, Herman A, Golan A, van der Ven H, Caspi E, Diedrich K. The comparison of early follicular and midluteal administration of long-acting gonadotrophin-releasing hormone agonist. *Fertil Steril* 1990;54:233–7.

5   Weeks AD. Gonadotrophin-releasing hormone agonists and the uterus [MD thesis]. University of Leeds; 1999.

6   Howell R, Dowsett M, King N, Edmonds DK. Endocrine effects of GnRH analogue with low dose hormone replacement therapy in women with endometriosis. *Clin Endocrinol* 1995;43:609–15.

7   Lemay A, Brideau NA, Forest JC, Dodin S, Maheux R. Cholesterol fractions and apolipoproteins during endometriosis treatment by a gonadotrophin releasing hormone (GnRH) agonist implant or by danazol. *Clin Endocrinol (Oxf)* 1991;35:305–10.

gave a paper on this two days later. There was much opposition to the practice of pain relief in labour, especially from the clergy, but he countered this by saying 'God put Adam to sleep to remove a rib and make Eve; therefore God was the first anaesthetist'. In 1853, Queen Victoria used chloroform in childbirth and this further enhanced Simpson's reputation. Edinburgh became a Mecca for women from all over Europe, who poured through Leith harbour and kept the Edinburgh hotels in business. His home was besieged by patients and in the midst of all this he continued with his writings, controversies, scientific work and lecturing. He developed a vacuum extractor, designed mid-cavity forceps and also became Professor of Archaeology and Antiquities. He had nine children, three of whom tragically died, and it all became too much for his wife, who withdrew to her room. In 1866, he accepted a baronetcy and although he was not elected Principal of the University, he was conferred the freedom of the City of Edinburgh. He died of cardiac failure in 1870 at the age of 59 years. Edinburgh was brought to a standstill by the huge funeral that was attended by 30 000 people.

With his pioneering work on pain relief and his interest in interventional obstetrics, Simpson would undoubtedly have been a subspecialist in fetal medicine had he lived a hundred years later and would have been in the forefront of the development of invasive procedures. It is this that I have called an intrauterine odyssey and I will now point out some of the main features on the map.

AMNIOCENTESIS

The odyssey begins with amniocentesis. The first reports appeared in the 1880s in the German literature as a means of withdrawing amniotic fluid for polyhydramnios. In the 1930s, it was used to inject X-ray contrast media for amniography and fetography. Bevis[1] then reported his studies on the bilirubin content of amniotic fluid in rhesus alloimmunisation in 1950. This was taken further by Liley[2] in New Zealand, who in 1961 published his charts, which became widely used for the management of rhesus disease. New diagnostic possibilities for amniocentesis were developed that led to its increasingly widespread use. In 1956, Fuchs and Riis[3] stained amniocytes for fetal sex chromatin. In 1965, Jeffcoate et al.[4] described the prenatal diagnosis of congenital adrenal hyperplasia in late pregnancy by finding high levels of steroid hormones in the amniotic fluid. In 1966, Steele and Breg[5] reported amniocyte culture and fetal chromosome analysis. This was soon followed by the first prenatal diagnosis of Down syndrome, which was confirmed after termination of pregnancy.[6] In 1972, Brock and Sutcliffe[7] showed that amniotic fluid had high αfetoprotein levels in the presence of fetal neural tube defects. Rapidly, other tests were developed on amniotic fluid for the prenatal diagnosis of inborn errors of metabolism, for the assessment of fetal maturity and to measure the lecithin/sphyngomyelin ratio for pulmonary maturity.

With this increasing use of amniocentesis, there was a need to evaluate the technique. In the 1970s, three major studies were published, two from the USA and one from the UK. They all used controls of different kinds but none was randomised. The two North American studies suggested that there was no increased risk of miscarriage following amniocentesis.[8,9] The UK Medical Research Council study,[10] on the other hand, found that there was an increased risk of miscarriage and in addition raised issues such as fetal trauma, pulmonary hypoplasia and musculoskeletal deformities. However, in none of these studies was ultrasound used as it is today, so that the techniques differed from present-day practice. The best study, which was randomised, was performed in Denmark and published in 1986.[11] This showed that the fetal loss rate was increased by 1% and it is still the most reliable evidence available, although some large cohort studies from individual operators suggest that the loss rate may be as low as 0.5%.

PLACENTAL ASPIRATION

Already in the 1960s other intrauterine interventions were being attempted. Alvares[12] and Aladjem[13] attempted transabdominal placental aspiration biopsy to study placental morphology and to diagnose hydatidiform mole. Mohr[14] described transcervical biopsy of the fetal membranes. Most of these procedures were performed before termination of pregnancy, and ultrasound was not available, so that their success rate was low. Furthermore, there were no clear-cut diagnostic indications and the procedures did not enter clinical practice at that time.

By the early 1970s it had become clear that haemoglobinopathies could be diagnosed prenatally if fetal blood was available. The placental aspiration techniques were adapted for this purpose and in 1972 Kan *et al.*[15] demonstrated that this was possible. In 1974,[16] this group in San Francisco published the first prenatal diagnosis of haemoglobinopathies. The technique, also called 'blind' aspiration or placentacentesis, involved passing a needle-tip to and fro through the chorionic plate in the hope of puncturing a fetal vessel. These samples nearly always consisted mainly of maternal blood and amniotic fluid and were a formidable challenge for the laboratory. Some 10% of patients needed a repeat procedure in order to obtain an adequate sample and there was also a 10% fetal mortality rate due to exsanguination.[17] This technique rapidly became obsolete when a more successful fetoscopic method was developed.

FETOSCOPY

Early attempts at fetoscopy either involved the transcervical passage of large endoscopes[18] or were transabdominal, using smaller endoscopes after exposing the uterus by laparotomy.[19–21] Their use was restricted to patients undergoing midtrimester termination of pregnancy because the risks to a continuing pregnancy were unknown. In 1973, Scrimgeour[22] published the first series of diagnostic cases. Through a laparotomy, in six patients, he attempted to examine the fetal spine for spina bifida. Again, intraoperative ultrasound was not available and the intervention failed in 50% of the cases. It was clear that the hazards outweighed any potential benefit.

However, in 1974 Hobbins and Mahoney[23] described a percutaneous ultrasound-guided technique. They used the Dyonics™ needlescope, which was a modified arthroscope, at 18–20 weeks of gestation. Fetal blood could be obtained by puncturing chorionic plate vessels under direct vision. However, it was believed that fetoscopy could be used only for posterior placentas and that placentacentesis was still required if the placenta was anterior.

Furthermore, although the quality of the blood samples was better than in those obtained by placentacentesis, they were usually diluted by amniotic fluid and often contaminated by maternal blood. The reason was that the approaching needle caused the chorionic plate vessels to collapse so that it was not possible to aspirate blood from within the lumen. The needle had to be withdrawn to allow the vessel to bleed into the amniotic fluid and it was this mixture that was aspirated. Haemoglobinopathies could thus be diagnosed from the fetal red cells but fetal plasma assays, of course, could not be performed. Several other centres in the USA, Europe and the UK adopted this method.

In 1978, Rodeck and Campbell published modifications of the technique for visualisation of fetal anatomy[24] (Figure 1) and, of more significance, for obtaining pure fetal blood samples in the second trimester[25] (Figure 2). The latter technique broke two cardinal safety rules but without, as it turned out, any harmful effects.

First, the umbilical cord was punctured at its placental insertion. The large vessels there were supported by Wharton's jelly, enabled aspiration of pure blood from within the lumen of the vessel and bled much less than the chorionic plate vessels that had no Wharton's jelly around them. Spasm

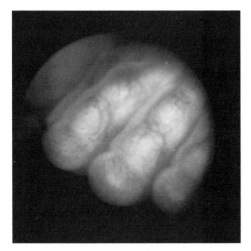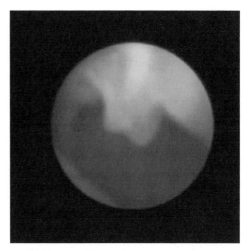

Figure 1 *Fetoscopic examination of the fetus at 15 weeks of gestation showing (A) fingers (B) the uvula*

of the umbilical cord vessels was never seen. Second, a lateral approach to the uterus was almost always chosen (a) so that an anterior placenta was not perforated, (b) because a posterior placenta was less likely to be damaged on entry and (c) because visualisation of the cord insertion was easier and better whatever the placental site. Complications related to bowel or uterine vessels were never encountered. The access to pure fetal blood samples with 100% reliability opened up new diagnostic possibilities and provided the basis for fetal medicine as a science. Soon afterwards, normal values for fetal haematology were established, including factors VIII and IX and other coagulation factors, and the prenatal diagnosis of the haemophilias was reported.[26]

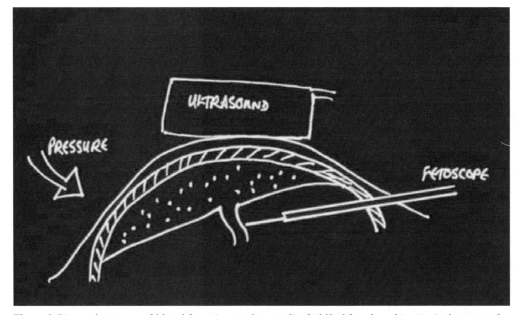

Figure 2 *Diagram showing successful lateral fetoscopic approach to sampling fetal blood from the cord insertion in the presence of an anterior placenta*

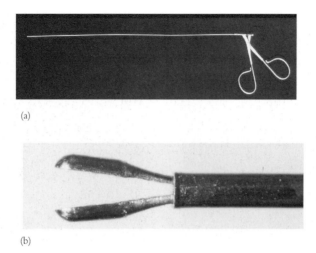

(a)

(b)

Figure 3 *Fetal skin biopsy: (a) fine 20-gauge biopsy forceps (b) close-up of jaws of forceps*

(a)

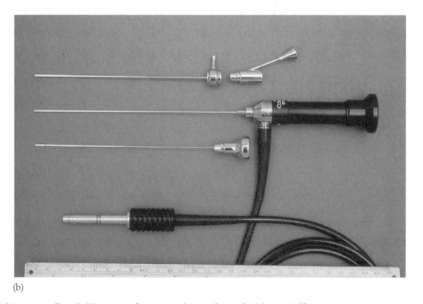

(b)

Figure 4 *(a) 21-gauge needle with 27-gauge tip for intravascular transfusion; (b) Olympus Selfoscope*

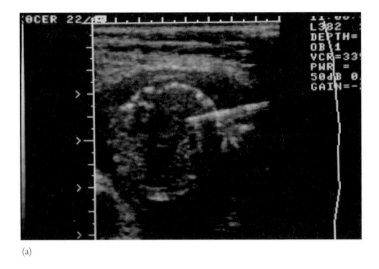

(a)

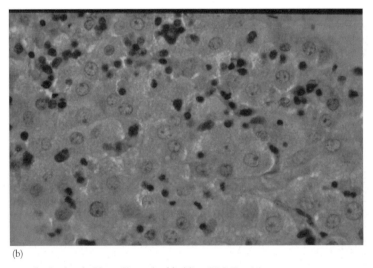

(b)

Figure 5 *(a) Outer needle placed in fetal liver; (b) sample of fetal liver (H & E stain)*

Initially, the cannula was triangular in cross-section and measured 2.2 mm by 2.4 mm. This accommodated only a 27-gauge needle, beside the endoscope. We modified it so that the cross-section was more oval, with diameters of 2.2 mm and 2.7 mm. This permitted the passage of fine biopsy forceps for fetal skin biopsy under direct vision and resulted in the first prenatal diagnosis of epidermolysis bullosa letalis[27] (Figure 3a, b and Figure 3c, Plate 2). We could also use a 21-gauge needle with a 27-gauge tip for the performance of the first percutaneous fetal intravascular transfusion,[28] (Figure 4) and a special aspiration needle for fetal liver biopsy[29] (Figure 5).

The versatility of this percutaneous ultrasound-guided fetoscopic approach was demonstrated by still further developments. It could be used from 15 weeks onwards, even up to 32 weeks, for transfusions. Selective feticide could be performed efficiently and safely by injecting 20 ml of air into the umbilical vein of the abnormal twin.[30] The increasing use of diagnostic ultrasound led to the identification of numerous fetal abnormalities that required further investigation, such as aspiration of a cyst or a large bladder and even occasionally fetal laparoscopy in hydrops or cystoscopy in obstructive uropathy. Between 1976 and 1986, we performed over 2000 fetoscopies at King's College Hospital, London, with a fetal loss rate as low as 2.4%. The vast majority were performed for fetal blood sampling but the indications were changing. By the early 1980s there was a massive increase in fetal blood sampling for rapid karyotyping of fetuses with malformations that had been detected by ultrasound. At the same time, advances in molecular biology meant that increasing numbers of genetic diseases could be diagnosed by DNA analysis, such as the haemoglobinopathies and the haemophilias, and progressively fetal blood sampling was replaced by chorionic villus sampling (CVS) for this group of patients.

CHORIONIC VILLUS SAMPLING

The earliest attempts at CVS were also transcervical and endoscopic and took place in patients undergoing termination of pregnancy.[31,32] The aim was to perform chromosome analysis but the success rate was not good. At this time amniocentesis was proving to be safe, successful and accurate and CVS was temporarily forgotten. However, a paper published in China in 1975[33] came to the attention of the West several years later. Fetal sexing was performed by Barr-body staining and the procedure seemed to be remarkably successful, even though a 'blind' transcervical aspiration technique was used. In 1982, Kazy,[34] then working in Russia, was the next to describe clinical cases of prenatal diagnosis of various genetic diseases either by transcervical aspiration or biopsy forceps. Meanwhile, the demonstration in 1981[35] that the fetal globin genes could be identified from chorionic villi indicated that the haemoglobinopathies could be diagnosed towards the end of the first trimester, i.e. much earlier than by fetal blood sampling. Several different techniques were developed and published in 1983: transcervical aspiration by the Portex™ catheter[36] or a silver cannula[37] and straight transcervical biopsy forceps.[38] Chromosome analysis from chorionic villi had been problematic because of difficulties in culturing villi but in 1983 Simoni et al.[39] described a rapid method whereby a karyotype could be obtained within 48 hours by 'direct' preparation. This led to a great increase in the numbers of patients having CVS.

Methods continued to evolve and in 1984 a transabdominal double-needle aspiration system was introduced (Smidt-Jensen and Hahnemann)[40] and in 1986 curved transcervical biopsy forceps (Rodeck)[41] (Figure 6). Progressively, many centres then moved towards transabdominal single-needle aspiration, which was the simplest but in some respects also the most problematic method.

EVALUATION OF CHORIONIC VILLUS SAMPLING

After some years and increasing numbers of patients having CVS, a number of problems became apparent. The first was mosaicism, which was found to be more common in the cytotrophoblast and therefore in the direct or short-term preparations. It occurred in about 1% of cases and was at least ten times more common here than in amniotic fluid. However, the dilemma was nearly always resolved by awaiting the results of the culture. Cytogenetics laboratories in general were more at ease handing amniotic fluid than villi. Another setback for CVS was the result of the MRC European trial published in 1991,[42] which showed a 4% excess in fetal loss rate compared to amniocentesis. Finally, the most serious problem was the suggestion that CVS was associated with

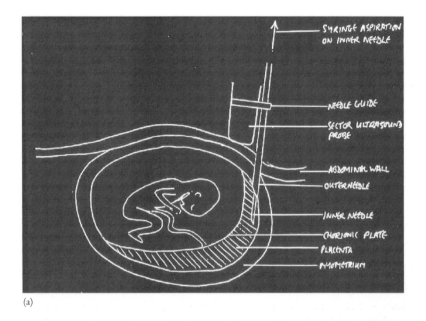

(a)

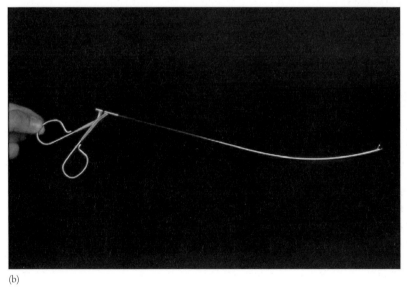

(b)

Figure 6 *(a) Diagram showing transabdominal CVS with needle entering (b) transcervical biopsy forceps*

severe fetal limb defects.[43] These limb defects occurred in several clusters around the world. Common factors appeared to be a combination of the very early gestation at which the procedure was performed (less than nine weeks) and a clumsy or excessively violent technique. This was further investigated[44] by measuring the rise in maternal serum α-fetoprotein as a surrogate of fetomaternal haemorrhage before and after transabdominal single-needle aspiration compared with transcervical biopsy forceps. The results showed a far larger amount of fetomaternal haemorrhage with the former technique and it was proposed that this could be a factor in the aetiology of limb defects.

In parallel with the development of CVS, there was also much interest in early amniocentesis, i.e. at 11–13 weeks. These various procedures have been subject to a number of large studies, most of them randomised, in addition to the UK MRC study.[42] They include a US study comparing transcervical CVS with conventional amniocentesis (i.e. at 15–16 weeks),[45] a Danish study comparing transabdominal and transcervical CVS and conventional amniocentesis,[46] a US study comparing transcervical and transabdominal CVS,[47] another Danish study comparing transabdominal CVS and early amniocentesis[48] and a Canadian trial comparing early and midtrimester amniocentesis.[49] The main points that emerge from these studies are:

- CVS should not be performed before ten weeks

- amniocentesis should not be performed before 15 weeks

- amniocentesis at 11–13 weeks causes more talipes and rupture of membranes

- where operators are equally proficient, fetal loss rates after transabdominal or transcervical CVS are the same

- the fetal loss rates for CVS and amniocentesis can be the same in the most experienced hands, but the learning curve for CVS is longer and, in general, the fetal loss rate is slightly higher

- amniocentesis is best for chromosome analysis, whereas CVS is most useful for genetic diseases and DNA-based diagnoses.

ULTRASOUND-GUIDED FETAL BLOOD AND TISSUE SAMPLING

As early as 1982, Bang et al.[50] described ultrasound-guided intrahepatic umbilical vein puncture and they transfused blood into a fetus. In 1983, Daffos et al.[51] published their method of umbilical vein puncture at the cord insertion by ultrasound-guided needling. This proved to be much easier than fetoscopic sampling and to be remarkably safe, with a fetal loss rate in experienced hands of 1–2%. Fetal blood sampling became far more widespread by this method than by fetoscopy and from 1986 onwards all other invasive procedures, such as fetal skin and liver sampling and other tissue and fluid aspiration, were carried out by ultrasound guidance (Figure 7). However, in the last five years there has been a progressive decline in invasive diagnostic procedures for a number of reasons:

(1)   molecular, i.e. genotypic, diagnosis is now available for almost all genetic diseases rather than phenotypic diagnosis, which can require fetal blood sampling

(2)   molecular techniques have become available for karyotyping: first fluorescence in situ hybridisation and then polymerase chain reaction

(3)   improvements in the non-invasive assessment of fetal anaemia and hypoxia.

FETAL THERAPY

The first example of direct fetal therapeutic intervention was reported by Liley in 1963.[52] This was a fetal intraperitoneal blood transfusion for rhesus alloimmunisation. After 1981, fetal intravascular transfusions were given fetoscopically[28] and from the mid-1980s they were given with ultrasound guidance (Figure 8).

Also in the 1980s several groups were developing in utero shunting procedures and 1982 saw the inception of the International Fetal Medicine and Surgery Society. In parallel, Harrison et al.[53] in San Francisco were developing open fetal surgery (see below).

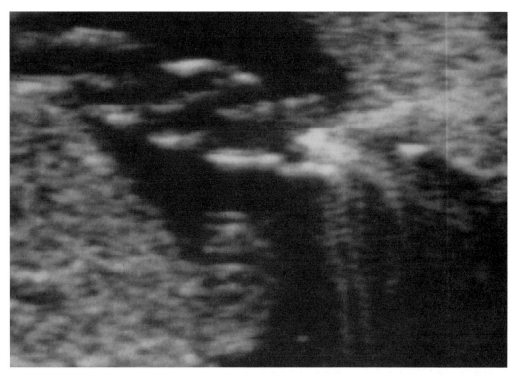

Figure 7 *Needle passing through anterior placenta and entering umbilical vein at cord insertion*

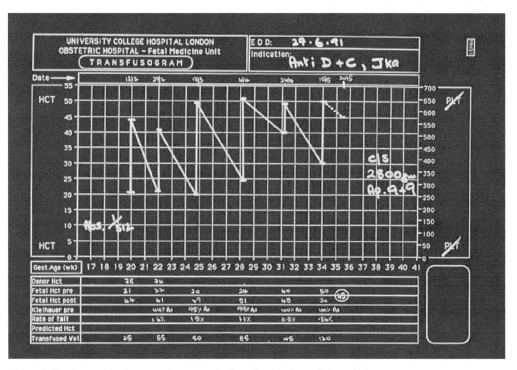

Figure 8 *Transfusogram showing course of treatment of a fetus affected by rhesus alloimmunisation*

Three types of shunt were attempted:

(1)   ventriculo-amniotic shunting for fetal hydrocephalus,[54] rapidly abandoned because of very poor results

(2)   vesico-amniotic shunts for posterior urethral valves[55] (now rarely performed because the criteria are highly selective and the majority of fetuses with this problem may not benefit from the procedure)

(3)   thoraco-amniotic shunting for fetal hydrothorax,[56] a valuable procedure that may be lifesaving for the fetus (Figure 9a, b and Figure 9c, Plate 2).

PROBLEMS WITH MULTIPLE PREGNANCY

Twin–twin transfusion syndrome

This serious complication occurs in about 25% of monochorionic twin pregnancies. The prognosis is poor and its pathogenesis is still poorly understood. De Lia *et al.*[57] proposed laser ablation of chorionic plate vessels, and Elliot *et al.*[58] reported serial aggressive amniotic drainage. Each method has proponents and it is still not clear which has the advantage in terms of fetal loss and long-term handicap due to cerebral damage. Both may be simplistic and research in this area is active.

Acardiac twin (twin reversed arterial perfusion)

In this rare complication, the healthy twin or pump twin has to perfuse the tissues of the acardiac fetus. The latter usually becomes grossly hydropic and the former may develop heart failure. Untreated, the mortality of the healthy twin approaches 80%. Many different methods of treatment have been tried, including hysterotomy and removal of the acardiac fetus, and different methods of occluding the umbilical circulation of the acardiac twin by embolisation, laser coagulation or cord ligation. Most of these methods are both difficult and ineffective. Monopolar thermocoagulation of the ultra-abdominal vessels of the acardiac fetus is the simplest, least invasive technique and has a good success rate (Figure 10).[59]

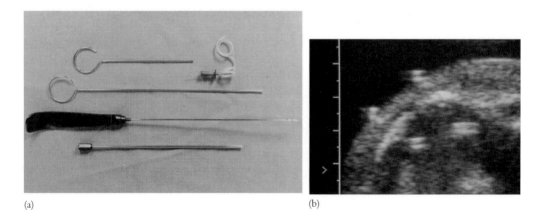

(a)   (b)

Figure 9 *(a) Equipment for fetal shunting; (b) thoraco-amniotic shunt in situ*

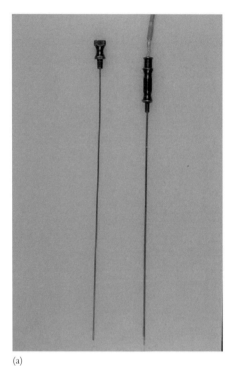
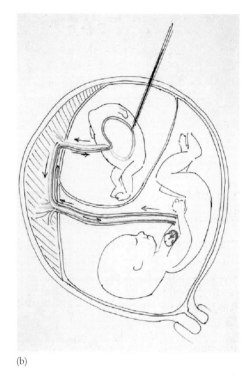

(a)   (b)

Figure 10 *Monopolar thermocoagulation of circulation to acardiac twin: (a) monopolar wire electrode and needle; (b) monopolar electrode in acardiac fetus*

OPERATIVE FETOSCOPY

Improvements in endoscopes, lenses, illumination systems and cameras have led to major progress in minimal-access surgery in many fields of medicine. This interest has spread to fetal medicine and surgery, beginning with laser ablation of chorionic plate vessels (see above). Other areas that have been explored are ligation of the umbilical cord in severe twin–twin transfusion syndrome or twin reversed arterial perfusion,[60] experimental tracheal ligation in congenital diaphragmatic hernia in order to promote pulmonary growth,[61] fetal cystoscopy and ablation of posterior urethral valves by laser or diathermy.[62] This work has been limited by the failure to establish appropriate indications for the procedures, by technical difficulties in performing them and by a high rate (up to 40%) of membrane rupture following the procedure. This field is being actively researched[63] and much of it is in animal models, from which significant improvements may emerge.

OPEN FETAL SURGERY

There has now been some 20 years' experience since the first procedures were carried out in San Francisco by Harrison *et al.*,[64] but there have been only a couple of hundred cases in total worldwide. Open fetal surgery has been performed for a variety of indications, most of which have subsequently been shown to be inappropriate or unnecessary. It is a major intervention for the mother, and the benefits to the fetus have often been unclear. Initially it was used for fetal obstructive uropathy, but it has been superseded by either insertion of shunts or conservative management. Congenital diaphragmatic hernia was regarded as a major indication[65] but diaphragmatic surgery was abandoned in favour of tracheal occlusion.[66] This, in turn, has also been shown to be of no benefit. Currently most interest is focused on fetal surgery to close spina bifida.[67] Initial results suggest that early fetal surgery may reduce the need for postnatal shunting but, as yet, there is nothing to suggest that walking or sphincter function are improved. It is hoped that a randomised trial will be funded to help clarify these issues.

CONCLUSION

This intrauterine odyssey has come to a temporary resting place, but it is still nearer the beginning than the end. It has seen a divergence between fetal diagnosis, which has become safer, less invasive, well-evaluated and heavily influenced by screening programmes, and fetal therapy, which is still very limited, has if anything become more invasive and is poorly evaluated. In the future we are likely to see developments in non-invasive diagnosis[68] and more effective treatment of fetal disease by *in utero* stem-cell transplantation[69] and/or fetal gene therapy.[70] With so much to learn about intrauterine life and so many challenges to face, this odyssey still has a very long way to go indeed.

Acknowledgements

There have been numerous mariners on this odyssey. It has been my privilege to work and publish with many of them and a pleasure to see 12 of them appointed to Chairs in the UK and different parts of the world. I am very grateful to Professor Andrew Calder for allowing me access to the Simpson archives in his department and to the Royal College of Obstetricians and Gynaecologists for inviting me to give this Oration.

References

1 Bevis DCA. The antenatal prediction of haemolytic disease of the newborn. *Lancet* 1952;ii:395–8.
2 Liley AW. Liquor-amnii analysis in the management of the pregnancy complicated by rhesus sensitization. *Am J Obstet Gynecol* 1961;82:1359–70.
3 Fuchs F, Riis P. Antenatal sex determination. *Nature* 1956;117:330.
4 Jeffcoate TNA, Fliegner JRN, Russel SN, Davis JC, Wade AP. Diagnosis of adrenogenital syndrome before birth. *Lancet* 1965;ii:553–5.
5 Steele MW, Breg WR Jr. Chromosome analysis of human amniotic-fluid cells. *Lancet* 1966;i:383–5.
6 Valenti C, Schutta EJ, Kahaty T. Prenatal diagnosis of Down syndrome. *Lancet* 1968;ii:220.
7 Brock DJH, Sutcliffe RG. Alphafetoprotein in the antenatal diagnosis of anencephaly and spina bifida. *Lancet* 1972;ii:197–9.
8 Simpson NE, Dallaire L, Miller JR, Siminovich L, Hamerton JL, Miller J, *et al.* Prenatal diagnosis of genetic disease in Canada: report of a collaborative study. *Can Med Assoc J* 1976;15:739–48.
9 National Institute of Child Health and Human Development. National Registry for Amniocentesis Study Group. Midtrimester amniocentesis for prenatal diagnosis safety and accuracy. *JAMA* 1976;236:1471–6.
10 Working Party on Amniocentesis. An assessment of hazards of amniocentesis. *Br J Obstet Gynaecol* 1978;85 Suppl 2:1–41.

11 Tabor A, Philip J, Madsen M, Bang J, Obel EB, Norgaard-Pedersen B. Randomised controlled trial of genetic amniocentesis in 4606 low risk women. *Lancet* 1986;i:1287–93.

12 Alvarez H. Diagnosis of hydratiform mole by transabdominal placental biopsy. *Am J Obstet Gynecol* 1996;95:538–41.

13 Aladjem S. Fetal assessment through biopsy of the human placenta. In: Pecile A, Finzi C, editors. *The Foeto-Placental Unit.* Amsterdam: Excerpta Medica; 1969. p. 392–402.

14 Mohr J. Foetal genetic diagnosis: development of techniques for early sampling of foetal cells. *Acta Pathol Microbiol Scand* 1968;73:73–7.

15 Kan YW, Valenti C, Giudotti R, Carnazza V, Rieder RF. Fetal blood sampling *in utero. Lancet* 1974;i:79–80.

16 Kan YW, Golbus M, Trecartin R, Furbetta M, Cao A. Prenatal diagnosis of homozygous β-thalassaemia. *Lancet* 1975;ii:790–92.

17 Fairweather DVI, Ward RHT, Modell B. Obstetric aspects of fetal blood sampling by needling or fetoscopy. *Br J Obstet Gynaecol* 1980; 87:87–99.

18 Westin B. Technique and estimation of oxygenation of the human fetus *in utero* by means of hysterophotography. *Acta Paediatr Scand* 1957;46:117.

19 Rocker I, Lawrence KM. Intrauterine fetal visualisation and blood sampling. In Murken JD, Stengel-Rutkowski S, editors. *Prenatal Diagnosis.* Stuttgart: Enke; 1979. p. 213.

20 Mandelbaum B, Ponterelli DA, Bruschenko A. Endoamnioscopy for prenatal transfusion. *Am J Obstet Gynecol* 1967;98:1140–43.

21 Valenti C. Antenatal detection of haemoglobinopathies. A preliminary report. *Am J Obstet Gynecol* 1973;115:851–3.

22 Scrimgeour JB. Other techniques for antenatal diagnosis. In: Emery AEH, editor, *Antenatal Diagnosis of Genetic Disease.* Edinburgh: Churchill Livingstone; 1973. p. 40–57.

23 Hobbins JC, Mahoney MJ. *In utero* diagnosis of hemoglobinopathies: technic for obtaining fetal blood. *N Engl J Med* 1974;290:1065–7.

24 Rodeck CH, Campbell S. Early prenatal diagnosis of neural-tube defects by ultrasound-guided fetoscopy. *Lancet* 1978;i:1128–9.

25 Rodeck CH, Campbell S. Sampling pure fetal blood by fetoscopy in second trimester of pregnancy. *BMJ* 1978;2:728–30.

26 Mibashan RS, Rodeck CH, Thumpston JK, Edwards RJ, Singer JD, White JM, *et al.* Plasma assay of fetal factors VIIIC and IX for prenatal diagnosis of haemophilia. *Lancet* 1979;1:1309–11.

27 Rodeck CH, Eady RAJ, Gosden CM. Prenatal diagnosis of epidermolysis bullosa letalis. *Lancet* 1980;1:949–52.

28 Rodeck CH, Kemp J, Holman CA, Whitmore DN, Karnicki J, Austin MA. Direct intravascular fetal blood transfusion by fetoscopy in severe rhesus isoimmunisation. *Lancet* 1981;1:625–7.

29 Rodeck CH, Patrick AD, Pembury ME, Tzannatos C, Whitfield AE. Fetal liver biopsy for prenatal diagnosis of ornathine carbamyl transferase deficiency. *Lancet* 1982;2:297–300.

30 Rodeck CH, Mibashan R, Abramowicz J, Campbell S. Selective fetocide of the affected twin by fetoscopic embolisation. *Prenat Diagn* 1982;2:189–94.

31 Kullander S, Sandahl B. Fetal chromosome analysis after transcervical placental biopsies during early pregnancy. *Acta Obstet Gynecol Scand* 1973;52:355–9.

32 Hahnemann N. Early prenatal diagnosis; the study of biopsy techniques and cell culturing from extraembryonic membranes. *Clin Genet* 1974;6:294–306.

33 Tietung Hospital of Anshan Iron and Steel Company, Anshan, China. Fetal sex prediction by sex chromatin of chorionic villi cells during early pregnancy. *Chinese Medical Journal* 1975;1:117–26.

34   Kazy Z, Rozovsky IS, Bakharev BA. Chorion biopsy in early pregnancy: a method of early prenatal diagnosis for inherited disorders. *Prenat Diagn* 1982;2:39–40.

35   Williamson R, Eskdale J, Coleman DV, Niazi M, Loeffler FE, Modell BM. Direct gene analysis of chorionic villi. A possible technique for first trimester antenatal diagnosis of haemoglobinopathies. *Lancet* 1981;ii:1125–7.

36   Ward RHT, Modell B, Petrou M, Karagozlu F, Douratsos E. Method of sampling chorionic villi in first trimester of pregnancy under guidance of real time ultrasound. *BMJ* 1983;286:1542–4.

37   Rodeck CH, Nicolaides KH, Morsman JM, McKenzie C, Gosden CM, Gosden JR. A single operator technique for first trimester chorion biopsy. *Lancet* 1983;2:1340–41.

38   Goossens M, Dumez Y, Katlan Y, Lupker M, Chabret C, Henrion R, et al. Prenatal diagnosis of sickle cell anaemia in the first trimester of pregnancy. *N Engl J Med* 1983;309:831–3.

39   Simoni G, Brambati B, Danesino C, Rosella F, Tertselli GL, Ferrari M, et al. Efficient direct chromosome analyses and enzyme determinations from chorionic villi samples in the first trimester of pregnancy. *Hum Genet* 1983;63:349–57.

40   Smidt-Jensen S, Hahnemann N. Transabdominal fine needle biopsy from chorionic villi in the first trimester. *Prenat Diagn* 1984;4:163–9.

41   Vaughan J, Rodeck CH. Interventional procedures. In: Dewbury K, Meire H, Cosgrove D, Farrant P, editors. Clinical ultrasound – a comprehensive text. *Ultrasound in Obstetrics and Gynaecology*. Edinburgh: Churchill Livingstone; 2001. p. 557–606.

42   Medical Research Council Working Party on the Evaluation of Chorion Villus Sampling. MRC European trial of chorion villus sampling. *Lancet* 1991;337:1491–6.

43   Firth HV, Boyd PA, Chamberlain P, MacKenzie IZ, Lindenbaum RH, Huson SM. Severe limb abnormalities after chorionic villus sampling at 56 to 66 days' gestation. *Lancet* 1991;337:726–63.

44   Rodeck CH, Sheldrake A, Beattie A, Whittle MJ. Maternal serum alphafetoprotein after placental damage in chorionic villus sampling. *Lancet* 1993;341:500–1.

45   Rhoads GG, Jackson LG, Schlesselman SE, de la Cruz FF, Desnick RJ, Golbus MS, et al. The safety and efficacy of chorionic villus sampling for early prenatal diagnosis of cytogenetic abnormalities. *N Engl J Med* 1989;320:609–17.

46   Smidt-Jensen S, Philip J. Comparison of transabdominal and transcervical CVS and amniocentesis: sampling success and risk. *Prenat Diagn* 1991;11:529–37.

47   Jackson LG, Zachary JM, Fowler SE, Desnick RJ, Golbus MS, Ledbetter DH, et al. A randomised comparison of transcervical and transabdominal chorionic villus sampling. The US NICDH CVS and Amniocentesis Study Group. *N Engl J Med* 1992;327:594–8.

48   Sundberg K, Bang J, Smidt-Jensen S, Brocks B, Lundsteen C, Parner J, et al. Randomised study of risk of fetal loss related to early amniocentesis versus chorionic villus sampling. *Lancet* 1997;350:697–703.

49   The Canadian Early and Midtrimester Amniocentesis Trial (CEMAT) Group. Randomised trial to assess the safety and fetal outcome of early and midtrimester amniocentesis. *Lancet* 1998;351:242–7.

50   Bang J, Bock JE, Trolle D. Ultrasound guided fetal intravenous transfusion for severe rhesus haemolytic disease. *BMJ* 1982;284:373–4.

51   Daffos F, Capella-Pavlovsky M, Forestier F. Fetal blood sampling via the umbilical cord using a needle guided by ultrasound. Report of 66 cases. *Prenat Diagn* 1983;3:271–7.

52   Liley AW. Intrauterine transfusion of the fetus in haemolytic disease. *BMJ* 1963;2:1107–9.

53   Harrison M, Makayama D, Nowall R, De Lorimier A. Correction of congenital hydronephrosis *in utero* II. Decompression reverses the effects of obstruction on the fetal lung

and urinary tract. *J Pediatr Surg* 1982;17:965–74.

54   Clewell WH, Manco-Johnson ML, Manchester DK. Diagnosis and management of fetal hydrocephalus. *Clin Obstet Gynecol* 1986;29:514–22.

55   Manning FA, Harrison MR, Rodeck CH. Catheter shunts for fetal hydronephrosis and hydrocephalus. Report of the International Fetal Surgery Registry. *N Engl J Med* 1986;315:336–40.

56   Rodeck CH, Fisk NM. Fraser DI, Nicolini U. Long-term *in utero* drainage for fetal hydrothorax. *N Engl J Med* 1988;319:1135–8.

57   De Lia JE, Cruikshank DP, Keye WR Jr. Fetoscopic neodymium: YAG laser occlusion of placental vessels in severe twin-twin transfusion syndrome. *Obstet Gynecol* 1990;75:1046–53.

58   Elliott JP, Urig MA, Clewell WH. Aggressive therapeutic amniocentesis treatment of twin-twin transfusion syndrome. *Obstet Gynecol* 1991;77:537–40.

59   Rodeck CH, Deans A, Jauniaux E. Thermocoagulation for the early treatment of pregnancy with an acardiac twin. *N Engl J Med* 1998;339:1293–5.

60   Quintero R, Reich H, Puder K, Bardicef M, Evans MI, Cotton DB, *et al.* Brief report: umbilical cord ligation of an acardiac twin by fetoscopy at 19 weeks of gestation. *N Engl J Med* 1994;330:469–71.

61   Di Fiore J, Fauza D, Slavin R, Peters CA, Fackler JC, Wilson JM. Experimental fetal tracheal ligation to reverse the structural and physiological effects of pulmonary hypoplasia in congenital diaphragmatic hernia. *J Pediatr Surg* 1994;29:248–54.

62   Quintero R, Hume R, Smith C, Johnson MP, Cotton DB, Romero R, *et al.* Percutaneous fetal cystoscopy and endoscopic fulguration of posterior urethral valves. *Am J Obstet Gynecol* 1995;172:206–9.

63   Deprest JAM, Ville Y. Obstetric endoscopy. In: Harrison MR, editor. *The Unborn Patient.* London: WB Saunders; 2001. p. 213–31.

64   Harrison MR, Adzick NS. The fetus as a patient: surgical considerations. *Ann Surg* 1990;213:279–91.

65   Flake AW. Fetal surgery for congenital diaphragmatic hernia. *Semin Paediatr Surg* 1996;5:266–74.

66   Harrison MR, Adzick NS, Flake AW, VanderWall KJ, Bealer JF, Howell LJ, *et al.* Correction of congenital diaphragmatic hernia *in utero*: VIII. Response of the hypoplastic lung to tracheal occlusion. *J Paediatr Surg* 1996;31:1339–48.

67   Sutton LN, Adzick NS, Bilanink LT, Johnson MP, Crombleholme T, Flake AW. Improvement in hindbrain herniation demonstrated by serial fetal magnetic resonance imaging following fetal surgery for myelomeningocele. *JAMA*;282:1826–31.

68   Holzgreve W, Hahn S. Fetal cells in cervical mucus and maternal blood. *Baillieres Best Pract Res Clin Obstet Gynecol* 2000;14:709–22.

69   Flake AW. *In utero* haematopoietic stem cell transplantation. In: Rodeck CH, Whittle MJ, editors. *Fetal Medicine: Basic Science and Clinical Practice.* Edinburgh: Churchill Livingstone; 1999. p. 887–97.

70   Themis M, Schneider H, Cook T, Adebakin S, Jessard S, Forbes S, *et al.* Successful expression of beta-galactosidase and factor IX transgenes in fetal and neonatal sheep after ultrasound-guided percutaneous adenovirus vector administration into the umbilical vein. *Gene Ther* 1999;6:1239–48.

4

Short cuts

John Bidmead and Linda Cardozo

Based on the Victor Bonney lecture given on 30 November 2000 at the Royal College of Obstetricians and Gynaecologists.

INTRODUCTION

Stress incontinence is a distressing symptom that has a major impact on a woman's quality of life. The history of surgical attempts to cure stress incontinence goes back thousands of years. Innumerable procedures have been described, with varying degrees of success. Only in recent years have the objective, long-term results of traditional surgical techniques been evaluated. More recently, a number of new procedures have been developed that aim to offer improved results with lower morbidity than conventional surgery.

Urinary incontinence is certainly not a recent problem, although there is little mention of it in the writings of ancient Egyptian and classical Greek physicians. The problem has probably existed since human beings adopted an upright posture and developed an increased brain size. This led to the need for women to deliver an infant with a large head through a narrow pelvic canal. Pelvic-floor muscles, originally developed simply for tail-wagging in quadrupeds, then had to provide support for all the abdominal organs and became increasingly susceptible to damage during childbirth.

Urinary incontinence resulting from obstructed labour and subsequent fistulae has probably occurred since prehistoric times, but was certainly a problem during the Egyptian empire. Douglas Derry from Cairo examined five mummies from the harem of Mentuhotep II of the 11th dynasty (2050 BC) and found that that of Queen Henhenit had a large vesicovaginal fistula, probably caused by the long labour that also led to her death.

Urinary incontinence continued to be a problem and is intermittently commented on in medical writing. Avicenna, in 1000 AD, wrote: 'In cases where women are married too young … the bulk of the fetus may cause a tear in the bladder which results in incontinence of urine which is incurable and remains so until death'. In 1597, Luiz de Mercato described the suffering of women with urinary fistulae: 'What an empty and tragic life is led by the affected victims and how great are their embarrassments … uncontrolled urine runs from the fistula with ease'. It is clear from both these statements that urinary incontinence was at this time regarded as an incurable problem.

Obstetric fistulae are still a major problem in parts of the developing world but, fortunately, are rarely seen in industrialised countries with high standards of intrapartum care. Stress incontinence, however, remains a problem.

There appears to have been little interest in investigating the causes and potential treatment of urinary incontinence until the 18th century. Historically, many different surgical techniques were developed with the aim of curing urinary incontinence, although given the inadequate understanding of the underlying causes of urinary incontinence and the absence of sterile technique, adequate anaesthesia and antibiotic cover, it is not surprising that these often failed disastrously. The fact that women were prepared to subject themselves to this type of surgery in the pre-anaesthetic, pre-antibiotic era is a chilling reminder of the misery that can be caused by urinary incontinence.

A variety of inventive procedures were described, mostly with the aim of causing urethral obstruction. For example, in 1892 Poussan described his technique of urethral advancement by: 'introducing a bougie into the urethra, resecting the external meatus and portion of the urethra, and then after torsion of the canal to 180° it is transplanted just below the clitoris'.

By the end of the 19th century, many surgeons had described their own variations on this theme, combining torsion of the urethra and advancement of the external urethral meatus. The results of this type of surgery are, perhaps fortunately, not well described.

Other techniques employed consisted of some form of urethrocleisis, combined with the deliberate creation of a vesicovaginal fistula or suprapubic cystotomy. The intention was to restore continence with some form of removable obturator, which could then be used to close the fistula or stoma. The most extreme form of this type of surgery was an attempt to create a vesicovaginal fistula together with a rectovaginal fistula and then to achieve urinary continence by performing a colpocleisis, a form of primitive rectal reservoir.

With the discovery of electricity, combinations of massage and electrical stimulation were used as a crude precursor to modern physiotherapy. Various forms of physical therapy, hydrotherapy, the ubiquitous leeches and the application of caustic solutions to the urethra and vagina were also employed.

As if to demonstrate that there is rarely anything completely new in surgery, injection of sclerosing and bulking agents into the urethra was used in the early 20th century. As Kelly wrote in 1913: 'For a long time surgeons have tried to relieve this condition by a variety of operations, some of them more or less bizarre, designed to act upon the external urethral orifice by contracting it, or to resect the vagina at the urethral orifice, or to kink the urethra in one way or another to tighten it. These operations rarely succeed. I have seen many patients subjected to them but none relieved'.[1]

It is no surprise that these early enthusiastic pioneers of continence surgery met with so little success, given the tools they had at their disposal and their poor knowledge or means of investigating the causes of incontinence. Investigation of the pathophysiology of incontinence dramatically improved with the development of two techniques, cystometry and cystoscopy.

CYSTOMETRY

Cystometry was pioneered by Mosso and Pellicani[2] in 1882, using a simple water-filled manometer attached to a smoked recording drum. Major advances were made when, in 1961, Enhörning proposed his theory of the correct transmission of intra-abdominal pressure in the prevention of stress incontinence.[3] As technology improved further, the appreciation of the potential mechanisms of incontinence increased. Bates et al.[4] developed the clinical use of combined videocystometry. Indeed, it was not until 1970, when Bates and Turner-Warwick[4] reported the relevance of abnormal detrusor activity and coined the term 'detrusor instability', that the role of abnormal detrusor activity as a cause of incontinence was fully appreciated.

CYSTOSCOPY

In 1893, Kelly developed the first cystoscope and also realised that 'air cystoscopy' could be performed in women using a silver cystoscope, by placing the patient in the knee–chest position.[5]

Air then spontaneously filled the bladder and allowed direct visualisation of the urothelium. In fact, it was Howard Kelly, a gynaecologist, who first inserted a ureteral catheter under direct vision. Improvements in rod lens technology led to further improvements in the design of cystoscopes and allowed the bladder neck to be studied. This led to Kelly describing the cystoscopic features of stress incontinence:

'The most common form of incontinence is the result of childbirth, entailing an injury to the neck of the bladder; it is occasionally seen in elderly nullipara and is most common after the age the age of forty. It is usually progressive, beginning with an occasional dribble, later becoming more frequent and occurring on slight provocation. In its incipiency a strain, cough or sneeze or getting up to get on a tram car starts a little spurt of urine which, in the course of time, initiates the act which empties the bladder … Sometimes the most suggestive picture that can be seen by a cystoscope is a gaping internal sphincter orifice which closes sluggishly. The key to successful treatment lies at the internal orifice of the urethra and in the sphincter muscle which controls the canal at this point.'

The forerunner of anterior colporrhaphy was probably first described by Schultz in 1888.[6] He described the excision of a triangular flap of vaginal skin and suture of the edges of the defect to narrow and elevate the anterior vaginal wall. Kelly[1] developed the technique of colporrhaphy further and described his now familiar bladder-neck plication: 'The torn or relaxed tissues of the vesical neck should be sutured together using 2 or 3 vertical mattress sutures of fine silk linen passed from side to side'. Following this, for many years, anterior colporrhaphy with some form of bladder-neck plication or buttressing was used to treat stress incontinence and until recently was regarded by many gynaecologists as the first-line surgical approach.

SLINGS

Operations using muscular and fascial strips to form suburethral slings were attempted at the beginning of the 20th century. In 1910, Goebell[7] and Stockell[8] suggested using the pyramidalis to form a muscular sling beneath the urethra. Other materials such as the gracilis muscle were also used with varying success. Aldridge[9] described his rectus fascia sling procedure in 1942 and, following this, sling procedures became established, particularly for secondary incontinence surgery.

Since Aldridge suggested the use of rectus fascia, many alternative sling materials have been tried. Natural materials such as fascia lata (autologous or donor), porcine dermis and collagen have all been used. Sling operations using synthetic materials such as silicon-based rubber strips or polyester, polyethylene and polytetrafluoroethylene meshes have all been described. There are many reports of success rates of 80–90% with slings, although they are associated with high rates of voiding difficulties and detrusor instability. Synthetic sling materials in particular can be associated with high rates of erosion into the vagina or urinary tract.

SUPRAPUBIC SURGERY

A suprapubic approach to surgical elevation of the bladder neck was first described by Marshall-Marchetti and Krantz in 1949.[10] This was initially reported in male patients with incontinence following radical prostatectomy. The retropubic space is entered via a low transverse suprapubic incision. The urethra and bladder neck are dissected free and sutures are taken to include the paraurethral tissues and urethral wall and are attached to the periosteum of the superior ramus. Subjective cure rates of 90% have been reported, but objective cure rates may be lower. However, the major complication of the Marshall-Marchetti Krantz (MMK) procedure is osteitis pubis, with a reported frequency of 5–7%.

In 1961, Burch[11] published a paper describing how, during a technically difficult attempted MMK procedure, he was unable to secure sutures into the periosteum. As an alternative, he hit upon the idea of supporting the urethra and bladder by elevation of the paravaginal tissue to the ipsilateral ileopectineal ligament; this technique, after modification, has become widely used today. Burch went on to describe a number of refinements to this technique and suggested the use of sterile milk instilled into the bladder to allow detection of any bladder injury.

As with many initial studies, Burch originally reported success rates of 100%; however, objective cure rates determined on the basis of postoperative urodynamic testing are usually lower. Hilton and Stanton[12] reported a 90% objective cure rate and Stanton and Cardozo[13] an 84% cure rate. Most published series suggest an objective cure rate of between 80% and 90%.

NEEDLE SUSPENSIONS

The first description of a needle bladder-neck suspension procedure was made by Pereyra in 1959.[14] He used a long needle to suspend sutures from the vagina to the fascia of the anterior abdominal wall. Originally these sutures were made of wire but, because these wire loops eventually cut through the vaginal wall, this technique was modified to include a helical plication of the paraurethral tissues. The degree of dissection was also extended to enter the retropubic space and mobilise the urethra and, in a series of modifications culminating in 1982, the suture material was changed to polypropylene.[15] In 1973, Stamey described the use of specially developed needles to suspend nylon sutures from the paraurethral tissues to the anterior abdominal fascia. Originally buffers of woven polyester were recommended to prevent the sutures cutting through weak paravaginal tissue. Many other variations on the theme of needle suspension have been proposed, most notably by Raz[16] in 1981.

During the 1980s, needle suspensions were commonly undertaken because they were easy to perform and gave good short-term results. It was considered unlikely that they would compromise the results of future surgery should it be required. In addition, the short hospital stay and low complication rate seemed attractive.

Unfortunately, longer-term follow-up studies have demonstrated the poor long-term results. In one study, Kevelighan et al.[17] followed up 259 patients who underwent a Stamey procedure at St James' Hospital, Leeds, over a ten-year period. Their subjective cure rates were 45% at two years, 18% at four years and only 6% at ten years. For this reason, needle suspensions have largely fallen out of favour except in frail or elderly patients.

The published results of all the various continence operations were examined in a series of meta-analyses by Jarvis in 1994, Black and Downs in 1996 and the American Urological Association in 1997. It became clear that suprapubic bladder-neck suspensions and slings gave the best results and these are currently regarded as the 'gold standard' procedures.

RECENTLY INTRODUCED SURGICAL TECHNIQUES

Attention has been directed at developing less invasive procedures, which will replicate the high cure rates of slings and colposuspension but with reduced morbidity, hospital stay and time taken to return to normal activities compared with conventional surgery.

Laparoscopic colposuspension

It is possible to perform colposuspension laparoscopically and, in theory, this should provide the same long-term success rates as an open colposuspension, with reduced morbidity and quicker recovery. A large multicentre randomised trial of laparoscopic and open colposuspension funded by the Medical Research Council is under way. This will eventually provide definitive evidence of the role of laparoscopic surgery in this area.

Injectable periurethral bulking agents

Injections of periurethral bulking agents are by no means a recent innovation. Periurethral injection of sclerosing agents (sodium morrhuate or cod liver oil) was described in 1938 by Murless,[18] although subsequent complications due to scarring and vaginal sloughing led to this being abandoned. Quackells also used paraffin in the 1950s.

Teflon® was the first widely used periurethral injectable material but was found to produce dense fibrous tissue and a granulomatous reaction, leading to urinary obstruction, urethral erosion and severe problems with any subsequent surgery. Teflon has also been shown to migrate from the injection site to local lymph nodes, lung and brain in postmortem studies.[19,20] As a result of these problems, Teflon is now rarely used. However, the encouraging initial results led to the use of alternative materials.

Autologous fat has been used as a urethral bulking agent. It has the advantage of being cheap and easy to obtain. However, fat is rapidly phagocytosed and, while initial results may be reasonable, longer-term results are disappointing; a recent report[21] of fatal fat embolism following periurethral fat injection casts further doubt on its use.

One of the most common materials used currently is gluteraldehyde cross-linked bovine collagen. This has not been shown to have any adverse effects due to migration but it does produce a local inflammatory response in which injected collagen is replaced with endogenous collagen.[22] Because of the inflammatory response produced by GAX collagen and the resorption of this material, repeated injections may be necessary to sustain continence.[23] Most studies report cure rates in the region of 40–60%.[24,25]

Another widely used injectable material consists of micronised silicone rubber particles suspended in a nonsilicone carrier gel.[26] This is currently marketed as Macroplastique® (Uroplasty, Reading, UK). The larger particle size of this material makes migration and displacement less likely and, in addition, the inert nature of the material makes a local inflammatory reaction less problematic. The silicone particles are designed to act as a bulking agent with local inflammatory response removing the carrier gel, encapsulating the silicon in fibrin and replacing the gel with collagen fibres. Cure rates reported with Macroplastique are similar to those with collagen but less of the material is required.

Other periurethral injectable materials have become available, including alternative extracts of bovine collagen, carbon-coated silicon particles, bone and ceramic materials and silicon balloons inflated after positioning in the periurethral tissues; however, there are insufficient data at present to compare these new materials.

Although injectable agents offer quick and easy treatment with low morbidity, their longer-term results have been disappointing; most studies report initial cures in the region of 40–60%. Given the poor long-term results, their use in younger, fit women is difficult to justify. While it might appear tempting to repeat injections every few years, not only is this extremely expensive, but the long-term effects of repeated injection are unknown. Repeated injections might lead to fibrosis and denervation of the urethral sphincter; recurrent incontinence would then be more difficult to treat with conventional surgery. Injectables are, however, invaluable in the frail elderly, in the treatment of secondary incontinence in women who have undergone multiple failed procedures or after radiotherapy where the urethra is fixed and scarred.

Most seemed to think that biophysical fetal assessment, intrapartum surveillance, labour management and neonatal care are as good or as bad as they are going to be. But that there will be huge advances in prenatal diagnosis, screening, genetics and treatment.

Perhaps the best message I got from any fetal medicine director was from Norman Smith in Aberdeen when he wrote: 'Dear Jim, prenatal screening is shambolic. Intrapartum surveillance has changed little since we were boys. Neonatology has peaked and needs to be rationalised. Molecular genetics is the key to it all. Best of luck, Norman. Aged 51?'.

Our younger members will be amazed that when I started out in my life as an obstetrician, progesterones were given to threatened miscarriage, Shirodkar sutures were used for women who had a previous miscarriage, women were not asked about choice, there were no fathers in labour ward, external cephalic version was carried out at 32 weeks, 70% of mothers were X-rayed, admission for static maternal weight or weight loss was the norm, with most maternity units having at least two or three antenatal wards, 24-hour urinary oestriols were used to assess fetal wellbeing and you would find out on the Monday that the baby had been sick on the previous Thursday. Valium was given for hypertension, natural labours were the norm, with eight percent caesarean section rates, general anaesthetics for caesarean section, anencephalics were diagnosed at delivery and consultants were never wrong.

However, let us not be too cocky. Twenty-five years from now the 'I don't believe it!' will be 'I don't believe you had invasive tests for trisomy? Screening for growth restriction with a tape measure? Screening for pre-eclampsia with a sphygmomanometer? Midwives and senior house officers looking after so-called low-risk pregnancy? Antenatal CTG to assess wellbeing? Detecting brain damage by looking at heart traces? Failed induction of labour? Specialist registrars in charge of labour wards? Listening to paediatricians? Obstetricians who couldn't scan? And someone suggested splitting obstetrics and gynaecology? I don't believe it'.

Diary entry

Monday 27 July 1942 '*Cable from Charlie saying he had arrived in Durban.*' But what effect did the terrible birth of baby Bill have on Joyce and Charlie?

Saturday 1 August 1942 '*Sister Radcliff came in at 6 and informed me I was going to go home tomorrow, bit of a blow, as I felt so weak*'

Thursday 17 August 1942 '*Feeling my old self again. Baby nine weeks old today*' and as you can see the baby was 9 lb 10 oz. But meanwhile Charlie is still in Africa and very much in love and missing his childhood sweetheart, his wife he hasn't seen since that fateful roast beef dinner. He hasn't seen his son.

Charlie penned many beautiful poems, songs and letters to Joyce while he was away. Here is just an example of one written two years after Bill's birth and before he has seen him:

> From the very hour I left dear
> I have been dreaming night and day,
> Longing for that great reunion,
> When I come home to stay.
> *Your Picture Is In My Heart*
> *Military Hospital, North Africa, 1944, Charlie.*

Diary entry

Thursday 4 January 1945 '*Sold the pram to Pamela for £10-10s. Monday May 7th.*'

Monday 7 May 1945 '*Tea in town. Hurried home as everyone expects the war to be over tomorrow.*'

Tuesday 8 May1945 '*Victory Day – Tuesday May 18th 1945 – put out three flags.*'

Charlie did indeed come home shortly afterwards and I am sure you would like there to be a happy ending to this story but it is not to be for, as the diaries tell us, Joyce had such a horrific time in labour and such terrible problems with her perineum that, also because of a lack of satisfactory contraception, she was never sexually active again. Charlie was shattered. Their physical relationship ended, followed swiftly by the emotional and the inevitable drifting apart. He took to the bottle, being described as arriving home 'squiffy' almost every night. He developed a duodenal ulcer but there was no ranitidine in those days and three years after coming home from the war the relationship had foundered. Charlie was drinking more and more, he had a massive gastrointestinal bleed and died at the age of 40 years, leaving Bill an only child and Joyce a widow.

But old sins do have long shadows. The sin of Eve and the resulting pain of labour can have long-lasting effects on many lives. For those for whom birth is a beautiful natural process – great. For those for whom it is not, we must continue to listen.

The future of obstetrics – is it an art? Is it a science? Which is better? Science has given us so much information that has shaped our practice. We have often reached the correct conclusion, but sadly the interpretation of scientific facts has not always been logical. Which is better? Neither – we need both. Thanks to science, the practice of obstetrics can indeed remain an art.

References

1   D James, personal communication.

2   Confidential Enquiries into Stillbirths and Deaths in Infancy. *5th Annual Report*. London: Maternal and Child Health Research Consortium; 1998.

3   McKenna D, Tharmaratnam S, Mahsud S, Bailie C, Harper A, Dornan J. A randomised controlled trial using serial directed real-time ultrasound to identify the at-risk fetus in a low risk population. *Prenatal and Neonatal Medicine* 2000;5:183.

4   Tucker JS, Hull MH, Howie PW, Reid ME, Barbour RS, Florey CD, *et al.* Should obstetricians see women with normal pregnancies? A multicentre randomised trial of routine antenatal care by general practitioners and midwives compared with shared care led by obstetricians. *BMJ* 1996;312:554–9.

5   F Manning, personal communication.

6

Totally forgettable contraception

John Guillebaud

Based on a lecture given on 14 September 2001 at the RCOG Celebration of Obstetrics and Gynaecology.

On 9 November 1965, millions of people living in 80 000 square miles of north-eastern USA and part of Canada suffered a total power blackout from 5.15 p.m. until the following day. Thousands were trapped in the New York subway and were not released until 4 a.m. the following morning. Nine months after these events, a measurable increase in the birth rate was reported in the same eight states. The reason given was: 'there wasn't anything else to do and they could not find their contraceptives in the dark'.

At that time the combined contraceptive pill was new and relatively infrequently used, having first been marketed in the USA in 1960 and in the UK in 1962. In 2002 many, but certainly not all, methods are ones that you do not have to find in the dark. What about 2100? If there were to be a power cut affecting the entire planet, would there be a further detectable increase in births nine months later? In theory, at least, by then this ought to be impossible, because we ought to have totally safe and 'forgettable' contraceptive technology plus complete availability for every couple who wanted to use it. If it were available to all and actually used by all, even if there was nothing else to do in a total power blackout but to go to bed with your partner, there would be absolutely no babies nine months later. Moreover, both induced abortions and emergency contraception in such a future contraceptive utopia should become redundant.

For the present, of course, reality is not like that. Accidents are caused by humans and most humans are still caused by accidents. Worldwide, with a total population already of 6.2 billion, such is the production rate of mostly 'accidental' humans that we have 80 million extra (above replacement) a year. This is down from the annual rate in the 1990s, but there are still more than two additions each second. A city (or, in reality, a slum) for one million people needs to be built somewhere every five days. While we pay lip service to the notion of 'quality of life', an extraterrestrial observer of this planet might well conclude that we strive more for 'quantity of human flesh'.

Every two minutes, a jumbo-jet-ful of humans arrives on the planet. This arrival, combined with the power of our advanced technology, means that we are, for the first time in recorded history, capable of having a collective planetary impact comparable to the global events of the whole biosphere. That humans are now appropriating around 40% of total photosynthesis and are able to influence climate change is just one aspect. Our collective environmental impact is already seriously harming our world and the varied flora and fauna with whom we should be sharing it more fairly.

I believe that the equation below should be taught to every young person.[1] It is a simple equation – factoring in the (only) three components there are to the environmental impact that we all have on this beautiful planet of ours … environmental impact: $I = P \times A \times T$ … where: P is for population, times A representing *per capita* 'affluence' (which unavoidably always means 'effluence', and the consumption of energy and resources), times T, which is the technology factor, *per capita*. This factor relates to the kind of technology used and how, on average, we humans succeed in minimising its impact through the use of greener, i.e. renewable rather than fossil-fuel, energy and greener ways of achieving our material culture.

REDUCING THE *T* FACTOR

You have heard of 'the 3 Rs'– *reading, writing and 'rithmetic*. There are also the environmental 4 Rs, namely:

- reuse

- repair

- refuse (the packaging and the many artefacts that are completely unnecessary but are constantly on sale)

- recycling – and, of course, bicycling (and travelling by train rather than by car).

By all these means, combined with the application of good science and appropriate low-energy technology, humanity should be reducing the *per capita T*. However, any scientist will tell you that there are strict limits to what reductions can foreseeably be delivered by technology alone.

REDUCING THE *A* FACTOR (*PER CAPITA* AFFLUENCE)

Can anyone honestly say that they would like less affluence than they have now? So if we can say that this view is representative of the current 'haves' of the planet, and I think it is, if we intend at least to keep our affluence, if not to strive actively to increase it (albeit in a 'greener' way with reduced *T*), what will happen to the world average *A* factor? There are over two billion 'have-nots' in the developing world – approximately one-third of the human population of the planet – who deserve to come out of degrading poverty through development. What is often overlooked is that, however 'sustainable' that development is, it has to create effluence and expend energy and resources. Thus, as an environmentalist, I find myself in the strange position of campaigning for the world average *A* factor in the equation to go up not down – for the sake of our two billion brothers and sisters living in such deprivation.

The *A* factor – *per capita* affluence – is thus destined to increase, partly for the good reason of sustainable development for the world's poorest – the have-nots – and partly for the extremely bad reason of increasing consumption and pollution by the haves. Ideally, the latter should cease. But what are we left with, to reduce the calamity of increasing global environmental impact? *P*, the population factor, the ever-increasing number of individual humans going routinely about their business and consuming, polluting and destroying habitats and biodiversity in the process. This is the only other potentially alterable factor – and it is a 'hot potato'. If mentioned at all, it is nearly always presented as a 'given' to be adapted to, rather than as a variable to be adjusted. This can be done non-coercively by making it a human right for every woman who wishes to control her fertility by using a contraceptive to be able to obtain one. The United Nations Family Planning Association (UNFPA) estimates that at present 350 million couples – one-third of all couples of reproductive age – do not have access to the range of contraceptive methods that we can choose from. We are failing to push at an open door; we are 'fiddling while Rome burns' and the planet is choking.

A major UN conference on the environment known as Rio-plus-10 or the Earth Summit is scheduled for September 2002 in Johannesburg. Yet, until some friends and colleagues of mine and

I became involved, the UK submission for that conference did not mention the word population anywhere.

My original home is a country called Rwanda. I was there in August, visiting my mother who was still there at the age of 86 years of age, working with my sister among the widows and orphans of the appalling genocide of 1994. I grew up speaking Kinyarwanda in preference to English, and some of my childhood playmates and adult friends were the first to die in April 1994. I believe that violence had as one of its non-proximate causes the fact that, when I was a child in the 1940s, Rwanda's population was only two million, whereas by 1994 it was eight million and rising; it was also in two implacably opposed groupings competing for the finite resources of a small land-locked country (Box A).

Increasing human numbers is not the cause of all world problems, but it is undoubtedly a great multiplier of most of them, including terrorism and poverty. It has been said since the attack on the World Trade Center of 11 September 2001 that terrorists should be disposed of like mosquitoes. But if we kill a thousand tonight, tomorrow there will be a thousand more mosquitoes. A far better course of action is to drain the swamp that is the breeding-ground for terrorism. In other words, we should deal with poverty by sustainable development. How can we ever expect to meet human needs sustainably unless we stabilise human numbers?

About 200 million people in our world are going to bed hungry tonight. We have to double the amount of food produced by 2025 to deal with world hunger. But are not food and water shortages, indeed every kind of resource shortage, in a strong sense primarily caused by 'people *longages*'…?

There is a small biological experiment from which some of our nephews and nieces might obtain a perverse pleasure, although repeating it is not recommended. It has been reported that if you get a saucepan, fill it about 4 cm deep with water, boil the water and then drop a frog into the water … it jumps out, unscathed. Now, if you complete the controlled trial (and this is where the experiment stops being ethical) with the same frog, the same saucepan, the same water and the same source of heat, put them all together at time zero and boil the water: what do you finish with? A boiled frog.

To any extraterrestrial observer the human race would seem exactly like frog number two, in its neglect of the threat posed by so many adverse if gradual trends – climate change, over-fishing, soil destruction, fossil fuel consumption – all exacerbated by the exponential growth in human numbers.

Box A *Human population increase and birth-planning: a key variable*

- Violence/genocide/terrorism
- Asylum-seeking
- Unemployment/mass economic migrations
- Maternal mortality
- Infant mortality
- Epidemic disease

- Food shortages, starvation
- Water shortages
- Shortages of all other basic resources and energy

- Poverty in the developing world
- Habitat destruction, conservation of the natural world, biodiversity

Every six hours, the equivalent of a jumbo jet of pregnant women crashes, killing everyone on board. That is maternal mortality: one a minute. As many women – around 3000 – die every two days as died in the events of 11 September 2001 in the USA. But we can and indeed do disregard those deaths. Is it not because they happen in ones and twos, to poor people, in rural areas – and, anyway, what do women matter? This is another example of our ability to disregard the gradual, however catastrophic. The real tragedy is that World Health Organization and others have calculated that about two-fifths of those deaths are happening to women who did not want to be pregnant in the first place. If we just pushed at the open door and made available to those 350 million of our sisters in the developing world the full range of contraceptives that are currently unavailable to them, that would be the most cost-effective among many necessary interventions to reduce maternal mortality. The tyranny of unwanted fertility is seen nowhere more clearly than in 50 million abortions each year. About half of these are unsafe abortions, with intolerable carnage and reproductive morbidity. These are at least potentially avoidable through voluntary contraception.

In this country we are more aware, perhaps, of the problem of teenage pregnancy. Given the ready availability of the methods, how can it be that the UK has six times as many live births to mothers aged 15–19 years as the Netherlands (Figure 1)? Why is this? First, sex is a powerful instinct, part of our animal nature. Second, the 'best' oral contraceptive – the word 'NO' – is hardly popular. Among young teenagers, should we not rediscover the possibility of 'selling' it, mildly, as

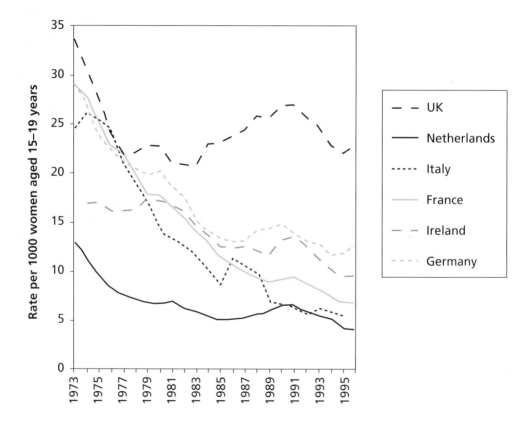

Figure 1 *Livebirth rate to women ages 15–19 years; various European countries 1973–1996; Crown copyright material reproduced with the permission of the Controller of HMSO and the Queen's Printer for Scotland*

a mighty good option that does avoid a lot of grief – through sexually transmitted infections (STIs), unplanned pregnancies and, in some ways more importantly, a lot of emotional trauma? But if that means 'the best', it should not stand in the way of 'the good', which is optional sex and relationships education in conjunction with the availability of good contraception. Years ago I got our local medical photography department to put a man's ejaculate in a teaspoon on the map of North America. When speaking to young people, I point out the sobering fact that if every sperm in there was able to find an egg, any normal man could populate the whole of North America on a single occasion.

AN APOCRYPHAL STORY ABOUT ADAM AND GOD

Apparently when God created Adam, he said: 'First, a bit of good news: I am going to create for you an organ. That organ is called the brain and with the brain you are going to be able to think and you can give names to all these wonderful animals and plants I am making for you'. So Adam said, 'Thank you, God. So what's the next bit of good news?' And God said to Adam, 'I am going to create for you another organ. This organ is called the penis. With the penis you will be able to have a lot of pleasure with your wife Eve. If you do things as I want you to, it will only be with your wife Eve, though if you do it right you will give her a lot of pleasure too. And the outcome of this, as I am God the creator, is that you will have children: I want you to bring them up to steward and care for this beautiful world'. So Adam said to God, 'That sounds like good news, too. So what's the bad news?' And God said to Adam, 'You will never be able to use both at the same time'.

This of course is the motif and the basis for this chapter. The story relates to the first man, because it is the male gender that has the worst problem in putting brains and genitalia together. Sex (of the genitals) is 'hot', whereas contraception (of the brain) is 'cold'. The combined pill is to contraception what the Hoover is to carpet-cleaners; it is the first thing we think of but not necessarily the best. It has the wrong 'default state' – conception. What the above fable tells us is that, for most people, the optimum would be forgettable contraception, requiring no continuing use of the brain over the years, having the correct default state – yet totally reversible whenever conception was really desired.

There is a wide range of contraceptive methods available in Britain at present.[2] The oral contraceptive pill, of course, gets a bad press and there was a detectable increase in induced abortions after October 1995, when there was that major scare to do with pills of the second and third generations. In the real world out there, the pill does not work all that well. It is too easy to stop and fail to restart in time, as well as to forget. Forgettable contraception means intrauterine devices (now joined by the intrauterine system), injectables, implants, with our present technology – and maybe, one day, reversible sterilisation and implantables for use by men.

So what about future methods?[2] There was an intriguing idea put forward about 15 years ago by Dr Stephen Kaali from New York University, which actually works. If you put a tiny electric battery in the cervix, the sperm are immobilised before they enter the cervical canal. There have also been experiments putting a battery in the vas deferens and so killing sperm in transit there. Switch off the battery and fertility returns. So why have we heard no more about this approach? If you go back to your A-level chemistry, you will recall that if you pass a current through any fluid that contains electrolytes you will get products at the anode and cathode. Those could be all kinds of things, including potential carcinogens, in a region such as the cervix where premalignant changes are common. So what about more promising ideas between now and 2100?

Figure 2 shows that there is huge potential for new interventions to control fertility, if you think of the new knowledge obtained in the field of artificial reproduction. What we are now learning

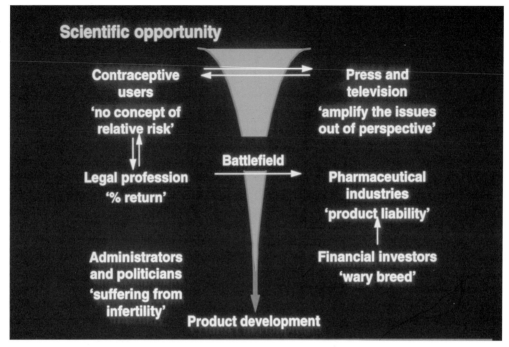

Figure 2 *Scientific opportunity, courtesy of Professor Denis Lincoln*

about the details of the processes of ovulation, fertilisation and implantation opens wide vistas of potential product development. However, as the figure shows, there is a battleground between groups with different agendas, leading to only a tiny number of new products emerging, despite the huge scientific potential.

Nevertheless, to be positive, there are some new products in the pipeline. The attributes of forgettability with reversibility mean, almost by definition, implantability. Some implants with those attributes already exist. Current versions are far from perfect, particularly with regard to the uterine bleeding pattern. But maybe by 2100 there could be an implant that you could put in at time zero – at the onset of sexual activity – when you didn't want a baby and then after ten to 15 completely adverse-effect-free years, when you did wish for a conception, you could switch it off, ideally all by yourself. That has to be the model that we should work towards if we are going to avoid surges in births or induced abortions following power blackouts or pill scares.

Implants may in future be placed in locations, other than subdermally. I could well be wrong, but I predict that one site will not become outdated even in 100 years – the uterine fundus. As gynaecologists we all know about the intrauterine system Mirena,™ which I call the 'future already present', the greatest single advance in my field since the pill. But it is still not recognised as such among the public at large: indeed, it seems perversely to be one of the nation's best-kept secrets. Again, in its present form, it is definitely not perfect. You have to warn each new user about early intermenstrual bleeding/spotting. My approach is to say, 'It is a package deal. Here is your Mirena and here are some weeks of time. You just have to accept several weeks or even six months of "dribbling" before it settles down'. Forewarned is forearmed. If you tell people how bad it might be to start with, then some may be ringing you up after three weeks saying, 'Gosh, it's stopped;

there must be something wrong!' It is a better idea for many than five years of the pill, for many reasons including its forgettability. Although we can say the pill has served us well, I predict that we will have little use for it by 2100.

But what about male systemic contraception? Forgettable contraception doesn't intrinsically have to be just for women. It should not be beyond the scope of human endeavour to produce by the year 2100 an implant that, at time zero, a young man could implant or have implanted and ten or 15 adverse effect-free years later remove, with total satisfaction and total reversibility. Indeed, a male progestogen implant plus depot testosterone ester combination shows promise in current trials. Note that I have avoided even suggesting a contraceptive pill for men, because most women feel it could be difficult to trust a man to remember to take it.

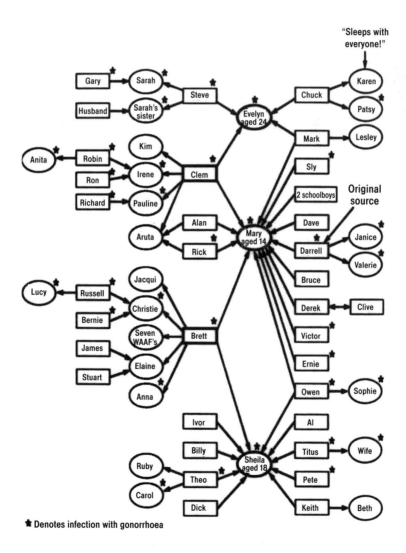

Figure 3 'Fun in the fens' – a contact training diagram' courtesy of Peter Greenhouse

Finally, we have must remember the issue of infection. Figure 3 documents a real STI network, an epidemic of gonorrhoea in the Fen country near Cambridge documented by Peter Greenhouse.[3] He did this work many years ago, but it remains highly relevant today. Every asterisk represented a case of gonorrhoea. In the current UK sexual infection context, the exact same story applies to chlamydia. Consider Anita, on the left of the diagram; let's say that Anita is 100% monogamous to her Robin. But unfortunately, Robin is not monogamous to her. He went with Irene, Irene went with Clem and Clem made the great mistake of sleeping with Mary aged 14 years – who is the source of every 'asterisk' in the picture. That is the real world. Figure 3 should in my view be on every school noticeboard. It should be regularly broadcast on TV and appear in the videos that our young people watch. If they could only appreciate what a dodgy situation exists out there, in all our metropolitan areas where, if you are not mutually monogamous, you are likely to pick up something much more hazardous to your health and future fertility than an asterisk!

In effect, there are really only three ways to have heterosexual sex, and I am not referring to the Kama Sutra. One is completely 'symmetrical' 100% mutual monogamy, where Robin is as faithful to Anita as she is to him. Otherwise there are only two ways, as depicted in Box B. Either use an effective method with condoms for STI prevention or use a condom as the primary method for both pregnancy and STI prevention and then use emergency contraception as may and indeed likely will become necessary.

Box B *Effective contraception*

EITHER:
Use a primary EFFECTIVE METHOD for pregnancy prevention, e.g. pill, implant, injection, intrauterine device or system   PLUS   CONDOMS for prevention of sexually transmitted infections

OR:
Use CONDOMS as primary method, for both pregnancy and prevention of sexually transmitted infections   PLUS   EMERGENCY CONTRACEPTIVE PILLS, for whenever condoms are not used, break or slip off

---

We should certainly be talking to our clients and patients along these lines. With our present technology, no single totally user-friendly method will do both jobs and prevent both conception and infection. Barriers are essential, but barriers unfortunately are not 100% and condoms slip off, break or are not used. So for the time being, we are still going to need postcoital contraception. Yet I do not believe that postcoital contraception will be needed, over the counter or not, in the ideal contraceptive future I envisage for 2100.

I have been involved for the last ten years in the Virucide Study Committee of the MRC. This committee is integral to the UK arm of what I think should take place on a greater scale worldwide – the search for vaginal microbicides. These would destroy HIV and all other pathogens in the vagina and be usable by the many women who cannot persuade their men to use condoms. We already have vaginal rings that are effective in delivering hormones. It should be possible in 2100 to have a small vaginal ring or an implant in the upper vagina slowly releasing a microbicide capable of killing all known sexually transmitted viruses and bacteria that would need replacement only every year, or indeed ten years. Quite a challenge! Yet it ought not to be beyond the wit of humankind by 2100 to produce a totally forgettable STI-preventer, as an adjunct to the forgettable pregnancy-preventer.

Thus we might arrive at a contraceptive and STI-free utopia through the slow-release vaginal microbicide just described, operating in a completely user-friendly undetectable way. It should not, of course, interfere in the slightest with the sensations of intercourse – hardly true of even the best present-day male or female condoms. This would also be a world with precisely zero unplanned pregnancies, no longer trying to accommodate ever more unplanned humans arriving to consume and pollute. With numbers stabilised, we might then meet needs through more appropriate 'greener' technology, which this fragile and beautiful planet would be able to sustain in the long term. Much more will be required than improved technology, of course – peace without terrorism will help, for a start – but let us at least dream and strive for a world in which, in short, we stop demolishing rain-forests and the other habitats for all our wildlife cousins, so that we may live, in Dame Barbara Ward's words of 30 years ago: 'full lives without dirtying a single stream'.

References

1   Hinrichsen D, Robey B. *Population and the Environment: The Global Challenge*. Population Reports Series M, No 15. Baltimore, MD: Johns Hopkins University School of Public Health, Population Information Program, Fall 2000:1–31.

2   Kubba A, Guillebaud J, Anderson R, MacGregor EA. Contraception (seminar). *Lancet* 2000;356:1913–19.

3   Greenhouse P. Study of contact training network for gonorrhoea. Unpublished report; 1977.

7

Surgery for intersex: where is the evidence?

Sarah M Creighton

Based on the William Blair-Bell Memorial Lecture given on 27 November 2002 at the Royal College of Obstetricians and Gynaecologists.

INTRODUCTION

In intersex conditions the dual pathways of sex determination and differentiation leading to a male or female child have not proceeded as expected. At some point the fetus has crossed from one pathway to the other or blended the two; hence an 'intersex' child, with internal and/or external physical characteristics of both sexes (Table 1).[1] The traditional medical management of these conditions has centred on trying to work out what has gone wrong in sexual development and to restore 'normality'. The child is classified as male or female, inappropriate gonadal tissue is removed and genital surgery is undertaken to make the genital appearance fit with the chosen sex of rearing. This management is now being criticised from ethical, social and clinical perspectives.[2–4]

The intervention of genital surgery in the treatment of intersex conditions needs urgent re-evaluation. The areas of surgery currently under most intense scrutiny are cosmetic surgery for ambiguous genitalia – especially childhood feminising genitoplasty and treatments for a shortened or absent vagina.

There is intense consumer dissatisfaction, with intersex peer support groups around the world expressing condemnation of infant genital surgery performed for cosmetic reasons.[5–7] Some adult patients feel damaged by their genital surgery and argue that many of these infant cosmetic procedures are unnecessary.[8] Despite this, little has changed in the medical management of intersex cases and the majority of clinicians, after thorough investigation and diagnosis, continue to recommend genital surgery to complement the sex of rearing.[9] A small number of clinicians are recommending greater caution with the surgical approach to the treatment of intersex conditions,[10,11] and one group has now called for a halt to infant genital surgery until the controversy is resolved.[4]

AIMS OF INFANT FEMINISING GENITOPLASTY

A standard infant feminising genitoplasty consists of removing some of the clitoris or phallus to reduce its size, constructing a vagina or opening the vaginal introitus and sometimes refashioning of the labia. Although generally accepted by clinicians and parents as a logical approach, there is little evidence of benefit or risk. Proponents of feminising genitoplasty in infancy cite the following as reasons to operate:

Table 1 *Intersex conditions*

Aetiology of condition	Conditions	Karyotype	Gonads
End-organ insensitivity to androgens	Complete androgen insensitivity syndrome	XY	Testes
	Partial androgen insensitivity syndrome	XY	Testes
Structural errors in the gonads (due to absent SrY or other autosomal testes determining genes, e.g. SOX9, WT1. SF1)	Swyers syndrome (complete gonadal dysgenesis)	XY	Streak gonads
	Denys-Drash syndrome	XY	Streak or dysgenetic testes
	Frasier syndrome	XY	Streak
Gonadal agenesis	Gonadal agenesis	XY	Absent
Errors in gonadal function, e.g. due to atypical cell lines or enzyme deficiencies	Mixed gonadal dysgenesis	5X/46XY	Bilateral dysgenetic testes or unilateral testis with contralateral streak or dysgenetic testis
	Mosaic turners	45X/46XY	Streak gonads
	5 alpha reductase deficiency	XY	Testes
	Leydig cell hypoplasia	XY	Testes with absent/reduced Leydig cells
	17β-hydroxysteroid dehydrogenase deficiency	XY	Testes
Simultaneous ovarian and testicular determination	True hermaphrodite	XX or XX/ XY or XY	Ovarian and testicular tissue separately or in an ovotestis
Excessive androgen production in *utero*	Congenital adrenal hyperplasia	XX	Ovaries
	Maternal virilising drug ingestion	XX	Ovaries
	Tumours, e.g. arrhenoblastomas, luteomas of pregnancy	XX	Ovaries
Miscellaneous	Cloacal extrophy	XY or XX	Testes or ovaries
	Traumatic loss of penis	XY	Testes
	Penile agenesis of unknown origin	XY	Testes

- a more stable gender identity development

- a better psychosexual and psychosocial outcome

- relief of parental anxiety

- provision of a vaginal introitus for psychological relief

- menstruation and intercourse in adolescence and adulthood

- stability in the child's gender development and congruity with sex of rearing.

Research by Joan Hampson, John Hampson and John Money at the Johns Hopkins University in the 1950s introduced the view that gender development – the process of identifying oneself as a male or a female – is mostly a function of postnatal environmental factors. They postulated that babies are psychosexually neutral at birth and have the potential to develop a male or female gender, depending on the way in which their parents treat them, the appearance of their genitalia as male or female and the way in which society perceives and reacts to their gender.[12] On the basis of 60 patients, the Hopkins group recommended that in all intersex cases, sex should be assigned solely on the basis of the external genital appearance as being suitable for male or female sexual function, and that all should then undergo early genital cosmetic surgery.[13] As the majority of intersex cases were felt to have inadequate male genitalia, infant feminising surgery became standard treatment.

Some clinicians and researchers agreed with this 'nurture' view,[14] or the overriding influence of environmental factors in gender differentiation. Others preferred the 'nature' view, or the predominantly biological determination of gender through fetal influences, mainly androgen exposure.[15] However, it is becoming clearer that gender identity differentiation is a complex and multifactorial process, involving prenatal influences and postnatal hormonal, social and psychological determinants.[16,17] The relative importance of external genital appearance in this process is unknown but may be minimal. Essentially, the aim of stabilising gender development with infant cosmetic surgery remains controversial, with a lack of evidence for the role of genital appearance in gender identity development.

Improved psychosocial and psychosexual outcomes and prevention of psychological distress

The expectation of current management is that infant feminising genitoplasty improves psychological outcomes. However, there are no data available to support this. There are no studies comparing the outcome in those who do and do not undergo genital surgery. The Johns Hopkins surgical management of intersex became standard treatment worldwide from the 1950s and the majority of the children underwent surgery. The medical literature is pervaded with the assumption that psychological outcomes are better after cosmetic surgery, with some even stating that gender assignment and surgery should be at an early age so that the child never needs to be aware that they were born with an intersex condition.[18] However, there is simply no available evidence at the moment that genital surgery improves psychological outcome. It has been suggested that all intersex children are at risk of psychological problems, irrespective of genital appearance and surgery.[19]

Relief of parental anxiety

Immediate relief of parental anxiety has been cited numerous times as one of the prime indications for feminising genitoplasty in childhood.[13,20] However, this does depend upon the clinician's reassurance that surgery will ensure good outcomes. It may be that, if parents are aware of the risks of surgery and the lack of evidence of good long-term outcomes, they will not choose surgery. However, their understandable anxiety may still be relieved in many ways, including full information, contact with other families and expert clinical psychological input.

Provision of a vaginal introitus for normal psychosexual development

The immediate aim of vaginal surgery, if performed as part of the infant feminising genitoplasty, is often to relieve parental anxiety.[21-23] Some clinicians believe that the vaginal introitus is also needed in order to stabilise gender development and to ensure normal psychosexual development.[18] There is an often unstated assumption in many surgical papers promoting infant vaginoplasty that the aim of vaginal surgery is simply to provide a passage for menstruation and sexual activity and that, by performing the surgery in infancy, the child can be 'cured' and spared the supposed psychological trauma of considering vaginal surgery later in adolescence or adulthood.[23] The literature is lacking in any evidence of the association between genital appearance and gender identity development and it is also unknown whether lack of a vaginal introitus in childhood and adolescence affects psychosexual development. This would seem unlikely, as women with Mayer-Rokitansky-Kuster-Hauser syndrome with congenital absence of the vagina are often unaware of their absent vagina in childhood and they do not have a higher rate of lesbian relationships or gender identity disorders.[24] There is also no evidence that infant vaginal surgery is less psychologically damaging than later vaginal surgery. On the contrary, there is evidence that hospitalisation, surgery and repeated vaginal examinations in young children can be psychologically traumatic and lead to long-term psychological damage.[25,26]

THE AVAILABILITY OF LONG-TERM DATA

In order to make sense of this difficult situation, objective data on long-term medical, psychological, psychosexual and quality-of-life outcomes from representative groups of intersex adults are required. Unfortunately there is little published work on any of these outcomes. The evidence that is available falls mainly into two groups: psychological follow-up mainly looking at gender and psychosexual outcomes in intersex cases and personal surgical series – with operating techniques and variable outcome measures – from clinicians. There are few studies of long-term outcomes that are not performed by the original surgeon(s), and open unbiased ascertainment in all the studies to date can be questioned. Follow-up studies of intersex adults have also been hampered by the widespread policy of non-disclosure (withholding of information on the intersex diagnosis from the patient), which leaves some intersex adults ignorant of their true diagnosis and absent from outcome studies.

CLITORAL SURGERY

The risk of damage to sexual function

Clinicians and parents worry about the possibility that clitoral surgery may damage adult sexual function. The clitoris is an erotically important sensory organ and its only known function is in contributing to female orgasm. However, sexual response is multifactorial and the exact contribution of the clitoral glans, clitoral hood and clitoral corpora to orgasm is poorly understood. Recent work on the neuroanatomy of the human fetal clitoris has demonstrated an extensive network of nerves completely around the tunica with multiple perforating branches entering the dorsal aspect of the corporeal body and glans.[27] It is clear that any incision to the clitoral glans, corpora or hood may risk damage to the innervation (Figure 1 – Plate 3). Other surgical risks are loss of the clitoral glans from vascular insufficiency and pain during sexual arousal in the remaining corporal tissue following either amputation of the corporal bodies at the pubic bifurcation[28] or recession of the corporal tissue.[29] Additionally, the effect on future sexual function of removing the paired clitoral corpora that make up the clitoral body is unknown.[30]

Literature review on clitoral surgery

There are over 100 papers on clitoral surgery in the medical literature; however, only a minority provides follow-up data on psychosexual outcomes. 'Long-term' results are sometimes reports of young patients who have not had an opportunity to be sexually active. The objectivity of all the follow-up reports to date is poor and the methods of assessment are either vague or unreported. The evidence from such studies is biased and unhelpful, with conclusions such as 'clitoral sensation was present in all'[29] or 'in all 10 the clitoris has normal sensation to touch'.[20] Some surgeons seem highly optimistic, describing genital surgery as achieving 'near normal cosmetic and functional results'.[31] There is only one study where attempts have been made to objectively evaluate clitoral sensory innervation after surgery.[32] In this study five out of six infants were shown to have preservation of a genital electromyographical response at the glans clitoris after stimulation of the clitoral dorsal neurovascular bundle, as assessed both before and immediately after clitoral reduction surgery. These patients were all children and so have not had any psychosexual evaluation. In addition, this study looked at conduction in large myelinated fibres rather than the more appropriate small-diameter myelinated and unmyelinated fibres.[33]

Two studies have looked in more detail at psychosexual function in intersex women after genital surgery. The first compared 34 women with congenital adrenal hyperplasia (CAH) to their non-CAH sisters.[34] The CAH group were less likely than their sisters to be sexually active and more likely to experience orgasmic dysfunction (33% orgasmic dysfunction versus 0%, respectively). The second study of 19 women with CAH compared with a control group of women with diabetes had similar findings.[35] Again, those with CAH had significantly less sexual experience and worse orgasmic dysfunction and they were more likely to report problems with penetration than those with diabetes – a group who are expected to have sexual dysfunction. They attributed their difficulties to their surgery.

A STUDY OF LONG-TERM SEXUAL FUNCTION IN INTERSEX CONDITIONS WITH AMBIGUOUS GENITALIA

Our study at University College London Hospital was of 37 adult women with a history of ambiguous genitalia.[36] Of the group, 24 had undergone feminising genital surgery and 13 had avoided surgery. All were assessed using the Golombok Rust Inventory of Sexual Satisfaction, which is a UK standardised questionnaire assessing seven areas of female sexual dysfunction, as well as giving an overall score. All patients also underwent gynaecological examination. Overall sexual function scores were poor in both groups when compared with a standard UK population of women; however, there were also significant differences between the two groups. Those who had undergone clitoral surgery were significantly less likely to achieve orgasm than those who had not had surgery (26% anorgasmia versus 0%, respectively). There was no difference in outcome with the type of clitoral procedure performed, although numbers of different procedures were small. Our study suggests that cosmetic surgery to the clitoris does not ensure improved adult sexual function and, of much more concern, this surgery may in fact damage sexual function. More work is needed in this area to try to differentiate between the possible psychological and surgical components to sexual dysfunction in intersex adults; however, at present the evidence suggests that clitoral surgery may damage adult sexual function.

VAGINOPLASTY

As discussed earlier, vaginoplasty has been considered an integral part of feminising genitoplasty in the management of ambiguous genitalia. It is commonly performed during the first one to two years of life despite the fact that the child will not menstruate for a further ten or so years (if indeed she has a uterus) and is unlikely to be sexually active until after puberty.

However, there might be an indication for early infant vaginoplasty if there were evidence that early vaginal surgery had better long-term anatomical, cosmetic and functional outcomes than delayed surgery. Most of the follow-up studies of vaginoplasty have looked at the exteriorisation of the vagina in CAH. Early studies of both vertical incision and Y-V plasty showed high rates (40–77%) of introital stenosis between five and 22 years after childhood surgery.[37–39] Later studies have produced even worse figures for introital stenosis (50–100%), perhaps reflecting the results with longer follow-up.[40–43] This has led to calls for vaginoplasty not to be performed in childhood and delayed until the patient is old enough to consent and the vaginal tissues have been oestrogenised.[42,43]

Outcome of feminising genital surgery in adolescence

At University College London Hospital we examined 44 adolescents (mean age 15 years) under general anaesthetic to evaluate cosmetic and anatomical outcome.[43] All had undergone feminising genital surgery for ambiguous genitalia; 43 of the 44 (98%) would require further treatment to the vagina prior to using tampons or undertaking sexual activity (Figure 2 – Plate 3). Ten girls would need to use dilators and the other 33 required more genital surgery. We also noted an extrordinary number of repeated surgical procedures prior to referral at adolescence for gynaecological assessment. Thirty-one percent had already had two or more vaginoplasties and 26% had had two or more clitoral procedures. We concluded that repeat procedures were common and could be avoided by deferring the primary vaginal procedure until adolescence.

Surgical options for vaginoplasty

There are numerous surgical procedures for vaginoplasty,[20] and the vast array of techniques attests to the lack of a single procedure with definably superior results. Outcome studies are scarce and most series in the literature are by a proponent of a certain technique reviewing the outcome of their series of cases, and concentrating mainly on surgical techniques and immediate postoperative outcome. There are few adult sexual function outcome data, and there is no information on adjunctive therapies used with surgery, such as oestrogen cream or vaginal dilators. The two procedures that have the most published follow-up data are the McIndoe-Reed procedure and intestinal transposition.

Graft lining of a neovagina

The McIndoe-Reed procedure, which lines a created vaginal space with a split thickness skin graft is probably the most widely used procedure. There are follow-up reports of this technique, although none contains objective assessment of sexual function. However, 'normal sexual function' has been reported in 80–90% of women after this technique.[44] Complications include vaginal soreness and dryness, contraction of the vagina (which is difficult to treat),[45] and dissatisfaction with the scar at the buttock or thigh donor graft site. In a second study of McIndoe vaginoplasties, 113 women were followed up from one to seven years postoperatively.[46] The study claimed that 90% were satisfied with their sexual functioning, although 42% had some degree of graft contracture.

Intestinal vaginoplasty

Intestine has been used in vaginal replacement for nearly 100 years.[47] Initial complications were major (including some deaths) and the technique fell out of favour. More recently the technique has become widely used again in intersex conditions and also following pelvic exenteration for cancer. Various parts of the intestine are recommended (e.g. ileum, caecum and sigmoid colon). There are some small studies available reporting good success rates. In one study, 18 of 19 patients undergoing sigmoidovaginostomy had a good result, with follow-up ranging from one to 15 years, with the remaining patient developing a stricture at the introitus.[48] In this study, sexual intercourse and orgasm were reported as 'normal' in all women, but no details were given of how this was assessed. Benefits of intestinal vaginoplasty over other methods are the reportedly low rates of vaginal contracture, although there is still the risk of introital stenosis, and the natural mucus-producing properties of bowel mucosa that reduce vaginal dryness. Drawbacks of intestinal vaginoplasty are the major surgery required and the excessive and sometimes offensive-smelling mucus discharge that can occur.

SEXUAL FUNCTION IN INTERSEX CONDITIONS: RECENT WORK[49]

The difficulty in assessing the effects of surgical procedures is compounded by the fact that there are few long-term adult outcome data on sexual function in women with intersex conditions. For example, the assumption has been that women with complete androgen insensitivity syndrome (CAIS) have essentially 'normal' sexual function.[50] This has not been our clinical experience and there are several factors that may contribute to sexual dissatisfaction. These are the physical problems of vaginal hypoplasia, hormonal factors including absent androgen effect and inadequate oestrogen replacement and psychological factors concerning self-esteem and body image. We studied 67 women with CAIS. All patients had a gynaecological and psychological assessment and a full review was undertaken of the hospital notes; 88% had areas of sexual dysfunction and 42% had areas of severe sexual dysfunction. This has not previously been reported and must be taken into account when planning services. The appropriate gynaecological, psychosexual and psychological expertise must be readily available.

CONCLUSION

Many factors affect the quality-of-life and long-term outcomes in intersex disorders. In the past, surgery was regarded as the cornerstone of treatment and parents and clinicians viewed it to a great extent as a 'cure'. Review of the current literature does not support the use of feminising infant genitoplasty as an effective treatment for stable gender or psychosexual development. However, the psychological benefits or risks of genital surgery remain unknown and data are desperately needed in this area. While immediate cosmetic results can be good, relieving the concern of both parents and clinicians, the evidence for satisfactory postpubertal cosmetic outcomes is not strong and more data are urgently needed. The vagina is not necessary for a young girl prior to menstruation or sexual intercourse. Even in those with a uterus, menstrual drainage usually occurs without complication via the urogenital sinus. Vaginal surgery should be deferred until later in life in the majority of cases. This should limit the total number of operations an individual undergoes, reduce the substantial risk of fibrotic introital stenosis and provide patients with greater choice of vaginal enlargement interventions at adolescence and allow them to be involved in the decisions.

Evidence is now emerging of damage to the future sexual function of the child from clitoral reduction. In the absence of firm evidence that infant feminising genital surgery benefits psychological outcome, the option of no infant genital surgery must be discussed with the family. Accurate information must be given to the patient and their family from the outset about the aims of the surgery and the risks to their child. Adequate and informed long-term psychological support should be available to all families, whether or not they elect to have surgery.

At present, the information available to allow parents and patients to make fully informed decisions is woefully inadequate. There is a desperate need for well-organised multicentre follow-up studies, involving adults who have and have not undergone surgery. Multidisciplinary professionals, consumers and peer-support groups must be involved in these studies to prevent the bias that is prevalent in previous outcome studies. We need to start to understand the full implications of caring for individuals with intersex conditions and improve our clinical services accordingly.

References

1   MacLean HE, Warne GL, Zajac JD. Intersex disorders: shedding light on male sexual differentiation beyond SRY. *Clin Endocrinol (Oxf)* 1997;46:101–8.

2   Dreger AD. 'Ambiguous sex'– or ambivalent medicine? Ethical issues in the treatment of intersexuality. *Hastings Cent Rep* 1998;28:24–35.

3   Kessler SJ. *Lessons from the Intersexed*. New Brunswick, NJ: Rutgers University Press; 1990.

4   Phornphutkul C, Fausto-Sterling A, Gruppuso PA. Gender self-reassignment in an XY adolescent female born with ambiguous genitalia. *Pediatrics* 2000;106:135–7.

5   Cull ML. UK CAH Support Group presentation to British Association of Paediatric Urologists Annual Meeting, 20 September 2000, Cambridge, UK.

6   Androgen Insensitivity Syndrome Support Group (AISSG) [www.medhelp.org/www.ais].

7   Intersex Society of North America [www.isna.org].

8   Chase C. Surgical progress is not the answer to intersexuality. *J Clin Ethics* 1998;9:385–92.

9   American Academy of Pediatrics. Committee on Genetics. Evaluation of the newborn with developmental anomalies of the external genitalia. *Pediatrics* 2000;106:138–42.

10   Creighton S. Surgery for intersex. *J R Soc Med* 2001;94:218–20.

11   Schober JM. Early feminizing genitoplasty or watchful waiting. *Journal of Pediatric and Adolescent Gynaecology* 1998;11:154–6.

12   Money J, Hampson JG, Hampson JL. An examination of some basic sexual concepts: the evidence of human hermaphroditism. *Bulletin of the Johns Hopkins Hospital* 1955;97:301–19.

13   Hampson JG. Hermaphroditic genital appearance, rearing and eroticism in hyperadrenocorticism. *Bulletin of the Johns Hopkins Hospital* 1955;96:265–73.

14   Ehrhardt AA, Meyer-Bahlburg HF. Effects of prenatal sex hormones on gender-related behavior. *Science* 1981;211:1312–18.

15   Imperato-McGinley J, Peterson RE, Gautier T, Sturla E. Androgens and the evolution of male-gender identity among male pseudohermaphrodites with 5alpha-reductase deficiency. *N Engl J Med* 1979;300:1233–7.

16   Meyer-Bahlburg HFL. Gender assignment in intersexuality. *Journal of Psychology and Human Sexuality* 1998;10:1–21.

17   Zucker KJ. Intersexuality and gender identity differentiation. *Annu Rev Sex Res* 1999;10:1–69.

18   Engert J. Surgical correction of virilised female external genitalia. *Prog Pediatr Surg* 1989;23:151–64.

19   Glassberg KI. The intersex infant: early gender assignment and surgical reconstruction. *Journal of Pediatric and Adolescent Gynaecology* 1998 11:151–4.

20   Karim RB, Hage JJ, Dekker JJ, Schoot CM. Evolution of the methods of neovaginoplasty for vaginal aplasia. *Eur J Obstet Gynecol Reprod Biol* 1995;58:19–27.

21   Oesterling JE, Gearhart JP, Jeffs RD. A unified approach to early reconstructive surgery of the child with ambiguous genitalia. *J Urol* 1987;138:1079–82.

22   Hinderer UT. Reconstruction of the external genitalia in the adrenogenital syndrome by means of a personal one-stage procedure. *Plast Reconstr Surg* 1989;84:325–37.

23   Hendren WH. Editorial comment. *J Urol* 1987;137:705.

24   Lewis VG, Money J. Gender-identity/role: G-I/R Part A: XY (androgen-insensitivity) syndrome and XX (Rokitansky) syndrome of vaginal atresia compared. In: Dennerstein L, Burrows GD, editors. *Handbook of Psychosomatic Obstetrics and Gynaecology*. Amsterdam, New York, Oxford: Elsevier Biomedical Press; 1983. p. 51–60.

25   Money J, Lamacz M. Genital examination and exposure experienced as nosocomial sexual abuse in childhood. *Journal of Nervous and Mental Disease* 1987;175:713–21.

26   Bonn M. The effects of hospitalisation on children: a review. *Curationis* 1994;17:20–4.

27   Baskin LS, Erol A, Li YW, Liu WH, Kurzrock E, Cunha GR. Anatomical studies of the human clitoris. *J Urol* 1999;162:1015–20.

28   Chase C. Re: Measurement of pudendal evoked potentials during feminizing genitoplasty: technique and applications. *J Urol* 1996;156:1139–40.

29   Allen LE, Hardy BE, Churchill BM. The surgical management of the enlarged clitoris. *J Urol* 1982;128:351–4.

30   Strohmenger P. Clitoridectomy or plastic reduction of the clitoris in the adrenogenital syndrome. *Monograms in Paediatrics* 1981;12:80–85.

31   Rink RC, Adams MC. Feminizing genitoplasty: state of the art. *World J Urol* 1998;16:212–18.

32   Gearhart JP, Burnett A, Owen JH. Measurement of pudendal evoked potentials during feminizing genitoplasty: technique and applications. *J Urol* 1995;153:486–7.

33   Lundberg PO. Physiology of female sexual function and effect of neurologic disease. In: Fowler CJ, editor. *Neurology of Bladder, Bowel and Sexual Dysfunction*. Woburn, MA: Butterworth Heinemann; 1999. p. 33–46.

34   Dittmann RW, Kappes ME, Kappes MH. Sexual behavior in adolescent and adult females with congenital adrenal hyperplasia. *Psychoneuroendocrinology* 1992;17:153–70.

35   May B, Boyle M, Grant D. A comparative study of sexual experiences. *Journal of Health Psychology* 1996;1:479–92.

36   Minto CL, Creighton S, Woodhouse C. Long-term sexual function in intersex conditions with ambiguous genitalia. British Association of Urological Surgeons Annual Meeting, 21 June 2001, Dublin. Abstract 049.

37   Jones HW Jr, Garcia SC, Klingensmith GJ. Secondary surgical treatment of the masculinized external genitalia of patients with virilizing adrenal hyperplasia. *Obstet Gynecol* 1976;48:73–5.

38   Sotiropoulos A, Morishima A, Homsy Y, Lattimer JK. Long-term assessment of genital reconstruction in female pseudohermaphrodites. *J Urol* 1976;115:599–601.

39   Allen LE, Hardy BE, Churchill BM. The surgical management of the enlarged clitoris. *J Urol* 1982;128:351–4.

40   Bailez MM, Gearhart JP, Migeon C, Rock J. Vaginal reconstruction after initial construction of the external genitalia in girls with salt-wasting adrenal hyperplasia. *J Urol* 1992;148:680–82.

41   Newman K, Randolph J, Anderson K. The surgical management of infants and children with ambiguous genitalia. Lessons learned from 25 years. *Ann Surg* 1992;215:644–53.

42   Alizai NK, Thomas DFM, Lilford RJ, Batchelor AGG, Johnson N. Feminizing genitoplasty for congenital adrenal hyperplasia: what happens at puberty? *J Urol* 1999;161:1588–91.

43   Creighton SM, Minto CL, Steele SJ. Objective cosmetic and anatomical outcomes at adolescence of feminising surgery for ambiguous genitalia done in childhood. *Lancet* 2001;358:124–5.

44   Rock JA, Reeves LA, Retto H, Baramki TA, Zacur HA, Jones HW Jr. Success following vaginal creation for Müllerian agenesis. *Fertil Steril* 1983;39:809–13.

45   Buss JG, Lee RA. McIndoe procedure for vaginal agenesis: results and complications. *Mayo Clin Proc* 1989;64:758–61.

46   Cali RW, Pratt JH. Congenital absence of the vagina. Long-term results of vaginal reconstruction in 175 cases. *Am J Obstet Gynecol* 1968;100:752–63.

47   Baldwin JF. The formation of an artificial vagina by intestinal transposition. *Ann Surg* 1904;40:398.

48   Martinez-Mora M, Isnard R, Castellvi A, Lopez-Ortiz P. Neovagina in vaginal agenesis: surgical methods and long term results. *J Pediatr Surg* 1992;27:10–14.

49   Minto CL, Creighton SM. Sexual function in adult women with complete androgen

angiogenesis is disturbed in menorrhagia, with increases in endothelial cell turnover, the number of small venules in the deep endometrium and inner myometrium in women with menorrhagia.[23,34] There are also changes in the proliferation of VSMC associated with the spiral arterioles, which may affect their function during menstruation.[35] We have identified a loss of normal ang-1 expression in the endometrium of women with menorrhagia, which may provide a molecular basis for the altered VSMC phenotype noted in this disorder (see below).[2]

ENDOMETRIOSIS

Endometriosis is characterised by impaired immunological clearance of ectopic endometrium (presumed to arise from retrograde menstruation) accompanied by abnormal adherence and implantation with concurrent increase in peritoneal fluid macrophages, immunokines and angiogenic factors (such as VEGF, transforming growth factor-β (TGF-β) and platelet-derived endothelial cell growth factor).[36] Several angiogenic-related disturbances, including upregulation and altered distribution of VEGF[37,38] and increased matrix-degrading proteases (uPA and MMP),[39] are detected in endometriosis, but it is not clear whether these changes occur early or late in this pathology.

REGULATION OF ENDOMETRIAL ANGIOGENESIS

Many angiogenic factors have been implicated in vascular proliferation of cycling endometrium, but their significance and precise role in endometrial angiogenesis remain for the most part obscure. While the menstrual cycle is under the overall control of oestrogen and progesterone, there is little evidence that they act as direct regulators of endometrial angiogenesis.[24,40] Here we review some of the factors implicated in endometrial angiogenesis and focus on two angiogenic growth factor families that play a central role in both physiological and pathological angiogenesis, the VEGF family and the angiopoietin-tie-2 system.

VASCULAR ENDOTHELIAL GROWTH FACTOR FAMILY

Discovered in the early 1980s as the potent vascular permeability-inducing agent in tumours,[41] VEGF(-A) is now recognised as a highly potent angiogenic factor that elicits a wide variety of functional activities, predominantly in endothelial cells. Five VEGF isoforms of different chain length ($VEGF_{121}$, $VEGF_{145}$, $VEGF_{165}$, $VEGF_{189}$ and $VEGF_{206}$) have been identified thus far.[42,43] Produced through differential mRNA splicing, these polypeptides form disulphide-linked anti-parallel homodimers and show a progressive increase in their affinity for heparan sulphate with chain length, which greatly affects their bioavailability.[44] While $VEGF_{121}$ does not bind heparan sulphate and is freely soluble, $VEGF_{189}$ is largely bound by heparan sulphate containing proteoglycans at the cell surface and in the ECM but may become available through proteolytic cleavage. VEGF expression is controlled by many growth factors (e.g. TGFα, EGF) cytokines (e.g. interleukin-1β, IL-1β) and hypoglycaemia, but the major physiological regulator appears to be tissue hypoxia, which stimulates VEGF transcription via the hypoxia inducible factor-1-α, and also increases VEGF mRNA stabilisation.[45-48]

Six VEGF family members have been identified (VEGF-A, -B, -C, -D, -E and placental growth factor/PlGF) that bind to one or more of three high-affinity tyrosine kinase receptors; VEGFR-1 (Flt-1), VEGFR-2 (Flk-1/KDR), VEGFR-3 (Flt-4) (Figure 1). While some family members (e.g. PlGF) bind only to one VEGFR, the potential for signal diversification within the cell is greatly enhanced by the formation of VEGF heterodimers (Figure 1). Most of the activities induced by

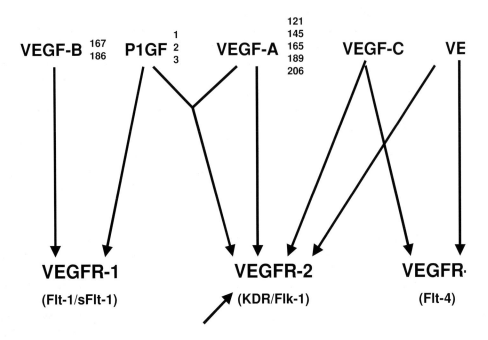

Figure 1 *Diagram showing the binding preferences of the vascular endothelial growth factor family (VEGF-A-E and PlGF) for their high-affinity receptor tyrosine kinases (VEGFR-1-3)*

the VEGFs, such as endothelial cell proliferation, differentiation, migration, survival and vessel permeability are mediated by VEGFR-2.[49] VEGFR-1 appears to act as a decoy receptor during embryological development but it plays an important role in VEGF signalling in the adult.[50–52] Our laboratory has recently reported that VEGFR-1 negatively regulates VEGFR-2, promoting the reorganisation of endothelial cells into capillary-like tube networks. We have shown that VEGFR-1 is responsible for branching angiogenesis.[50] VEGFR-1 is also produced as a soluble truncated extracellular domain splice variant (sVEGFR-1), which acts as a decoy receptor (deceptor) reducing VEGF activity by sequestration and dominant-negative receptor inhibition. VEGFR-3 is localised mainly to the lymphatic endothelium of the adult, where it mediates lymphangiogenesis stimulated by VEGF-C and VEGF-D.[53] In addition to the high-affinity VEGFRs, some VEGF family members (e.g VEGF$_{165}$ and PlGF) also bind to the cell surface glycoproteins neuropilin-1 and -2 (semaphorin/collapsin receptors), which appear to modulate VEGF binding to VEGFR-2 to enhance endothelial cell proliferation.[54]

Expression of vascular endothelial growth factor and its receptors in endometrium

There is some contradictory evidence in the literature with regard to the temporal and spatial expression of VEGF and cognate receptors in human endometrium during the menstrual cycle. This may in part be due to differences in the antibodies used for immunolocalisation and the stages of the cycle examined. The majority of endometrial VEGF appears to be produced by the glandular epithelium and, to a lesser extent, stromal cells.[1,42,55] Some early studies failed to demonstrate a correlation between VEGF expression and angiogenesis occurring in proliferative human endometrium.[57] However, recent investigations have identified a peak of VEGF expression during the menstrual phase (days one to three) of the cycle,[1,56] which is induced by the hypoxia that ensues following the constriction of the spiral arterioles in conjunction with TGFα and IL-1β.[1,58]

Patterns of VEGF expression in the mouse uterus suggest that it is under the regulation of oestrogen.[61] Consistent with these findings, oestrogen response elements have been identified in the regulatory regions of VEGF[43] and oestradiol and progestins induce VEGF expression in the rat uterus.[62] In addition, elevated VEGF levels and changes in endometrial microvessel density have been observed in women with levonorgestrel implants. It is unlikely that the sex steroids play a direct role in inducing VEGF during the menstrual phase when their levels are low,[1] but progesterone may be responsible for the upregulation of VEGF observed during the secretory phase of the cycle.

Normal eutopic endometrium contains numerous lymphomyeloid cells (macrophages, eosinophils, neutrophils, mast cells, natural killer cells and T and B lymphocytes), which increase dramatically during the secretory and premenstrual phases.[63] Infiltrating leucocytes (e.g. macrophage) provide a source of VEGF and other angiogenic factors in inflammatory conditions,[65] and oestrogen promotes the recruitment of macrophages to the endometrium and increases their level of VEGF expression.[24,27] However, circulating leucocytes may be particularly important in the endometrium, where intussusception and elongation are thought to be the major mechanisms of angiogenesis. Indeed, activated neutrophils release VEGF[63] and are associated with focal VEGF expression within microvessels undergoing angiogenesis in the subepithelial capillary plexus and functionalis layers during the proliferative phase.[61,64,65]

VEGFR mRNAs are reported to be present throughout the menstrual cycle. VEGFR-1 and VEGFR-2 are largely restricted to the endothelium but have also been identified in the VSMCs and glandular epithelium of the endometrium. Recent studies have detected maximal VEGFR expression during the menstrual phase corresponding to the highest VEGF expression.[1,66–69] The peak of VEGF, VEGFR-1, sVEGFR-1 and VEGFR-2 receptor expression observed by Graubert et al.[1] during the menstrual phase precedes increases in VEGFR-2 phosphorylation, endometrial blood vessel density[67] and maximal endothelial cell proliferation[69] during the late menstrual and early proliferative phases. Levels of sVEGFR-1 are also significantly elevated during the secretory phase.[1,69] Consistent with its role as an inhibitor of VEGF activity, sVEGFR-1 expression was inversely correlated with degree of VEGFR-2 phosphorylation, suggesting that it may mediate endometrial repair during the menstrual phase.[1] In addition, VEGFR-1 is expressed on monocytes/macrophages and VEGF stimulates monocyte migration. Infiltrating macrophages have been recognised as a significant source of VEGF and other angiogenic factors in many angiogenic situations.[37]

VEGF-induced angiogenesis is mediated by nitric oxide (NO), as VEGF fails to induce nevascularisation in NO synthase knock-out mice.[70] There are temporal and spatial variations in the expression of the inducible isoform of NO synthase (iNOS), which is maximal in glandular epithelium during the late-secretory and menstrual phases of the cycle. However, this is virtually absent in the proliferative phase, while the constitutive endothelial cell-specific NOS (eNOS) does not vary during menses.[71] Interestingly, NO synthase may be upregulated in the endometrium of women with menorrhagia.[72]

Endometrial expression of other vascular endothelial growth factor family members

VEGF-C and VEGF-D bind to VEGFR-2 and VEGFR-3 (Figure 1), which is largely restricted to lymphatic endothelial cells and involved in lymphangiogenesis in the adult.[53,73] VEGFR-3 is not expressed in the endometrial endothelium but is detected in infiltrating natural killer cells, which also co-express VEGF-C and PlGF.[61] Increases in VEGF-C and PlGF levels correspond to the infiltration and proliferation of these cells into secretory endometrium. While VEGF-B is not present in endometrium, VEGF-D is detected in the stroma and glandular epithelium.

ANGIOPOIETINS

The angiopoietins (ang-1–4) were identified as ligands for the largely endothelial-restricted tie-2 tyrosine kinase receptor. Tie-2 is essential for vascular development and is highly expressed in endothelium during both physiological and pathological angiogenesis.[74] While relatively little is known about ang-4 and its murine homologue ang-3,[7,75] ang-1 and ang-2 have been more extensively investigated. Ang-1 binding activates tie-2 signalling, leading to migration, sprouting, organisation into capillary-like tubule networks and survival of cultured endothelial cells,[76–80] and promotes vessel growth, branching, maturation, survival and integrity in vivo.[11,74,81–84] In contrast, ang-2 acts as a natural inhibitor of tie-2 signalling, leading to vessel destabilisation and neovascularisation in the presence of VEGF, or vascular regression in its absence.[14,83] Evidence supporting this antagonistic relationship is provided by gene knockout or overexpression studies in transgenic mice[74,82,83] and indicates a requirement for tight control over tie-2 signalling. However, recent studies have demonstrated that ang-2 may also directly promote changes in endothelial cell activity, depending on local concentration,[85] and is required for the development of lymphatics.[4,86] While little is known about the factors that regulate ang-1 expression, ang-2, like VEGF, is upregulated by hypoxia growth factors and cytokines.[87]

The ang-1/tie-2 system is believed to promote the close association of endothelial and mesenchymal perivascular cells (pericytes and VSMCs). Ang–1 produced by perivascular cells may stimulate VSMC mitogen (e.g. platelet-derived growth factor and heparin-binding epidermal growth factor) secretion in the endothelium to initiate and maintain the close association of perivascular cells.[14] Both ang-1 and ang-2 appear to increase the angiogenic activity of VEGF in vivo. While VEGF alone promotes the formation of leaky immature/unstable vessels, the addition of ang-1 stabilises newly formed vessels countering VEGF or cytokine-induced vascular leakage. This is presumably through the enhancement endothelial cell interactions with the ECM and perivascular cells and increases vessel diameter and branching.[7,84] Thus, the angiopoietins are thought to complement the actions of VEGF by providing permissive signals that result in the stabilisation and maturation of nascent blood vessels or destabilisation of vessels, initiating angiogenesis in the presence of VEGF or leading to vascular regression in its absence.[14]

Angiopoietins and tie-2 in human endometrium

Tie-2 is critically involved in the process of intussusception,[11] which has been identified as a mechanism of endometrial angiogenesis.[19] We recently examined the expression of ang-1/-2 and tie-2 in human endometrium.[2] Consistent with other studies,[61,88,89] tie-2 mRNA and protein was detected in endothelium and to a lesser extent the stroma,[2] although we also observed tie-2 in the glandular epithelium. Ang-1 was most abundant in the stroma surrounding blood vessels during the early proliferative phase, where relatively low levels of ang-2 were detected. Ang-1 transcripts were localised in the stroma surrounding tie-2-positive (ang-1 negative) vessels that along with the stroma were stained positively for ang-1 protein, demonstrating the paracrine nature of this ligand-receptor system and indicating its involvement in the initial distinct phase of angiogenesis in proliferative endometrium.

9

Fetal awareness

James Drife

Based on the lecture given at the FIGO World Congress of Obstetrics and Gynaecology, Washington DC, September 2000.

INTRODUCTION

When women ask us about the effects of playing music or reading to their baby in the womb, can we give them an evidence-based answer? We know that in late pregnancy the fetus can react to touch and loud sound[1,2] and that the newborn baby possesses all five senses. But we become rather vague when we try to define the gestation at which the senses develop and we have little idea of what – if anything – the fetus understands of the stimuli that reach it within the uterus. None of us can remember intrauterine life, but does that allow us to dismiss suggestions that some memories may be laid down before birth?

The most basic stimulus is pain. From time to time over the last two decades, clinicians and scientists have argued the question of whether or not the fetus can feel pain,[3–5] but we seem to be no nearer an answer now than we were twenty years ago.[6] The issue is sometimes raised as part of the abortion debate,[7,8] but it is also relevant to specialists who carry out procedures on the fetus and who have to decide whether anaesthesia is necessary. The question of fetal pain raises complex issues, ranging from developmental neuroanatomy to philosophical discussion about the nature of the self.[9]

NEUROANATOMY

'Awareness depends upon the structural and functional integration of the cerebral cortex with other parts of the central nervous system and the peripheral nervous system.'[10] The cerebral cortex matures relatively late in intrauterine life compared with the rest of the nervous system. The development of the nervous system will now be summarised, but it is fair to say at the outset that there have been few advances in knowledge since an authoritative review by the Royal College of Obstetricians and Gynaecologists Working Party was published in 1997.[10]

Peripheral sensory nerves

Sensory innervation of the skin begins early in the first trimester and develops in a cephalocaudal pattern. Neuronal free ending receptors in and around the mouth can be found at eight to nine weeks of gestation, and tactile receptors on the face, palms of the hands and soles of the feet can be detected by 11 weeks.[11] The first sensory fibres grow into the spinal cord at 14 weeks of gestation. According to animal studies, these transmit touch and not pain. The small C-fibres that transmit pain do not form connections in the spinal cord until after 19 weeks of gestation.[10]

Visual pathways

Rods are present in the retina by the fourth month of pregnancy and synapses appear on the rods at 18 weeks of gestation. At 20–24 weeks, the fetal eyelids open and the macule starts to develop, although its development does not become complete until a few months after birth.[12]

The visual pathway runs from the retina to the lateral geniculate nucleus (LGN) in the thalamus and thence to the occipital cortex. Fibres in the optic tract reach the precursor of the LGN by about seven weeks of gestation, and synapses between these fibres and LGN cells are formed by about 13–14 weeks.[10,13] At this stage, the LGN is a homogeneous collection of cell bodies and the development of its characteristic eye-specific layers only begins to be evident at about 22 weeks of gestation.[13]

A recent study of fixed brains from fetuses of 20–22 weeks of gestation showed that the axons from the retina entering the LGN were already organised at 20 weeks, and confirmed that the lamination of the LGN did not begin until 22 weeks. Axons from the thalamus densely innervated the subplate of the visual cortex but did not extend into the cortex itself. Animal studies have shown a similar 'waiting period' during which axons synapse in the subplate for days or weeks before entering the cortical plate.[13]

In summary, human visual connections are partially formed by mid-gestation and undergo further refinement during and after this period.

Auditory pathways

Details of the anatomical development of auditory pathways in the human are less clear. The otic vesicle divides into two parts by the fifth week, the semicircular canals stem out of the utricles by the sixth week and the vestibular apparatus is morphologically mature by 14 weeks. The cochlea is morphologically fully developed by the tenth week but it only seems to become functional at 18–20 weeks.[11]

The middle ear is formed by the end of the mid-trimester, with the ossicles being of adult size by the eighth month of pregnancy. In animals, there is some delay between anatomical development and functional maturity, due to completion of the myelination process, the formation of synapses and the initiation of enzyme activity. It is thought, but not proved, that a similar delay occurs in the human. Myelination begins during the 20th week of pregnancy but is not completed until after birth.[14]

Thalamus

All sensory pathways, including painful stimuli from peripheral nerves, are transmitted through the thalamus. From six to eight weeks of gestation, the thalamus begins to differentiate into its ventricular, intermediate and mantle zones, and formation of thalamic nuclei begins at ten to 14 weeks. Myelination first occurs in the thalamus at 25 weeks. Only 40% of the synaptic input of the thalamus is from sensory pathways, however, and the remaining 60% is from the cerebral cortex, in the form of descending connections, which do not reach the thalamus before 20–21 weeks of gestation. Full thalamic function depends on this feedback from the cortex, and therefore its function beyond a simple relay does not begin before 22 weeks. It has been suggested that the thalamus alone, without cortical connections, can produce sensations of pain or discomfort, but there is no evidence to support this.[10]

Cerebral cortex

Axons begin to grow into the primitive cortex from as early as 16 weeks of gestation, but they do not carry sensory information and are probably involved in the growth and guidance of neural connections in the immature cortex. Thalamocortical connections first penetrate the frontal cortical plate at 26–34 weeks. New neurones are still being generated at 34 weeks and the formation of synapses continues for two years, stimulated and modified by sensory experience. Indeed, structural and functional development of the nervous system continues until adult life.[10]

The formation of gyri and sulci on the surface of the brain begins at the second month of intrauterine life and continues until the end of pregnancy and even after birth. It can be studied by ultrasound and by magnetic resonance imaging (MRI). A recent MRI study confirmed a precise timetable for the appearance of secondary and tertiary sulci between 22 and 38 weeks of gestation. All primary and most of the secondary sulci are present by 34 weeks.[15]

NEUROPHYSIOLOGY

Fetal movements

Spontaneous fetal movements can be seen during ultrasound scanning from 7.5–8.0 weeks of gestation.[10] Spontaneous twitching of the trunk and head begin at the seventh week of pregnancy and limb movements, which first occur at the tenth week, appear co-ordinated by the 16th week. The amount of fetal activity increases until 32 weeks and then remains constant or decreases. Fetal breathing movements begin as early as 11 weeks and remain irregular during the first half of pregnancy. Slow eye movements have been observed at 16 weeks and rapid eye movements at 23 weeks. After 32 weeks, repetitive or nystagmoid eye movements occur. Eye inactivity becomes more common after 36 weeks.[1]

Reflex responses

Reflex responses to touching the region of the mouth have been reported in fetuses after first-trimester termination of pregnancy, although such fetuses are clearly not in a physiological condition.[10] Anencephalic fetuses respond to touch by moving, although they possess only simple spinal reflexes.[12] Neonates of less than 30 weeks of gestation show a flexor response to painful stimuli such as a pinprick in the leg.[16]

Behavioural states

By observing fetal body movements, eye movements and heart-rate patterns, Nijhuis described four fetal behavioural states, which are usually thought of as corresponding to sleep, rapid-eye-movement (REM) sleep and wakefulness.[1,17] The states are called '1F' to '4F' (the letter 'F' denoting the fetal state to distinguish it from the neonatal state). In State 1F, the heart rate is stable within a narrow range, eye movements are absent and body movements are incidental. In the other three states, eye movements are present, and in State 4F the heart-rate pattern is unstable with large long-lasting accelerations, and body movements are continuous. States 1F and 4F are generally thought of as corresponding to deep sleep and full wakefulness respectively, with the other two representing intermediate states. A fetus at 28–32 weeks of gestation, or a premature baby, spends more time in REM sleep than a mature fetus or neonate.[12]

Recently, functional MRI, an established technique for investigating adult brain activity, has been used to provide direct evidence of fetal cortical brain activity *in utero*. In a study of four fetuses, Hykin et al.[18] reported a change in brain activity in response to a stimulus in the form of a recording of a nursery rhyme read by the mother. The response to such stimuli is further discussed below.

THE SENSES

In late pregnancy, the fetus can respond to bright light and to sound, and the response varies depending on its behavioural state.[12] Less is known about the senses of taste and smell.

Sight

In a study of the effects of external light in the last month of pregnancy, a flashlight was applied to the maternal abdomen and the fetal heart rate and body movements were observed. A response (in the form of an acceleration of the heart rate) was seen in over 80% of cases when the fetus was in state 2F or 3F, but in only 4% of cases when the fetus was in state 1F.[19]

Input from the retina is important in controlling circadian rhythmicity, and by 36 weeks of gestation a direct pathway exists from the retina to the suprachiasmatic nuclei (SCN), the site of the biological clock. These nuclei are present by mid-gestation. In animals the SCN begin oscillating in synchrony with the external light–dark cycle in utero, but it is not known whether this occurs in humans, or whether fetal circadian rhythm is responsible for the fact that spontaneous labour occurs more frequently at night in humans. Increasing attention is, however, being paid to the importance of circadian rhythms in the lighting of neonatal nurseries caring for preterm babies.[20]

Hearing

Most of the research on fetal responses in utero has used sound as the stimulus. At 22 weeks, the fetus shows no response, but an increase in the fetal heart rate in response to sound has been reported as early as 26 weeks of gestation.[12] In a study of low-risk and high-risk fetuses between 27 and 36 weeks, the onset of cardiac accelerations and body-movement responses occurred at 30 weeks of gestational age. The threshold for a cardiac response in low-risk fetuses decreased from 105–110 decibels at 33 weeks to 100–105 decibels at 36 weeks.[21]

Some investigators have concluded that the intrauterine environment contains background noise, mainly maternal bloodflow, at a level of around 72 decibels and that external sound is so attenuated inside the uterus that it only rarely reaches levels exceeding the background noise: therefore that only loud external sounds (over 100 decibels) produce a sensory stimulus to the fetal ear.[12] These stimuli need to be within the frequency range audible to humans, and there is no evidence that ultrasound waves affect fetal activity.

However, Damstra-Wijmenga[22] reported that when a woman at 39 weeks of gestation placed a small microphone high in her vagina and spoke some sentences in her usual tone of voice, her voice was audible and identifiable on the resulting tape-recording and the background noise was much less loud than expected. A similar conclusion had previously been reached by French investigators,[23] who reported that human voices emerge above the basal noise, that the male voice, being lower, is better transmitted than the female voice and that syllables and the tune of a lullaby could be recognised.

The fetal response to loud sound in late pregnancy is reasonably consistent. In one study of fetuses in the last month of pregnancy, sound stimuli always produced a fetal heart-rate response,[19] and in another they always produced a response in terms of movement.[12] These responses can therefore be used clinically to check the condition of the fetus. Physiological purists point out that the fetus may be responding to vibration as well as sound, hence the term 'vibroacoustic' for the stimuli used in clinical practice, mainly in the USA.

Brain stem auditory evoked potentials have been recorded from the human fetus during labour in response to clicks delivered on the mother's abdomen at an intensity of 120 decibels.[24] This has been suggested as a possible screening tool for detecting severe neurological damage before birth.

It is now being increasingly appreciated that newborn babies are sensitive to sound. Large nurseries are not traditionally the most silent area of a hospital, and awareness of the effects of noise on the neonate has recently led to the development of criteria for permissible noise levels in hospital nurseries.[25]

Taste and smell

Morphologically mature taste buds are first seen at 12 weeks, spread out over the whole of the oral cavity, and later they are concentrated on the tip of the tongue and the circumvallate papillae.[12] The olfactory bulbs of fetal rats can take up and distribute odour molecules towards the end of pregnancy, suggesting that the sense of smell can function *in utero*.[1] Injection of saccharine into the amniotic fluid increases fetal swallowing and a bad-tasting substance decreases swallowing.[12]

TOUCH, PAIN AND THE STRESS RESPONSE

Tactile stimulation of the human fetus can elicit reflex responses at $10^1/_2$ weeks.[12] In late pregnancy, the fetal response to touch can be demonstrated by 'shaking the fetus awake' through the maternal abdomen.[1]

The question of whether the fetus can feel pain raised considerable controversy during the 1990s. On a scientific level, the reason for the debate is that pain is essentially a subjective phenomenon and cannot be directly measured objectively. Anand and Hickey[16] summarised the reasons why during the 1980s it was generally assumed that the neonate (and by implication the fetus) could not feel pain. Early neurological studies had concluded that neonatal responses to painful stimuli did not involve the cerebral cortex, that neonates had no memory of pain and, on a theoretical basis, that a high pain threshold was necessary to protect the fetus from pain during birth.

Reporting from the Department of Anaesthesia at Harvard and the Children's Hospital in Boston, these authors went on to summarise the evidence that pain perception is possible *in utero*. Neurochemical transmitters, such as substance P, that are involved in the transmission of pain impulses, are present in the fetal central nervous system from an early stage of development. Endorphins may be secreted in mid-pregnancy and their levels in the umbilical cord after delivery are three to five times higher than plasma levels in the resting adult. After vacuum extraction or breech delivery, the cord levels are higher still. Endorphin levels fall again during the neonatal period. Cardiovascular and cutaneous responses to painful stimuli in the neonate can be modified by anaesthesia. Anand and Hickey[16] argued that a neonate's movements, facial expressions and tone of crying in response to noxious stimuli can be distinguished from its responses to other stimuli, such as hunger or fear. As for the absence of memory of pain, they pointed out that, in the adult, the memory of pain is also poor.

The other major line of evidence cited in favour of pain perception by the fetus was the hormonal and metabolic response of the neonate to noxious stimuli. In 1994, Giannakoulopoulos *et al.*[26] published the first direct study of the biochemical response to such stimuli in the fetus itself. They examined cortisol and beta-endorphin concentrations in plasma obtained from fetuses undergoing clinically indicated intrauterine blood sampling between 20 and 34 weeks of gestation at Queen Charlotte's and Chelsea Hospital, London. Forty-six fetuses were included in the study, of which 21 had blood taken from the placental cord insertion (where no pain receptors exist) and 23 had blood taken from an intrahepatic vein by a needle inserted through the fetal abdominal wall. There was a rapid increase in cortisol and beta-endorphin concentrations among fetuses experiencing intrahepatic vein puncture but no change among the placental vein group. Giannakopoulos et al.[26] suggested that this raises the possibility that the fetus feels pain in utero and may benefit from anaesthesia or analgesia during invasive procedures.

In an accompanying editorial, Clark[27] pointed out that in other circumstances biochemical responses to stress can occur when analgesia is adequate, and that unconscious patients can show responses to putatively painful stimuli. Clark also commented that intervention to prevent putative pain could cause harm. In subsequent correspondence in the Lancet, Derbyshire[28] argued that pain is a multidimensional experience incorporating sensory, emotional and cognitive factors that have to be learned after birth. He contended that pain networks are dynamic structures that are continually changing throughout a person's life, citing the example of Indian mystics for whom the insertion of metal hooks in the skin is apparently painless. Another Lancet correspondent questioned the relevance of Giannakopoulos's results to mid-trimester termination of pregnancy.[29] Two years later, the controversy resurfaced in the British Medical Journal, again without any clear conclusion being reached.[5,30-36]

FETAL MEMORY

In a subsequent review article, the Queen Charlotte's group reviewed evidence that fetuses may indeed remember pain after birth.[37] In animal studies, rats exposed to stress perinatally secrete more corticosterone than controls in stressful situations later in life. Primates exposed to stress in the latter third of pregnancy secrete higher levels of cortisone and adrenocorticotropic hormone when stressed as neonates. In humans, babies born by instrumental delivery have a greater rise in salivary cortisol and cry for longer than those delivered normally, while those born by elective caesarean section show the opposite trend, with lower levels of cortisol compared with normal controls.[37]

Moving away from the question of pain, the debate about whether the human fetus can lay down other memories has gone on for centuries.[38] Psychologists have reported cases in which subjects apparently recalled prebirth experiences using techniques such as hypnosis or drugs such as lysergic acid diethylamide. Such memories are difficult to verify, however, and these clinical reports remain unreliable.[38] The vast majority of people cannot recall fetal memories but, theoretically, this may be because such memories do exist but 'cannot be voluntarily retrieved since they had been stored according to a processing mode that is not directly compatible with the functioning of the aroused child or adult brain'.[11]

Experimental studies on fetal learning have looked at three areas – habituation, classical conditioning and 'exposure learning'. Habituation is the decrease in response following repeated exposure to the same stimulus – usually, in such experiments, a loud sound. In a recent study from the Nijmegen group,[39] 17 of 19 fetuses at term showed a reduced response to repeated application of a vibroacoustic stimulus, not only on the initial test but also ten minutes later and 24 hours later. The investigators concluded that this suggests the existence of short-term memory in utero. It is possible, however, that a decrease in response may be due simply to peripheral neural processes such as motor fatigue or sensory adaptation, or both. This was addressed in studies in which a vibroacoustic stimulus was altered in pitch: repeating the stimulus at one tone led to a diminished response but then altering the tone produced a full response, suggesting the existence of true habituation involving central neural processes.[40]

The earliest stage at which fetuses have been shown to habituate is 22 weeks of gestation. Fetuses early in the third trimester take longer to habituate than those nearer term. Again, it is possible that this trend results from maturation of the motor response rather than from the habituation process. Female fetuses have shown evidence of earlier habituation than males. Using the habituation mechanism, some researchers have concluded that the fetus can distinguish between speech sounds ('bibi' and 'baba') and between male and female voices. Such discrimination is not evident at 27 weeks but has been found at 35 weeks.[40]

There is some evidence that fetal habituation can be modified by maternal circulating beta-endorphins, which suggests that maternal stress may influence the habituation process, at least in experimental circumstances. There is also evidence that habituation can be affected by corticotrophin-releasing hormone (CRH), which is synthesised and released by the placenta. In one study, the concentration of CRH in maternal serum was found to correlate with the response of the fetus to a vibroacoustic stimulus – a high CRH level being associated with the least responsiveness.[41]

Classical conditioning has been studied in animal experiments using the sense of taste. Fetal rats exposed to apple juice along with an unpleasant-tasting substance *in utero* showed an aversion to apple juice as neonates, suggesting that conditioning can take place in the womb.[1,42]

As regards exposure learning in humans, investigators in both France and America concluded in the 1980s that the newborn baby shows a preference for its mother's voice, to which it has become familiar through prenatal exposure. Experiments on newborns can be done using non-nutritive nipples, in which suckling produces not milk but an auditory stimulus through headphones. In such studies, newborn babies showed a preference for a story repeatedly read to them in the last six weeks of pregnancy, rather than an unfamiliar story.[1] There are anecdotal reports of fetuses showing preferences for different types of music but these have not yet been confirmed.[2]

DRUGS AND ANAESTHESIA

Intrauterine exposure to drugs can modify the fetal response to vibroacoustic stimulation and may have longer-lasting effects on the baby. Betamethasone transiently suppresses fetal movements and also transiently suppresses the startle response to vibroacoustic stimulation.[43] Intrauterine exposure to cocaine may have effects later in life: in animal experiments, rabbits exposed to cocaine *in utero* showed impaired behavioural learning as adults.[44]

The effects of anaesthetic agents on the fetus are not known. General anaesthesia has been used for many years if a woman requires a surgical procedure in mid-pregnancy and no adverse effects have been reported. Nevertheless, the Royal College of Obstetricians and Gynaecologists working party on fetal awareness commented that 'it is possible that opioid exposure at a critical stage of neural plasticity might alter the normal course of receptor development'.[10] The working party called for urgent research on this subject, but it appears that no such research has been published as yet.

RELEVANCE TO CLINICAL PRACTICE

Tests of fetal responsiveness to vibroacoustic stimuli are not widely used in the UK, presumably because their predictive value is in doubt. There are tantalising suggestions that postnatal outcome may be predicted by tests of fetal habituation – for example, fetuses affected by Down syndrome take longer to habituate than unaffected fetuses[45] – but again such tests have not been shown to have the sensitivity and specificity needed for today's obstetric practice.

The main implications of fetal awareness for clinical practice centre around the question of whether and when anaesthesia is required for procedures on the fetus. The Royal College of Obstetricians and Gynaecologists guidelines[10] that were published in 1997 and widely publicised at that time[46] have not yet been superseded. A major conclusion of the working party was that: 'The minimum stage of structural development which is necessary – but not that which is sufficient – to confer awareness upon the developing fetus … has not begun before 26 weeks of gestation'.

To allow for the difficulty of accurately assessing gestation, the working party recommended that 'practitioners who undertake diagnostic or therapeutic surgical procedures upon the fetus at or after 24 weeks of gestation … consider the requirements for fetal analgesia and sedation'. In such cases, the doctor also has to consider the effects of drugs on the mother and their possible long-term effects on the developing fetal brain. The latter consideration does not apply to another recommendation of the working party, that 'practitioners who undertake termination of pregnancy at 24 weeks or later should consider the requirements for feticide or fetal analgesia and sedation'. Such cases are very few, and there seems little rationale for fetal sedation in terminations involving vaginal delivery of the intact fetus.

In summary, then, our knowledge of fetal awareness remains far from complete and the answer to the question posed in the first sentence of this chapter is still vague. There is some evidence to suggest that the fetus learns to recognise the maternal voice, but we do not know what the implications of this are for the development of the baby and child. Calls for further research in this field have been made, but we should also recognise that some debates, particularly that on abortion, will never be resolved and some questions – particularly the question of what is going on inside the head of the unborn baby – are unlikely ever to be answered.

References

1   Drife JO. Can the fetus listen and learn? *Br J Obstet Gynaecol* 1985;92:777–9.

2   Gerhardt KJ, Abrams RM. Fetal exposures to sound and vibroacoustic stimulation. *J Perinatol* 2000;20:S21–30.

3   Richards T. Can a fetus feel pain? *BMJ* 1985;291:1220–1.

4   Marple-Horvat DE. Pain and the fetus. *Nature* 1988;334:190.

5   Derbyshire SWG, Furedi A. Do fetuses feel pain? 'Fetal pain' is a misnomer. *BMJ* 1996;313:795.

6   Valman HB, Pearson JF. What the fetus feels. *BMJ* 1980;280:233–4.

7   Goodman NW. Changing tactics in the abortion argument: does a fetus feel pain? *Br J Hosp Med* 1997;58:550.

8   Kmietowicz Z. Antiabortionists hijack fetal pain argument. *BMJ* 1996;313:188.

9   Szawarski Z. Do fetuses feel pain? Probably no pain in the absence of 'self'. *BMJ* 1996;313:796–7.

10   Royal College of Obstetricians and Gynaecologists. *Fetal Awareness. Report of a Working Party.* London: RCOG Press; 1997.

11   Lecanuet JP, Schaal B. Fetal sensory competencies. *Eur J Obstet Gynecol Reprod Biol* 1996;68:1–23.

12   Timor-Tritsch IE. The effect of external stimuli on fetal behaviour. *Eur J Obstet Gynecol Reprod Biol* 1986;21:321–9.

13   Hevner RF. Development of connections in the human visual system during fetal mid-gestation: a Dil-tracing study. *J Neuropathol Exp Neurol* 2000;59:385–92.

Table 4 *Summary of drugs permitted and to be avoided during pregnancy*

Drug type	Permitted	To be avoided
Immunosuppressives	Azathioprine	Cyclophosphamide
	Cyclosporin	Methotrexate
		MMF
Corticosteroids	Prednisone/prednisolone	Dexamethasone[a]
	Methyl-prednisolone	
Antimalarials	Hydroxychloroquine	Chloroquine
Antihypertensives	Methyl-dopa	ACE inhibitors
	Labetalol	Diuretics
	Nifedipine	
Anticoagulant and anti-aggregants	Heparin and LMWH	Warfarin
	Aspirin (low-dose)	
Other	Immunoglobulins	NSAIDs (third trimester)
	Vitamin D	

[a] except for *in utero* treatment of fetal myocarditis, hydrops fetalis or immature babies; MMF = mycophenolate mofetil; ACE = angiotensin converting enzyme; LMWH = low molecular weight heparins; NSAIDs = nonsteroidal anti-inflammatory drugs

that prophylactic steroids lower the frequency of flares, and there are significant adverse effects during pregnancy – premature rupture of membranes, infections, intrauterine growth restriction, hypertension, gestational diabetes mellitus, osteoporosis and avascular necrosis.[11] There is enough experience with hydroxychloroquine to say that it is safe for the fetus.[65–67] Our experience during more than ten years using this drug in pregnant women has not resulted in any case of malformation attributed to hydroxychloroquine. Furthermore, hydroxychloroquine persists in human tissues long after it is discontinued and its withdrawal can result in SLE flares that may be severe.[68] Therefore, we maintain hydroxychloroquine during the entire pregnancy in women who are already taking it.

Specific therapy for lupus flares depends on severity and specific organ involvement. Rash and arthritis can be managed with nonsteroidal anti-inflammatory drugs (NSAIDs), low-dose prednisolone (up to 10 mg/day) or hydroxychloroquine. NSAIDs must be used with caution in women on anticoagulants and in those with renal disease, due to the risk of gastrointestinal bleeding and deterioration of renal function, respectively. In addition they must be stopped in late pregnancy due to the risk of premature closure of ductus arteriosus.[69] NSAIDs are usually avoided in lupus pregnancies. Serosistis usually responds to low-dose prednisolone and/or hydroxychloroquine.

Visceral involvement, such as renal or neuropsychiatric, and other severe manifestations such as cutaneous vasculitis need a more aggressive treatment. In these cases higher doses of prednisolone are used. However, the high toxicity of steroids is enhanced during pregnancy. Thus we strongly advise against maintaining moderate to high doses for more than a few weeks. In order to achieve the goal of rapid tapering of prednisolone without leaving lupus untreated, we advocate early use of azathioprine. This is usually well tolerated and has been used in many pregnant women with autoimmune diseases or organ transplantations. Other authors recommend pulses of methyl-prednisolone,[70] although in this case careful monitoring of blood pressure and glucose levels is mandatory.

If these measures do not control disease activity, aggressive immunosuppressive treatment and pregnancy termination may be indicated. Cyclophosphamide and methotrexate are contraindicated during pregnancy. Cyclosporine is safe during pregnancy and can be considered in individual cases with severe but non-life-threatening disease. It is recommended by some authors for treating azathioprine-resistant nephritis before resorting to delivery.[70] Mycophenolate mofetil is an immunosuppressive agent that is being increasingly used in severe unresponsive cases of SLE.[71] There is a recent report of a transplanted women who received this drug during early pregnancy having a premature baby who was born with hypoplastic nails in fingers and toes, bilaterally shortened fifth fingers and aberrant blood vessels between trachea and oesophagus.[72] Renal transplant patients receiving mycophenolate are advised to avoid pregnancy. Therefore, mycophenolate must not be used during pregnancy in lupus women.

Pregnancy loss in antiphospholipid syndrome

Two small randomised studies showed that the combination of prednisone and aspirin resulted in more adverse effects than aspirin alone[73] or aspirin plus heparin.[74] Other studies have confirmed the unacceptably high rate of toxicity associated with prednisone use during pregnancy, including prematurity.[43,75] Therefore, prednisone is reserved for SLE manifestations and specific APS features such as thrombocytopenia or haemolytic anaemia.

Immunoglobulins have been advocated by some authors as a useful therapy for pregnancy loss in APS.[76] A randomised controlled study has investigated the effect of adding human intravenous immunoglobulin (IVIG) to the aspirin–heparin combination.[77] Since the study was small (16 patients), none of the differences between the two groups was significant. However, some of the results were interesting: patients treated with IVIG had a higher incidence of pre-eclampsia (44% versus 11% in the placebo group) and preterm delivery (100% and 33% respectively), although babies born to mothers treated with IVIG had less fetal distress (0% versus 33%) and a lower risk of admission to an intensive care unit (14% versus 44%). In addition, IVIG treatment is extremely expensive. Therefore, although IVIG may be used in individual patients in whom other therapies have failed, it is not used routinely in APS pregnancies.

Aspirin and heparin are thus the two main drugs used in the management of APS associated pregnancy loss. In fact, the improved obstetric outcome in women with APS, most of them treated with different combinations of these two drugs, is impressive despite the high rate of complications such as prematurity and hypertension (Table 3). However, there is no consensus regarding the optimal therapeutic schedule. Some authors treat (successfully) recurrent early miscarriage with low-dose aspirin only.[30,48] However, two controlled studies have found that adding heparin to aspirin improves obstetric results in women with a history of early recurrent miscarriage, low-titer aCL and lack of thrombotic complications,[78,79] while a similar randomised trial has found no difference between aspirin alone and aspirin combined with dalteparin.[80] To complicate the picture, one randomised trial has not shown any benefit in adding aspirin to supportive obstetric care in women with recurrent miscarriage and aPL (most of them had low-titre aCL).[81] A summary of these trials is shown in Table 5.

We do not believe that the 'no therapy' option is applicable to women with definite forms of APS (i.e. those with persistent medium to high levels of aCL and history of fetal death).[82] On the other hand, it is a matter of discussion whether heparin should be added to all patients with APS, as some authors advocate.[83,84] Until more studies clarify these issues, our practice is as follows:[5]

- aPL-positive women with no history of thrombosis or pregnancy loss

  Although there is no evidence of benefit, we recommend low-dose aspirin because of its low toxicity.

- Women with APS and history of first-trimester pregnancy losses only

Table 5 *Controlled studies of aspirin and heparin to treat pregnancy loss in antiphospholipid syndrome*

Study[a]	Year	Patients (n)	Treatment (group 1)	Treatment (group 2)	Live births (group 1) (%)	Live births (group 2) (%)	Difference	Comments
Kutteh[79]	1996	50	AAS 81 mg/day + Hep 5000 u bd	AAS 81 mg/day	44	80	Significant	Women with LA excluded
Rai et al.[78]	1997	90	AAS 75 mg/day + Hep 5000 u bd	AAS 75 mg/day	42	71	Significant	Most women LA + with aCL –
Farquharson et al.[80]	2001	98	AAS 75 mg/day + Dalteparin 5000 u/day	AAS 75 mg/day	72	78	Non-significant	Published in abstract form
Pattison et al.[81]	2000	40	AAS 75 mg/day	Placebo	80	85	Non-significant	All received supportive obstetric care

[a] all were randomised controlled trials except the study by Kutteh in which treatments were assigned consecutively; AAS= aspirin; aCL = anticardiolipin antibodies; bd = twice daily; Hep= heparin; LA = lupus anticoagulant

We treat these patients with low-dose aspirin alone. In view of recent trials,[78,79] adding heparin may be appropriate, although benefit beyond the first 13 weeks is not clear.

- Women with APS and history of fetal death

  We add subcutaneous dalteparin at a fixed dose of 5000 u daily throughout pregnancy without monitoring anti-Xa levels.

- Women with APS and pregnancy failure while taking aspirin

  These women are offered dalteparin 5000 u daily (plus low-dose aspirin) during the whole of the next pregnancy.

- Women with APS and thrombosis (irrespective of obstetric history)

  Most of these women will be already receiving oral anticoagulation. Since warfarin is contraindicated during the first trimester of pregnancy, we switch to aspirin plus subcutaneous LMWH (dalteparin), at a fixed dose of 5000 u daily, which is doubled at 16–20 weeks. We do not routinely determine anti-Xa levels.

- Women with APS and recurrent thrombosis during pregnancy

  Patients with previous stroke may present with neurological symptoms during pregnancy despite maximal doses of dalteparin 5000 u twice a day. In these cases we increase the dose of dalteparin to a maximum of 18 000 u a day. If symptoms persist, warfarin is reintroduced in the second trimester, with a target INR of 2.5. Close monitoring of anticoagulation is needed to help prevent fetal bleeding.

In women receiving dalteparin for thromboprophylaxis (i.e. with previous history of thrombosis), the drug is omitted in labour, and then 5000 u is given as soon after delivery as is permitted by the timing of epidural anaesthesia. Heparin is continued on a twice-daily basis for three days, and then continued at 5000 u daily until warfarin is re-started. Calcium, 1000 mg/day, plus vitamin D3, 400 iu/day, are given to every woman treated with heparin (see below).

Treatment with IVIG or even low-dose prednisolone or azathioprine may be considered for women with persistent pregnancy losses despite full treatment with aspirin and heparin. These approaches are mostly experimental.

PREGNANCY, HEPARIN AND OSTEOPOROSIS

The complex relationship between pregnancy, osteoporosis and heparin treatment has been reviewed recently.[64] Calcium demands rise during pregnancy. This may result in an increased turnover from bone, especially during the first and second trimesters. However, the process usually reverses during the third, resulting in only minor reductions of bone mineral density (BMD) after normal pregnancy.[85] Lactation may result in a delayed recovery of BMD.[86] Although the risk for symptomatic osteoporosis is not high during pregnancy, it may be increased in women with low preconceptual BMD or those treated with drugs that favour bone loss.

Heparin is frequently used in pregnant women with APS. The effect of heparin on bone is not completely defined, although osteoporosis is included among its adverse effects.[87] However, there may be a differential effect related to age,[87,88] and bone fractures are rare in pregnant women receiving heparin: Dahlman *et al.*[89] studied 184 women treated with unfractionated heparin during pregnancy, 2.2% of whom suffered vertebral fractures in the puerperium. This complication is even rarer with LMWH. A recent systematic review that analysed 486 women who received different LMWH during pregnancy (nadroparin, enoxaparin, dalteparin, reviparin or tinzaparin) has reported only one case of vertebral fractures, resulting in a frequency of 0.2%.[31]

Since heparin is essential for a subset of pregnant women with SLE and APS, its use should not be limited for fear of complications such as osteoporosis.[64] Steroids, drugs that lower BMD to a greater extent than heparin, must be limited as much as lupus activity allows and never be used to treat features of APS other than thrombocytopenia or haemolytic anaemia. The concomitant administration of calcium plus vitamin D, the use of LMWH rather than unfractionated heparin and adherence to strict guidelines regarding indications for heparin use are also measures that can lower the frequency of serious adverse effects. Finally, women deemed to be at increased risk because of preconceptual low BMD should receive advice regarding lactation, whose deleterious effects on bone mass can be more pronounced that those of heparin itself.[64]

References

1   Hochberg MC. Updating the American College of Rheumatology revised criteria for the classification of systemic lupus erythematosus. *Arthritis Rheum* 1997;40:1725.

2   Hughes GRV. Is it lupus? The St. Thomas' Hospital 'alternative' criteria. *Clin Exp Rheumatol* 1998;16:250–2.

3   Wilson WA, Gharavi AE, Koike T, Lockshin MD, Branch DW, Piette JC, *et al.* International consensus statement on preliminary classification criteria for definite antiphospholipid syndrome: report of an international workshop. *Arthritis Rheum* 1999;42:1309–11.

4   Hughes GRV. The antiphospholipid syndrome: ten years on. *Lancet* 1993;342:341–4.

5   Ruiz-Irastorza G, Khamashta MA, Hughes GRV. Systemic lupus erythematosus and antiphospholipid syndrome during pregnancy: maternal and fetal complications and their management. *IMAJ* 2000;2:462–9.

However, most units admit patients with abnormal biochemistry and perform daily CTGs and weekly biophysical profiles and Doppler assessment of umbilical bloodflow patterns.

The literature indicates that stillbirth occurs late in pregnancy,[28] so labour should be induced at 38 weeks or when fetal lung maturity has been achieved. This policy of active management decreases the postnatal mortality rate. It should be noted that the intrapartum CTG also appears to be an unreliable indicator of fetal compromise.[23] Neonatal vitamin K should be given immediately postpartum.

Causes of fetal distress, prematurity and death continue to be debated. Some authorities implicate an acute hypoxic event rather than chronic uteroplacental insufficiency because there is no evidence of intrauterine growth restriction. There may be defective nutrition of the fetoplacental unit induced by vasoconstrictive effects of bile acids on the chorionic veins. Bile acids have been shown to stimulate colonic motility in animals but no correlation was found in humans. Recent work[29] has demonstrated that the addition of the bile acid taurocholate to rat cardiomyocytes caused a decreased rate of contraction and cells ceased to beat synchronously, thus suggesting that an increase in taurocholate in fetal serum may result in the development of a fetal dysrhythmia and in sudden intrauterine death.

Prognosis

Recurrence occurs in up to 50% and disease may be more or less severe. Women should be advised to avoid the oral contraceptive pill. In a prospective study from France, pruritus recurred in 45% of multiparae and in 63% of primiparae who became pregnant again. However, pruritus was not noted in any of the 44 French women who had taken oestrogens as oral contraceptive therapy prior to the pregnancy that evolved into obstetric cholestasis.[12]

MANAGEMENT OF PRURITUS ASSOCIATED WITH CHOLESTASIS

The extensive list of medications used to control pruritus is indicative of their lack of success: cholestyramine, phenobarbitone, ursodeoxycholic acid (UDCA), charcoal, ultraviolet light, corticosteroids, plasma exchange, evening primrose oil, epomediol and S-adenosylmethionine (SAM) have all been tried, mostly in uncontrolled studies with disappointing results.

Cholestyramine is an anion exchange resin that interrupts the enterohepatic circulation of bile acids by binding. However, it also binds the fat-soluble vitamins, resulting in vitamin K deficiency. The effect on pruritus is minimal and there is an increased risk of antepartum fetal haemorrhage, as well as intrapartum or postpartum haemorrhage in the mother.[30]

Phenobarbitone and antihistamines, while mildly effective, are sedating and can cause respiratory problems in the newborn. A randomised double-blind placebo-controlled trial of 48 women in Finland with obstetric cholestasis found that guar gum, a dietary fibre that binds bile acids, prevented worsening of pruritus and elevation of bile acids.[31]

Dexamethasone inhibits fetoplacental hormone synthesis. A single study demonstrated significant improvement of pruritus, levels of bile acids and ALT in ten women treated with dexamethasone 12 mg taken four times daily for seven days.[32]

SAM improves cholestasis in animal studies. SAM influences the composition and fluidity of hepatocyte plasma membranes but also methylation and biliary excretion of hormone metabolites. Studies have been small, with conflicting results.

Aspirin appears to be more effective than chlorpheniramine for relief of itching when there is no rash but in the presence of a rash chlorpheniramine may be more effective.[33]

UDCA decreases pruritus found in chronic cholestatic disease. It is a naturally occurring hydrophilic bile acid that can affect both clinical and biochemical indices. In obstetric cholestasis, UDCA normalises the CA/CDCA ratio and decreases plasma concentrations and urinary excretion rates of sulphated steroid metabolites. It restores impaired bile acid transport across the trophoblast in obstetric cholestasis and decreases delivery of bile acids to the fetus. To date, UDCA decreases both biochemical abnormalities and pruritus in all reported small studies, without adverse effects on the newborn.[34,35] There are no adverse effects other than mild diarrhoea in the mother. The risk of teratogenicity is minimised, as treatment is usually in the third trimester. The results of future large randomised controlled trials to approve the use of UDCA for treatment of this condition are awaited.

References

1   Clark TJ, Dwarakanath L, Weaver JB. Pruritus in pregnancy and obstetric cholestasis. *Hosp Med* 1999;60:254–60.

2   Goodlin RC, Anderson JC, Skiles TL. Pruritus and hyperplacentosis. *Obstet Gynecol* 1985;66:36–8.

3   Vaughan Jones SA, Hern S, Nelson-Piercy C, Seed PT, Black MM. A prospective study of 200 women with dermatoses of pregnancy correlating clinical findings with hormonal and immunopathological profiles. *Br J Dermatol* 1999;141:71–81.

4   Holmes RC, Black MM. The specific dermatoses of pregnancy. *J Am Acad Dermatol* 1983;8:405–12.

5   Briggs GG, Freeman RK, Yaffe SJ. *Drugs in Pregnancy and Lactation.* 5ᵗʰ ed. Baltimore, MD: Lippincott, Williams and Wilkins; 1998.

6   Shornick JK, Black MM. Fetal risks in herpes gestationis. *J Am Acad Dermatol* 1992;26:63–8.

7   Fagan EA. Intrahepatic cholestasis of pregnancy. *Clin Liver Dis* 1999;3:603–32.

8   Locattelli A, Roncaglia N, Arreghini A, Bellini P, Vergani P, Ghidini A. Hepatitis C virus infection is associated with a higher incidence of cholestasis of pregnancy. *Br J Obstet Gynaecol* 1999;106:498–500.

9   Janczewska T, Olsson R, Hultcrantz R, Broome U. Pregnancy in patients with primary sclerosing cholangitis. *Liver* 1996;16:326–30.

10   Reyes H, Gonzalez MC, Ribalta J, Aburto H, Matus C, Schramm G, *et al.* Prevalence of intrahepatic cholestasis of pregnancy in Chile. *Ann Intern Med* 1978;88:487–93.

11   Jansen PLM, Mullen M. The molecular genetics of familial intrahepatic cholestasis. *Gut* 2000;47:1–5.

12   Bacq Y, Sapey T, Brechot M, Pierre F, Fignon A, Bubois F. Intrahepatic cholestasis of pregnancy: a French prospective study. *Hepatology* 1997;26:358–64.

13   Gonzalez MC, Reyes H, Arrese M, Figueroa D, Lorca B, Andresen M, *et al.* Intrahepatic cholestasis of pregnancy in twin pregnancies. *J Hepatol* 1989;9:84–90.

14   Hirvioja ML, Kivinen S. Inheritance of intrahepatic cholestasis of pregnancy in one kindred. *Clin Genet* 1993;43:315–17.

15   Olsson R, Tysk C, Aldenborg F, Holm B. Prolonged postpartum course of intrahepatic cholestasis of pregnancy. *Gastroenterology* 1993;105:267–71.

16   Raine-Fenning N, Kilby M. Obstetric cholestasis. *Fetomaternal Medicine Review* 1997;9:1–17.

17   Heikkinen J. Serum bile acids in the early diagnosis of intrahepatic cholestasis of pregnancy. *J Hepatol* 1995;22:66–70.

18   Heikkinen J, Maentausta O, Ylostalo P, Janne O. Changes in serum bile acid concentrations

during normal pregnancy, in patients with intrahepatic cholestasis of pregnancy and in pregnant women with itching. *Br J Obstet Gynaecol* 1981;88:240–5.

19   Girling JC, Dow E, Smith JH. Liver function tests in pre-eclampsia; importance of comparison with reference range derived for normal pregnancy. *Br J Obstet Gynaecol* 1997;104:246–50.

20   Jones EA, Bergasa NU. The pruritus of cholestasis: from bile acids to opiate antagonists. *Hepatology* 1990;11:884–7.

21   Confidential Enquiry into Stillbirths and Deaths in Infancy. *5th Annual Report*. London: Maternal and Child Health Research Consortium; 1998.

22   Fisk NM, Storey GNB. Fetal outcome in obstetric cholestasis. *Br J Obstet Gynaecol* 1988;95:1137–43.

23   Shaw D, Frohlich J, Wittman BA, Willms M. A prospective study of 18 patients with cholestasis of pregnancy. *Am J Obstet Gynecol* 1982;142:621–5.

24   Glasinovic JC, Mannovic I, Vella P, Ahumada E, Valditia MT, Gomez X, *et al.* Association between urinary infection and cholestasis of pregnancy. *Rev Med Chile* 1982;110:547–9.

25   Rioseco AJ, Ivankovic MB, Manzur A, Hamed F, Kato SR, Parer JT, *et al.* Intrahepatic cholestasis of pregnancy: a retrospective case–control study of perinatal outcome. *Am J Obstet Gynecol* 1994;170:890–5.

26   Fisk NM, Bye WB, Storey GN. Maternal features of obstetric cholestasis: 20 years' experience at King George V Hospital. *Aust N Z J Obstet Gynaecol* 1988;28:172–6.

27   Alsulyman OM, Ouzounian JG, Ames-Castro M, Goodwin TM. Intrahepatic cholestasis of pregnancy: perinatal outcome associated with expectant management. *Am J Obstet Gynecol* 1996;175:957–60.

28   Reid R, Ivey KJ, Rencoret RH, Storey B. Fetal complications of obstetric cholestasis. *BMJ* 1976;1:870–2.

29   Williamson C, Gorelik J, Eaton BM, Lab M, de Swiet M, Korchev Y. The bile acid taurocholate impairs rat cardiomyocyte function: a proposed mechanism for intra-uterine fetal death in obstetric cholestasis. *Clin Sci (Colch)* 2001;100:363–9.

30   Sadler LC, Lane M, North R. Severe fetal intracranial haemorrhage during treatment with cholestyramine for intrahepatic cholestasis of pregnancy. *Br J Obstet Gynaecol* 1995;102:169–70.

31   Gylling H, Riikonen S, Nikkila K, Savonius H, Miettinen TA. Oral guar gum treatment of intrahepatic cholestasis of pregnancy and pruritus in pregnant women: effects on serum cholestanol and other non-cholesterol steroids. *Eur J Clin Invest* 1998;28:359–63.

32   Hirvioja ML, Tuimala R, Vuori J. The treatment of intrahepatic cholestasis of pregnancy by dexamethasone. *Br J Obstet Gynaecol* 1992;99:109–11.

33   Young GL, Jewell D. Antihistamine versus aspirin for itching in late pregnancy. *Cochrane Database Syst Rev* 2000; (2): CD000027.

34   Palma J, Reyes H, Ribalta J, Hernandez I, Sandoval L, Almina R, *et al.* Ursodeoxycholic acid in the treatment of cholestasis of pregnancy: a randomised double blind study controlled with placebo. *J Hepatol* 1997;27:1022–8.

35   Diaferia A, Nicastin PL, Tartagni M, Loizzi P, Facovizzi C, Di Leo A. Ursodeoxycholic acid therapy in pregnant women with cholestasis. *Int J Gynecol Obstet* 1996;52:133–40.

12

Anti-oxytocic tocolytic agents

Ronald F Lamont and Philippa Greenfield

THE IMPACT OF PRETERM BIRTH

Preterm birth is the major cause of perinatal mortality and morbidity in the developed world. Approximately 13 million preterm births occur worldwide each year, from an incidence of nearly 12.0% in North America to 5.6% in Western Australia and New Zealand. Europe has approximately 400 000 preterm births each year, with an incidence of 5.8%. Excluding the small proportion of women to whom high-quality antenatal care is not available, as well as those delivered electively preterm, those in whom intervention is contraindicated or who are too far advanced in labour for intervention, it is estimated that there are approximately 100 000 potentially preventable preterm births in Europe annually.[1]

The perinatal mortality and morbidity associated with preterm births decreases with advancing gestational age. Only 20% of babies born at 28 weeks of gestation survive, whereas by 30 weeks of gestation 90% of babies survive. Although nearly 50% of preterm births occur after 35 weeks of gestation, nearly all the mortality and morbidity associated with preterm birth occurs before this time.[2] Between March and December 1995 in Great Britain and Ireland, the Epicure study recorded the outcome of over 1100 babies born before 26 weeks of gestation.[3] Approximately 65% of these babies died in the delivery suite or on the neonatal intensive care unit (NICU). When the survivors were followed up to the age of 30 months, approximately 50% had some form of handicap and in 50% of these the disability was severe. As a result, only 13% of babies born between 22 and 26 weeks of gestation could be shown to have survived intact.[3] Between the gestational ages of 23 and 27 weeks, neonatal survival increases at a rate of 3% per day with a concordant reduction in neonatal morbidity. The prevalence of handicap decreased with gestational age from 31% at 23 weeks to 7% at 27 weeks.[4]

In the USA, the short-term cost of neonatal intensive care is estimated to be approximately US$10,000 per baby per week, an annual cost of nearly US$5 billion. Severely disabled babies requiring lifelong residential care may cost up to US$450,000 over their lifetime. The psychological and social impact of preterm birth is immeasurable but it has profound effects on the infant, parents and extended family.[5] The rationale for the use of tocolytic therapy is to prolong pregnancy, ideally in the long term to permit growth and maturation. In the short term, it is hoped that delivery will be delayed sufficiently to allow administration of a full course of antepartum glucocorticoids and to arrange transfer of the baby, *in utero*, to centres with NICU facilities. Babies transferred *in utero* have statistically significantly lower mortality and morbidity than babies transferred neonatally.[6] Antepartum administration of glucocorticoids significantly reduces the incidence of idiopathic respiratory distress syndrome (IRDS), intraventricular haemorrhage and necrotising enterocolitis, particularly when an optimal course of steroids has been administered.[7]

Until recently, the only tocolytics licensed for use in the UK were the beta$_2$ agonists, ritrodrine hydrochloride and salbutamol. By stimulating beta$_2$ receptors in the myometrium, ritrodrine induces smooth muscle relaxation. A meta-analysis has shown that beta$_2$ agonists can prolong labour and hence gestation for 48 hours or so but have not been shown to be associated with a reduction in perinatal mortality or morbidity.[8] This was subsequently confirmed by the Canadian preterm labour investigators' group[9] and thought to be a result of the suboptimal use of the delay to arrange an *in utero* transfer or administer antepartum glucocorticoids. Unfortunately, due to the lack of specificity, beta$_2$ agonists also cause cardiovascular, metabolic and constitutional adverse effects. High doses of beta$_2$ agonists can be used to treat asthmatic attacks without the risk of pulmonary oedema, but pregnant women by nature of their physiological adaptations to pregnancy are already at increased risk of pulmonary oedema. If they are exposed to beta-agonists, either inappropriately or without the appropriate monitoring, they have a much higher risk of serious adverse effects, including pulmonary oedema. The Royal College of Obstetricans and Gynaecologists recommendations[10] for the monitoring of women receiving intravenous beta-agonists for the treatment of spontaneous preterm labour are:

* maternal pulse at least every 15 minutes
* maternal blood pressure initially every 15 minutes
* maternal blood glucose initially every four hours
* strict record of maternal fluid balance (input/output chart)
* maternal serum urea and electrolytes at least every 24 hours
* auscultation of maternal lung fields every four hours.

If the preterm labour is due to multiple pregnancy or associated with increased tissue permeability due to infection and/or inflammation, the following risks of pulmonary oedema are much higher:[11]

* maternal factors: fluid balance, posture
* fetal factors: multiple pregnancy
* tocolytic factors: positive fluid balance (drug-induced fluid retention or iatrogenic fluid overload), cardiovascular effects, metabolic effects, concomitant use of glucocorticosteroids
* fetomaternal infection: increased tissue permeability, adult respiratory distress.

As a result of these common and occasionally serious adverse effects, many obstetricians find the use of beta-agonists unacceptable. This has led to the use of non-licensed tocolytic agents such as prostaglandin synthetase inhibitors, magnesium sulphate, nitric oxide donors or calcium channel blockers. Since these agents are not specifically developed to inhibit uterine contractions, they all have fetomaternal adverse effects. None has been subjected to well-conducted studies of sufficient sample size to provide the evidence base required to satisfy regulatory bodies. The evidence pertaining to the efficacy and safety of these non-licensed drugs as well as beta agonists has recently been comprehensively reviewed.[12]

The perfect tocolytic agent that is completely safe for the mother and the fetus and that will inhibit uterine contractions in every case and stop preterm labour is yet to be discovered. Recent research into a new group of tocolytic agents – the oxytocin antagonists – has led to the introduction of a new licensed drug, atosiban (Tractocile®, Ferring, Copenhagen) for the treatment of preterm labour. This review outlines the rationale behind, the development and the clinical experience of the use of oxytocin antagonists for the treatment of spontaneous preterm labour.

DEVELOPMENT OF OXYTOCIC ANTAGONISTS

Oxytocin is a potent stimulator of myometrial contractility and a role for the hormone and its receptor in human parturition has been postulated.[13–17] This contractile effect on the myometrium is partly due to increased oxytocic receptors, together with pulsatile release of oxytocin from the posterior pituitary gland, secretion from peripheral tissues and increased prostaglandin release from the decidua and fetal membranes. Since the early 1950s,[18] modification of the oxytocin molecule has been undertaken, resulting in many analogues and antagonists. Oxytocin was the first peptide hormone to be used in a clinical setting and, while oxytocic receptor antagonists have contributed to the understanding of the physiology and pathophysiology of the hormone, until recently none has emerged as a potentially therapeutically useful drug. Initial modifications resulted in partial uterotonic antagonism. Further changes to the parent nonapeptide molecule led to analogues that showed full antagonism in animal models. Eventually, one of these analogues was found to inhibit vasopressin-stimulated uterine contractions in non-pregnant healthy women.[19]

Despite being a full antagonist *in vitro* and in animal models, this analogue was partially agonistic in women. Further developments led to two modified oxytocin molecules with higher receptor affinity for human myometrium, both of which lacked agonism in human species, and thus were full antagonists. One of these – atosiban – was more potent than the other and was chosen for clinical evaluation in dysmenorrhoea and preterm labour.

Pharmacochemistry of oxytocin and oxytocin antagonists

Oxytocin is a nonapeptide consisting of a ring of six aminoacids and a tail of three aminoacids, which differs from the other principal hormone of the neurohypophysis, arginine vasopressin (AVP), at positions 3 and 8 of the amino-acid sequence. Atosiban is an analogue of oxytocin that is modified at the 1, 2, 4 and 8 positions of the parent molecule (Figure 1). Since oxytocin and AVP share substantial structural similarities, the receptor-binding specificities of these two hormones are not absolute and there is some crossover in their physiological effects. As a result, most oxytocic antagonists resemble atosiban in not being totally specific in their action. They therefore exhibit some antagonism towards the vasopressor and antidiuretic effects of arginine vasopressin because of an affinity for both V1a (AVP receptors in vascular and uterine tissues) and V_2 (AVP receptors in renal tissue) receptors. Hirst et al.[20] demonstrated in pregnant rhesus monkeys that plasma oxytocin levels displayed a circadian rhythm with a maximum oxytocic concentration at midnight and that this pattern correlated well with uterine activity. This nocturnal uterine activity was abolished by an infusion of atosiban, which may be relevant in human term labour, which begins with greater frequency at night, reflecting a similar nocturnal peak of oxytocin in women.[21]

The mechanism of oxytocin and the effect of antagonists

As in smooth muscle elsewhere in the body, myometrial contractions are regulated by changes in intracellular free calcium ion (Ca^{2+}) concentration. Myometrial contractility may be reduced by decreasing intracellular free Ca^{2+}, either by inhibiting the release of intracellular cytosolic Ca^{2+} or by decreasing the influx of extracellular ions through voltage gated channels. Oxytocin initiates contractility through two mechanisms and involves prostaglandins.[22] The primary action of oxytocin on the uterus is via membrane-bound receptors on myometrial cells, which by means of secondary messages results in the release of Ca^{2+} from the sarcoplasmic reticulum.[23] Intracellular

12   Besinger RE, Iannucci TA. Tocolytic therapy. In: Elder MG, Romero R, Lamont RF, editors. *Preterm Labour*. New York: Churchill Livingstone; 1997. p. 243–97.

13   Zingg H, Lefebvre D, Giaid A. Uterine oxytocin gene expression: a novel framework for oxytocin action. *Regul Pept* 1993;45:43–6.

14   Fuchs AR, Romero R, Deefe D, Parra M, Oyarzun E, Behnke E. Oxytocin secretion and human parturition: pulse frequency and duration increase during spontaneous labor in women. *Am J Obstet Gynecol* 1991;165:1515–23.

15   Fuchs AR, Fuchs F, Husslein P, Soloff MS. Oxytocin receptors in the human uterus during pregnancy and parturition. *Am J Obstet Gynecol* 1984;150:734–41.

16   Soloff M, Fuchs AR, Fuchs F. Oxytocin receptors and the onset of parturition. In: Albrecht E, Pepe G, editors. *Perinatal Endocrinology*. Baltimore, MD: Perinatology Press; 1985. p. 289–311.

17   Åkerlund M, Stromberg P, Hauksson A, Andersen LF, Lyndrup J, Trojnar J, et al. Inhibition of uterine contractions of premature labour with an oxytocin analogue. Results from a pilot study. *Br J Obstet Gynaecol* 1987;94:1040–44.

18   Du Vigneaud V, Ressler C, Trippett S. The sequence of amino acids in oxytocin, with a proposal for the structure of oxytocin. *J Biol Chem* 1953;205:949–57.

19   Åkerlund M, Stromberg P, Forsling ML, Melin P, Vilhardt H. Inhibition of vasopressin effects on the uterus by a synthetic analogue. *Obstet Gynecol* 1983;62:309–12.

20   Hirst JJ, Chibbar R, Mitchell B. Role of oxytocin in the regulation of uterine activity during pregnancy and in the initiation of labor. *Semin Reprod Endocrinol* 1993;11:219–33.

21   Fuchs AR, Behrens O, Liu HC. Correlation of nocturnal increase in plasma oxytocin with a decrease in plasma estradiol/progesterone ratio in late pregnancy. *Am J Obstet Gynecol* 1992;167:1559–63.

22   Fuchs AR, Fuchs F, Husslein P, Soloff MS, Fernstrom MJ. Oxytocin receptors and human parturition: a dual role for oxytocin in the initiation of labor. *Science* 1982;215:1396–8.

23   Thornton S, Gillespie JI, Anson LC, Greenwell JR, Melin P, Dunlop W. The effect of the oxytocin antagonists, CAP 476 and F327, on calcium mobilisation in single cultured human myometrial cells. *Br J Obstet Gynaecol* 1993;100:581–6.

24   Thornton S, Davison JM, Baylis PH. Plasma oxytocin during the first and second stages of spontaneous human labor. *Acta Endocrinol (Copenh)* 1992;126:425–9.

25   Moore JJ, Dubyak GR, Moore RM, Kooy DV. Oxytocin activates the inositol-phospholipid-protein kinase-C system and stimulates prostaglandin production in human amnion cells. *Endocrinology* 1988;123:1771–7.

26   Ivanisevic M, Behrens O, Helmer H, Demarest K, Fuchs AR. Vasopressin receptors in human pregnant myometrium and decidua: interactions with oxytocin and vasopressin agonists and antagonists. *Am J Obstet Gynecol* 1989;161:1637–43.

27   Maggi M, Fantoni G, Baldi E, Cioni A, Rossi S, Vannelli GB, et al. Antagonists for the human oxytocin receptor: an *in vitro* study. *J Reprod Fertil* 1994;101:345–52.

28   Jenkin G. Oxytocin and prostaglandin interactions in pregnancy and at parturition. *J Reprod Fertil Suppl* 1992;45:97–111.

29   Clyman RI. Ontogeny of the ductus arteriosus response to prostaglandins and inhibitors of their synthesis. *Semin Perinatol* 1980;4:115–24.

30   Phaneuf S, Asboth G, Mackenzie IZ, Melin P, Lopez-Bernal A. Effect of oxytocin antagonists on the activation of human myometrium *in vitro*: Atosiban prevents oxytocin-induced desensitization. *Am J Obstet Gynecol* 1994;171:1627–34.

31   Abrams LS, Goodwin TM, Miller L, Wegelein RC, Klamarides D, North L, et al. Pharmacokinetics of atosiban in pregnant women. *Pharmacol Res* 1993;10:5335.

32   Andersen L F, Lyndrup J, Akerlund M, Melin P. Oxytocin receptor blockade: a new principle in the treatment of preterm labour. *Am J Perinatol* 1989;6:196–9.

33   Goodwin TM, Valenzuela G, Silver H, Hayashi R, Creasy GW, Lane R. Treatment of preterm labour with the oxytocin antagonist atosiban. *Am J Perinatol* 1996;13:143–6.

34   Goodwin TM, Paul R, Silver H, Spellacy W, Parsons M, Chez R, *et al.* The effect of the oxytocin antagonist atosiban, on preterm uterine activity in the human. *Am J Obstet Gynecol* 1994;170:474–8.

35   Goodwin TM, Valenzuela G, Silver H, Creasy G. Dose ranging study of the oxytocin antagonist atosiban in the treatment of preterm labour. *Obstet Gynecol* 1996;88:331–6.

36   Romero R, Sibai BM, Sanchez-Ramos L, Valenzuela GJ, Veille JC, Tabor B, *et al.* An oxytocin receptor antagonist (atosiban) in the treatment of preterm labour: a randomised, double-blind, placebo-controlled trial with tocolytic rescue. *Am J Obstet Gynecol* 2000;182:1173–83.

37   Valenzuela GJ, Sanchez-Ramos L, Romero R, Silver HM, Koltun WD, Millar L, *et al.* Maintenance treatment of preterm labour with the oxytocin antagonist atosiban. *Am J Obstet Gynecol* 2000;182:1184–90.

38   The Worldwide Atosiban versus Beta-agonists Study Group. Effectiveness and safety of the oxytocin antagonist atosiban versus beta adrenergic agonists in the treatment of preterm labour. *BJOG* 2001;108:133–42.

13

Group B streptococcus and pregnancy

Rhona Hughes and Albert Mifsud

INTRODUCTION

Since the 1970s, group B streptococcal (GBS) disease has become the most prevalent life-threatening neonatal infection in the industrialised world, affecting between 0.5 and 0.3 infants per 1000 live births, with substantial morbidity and mortality.[1] As a result, professional bodies in the USA have published consensus guidelines on the prevention of the disease,[2] and numerous obstetric units in the UK[3] and elsewhere[4-6] have introduced local prophylaxis policies.

There is a belief in the UK that the condition is less common here, although this is based on historical data[7] and has recently been questioned by several authorities.[8,9] Evidence from the USA and Australia suggests that neonatal GBS disease is more common in the infants of women under the age of 20 years and in ethnic minorities,[10,11] both groups that have probably been under-represented in British studies.[7,12] It is anticipated that better UK data will be provided by a 12-month nationwide study of culture-confirmed invasive GBS neonatal disease. This was completed in February 2001, and was conducted by the British Paediatric Surveillance Unit.[13] At the time of writing, results are being analysed.

In this chapter the epidemiology of the disease is discussed, as well as the evidence regarding various strategies for reducing the burden of the disease by preventing transmission of the causative organism from mother to infant.

THE ORGANISM

The group B streptococcus or *Streptococcus agalactiae* is a facultative anaerobic Gram-positive coccus. There are eight distinct serotypes, of which types Ia, III and V account for 70–80% of cases of invasive neonatal disease in the USA[14,15] and the UK.[16] In the laboratory, the organism can be cultured readily on most routine media (Figures 1 and 2 – Plate 4), but selective and enrichment media are available to improve isolation rates.

THE CLINICAL SPECTRUM

Maternal colonisation

The micro-organism is a normal commensal of the female genital tract and can be recovered from 10–25% of pregnant women in most populations of women in the UK[17] and worldwide,[18,19] regardless of the stage of pregnancy. Carriage is intermittent and repeat sampling during pregnancy increases the number of carriers identified to up to 30%.[20,21] The gastrointestinal tract is the primary reservoir and spread is transperineal, so that rectal and low vaginal swabs have a higher yield than high vaginal or cervical swabs.[22]

Neonatal colonisation

Between 3% and 12% of neonates are colonised with GBS during the first week of life. This figure rises to 35–70% of the infants of colonised mothers.[21,23] These infants are usually colonised with the same serotype as their mother.[24] Vertical transmission is more likely if mothers are heavily colonised,[23] if there is cervical carriage,[25] or if there is GBS bacteriuria.[26] Administration of effective intrapartum chemoprophylaxis to the mother can eliminate transmission of the organism to the neonate, although some babies will acquire the organism after the first 24 hours of life.[27] Transmission of GBS following intrapartum chemoprophylaxis has been described, but this usually follows inadequate dosing regimens.[28]

Neonatal invasive disease

Invasive disease can be divided into early- and late-onset disease. Early-onset (EOGBS) disease, which accounts for 80% of cases, occurs in the first week of life and is due to vertical transmission. In 95% of cases, it presents within the first 24 hours of life, most frequently as pneumonia or septicaemia.[29] Late-onset disease occurs after the first week and affected infants usually present with septicaemia or meningitis. It is due to either vertical (approximately 50% of cases[18]) or nosocomial spread from hospital staff or other adults or infants. As a result, the serotypes of the causative organisms in late-onset disease do not always reflect those present in the mother's genital tract.

Prior to the widespread introduction of interventions to reduce EOGBS disease, the incidence of the disease in 'active surveillance' areas in the USA had been reported as 1.0 to 2.3 per 1000 live births in 1991 to 1992,[10,30] while the rate reported by the Australasian Study Group for Neonatal Infections was 2.0 per 1000 live births over 1991–1993.[31] The same investigators have shown rates of EOGBS to have fallen to 0.39 (1998–1999)[32] and 0.5 (1995–1997),[31] respectively, a few years later. These reductions have coincided with the introduction and implementation of consensus guidelines[2,33,34] resulting in the increased use of intrapartum penicillin or ampicillin in women considered to be at higher risk of infecting their infants. To date, six studies of EOGBS disease in the UK have been published, and rates of 0.24–1.15 per 1000 live births have been reported (Table 1).

With the exception of the multicentre study, most of these studies covered a restricted geographical area, so that extrapolation of these results to the rest of the country may not necessarily be applicable. In order to address this, one of the authors (AJM) set up a retrospective ten-year study of the incidence of EOGBS in seven centres in London. Preliminary analysis of the results indicates that the incidence of EOGBS in London from 1990 to 1999 was 0.85 per 1000

Table 1 *Published UK studies of proven early- and late-onset group B streptococcal invasive disease*

Centre	Live births (*n*)	Neonatal disease (incidence per 1000 live births)		Study period	Reference
		Early-onset	Late-onset		
Aberdeen	9 764	0.72	0.10	1972–74	Reid[35]
26 centres, England and Scotland	226 899	0.24	0.05	1978–79	Mayon-White[7]
Oxford	74 920	0.56		1985–96	Moses et al.[12]
Sunderland	10 525	0.95	0.47	1995–97	Bignardi[36]
Wessex	63 585	1.00		1992–97	Halliday et al.[37]
Bedfordshire	24 267	1.15		1993–98	Beardsall et al.[38]

live births. On this basis and on the basis of limited UK data demonstrating an incidence of 0.5–1.15 per 1000 live births (Table 1), a risk-based screening approach could be justified on a cost basis in UK, but not a microbiological screening-based approach.

Medicalisation of labour

Normal labour is a physiological, not a pathological, process and this remains true for the majority of women colonised with GBS. The introduction of four-hourly intravenous antibiotics can medicalise an otherwise normal labour. It is likely to mean that the woman is no longer eligible to deliver in a midwife-run unit or at home and may thus have a less positive birth experience.[81,82] It is recognised that interventions during labour reduce maternal satisfaction with labour.[83] This may seem a trivial concern compared with the possibility of neonatal disease. However, this risk may be perceived as relatively low (approximately one in 200 in women known to be colonised)[46] and, after counselling, some women will decline administration of intrapartum antibiotics.[34]

Increased demands for prenatal counselling and increased maternal anxiety

If approximately 20–25% of women in labour were to be offered intrapartum antibiotics (whether a screening or risk-based strategy was adopted) it would become necessary to inform all women at booking of this possibility. Women attending booking clinics already receive a large amount of information regarding screening for HIV, hepatitis B, rubella and syphilis infections, chromosomal disorders, neural tube defects and other fetal structural abnormalities. It has been demonstrated that 'low-risk' women retain little of this information[84,85] and that prenatal screening tests cause 'significant negative psychosocial effects'.[86] This would presumably be the case if a policy of universal screening for GBS carriage were adopted.

Medicalisation of the neonatal period

An increasing use of intrapartum antimicrobial agents may have a substantial impact on the clinical management of the well neonate.[87,88] Some paediatricians advise a 48-hour inpatient observation period or routine additional diagnostic tests for the asymptomatic infant of a mother who has received intrapartum antibiotics.[88] There is currently no evidence to support this practice, and it has been argued that a 48-hour stay is not necessary, because infants will display evidence of infection with GBS within the first 24 hours of life.[89] If a mother has received 'inadequate' prophylaxis, i.e. if she delivers within two to four hours of the first dose of antibiotic or receives no chemoprophylaxis contrary to local guidelines, many neonatologists feel uneasy about sanctioning an early discharge from hospital. Again, there is no current evidence to support the use of extra interventions for these infants.[89,90]

It has been demonstrated that a screening-based approach is associated with less neonatal intervention than a risk-based approach,[55,91,92] but that both approaches are associated with more intervention in the healthy neonate than would be the case without these guidelines.[87,88]

Failure to prevent disease

In common with most medical interventions, intrapartum antimicrobial prophylaxis does not prevent 100% of cases of EOGBS disease,[93] probably because of failure to eradicate an established fetal infection. More than 80% of treatment failures are associated with chorioamnionitis or maternal fever.[29] Intrapartum prophylaxis causes only a temporary reduction in neonatal colonisation[27] and therefore has no influence on the incidence of late-onset GBS disease, which is an important cause of neonatal mortality and serious morbidity.[1]

OTHER STRATEGIES

Vaginal disinfectants

These have been used in research trials in Sweden[94] and Malawi[95] and are less invasive than intrapartum antibiotics. The Malawi study demonstrated a significantly reduced rate of admission for neonatal sepsis associated with disinfectant use but an effect on GBS disease has not been demonstrated.

Postnatal antibiotic prophylaxis

In some centres postnatal penicillin is given to all infants[96] or to the infants of colonised mothers without intrapartum risk factors.[97] The strategy does reduce the incidence of EOGBS disease in term infants but has no effect on the disease in low-birthweight infants or on late-onset disease.[1] Universal postpartum prophylaxis has been shown to increase overall mortality rates due to mortality attributable to penicillin-resistant pathogens[80] and has not, therefore, been widely adopted.

Vaccines

Studies in the 1970s established a relationship between low levels of maternal antibodies to GBS capsular polysaccharides and susceptibility of the infant to invasive GBS infection.[44] It has been suggested that this relationship explains the increased risk of GBS disease in infants born to teenagers, who tend to have lower anti-GBS antibody levels.[98] The identification of the association prompted research on GBS polysaccharide antigens and resulted in production of purified polysaccharides and, more recently, conjugated vaccines against the major serotypes causing the disease.[1] A vaccine specific for serotype III has been produced and has been shown to cause a four-fold or greater rise in antibody levels in 90% of volunteers.[99] The antibody crossed the mouse placenta and protected neonatal mice from lethal challenge with type III organisms.[99] A vaccine specific for serotypes Ia and Ib has also been produced with encouraging results.[100]

For statistical validation purposes, sample sizes for trials to measure the clinical protective efficacy of vaccines against invasive GBS disease would be prohibitively large given the low incidence of the disease. In view of this, research has focused on surrogates for clinical protection through a variety of immunological assays. GBS colonisation may also be a useful surrogate. At present the optimum timing for vaccination has not been established.

In addition to the above considerations, there has been a shift in the serotypes of strains causing disease, which creates a challenge for vaccine development.[1] Serotype V was first recognised in USA in 1993 and is now identified as responsible for approximately 10% of neonatal disease.[1]

MATERNAL DISEASE

Preterm delivery

The relationship between GBS and preterm delivery is complex and it is difficult to establish causality. Preterm prelabour rupture of the fetal membranes is strongly associated with EOGBS disease.[1] This may be due to the fact that antibody transport across the placenta is reduced in early pregnancy, so that infants born prematurely have less protection from maternal antibodies.[1] GBS, antenatal screening cultures in predicting genital group B streptococcal colonization at delivery. *Obstet Gynecol* 1996;88:811–15.

60   Badri MS, Zawanch S, Cruz AC, Mantilla G, Baer H, Spellacy WN, *et al.* Rectal colonization with group B streptococcus: relation to vaginal colonization of pregnant women. *J Infect Dis* 1977;135:308–12.

61   Baker CJ, Goroff DK, Alpert S, Crockett VA, Zinner SH, Evrard JR, *et al.* Vaginal colonization with group B streptococcus: a study in college women. *J Infect Dis* 1977;135:392–7.

62   Mercer BM, Taylor MC, Fricke JL, Baselski VS, Sibai BM. The accuracy and patient preference for self-collected group B Streptococcus cultures. *Am J Obstet Gynecol* 1995;173:1325–8.

63   Mohle-Boetani JC, Schuchat A, Plikaytis BD, Smith JD, Broome CV. Comparison of prevention strategies for neonatal group B streptococcal infection. A population-based economic analysis. *JAMA* 1993;270:1442–8.

64   Watt JP, Schuchat A, Erickson K, Honig JE, Gibbs R, Schulkin J. Group B streptococcal disease prevention practices of obstetricians-gynaecologists. *Obstet Gynecol* 2001;98:7–13.

65   Bloom KC, Ewing CA. Group B streptococcal disease screening and treatment during pregnancy: nurse-midwives' consistency with 1996 CDC recommendations. *J Midwifery Women's Health* 2001;46:17–23.

66   Brocklehurst P. UK national survey of maternity units to determine their policies for managing group B streptococcus infection in pregnancy. 2000 (unpublished report).

67   Peralta-Carcelen M, Fargason CA Jr, Coston D, Dolan JG. Preferences of pregnant women and physicians for 2 strategies for prevention of early-onset group B streptococcal sepsis in neonates. *Arch Pediatr Adolesc Med* 1997;151:712–18.

68   American Academy of Pediatrics Committee on Infectious Diseases and Committee on Fetus and Newborn. Guidelines for prevention of group B streptococcal (GBS) infection by chemoprophylaxis. *Pediatrics* 1992;90:775–8.

69   Hankins GV, Chalas E. Group B streptococcal infection in pregnancy: ACOG's recommendations. *ACOG Newsletter* 1993;37:2.

70   McLaughlin K, Crowther C. Universal antenatal group B streptococcus screening? The opinions of obstetricians and neonatologists within Australia. *Aust N Z J Obstet Gynaecol* 2000;40:338–40.

71   Hager WD, Schuchat A, Gibbs R, Sweet R, Mead P, Larsen J.W. Prevention of perinatal group B streptococcal infection: current controversies. *Obstet Gynecol* 2000;96:141–5.

72   Stiller RJ, Vander VS, Laifer SA, Whetham JC. Indicated preterm birth: a possible contribution to group B streptococcal sepsis prophylaxis protocol failures. A case report. *J Perinatol* 2000;20:316–17.

73   Heim K, Alge A, Marth C. Anaphylactic reaction to ampicillin and severe complication in the fetus. *Lancet* 1991;337:859–60.

74   Rouse DJ, Andrews WW, Lin FY, Mott CW, Ware JC, Philips JB. Antibiotic susceptibility profile of group B streptococcus acquired vertically. *Obstet Gynecol* 1998;92:931–4.

75   Levine EM, Ghai V, Barton JJ, Strom CM. Intrapartum antibiotic prophylaxis increases the incidence of gram-negative neonatal sepsis. *Infect Dis Obstet Gynecol* 1999;7:210–13.

76   McDuffie RS, McGregor JA, Gibbs RS. Adverse perinatal outcome and resistant Enterobacteriaceae after antibiotic usage for premature rupture of the membranes and group B streptococcus carriage. *Obstet Gynecol* 1993;82:487–9.

77   Joseph TA, Pyati SP, Jacobs N. Neonatal early-onset Escherichia coli disease. The effect of intrapartum ampicillin. *Arch Pediatr Adolesc Med* 1998;152:35–40.

78   Towers CV, Carr MH, Padilla G, Asrat T. Potential consequences of widespread antepartal use

of ampicillin. *Am J Obstet Gynecol* 1998;179:879–83.

79   Mercer BM, Carr TL, Beazley DD, Crouse DT, Sibai BM. Antibiotic use in pregnancy and drug-resistant infant sepsis. *Am J Obstet Gynecol* 1999;181:816–21.

80   Benitz WE, Gould JB, Druzin ML. Antimicrobial prevention of early-onset group B streptococcal sepsis: estimates of risk reduction based on a critical literature review. *Pediatrics* 1999;103:e78.

81   Waldenstrom U, Nilsson CA. Experience of childbirth in birth center care. A randomized controlled study. *Acta Obstet Gynecol Scand* 1994;73:547–54.

82   Shields N, Turnbull D, Reid M, Holmes A, McGinley M, Smith LN. Satisfaction with midwife-managed care in different time periods: a randomised controlled trial of 1299 women. *Midwifery* 1998;14:85–93.

83   Waldenstrom U. Experience of labor and birth in 1111 women. *J Psychosom Res* 1999;47:471–82.

84   Marteau TM, Johnston M, Plenicar M, Shaw RW, Slack J. Development of a self-administered questionnaire to measure women's knowledge of prenatal screening and diagnostic tests. *J Psychosom Res* 1988;32:403–8.

85   Browner CH, Preloran M, Press NA. The effects of ethnicity, education and an informational video on pregnant women's knowledge and decisions about a prenatal diagnostic screening test. *Patient Educ Couns* 1996;27:135–46.

86   Santalaahti P, Latikka AM, Ryynanen M, Hemminki E. Women's experiences of prenatal serum screening. *Birth* 1996;23:101–7.

87   Pylipow M, Gaddis M, Kinney JS. Selective intrapartum prophylaxis for group B streptococcus colonization: management and outcome of newborns. *Pediatrics* 1994;93:631–5.

88   Wiswell TE, Stoll BJ, Tuggle JM. Management of asymptomatic, term gestation neonates born to mothers treated with intrapartum antibiotics. *Pediatr Infect Dis J* 1990;9:826–31.

89   Mecredy RL, Wiswell TE, Hume RF. Outcome of term gestation neonates whose mothers receive intrapartum antibiotics for suspected chorioamnionitis. *Am J Perinatol* 1993;10:365–8.

90   Gotoff SP. Chemoprophylaxis of early-onset group B streptococcal disease in 1999. *Curr Opin Pediatr* 2000;12:105–10.

91   Davis RL, Hasselquist MB, Cardenas V, Zerr DM, Kramer J, Zavitkovsky AS. Introduction of the new Centers for Disease Control and Prevention group B streptococcal prevention guideline at a large West Coast health maintenance organization. *Am J Obstet Gynecol* 2001;184:603–10.

92   Share L, Chaikin S, Pomeranets Kiwi R, Jacobs M, Fanaroff AA. Implementation of guidelines for preventing early-onset group B streptococcal infection. *Semin Perinatol* 2001;25:107–13.

93   Benitz WE, Gould JB, Druzin ML. Preventing early-onset group B streptococcal sepsis: strategy development using decision analysis. *Pediatrics* 1999;103:e76.

94   Burman LG, Christensen P, Christensen K, Fryklund B, Helgesson AM, Svenningsen NW, *et al.* Prevention of excess neonatal morbidity associated with group B streptococci by vaginal chlorhexidine disinfection during labour. The Swedish Chlorhexidine Study Group. *Lancet* 1992;340:65–9.

95   Taha TE, Biggar RJ, Broadhead RL, Mtimavalye LA, Justesen AB, Liomba GN, *et al.* Effect of cleansing the birth canal with antiseptic solution on maternal and newborn morbidity and mortality in Malawi: clinical trial. *BMJ* 1997;315:216–19.

96   Siegel JD, Cushion NB. Prevention of early-onset group B streptococcal disease: another

look at single-dose penicillin at birth. *Obstet Gynecol* 1996;87:692–8.

97   Gotoff SP, Boyer KM. Prevention of early-onset neonatal group B streptococcal disease. *Pediatrics* 1997;99:866–9.

98   Campbell JR, Hillier SL, Krohn MA, Ferrieri P, Zaleznik DF, Baker CJ. Group B streptococcal colonization and serotype-specific immunity in pregnant women at delivery. *Obstet Gynecol* 2000;96:493–503.

99   Kasper DL, Paoletti LC, Wessels MR, Guttormsen HK, Carey VJ, Jennings HJ, *et al.* Immune response to type III group B streptococcal polysaccharide-tetanus toxoid conjugate vaccine. *J Clin Invest* 1996;98:2308–14.

100   Baker CJ, Paoletti LC, Wessels MR, Guttormsen HK, Rench MA, Hickman ME, *et al.* Safety and immunogenicity of capsular polysaccharide-tetanus toxoid conjugate vaccines for group B streptococcal types Ia and Ib. *J Infect Dis* 1999;179:142–50.

101   Parry S, Strauss JF III. Premature rupture of the fetal membranes. *N Engl J Med* 1998;338:663–70.

102   Kenyon S, Boulvain M. Antibiotics for preterm premature rupture of membranes. *Cochrane Database Syst Rev* 2000;(2):CD001058.

103   Kenyon SL, Taylor DJ, Tarnow-Mordi W. Broad-spectrum antibiotics for pre-term, prelabour rupture of fetal membranes: the ORACLE I randomised trial. *Lancet* 2001;357:979–88.

104   Blanco JD, Gibbs RS, Castaneda YS. Bacteremia in obstetrics: clinical course. *Obstet Gynecol* 1981;58:621–6.

105   Regan JA, Klebanoff MA, Nugent RP, Eschenbach DA, Blackwelder WC, Lou YG, *et al.* Colonization with group B streptococci in pregnancy and adverse outcome. VIP Study Group. *Am J Obstet Gynecol* 1996;174:1354–60.

106   Klebanoff MA, Regan JA, Rao AV, Nugent RP, Blackwelder WC, Eschenbach DA, *et al.* Outcome of the Vaginal Infections and Prematurity Study: results of a clinical trial of erythromycin among pregnant women colonized with group B streptococci. *Am J Obstet Gynecol* 1995;172:1540–45.

107   Locksmith GJ, Clark P, Duff P. Maternal and neonatal infection rates with three different protocols for prevention of group B streptococcal disease. *Am J Obstet Gynecol* 1999;180:416–22.

108   Pass MA, Gray BM, Khare S, Dillon HC. Prospective studies of group B streptococcal infections in infants. *J Pediatr* 1979;95:437–43.

14

Cystic fibrosis and pregnancy outcome

Frank P Edenborough and William E Mackenzie

INTRODUCTION

Once a condition known solely to paediatricians, in the last two decades cystic fibrosis has entered the world of adult medicine. Median survival in cystic fibrosis has increased to about 30 years in the UK, and obstetricians and physicians are therefore now having to address issues surrounding the reproductive health of women with this condition.

A woman with cystic fibrosis wants to know the answers to a number of questions, namely:

- Can I have a baby?

- Will it have cystic fibrosis?

- Will it be affected by my cystic fibrosis?

- Will my cystic fibrosis be affected by the pregnancy?

Within the last five years, many more data have become available to enable medical professionals to answer these questions.

HISTORICAL PERSPECTIVE

Cystic fibrosis is the most common severe autosomal recessive disorder in the Caucasian population occurring in one in 2500 live births.[1,2] It has a carrier status frequency of about 1:25 in the general population. The prognosis for patients with cystic fibrosis has improved dramatically over the last two decades and because of this many more patients are surviving into adulthood and seeking continued care from physicians. The proportion of cystic fibrosis patients who are adults is projected to rise significantly over the next decade. In the UK, there are about 7500 people with cystic fibrosis, one-third of whom are over the age of 16 years. Median survival for cystic fibrosis patients has risen from 20 years for those born in 1970 to a projected 40 years for those born in 2000, and it can be expected to improve further in years to come.

The reasons for these dramatic improvements are multifactorial and include earlier diagnosis, improved management of neonatal meconium ileus obstruction, routine physiotherapy, better nutritional support, development of effective antipseudomonal antibiotics and the trend towards specialist treatment centres. Heart-lung and double-lung transplantation has further extended the lives of a fortunate few, although lack of donor organs precludes these procedures from being available for all those for whom they are suitable.

GENETICS

A genetic basis for cystic fibrosis was suspected as long ago as Andersen's original description in 1938.[3] The discovery of the cystic fibrosis gene on the long arm of chromosome 7, described in 1989,[4-6] rather than simplifying our knowledge of the genetics of cystic fibrosis, has, through subsequent research, revealed a complex picture of genetic diversity. To date, more than 900 different gene defects have been described, all of which, either in homozygous or compound homozygous form, result in the phenotypes that we recognise as cystic fibrosis.

There are marked geographical variations in the frequency of some cystic fibrosis gene defects. The most common defect, a three base pair deletion causing the loss of a single phenylalanine residue at position 508 in the protein chain, has been labelled as the delta-F508 deletion.[7] This mutation accounts for about 70% of cystic fibrosis mutations in North America and slightly more in European populations. In the UK, the overall incidence of delta-F508 is 76%, rising to 81% in the north-west of England.

The normal gene codes for production of a complex protein, the cystic fibrosis transmembrane conductance regulator (CFTR) protein, which is involved in the regulation of the passage of chloride ions across the apical membranes of cells where the gene is expressed.[8] Although the relationship between genotype and phenotype is far from fully elaborated, it does appear that the delta-F508 homozygous state in general produces more severe disease than the delta-F508/other, compound heterozygote.[7] The presence of pancreatic insufficiency (itself clinically associated with poorer lung function than pancreatic sufficiency) appears to be well correlated with the delta-F508 homozygous state, although this relationship is not absolute. There is no clear relationship between the severity of lung disease *per se* and genotype.

Characterisation of the cystic fibrosis gene now allows prenatal testing via chorionic villus sampling at 11 weeks of gestation. For specific mutations that can be identified, accuracy should be 100%. Furthermore, testing for carrier status in a partnership with an affected partner (usually the female, since 98% of males are infertile due to congenital bilateral absence of the vas deferens) is now possible.[9,10] There is a large number of rare mutations that are not routinely tested for and an absolute 'all-clear' therefore cannot be given. Technology now exists for population-wide heterozygote screening with increasing sensitivity as commercial kits testing for increasing numbers of defects become available. A combination of carrier detection and prenatal diagnosis incorporated in programmes of prenatal screening has the potential to reduce the birth incidence of cystic fibrosis in the future.

CLINICAL FEATURES OF CYSTIC FIBROSIS

The cardinal features of cystic fibrosis are those of chronic lung disease and pancreatic exocrine insufficiency. Although the clinical picture of cystic fibrosis is highly variable, by adulthood nearly all patients will exhibit respiratory symptoms and most will have advanced pulmonary disease.[11] Clinically significant exocrine pancreatic insufficiency (requiring treatment with enzyme supplements) is present in about 90% of cystic fibrosis adults; there is some evidence that exocrine pancreatic function in cystic fibrosis may decline with age.

In the lungs the condition is dominated by tenacious mucus, which becomes chronically infected with a variety of organisms, leading to repeated respiratory exacerbations, chronic inflammation, progressive bronchiectasis, declining respiratory function and death from respiratory failure. Pancreatic, bowel and hepatobiliary involvement lead to abnormal digestion, malabsorption, steatorrhoea and undernutrition, which may be further compromised by diabetes mellitus and biliary cirrhosis.

Although the abnormal CFTR protein is expressed in the fallopian tubes, endometrium and cervix, these organs are usually little affected. The ovaries are structurally normal and development of the pituitary gonadal hormonal axis, although delayed by up to two years, is normal, so fertility in a woman with cystic fibrosis may be relatively unaffected.

PREGNANCY IN CYSTIC FIBROSIS

The first pregnancy in a woman with cystic fibrosis was described in 1960, when death before school age was usual.[12] However, since the 1990s, when median survival has increased to about 30 years in the Western world, the numbers of pregnancies in women with cystic fibrosis has been increasing rapidly. In the USA, approximately 140 pregnancies have been reported annually since 1991, accounting for 3–4% of women aged 17 years and over per year.[13]

Early reports of pregnancy showed poor fetal outcomes and a deterioration in the woman's condition, especially in women with more severe disease, although recent reports[14,15] suggest that outcomes for the woman and her child have improved.

Between 1991 and 1994, the North American Cystic Fibrosis Foundation Data Registry reported 119–140 pregnancies per year, with over 70% of pregnancies resulting in live births and a 30% therapeutic termination rate. Approximately 25% of deliveries were premature and the number of stillbirths fell from 10% to 0% (Table 1). The increase in live births may be due to improvements in obstetric and neonatal care, allowing the survival of infants born increasingly prematurely to women with advanced cystic fibrosis.

Table 1 *Outcome of 69 UK pregnancies contrasted with US data*

	USA		UK
	1982	1994	1996
Mothers/pregnancies (n)	100/121	87/87	55/69
Completed pregnancies (%)	75	71	70
Viable births (%)	89	100	100
Term birth (%)	73	not known	54
Preterm birth (%)	27	not known	46
Perinatal deaths (%)	11	0	0
Stillbirths (%)	6	0	0
Neonatal deaths (%)	5	0	0
Abortions (%)	25	29	30
Miscarriage (%)	6	not known	10
Terminations (%)	19	not known	20
Birth defects (%)	0	0	4
Maternal deaths < 24 months (%)	15	NA	5

EFFECTS OF PREGNANCY ON LUNG FUNCTION

Early reports suggested poorer outcome for mother and infant and were related to pancreatic status, nutrition and lung function.[16,17] In the last two decades, pregnancy has become increasingly successful in pancreatic insufficient women because of better nutritional care, including oral and enteral tube feeding with enzyme supplementation. There is little doubt that pregnancy is likely to be more complicated in those with advanced lung disease but the magnitude of any potential effect and whether pregnancy adversely affects those with poor lung function is still debated.

Controlled studies are few and conflicting. Ahmed et al.[18] and Frangiolias et al.,[19] reporting on 13 and seven pairs of patients and non-pregnant controls respectively, matched for age, lung function and in the latter weight, height, pancreatic status and sputum microbiology noted no statistically significant decline in percentage of forced expiratory volume in one second (FEV_1) and percentage of forced vital capacity (FVC) up to two years after delivery. However, Ahmed's group had better prepregnant clinical status than controls but despite this had a greater decline in all parameters during pregnancy, including an increased number of exacerbations. In Frangiolas's group, the greatest declines in almost all parameters were seen in the two patients with $\%FEV_1$ of less than 70%, leading them to conclude that certain individuals experienced 'progressive deterioration out of keeping with their clinical course prepregnancy'.

The largest study to date from the American Cystic Fibrosis Database,[20] with 258 completed pregnancies matched with 889 controls, potentially has the statistical power to resolve the issue. However, the data, being based on annual review data, may mask individual changes. To date they have reported no difference in rates of decline in FEV_1 or survival at two years, noting that survival was reduced in cases and controls with poor weight and lung function and that diabetes is a significant adverse determinant for mother and infant; however, the analysis has yet to be published in detail.

A study from Canada[14] reviewed all women with cystic fibrosis attending the Toronto Cystic Fibrosis clinic from 1961 to 1998. Their overall mortality among cystic fibrosis patients was 19%. They concluded that, when adjusted for the same parameters, pregnancy did not affect survival compared with the entire cystic fibrosis population. They found the decline in FEV_1 in the pregnant population to be comparable to that in the total cystic fibrosis population. By contrast, Edenborough et al.[15] found that in pregnant women with cystic fibrosis who delivered a baby prematurely there was a fall-off in lung function in pregnancy that was worse than in non-pregnant controls and they concluded that pregnancy exerted an adverse effect on women with poor lung function.

There is general agreement that in severe disease the presence of pulmonary hypertension and cor pulmonale, which are both associated with a poor prognosis for the woman and her infant, should be regarded as absolute contraindications and lead obstetricians and cystic fibrosis physicians to counsel against pregnancy. Most authors agree that a prepregnant FEV_1 of 50% and under is a relative contraindication and pregnancy should be discouraged. Above 90%, FEV_1 pregnancy is likely to be normal and between 60–80% FEV_1 most pregnancies can be expected to have a successful obstetric outcome but with increased obstetric and maternal complications seen with poorer lung function.

EFFECT OF CYSTIC FIBROSIS ON PREGNANCY

'Fertility in females is 20% that of normal women' is an often-quoted statistic but, as previously shown, cystic fibrosis has a minimal effect on the female reproductive tract and all menstruating women should be considered fertile. Similarly, the effect of cystic fibrosis on pregnancy itself appears to be much less than previously believed.

In large reported series, cystic fibrosis does not appear to increase the prematurity rate significantly, although most women who carried a pregnancy to term had mild to moderate disease.[14]

Obstetric complications tend to occur in sicker women. The extra calorific demands of pregnancy, as well as nausea and vomiting, may result in weight loss and, in some women with poor prepregnancy body mass indices, enteral or parenteral feeding may be necessary.

In one series of nine women with a body mass index greater than 18 kg/m², five miscarried or underwent termination of pregnancy and four delivered prematurely.[15] The effect of cystic fibrosis on pregnancy in women who are also affected by diabetes is not entirely clear from the literature, as the numbers of such women are small. Diabetes not resulting from cystic fibrosis has well-known effects on pregnancy, namely fetal death, prematurity and an increased maternal morbidity. When combined with cystic fibrosis, diabetes appears to increase the tendency to shorter gestation, an increased caesarean section rate and a greater use of antibiotics.

Pregnancy in women with cystic fibrosis should be planned and preferably take place in units with physicians experienced in the care of cystic fibrosis patients. Teamwork between the physicians, physiotherapists, obstetricians and anaesthetists is important.

As previously indicated, close attention needs to be paid to the mother's nutritional status throughout pregnancy, with admissions for nutritional supplements when necessary as well as aggressive treatment of respiratory infections. The risk to the fetus from poor maternal health is probably greater than the possible teratogenic risk of such drugs.

The usual obstetrics tests associated with high-risk pregnancy should be applied. All patients should be tested for glucose intolerance by the late mid-trimester. Decisions about induction of labour should usually be taken for obstetric reasons and not just because the woman has cystic fibrosis. Many women with mild to moderate disease will tolerate labour well and a normal delivery can be expected. Where labour has to be induced or preterm delivery by caesarean section is required, the whole team will need to be involved in that decision, as such women will often need intensive medical management before the birth.

Epidural anaesthesia is recommended for most labouring women, as it can minimise fatigue in the first stage as well as facilitate second-stage interventions. Anaesthesia in cystic fibrosis has been discussed by Howell et al.[21]

COUNSELLING

Ideally, the advice of geneticists should be sought when a woman with cystic fibrosis is contemplating pregnancy, and her partner should be tested before conception. All unaffected children will, of course, be carriers of the disease. Couples should realise that in the presence of severe cystic fibrosis, pregnancy may shorten the life of the woman and in certain circumstances, where alternative methods of contraception are not accepted, sterilisation of the nulliparous woman should be discussed.

As it remains unclear whether pregnancy affects the maternal prognosis directly, a certain degree of caution is wise in discussions about maternal outcome, but pregnancy is safe for women with mild cystic fibrosis, especially where the FEV_1 is greater than 70%. As Gilljam[14] observed, some women experienced their best health during pregnancy while others described the onset of deteriorating health. They believe that this reflects the variable nature of cystic fibrosis with stability over years in some patients and acute deterioration in others. In moderate disease, the obstetric outcome is likely to be satisfactory, although there is some evidence that if the birth is premature there is an increased risk to maternal health.

Although cystic fibrosis patients will undergo varied and intensive antibiotic treatment, as well as treatment with other drug regimens during their pregnancy, there are no data about any increased incidence of congenital anomalies. None of the drugs used in cystic fibrosis has previously been associated with causing fetal anomalies. Within one study there were three cases of fetal anomaly.[15] Two babies were born with non-fatal heart defects and one pregnancy was terminated at 19 weeks because of a diaphragmatic hernia and polysplenia. To date, this is the only large study that has reported on fetal anomalies in babies born to women with cystic fibrosis. Until much larger series have been published and confounding variables controlled for, the general impression is that there is no causal association between cystic fibrosis, its treatment and the subsequent development of fetal anomalies during pregnancy.

BREASTFEEDING

Women with cystic fibrosis can breastfeed successfully. Breast milk from such women has a normal electrolyte composition and, although it is said to have a slightly lower fat content than normal, it is satisfactory for infant feeding.[22,23] It is recommended that breastfeeding be attempted, even if partial and requiring augmentation with formula feed, although careful attention needs to be paid to maternal nutrition. If the extra calorific burden of breastfeeding leads to difficulty in maintaining maternal weight, then breastfeeding should be reconsidered.

CONCLUSION

Pregnancy in women with cystic fibrosis should be planned, and requires good teamwork between the obstetrician and the mother's cystic fibrosis carers. As more patients with cystic fibrosis become pregnant, and as larger numbers are studied, the exact effect of pregnancy in women with cystic fibrosis with moderate to severe disease will become clearer. The general consensus from most studies at present is that pregnancy is well tolerated in women with all but the most severe cystic fibrosis. Good lung function will predict a full-term pregnancy with few sequelae. Poor lung function is associated with a poorer obstetric outcome and an increased fetal and maternal morbidity. The long-term effect of pregnancy on lung function in women with cystic fibrosis remains unclear.

References

1   Dodge JA, Morison S, Lewis PA, Coles EC, Geddes D, Russell G, *et al.* Incidence, population, and survival of cystic fibrosis in the United Kingdom 1968-95. *Arch Dis Child* 1997;77:493–6.

2   Walters S. *Association of CF Adults (UK) Survey, 1994: Analysis and Report.* Birmingham: University of Birmingham; 1995. p. 3.1–3.3.

3   Anderson DH. Cystic fibrosis of the pancreas and its relation to coeliac disease. A clinical and pathological study. *Am J Dis Child* 1938;56:344–99.

4   Rommens JM, Iannuzzi MC, Kerem B-S, Drumm ML, Melmer G, Dean M, *et al.* Identification of the cystic fibrosis gene: chromosome walking and jumping. *Science* 1989;245:1059–65.

5   Riordan JR, Rommens JM, Kerem B-S, Alon N, Rozmahel R, Grzelcak Z, *et al.* Identification of the cystic fibrosis gene: cloning and characterisation of complementary DNA. *Science* 1989;245:1066–73.

6   Kerem B-S, Rommens J, Buchanan JA, Markiewicz D, Cox TK, Chakravarti A, *et al.* Identification of the cystic fibrosis gene: genetic analysis. *Science* 1989;245:1073–80.

7   Kerem E, Corey M, Kerem B-S, Rommens J, Markiewicz D, Levison H, *et al.* The relation between genotype and phenotype in cystic fibrosis – analysis of the most common mutation (delta F508). *N Engl J Med* 1990;323:1517–22.

8   Tizzano EF, Silver MM, Chitayat D, Benichou JC, Buchwald M. Differential cellular expression in cystic fibrosis transmembrane regulator in human reproductive tissues. Clues for the infertility in patients with cystic fibrosis. *Am J Pathol* 1994;144:906–14.

9   Kaplan E, Shwachman H, Perlmutter A, Rule A, Khaw KT, Holsclaw D. Reproductive failure in males with cystic fibrosis. *N Engl J Med* 1968;279:65-9.

10   Taussig LM, Lobeck CC, di Sant'Agnese PA, Ackerman DR, Kattwinkel J. Fertility in males with cystic fibrosis. *N Engl J Med* 1972;287:586–9.

11   Corey M, McLaughlin FJ, Williams M, Levison H. A comparison of survival, growth, and pulmonary function in patients with cystic fibrosis in Boston and Toronto. *J Clin Epidemiol* 1988;41:583–91.

12   Siegel B, Siegel S. Pregnancy and delivery in a patient with cystic fibrosis of the pancreas. *Obstet Gynecol* 1960;16:438–40.

13   Hilman BC, Aitken M, Constantinescu M. Pregnancy in patients with cystic fibrosis. *Clin Obstet Gynecol* 1996;38:70–86.

14   Gilljam M, Antoniou M, Shin J, Dupius A, Corey M, Tullis E. Pregnancy in cystic fibrosis – fetal and maternal outcome. *Chest* 2000;118:85–91.

15   Edenborough FP, Mackenzie WE, Stableforth DE. The outcome of 72 pregnancies in 55 women with cystic fibrosis in the United Kingdom 1977–1996. *Br J Obstet Gynaecol* 2000;107:254–61.

16   Weinberger SE, Weiss ST, Cohen WR, Weiss JW, Johnson TS. Pregnancy and the lung. *Am Re Respir Dis* 1980;121:559–77.

17   Milne JA. The respiratory response to pregnancy. *Postgrad Med J* 1979;55:318–24.

18   Ahmed R, Wielinski CL, Warwick WJ. Effect of pregnancy on CF. *Pediatric Pulmonology* 1995; Suppl 12:289.

19   Frangiolas DD, Nakielna EM, Wilcox PG. Pregnancy in cystic fibrosis: a case-controlled study. *Chest* 1997;111:963–9.

20   FitzSimmons SC, Fitzpatrick S, Thompson B, Aitkin M, Fiel S, Winnie G, *et al.* A longitudinal study of the effects of pregnancy on 325 women with cystic fibrosis. *Pediatric Pulmonology* 1996; Suppl 13:99–101.

21   Howell PR, Kent N, Douglas MJ. Anaesthesia for the parturient with cystic fibrosis. *Int J Obstet Anaesth* 1993;2:152–8.

22   Alpert SE, Cornier AD. Normal electrolyte and protein content in milk from mothers with cystic fibrosis: an explanation for the initial report of elevated milk sodium concentration. *J Pediatrics* 1983;102:77–80.

23   Shiffman ML, Seale TW, Flux M, Rennert OR, Swender PT. Breast milk composition in women with cystic fibrosis: report of two cases and a review of the literature. *Am J Clin Nutr* 1989;49:612–17.

Plate 9

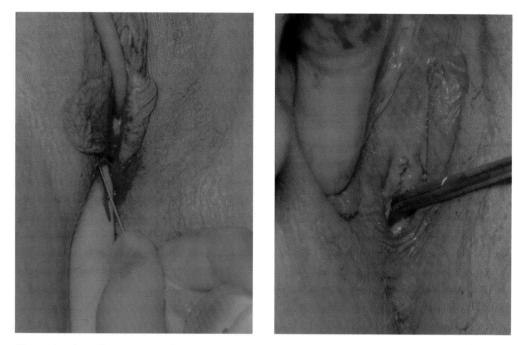

Figures 8 and 9, Chapter 21 *'Cough testing' is undertaken after tape placement in a patient operated under local anaesthesia; it is important that an instrument is placed between the tape and the urethra whenever tape adjustments are made, and during withdrawal of the polyurethane sheath, to preclude undue tightening of the tape*

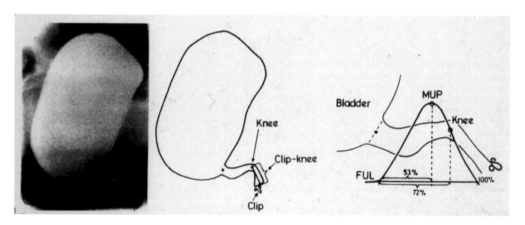

Figure 10, Chapter 21 *Lateral cystogram (left) and resting urethral pressure profile (right) to demonstrate the 'urethral knee'; reproduced with permission from Springer[4]*

Plate 10

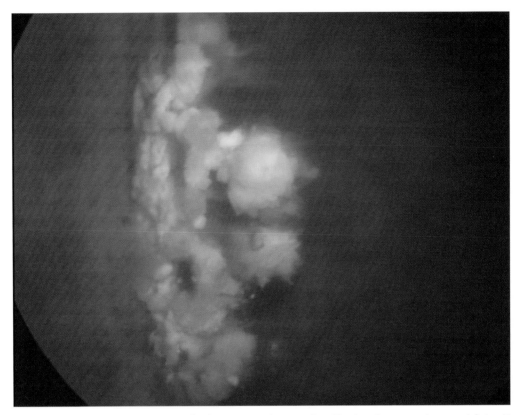

Figure 12, Chapter 21 *TVT tape encrusted with stone in a patient presenting with pain and recurrent urinary tract infection 15 months after surgery*

Plate 11

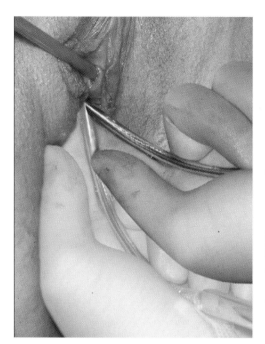

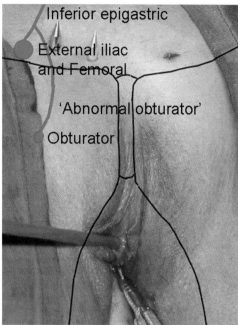

Inferior epigastric

External iliac and Femoral

'Abnormal obturator'

Obturator

Figures 13 and 14, Chapter 21 *Superimposed photographs to indicate correct and incorrect needle orientation of the TVT needle as it passes through the retropubic space; too lateral an insertion track brings the needle in closer proximity to major vessels (shown in overlay) and increases the risk of vascular injury*

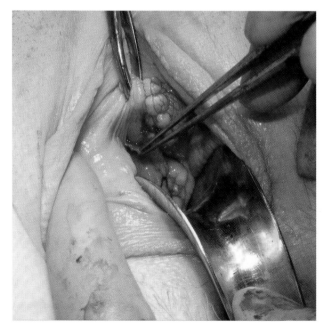

Figure 15, Chapter 21 *Perforation of the lateral vaginal sulcus by TVT tape*

Plate 12

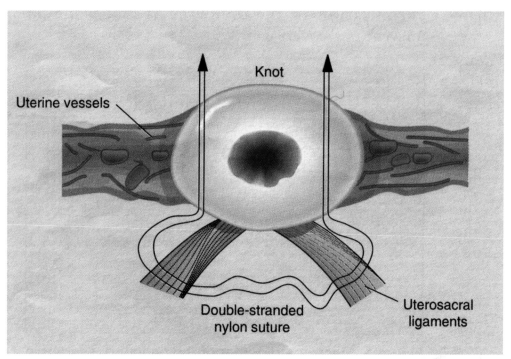

Figure 2, Chapter 22 *Schematic diagram of insertion of transabdominal cerclage; reproduced by kind permission of* Hospital Medicine[18]

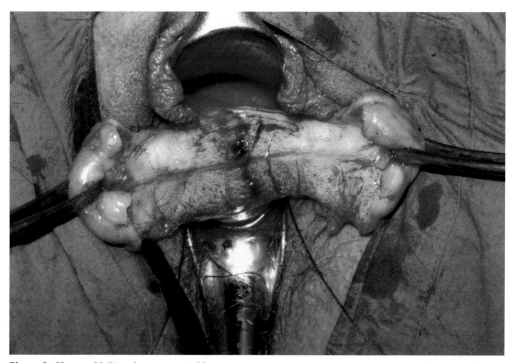

Figure 2, Chapter 23 *Bisected uterus at vaginal hysterectomy*

ERRATUM

Due to an error these figures were printed incorrectly and should be as shown here.

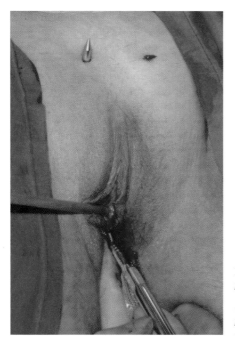

Figure 5, Chapter 21, Plate 7 *Once the endopelvic fascia is perforated, the needle orientation is then adjusted and the handle lowered (compare position of handle with Figure 4); the needle is kept in contact with the posterior surface of the symphysis at all times as the needle is passed through the retropubic space; it is then eased through the rectus sheath to emerge from the suprapubic incision*

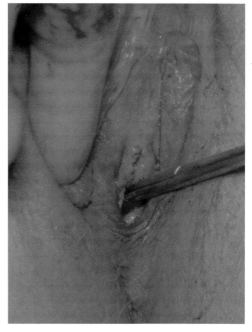

Figures 8 and 9, Chapter 21, Plate 9 *'Cough testing' is undertaken after tape placement in a patient operated under local anaesthesia; it is important that an instrument is placed between the tape and the urethra whenever tape adjustments are made, and during withdrawal of the polyurethane sheath, to preclude undue tightening of the tape*

15

Tokophobia: a profound dread and avoidance of childbirth – from *Genesis* to the Sentinel Audit

Kristina Hofberg

HISTORICAL INTRODUCTION

Tokophobia is not a modern-day phenomenon. Fear of parturition was described by Marcé in 1858.[1] He said: 'If they are primiparous, the expectation of unknown pain preoccupies them beyond all measure, and throws them into a state of inexpressible anxiety. If they are already mothers, they are terrified of the memory of the past and the prospect of the future'.

It is well-known that pregnancy may be a time of considerable anxiety, especially in the third trimester.[2,3] Osiander[4] described a woman in 1797 who, in the course of a long and painful labour, opened her own abdomen, extracted the baby and recovered. In 1907, Sigwart[5] described a labouring woman 'gripped by the fear of death. She imagined that no one could help her in her pain, and the doctor would come and tear her to pieces'.

Although the pain and danger of parturition have been greatly reduced since Osiander and Sigwart, women still suffer the fear of death during delivery.[6] When fear of childbirth precedes pregnancy and is so intense that 'tokos' (childbirth) is avoided whenever possible, it is a phobic state called 'tokophobia'.[7] Tokophobia may affect women from childhood into old age.

PSYCHOLOGICAL AND SOCIAL CONSIDERATIONS

Social culture

An integral part of British religious culture and education is the fate of Adam and Eve.[8] Eve was punished. God said, 'I will greatly increase your pains in childbearing: with pain you will give birth to children'. The concepts of pain, punishment and parturition may become closely integrated in childhood teaching. This may be further highlighted for girls when their parents have a negative attitude towards sexuality.[9]

Kitchen culture

Mothers of young children often find friends with babies. Meetings lead to discussion of childbirth. Women accurately recall details of childbirth 20 years later.[10] Meanwhile, children listen, again and again. This is kitchen culture. If deliveries have been traumatic, mothers narrate horror stories. Fear of childbirth may be transmitted over generations,[11] and represent a second-generation effect of a mother's own unresolved frightening experience.[12] Women's reproductive adaptations resemble their mothers'. This suggests a psychological heredity.[13]

Theories of anxiety

A phobia is an avoidance response. It may be learned through frightening experiences, vicariously by seeing others' fearful responses or through instruction.[14] Zar[15] used the work of Lazarus[16] to investigate fear of childbirth. She suggested that a pregnant woman's expectations of the delivery are relevant to how she experiences it and behaves throughout. Furthermore, her appraisal of the last delivery will include the anxiety associated with it and indicate the level of fear for a future delivery. Fear of childbirth has been associated with anxiety proneness in general[17] and may belong to the family of anxiety disorders.

Childhood sexual abuse

Baker and Duncan[18] reported that 12% of women described being sexually abused before the age of 16 years. Psychological morbidity secondary to childhood sexual abuse may be immense and diverse with increased rates of sexual dysfunction,[19] anorexia[20] and post-traumatic stress disorder (PTSD).[21] A history of childhood sexual abuse could be associated with an aversion to gynaecological examinations, including routine smears or obstetric care. The trauma of vaginal delivery, or even the contemplation of it, may cause a resurgence of distressing memories. This can lead to dread and avoidance of childbirth, even when a woman wants a baby.[7]

CLASSIFICATION AND NATURE OF THE DISORDER

Tokophobia has been classified into primary tokophobia, secondary tokophobia and tokophobia as a symptom of depression.[7]

Primary tokophobia

When dread of childbirth predates the first conception, this is called primary tokophobia. The dread of childbirth may start in adolescence or early adulthood. Sexual relations may be normal but contraceptive use is often overscrupulous.[7]

Some women never overcome their fear of childbirth. Some adopt. Some feel shame at their perceived inadequacy. They enter the menopause having never delivered a much-desired baby. They mourn this loss into old age.

Case 1

A 35-year-old woman had been married for ten years. She had never become pregnant because she was terrified of childbirth. She thought she would lose control and humiliate herself. She believed that she would die. She had a normal sexual relationship with her husband. For contraception they used condoms, spermicide and the oral contraceptive pill. In primary tokophobia, pregnancy is avoided to prevent parturition. Some women take drastic measures to avoid childbirth.

Case 2

A 16-year-old girl watched an educational video at school on childbirth. She was terrified. She vowed she would never deliver a baby. At the age of 25 years, she was engaged to be married. She conceived by accident. She secretly planned a termination of pregnancy. She was clear that she in 1897, described depression following a severe labour, with resulting phobia for pregnancy. In 1978, Bydlowski and Raoul-Duval[60] described ten cases of '*névrose traumatique post-obstetricale*' in women who endured long, painful deliveries. They stated: 'Parturition – especially the first – can, by its obligatory violence and confrontation with an imminent and lonely death, put the mother under extreme stress'.

They suggested that the aftermath of delivery trauma was intensified in subsequent pregnancy. These traumatised women avoided childbirth. Some suffered nightmares so terrifying that they were unable to sleep.[61] Postnatal women report the delivery as a stressor.[62] The clinical picture and course of PTSD after childbirth was described in four cases in 1995.[63] It has been suggested that PTSD may follow deliveries that 'need not have been abnormal from the clinician's perspective'.[64] In addition, 'some have aborted much wanted pregnancies because they are unable to deal with the idea of another delivery'.

It was reported that almost 2% of women have a post-traumatic stress symptom profile related to childbirth during the first year postpartum.[22] Furthermore, one-third of women suffered 'serious post-traumatic intrusive stress reactions' one to two months after a caesarean section.[65] As a consequence, post-delivery stress clinics have been developed.[66] In tokophobia, the incidence of PTSD was high in women not granted their choice of mode of delivery.[7]

Sterilisation

Early researchers investigating the outcome of sterilisation recognised a special group of women with an intense fear of pregnancy. Binder[67] in 1937 described 18 women sterilised for this reason. All but one were fully satisfied. In 1955, Hoppeler[68] studied 100 women in Zurich. He found that the greater the fear of pregnancy, the lower the risk of regret. Ekblad[69] addressed the issue of 'fear of pregnancy' as a reason for requesting sterilisation, stating: 'Many of the women examined had suffered before the sterilisation from a pronounced fear of pregnancy which had adversely affected their sexual life and had contributed to marital troubles. This fear of pregnancy was often an important reason for the women themselves wishing to be sterilised'.

It could be speculated that some of these women had tokophobia and had rid themselves of the danger of having to face their phobic situation. It would be valuable to investigate the motives of childless women presenting for sterilisation. Some may suffer from tokophobia and respond to a psychological approach to their situation. Some women with tokophobia will request sterilisation as a means of managing their intense fear of childbirth.[7] Tokophobic women will be ambivalent about this decision if they still desire motherhood.

CONCLUSION

Tokophobia is a harrowing condition. Women with tokophobia may present to obstetricians demanding delivery by caesarean section without obvious medical indication. They may also request a termination of pregnancy or sterilisation when the fear is of parturition rather than parenting a baby. Refusal of the delivery of choice may lead to a further psychological trauma if they are subjected to a vaginal delivery against their will. These women may then be more vulnerable to PTSD and postnatal depression. This psychological morbidity may deleteriously affect both their relationship with the baby and the baby's own development.[70]

Further research investigating the heterogeneous nature of the condition and the initiation of intervention trials is urgently needed. Until then, tokophobia requires recognition and close liaison between the obstetrician and psychiatrist to assess a balance between surgical and psychiatric morbidity.

Acknowledgements

I would like to thank Emeritus Professor Ian Brockington for his enthusiastic interest and support with all the work on tokophobia, without whom 'tokophobia' would never have been described. I would also like to thank Mr Simon Jenkinson FRCOG, Consultant Obstetrician and Gynaecologist, Worcestershire Acute NHS Trust, for all his help with this work, and Dr Abid Khan, my trainer, for his support while I worked on this chapter. I would also like to thank the South Stafford Healthcare NHS Trust, my employer during this time.

References

1   Marcé LV. *Traité de la Folie des Femmes Enceintes, des Nouvelles Accouchées et des Nourrices.* Paris: Baillière; 1858.

2   Lubin B, Gardiner S, Roth A. Mood and somatic symptoms during pregnancy. *Psychosom Med* 1975;37:136–46.

3   Heymans H, Winter ST. Fears during pregnancy. An interview study of 200 post-partum women. *Israeli Journal of Medical Science* 1975;11:1102–5.

4   Osiander FB. *Neue Denkwürdigkeiten für Ärzte und Geburtshelfer.* Göttingen: Rosenbusch; 1797.

5   Sigwart W. Selbstmordversuch während der Geburt. *Archiv für Psychiatrie und Nervenkrankheiten* 1907;42:249–56.

6   Fava GA, Grandi S, Michelacci L, Saviotti F, Conti S, Bovicelli L, et al. Hypochondriacal fears and beliefs in pregnancy. *Acta Psychiatry Scand* 1990;82:70–72.

7   Hofberg KM, Brockington IF. Tokophobia: an unreasoning dread of childbirth. A series of 26 cases. *Br J Psychiatry* 2000;176:83–5.

8   Holy Bible, King James Version. *Genesis* Chapter 3, verse 6.

9   Areskog B, Uddenberg N, Kjessler B. Background factors in pregnant women with and without fear of childbirth. *J Psychosom Obstet Gynaecol* 1983;2:102–8.

10 Simkin P. Just another day in a woman's life? Part II: Nature and consistency of women's long term memories of their first birth experiences. *Birth* 1992;2:64–81.

11 Benoit D, Parker KCH. Stability and transmission of attachment across three generations. *Child Devel* 1994;65:1444–56.

12 Ryding EL. Investigation of 33 women who demanded a cesarean section for personal reasons. *Acta Obstet Gynecol Scand* 1993;72:280–85.

13 Uddenberg N. Reproductive adaptation in mother and daughter. A study of personality development and adaptation to motherhood. *Acta Psychiatry Scand Suppl* 1974;254:1–115.

14 Rachman S. The conditioning theory of fear-acquisition: a critical examination. *Behav Res Ther* 1977;15:375–87.

15 Zar M. Diagnostic aspects of fear of childbirth. *Linköping Studies in Education and Psychology* 2001. Dissertation No 78.

16 Lazarus RS. *Emotion and Adaptation.* New York: Oxford University Press; 1991.

17 Wijma K, Wijma B. Changes in anxiety during pregnancy and after delivery. In: Wijma K, von Schoultz B, editors. *Reproductive Life. Advances in Research in Psychosomatic Obstetrics and Gynaecology.* Lancaster: Parthenon Publishing Group; 1992. p. 81–8.

18 Baker AW, Duncan SP. Sexual abuse in childhood: a study of prevalence in Great Britain. *Child Abuse Negl* 1985;9:457–67.

19 Oppenheimer R, Howells KJ, Palmer RL, Chaloner DA. Adverse sexual experiences in childhood and clinical eating disorders: a preliminary description. *J Psychiatry Res* 1985;19:357–61.

References

1   Paterson-Brown S. Should doctors perform an elective caesarean section on request? Yes, as long as the woman is fully informed. *BMJ* 1998;317:462–3.

2   Amu O, Rajendran S, Bolajii II. Should doctors perform an elective caesarean section on request? Maternal choice alone should not determine method of delivery. *BMJ* 1998;317:463–5.

3   Leitch CR, Walker JJ. The rise in caesarean section rate: the same indications but a lower threshold. *Br J Obstet Gynaecol* 1998;105:621–6.

4   Porreco RP, Thorp JA. The cesarean birth epidemic: trends, causes, and solutions. *Am J Obstet Gynecol* 1996;175:369–74.

5   Johnson SR, Elkins TE, Strong C, Phelan JP. Obstetric decision-making: responses to patients who request caesarean delivery. *Obstet Gynecol* 1986;67:847–50.

6   Cotzias CS, Paterson-Brown S, Fisk NM. Obstetricians say yes to maternal request for elective caesarean section: a survey of current opinion. *Eur J Obstet Gynecol Reprod Biol* 2001;97:15–16.

7   Stewart MA. Effective physician-patient communication and health outcomes: a review. *CMAJ* 1995;152:1423–33.

8   Kravitz RL, Melnikow J. Engaging patients in medical decision making. *BMJ* 2001;323:584–5.

9   Murray E, Davis H, Tai SS, Coulter A, Gray A, Haines A. Randomised controlled trial of an interactive multimedia decision aid on hormone replacement therapy in primary care. *BMJ* 2001;323:490–93.

10 Murray E, Davis H, Tai SS, Coulter A, Gray A, Haines A. Randomised controlled trial of an interactive multimedia decision aid on benign prostatic hypertrophy in primary care. *BMJ* 2001;323:493–6.

11 Deyo RA. A key medical decision maker: the patient. *BMJ* 2001;323:466–7.

12 Hall MH. When a woman asks for a caesarean section. *BMJ* 1987;294:201–2.

13 Wackerhausen S. What is natural? Deciding what to do and not to do in medicine and healthcare. *Br J Obstet Gynaecol* 1999;106:1109–12.

14 Lilford RJ, Van Coeverden de Groot HA, Moore PJ, Bingham P. The relative risks of caesarean section (intrapartum and elective) and vaginal delivery: a detailed analysis to exclude the effects of medical disorders and other pre-existing physiological disturbances. *Br J Obstet Gynaecol* 1990;97:883–92.

15 Sachs BP, Yeh J, Acker D, Driscoll S, Brown DAJ, Jewett JF. Caesarean section-related maternal mortality in Massachusetts, 1954–1985. *Obstet Gynecol* 1988;71:385–8.

16 Hopkins L, Smaill F. Antibiotic prophylaxis regimens and drugs for prophylaxis. *Cochrane Database Syst Rev* 2000;(2):CD 001136.

17 Royal College of Obstetricians and Gynaecologists. *Prophylaxis Against Thromboembolism in Gynaecology and Obstetrics. Report of a Working Party*. London: RCOG; 1995.

18 Lewis G, Drife J, editors. *Why Mothers Die. Report on Confidential Enquiries into Maternal Deaths in the United Kingdom 1994–1996*. London. The Stationery Office; 1998. p. 48–55.

19 Lewis G, Drife J, editors. *Why Mothers Die. The Confidential Enquiries into Maternal Deaths in the United Kingdom 1997–1999*. London: RCOG Press; 2001. p. 317–22.

20 Hofmeyr GJ, Hannah ME. Planned caesarean section for term breech delivery. *Cochrane Database Syst Rev* 2001;(3):CD0000116.

21   Meyer S, Schreyer A, de Grandi P, Hohlfeld P. The effects of birth on urinary continence mechanisms and other pelvic-floor characteristics. *Obstet Gynecol* 1998;92:613–18.

22   Wilson PD, Herbison RM, Herbison GP. Obstetric practice and the prevalence of urinary incontinence three months after delivery. *Br J Obstet Gynaecol* 1996;103:154–61.

23   Sultan AH, Kamm MA, Hudson CN, Thomas JM, Bartram CI. Anal sphincter disruption during vaginal delivery. *N Engl J Med* 1993;329:1905–11.

24   Fynes M, Donnelly V, Behan M, O'Connell PR, Herlihy CO. Effect of second vaginal delivery on anorectal physiology and faecal incontinence: a prospective study. *Lancet* 1999;354:983–6.

25   Fynes M, Donnelly V, O'Connell PR, Herlihy CO. Cesarean delivery and anal sphincter injury. *Obstet Gynecol* 1998;92:496–500.

26   MacArthur C, Bick DE, Keighley MRB. Faecal incontinence after childbirth. *Br J Obstet Gynaecol* 1997;104:46–50.

27   MacArthur C, Glazener CMA, Wilson PD, Herbison GP, Gee H, Lang GD, et al. Obstetric practice and faecal incontinence three months after delivery. *BJOG* 2001;108:678–83.

28   Faltin DL, Sangalli MR, Roche B, Floris L, Boulvain M, Weil A. Does a second delivery increase the risk of anal incontinence? *BJOG* 2001;108:684–8.

29   Olsen AL, Smith VJ, Bergstrom JO, Colling JC, Clark AL. Epidemiology of surgically managed pelvic organ prolapse and urinary incontinence. *Obstet Gynecol* 1997;89:501–6.

30   MacLennan AH, Taylor AW, Wilson DH, Wilson D. The prevalence of pelvic floor disorders and their relationship to gender, age, parity and mode of delivery. *BJOG* 2000;107:1460–70.

31   Clement S. Psychological aspects of caesarean section. *Best Pract Res Clin Obstet Gynaecol* 2001;15:109–26.

32   Glazener CMA, Abdalla M, Stroud P, Naji S, Templeton A, Russell IT. Postnatal maternal morbidity: extent, causes, prevention and treatment. *Br J Obstet Gynaecol* 1995;102:282–7.

33   Unicef UK Baby Friendly Initiative [www.babyfriendly.org.uk/guid-pol.htm].

34   Nielsen TF, Hagberg H, Ljungblad U. Placenta praevia and antepartum haemorrhage after previous caesarean section. *Gynecol Obstet Invest* 1989;27:88–90.

35   Taylor VM, Kramer MD, Vaughan TL, Peacock S. Placenta praevia and prior caesarean delivery: how strong is the association? *Obstet Gynecol* 1994;84:55–7.

36   Ananth CV, Smulian JC, Vintzileos AM. The association of placenta praevia with history of caesarean delivery and abortion: a metaanalysis. *Am J Obstet Gynecol* 1997;177:1071–8.

37   Clark SL, Koonings PP, Phelan JP. Placenta praevia/accreta and prior caesarean section. *Obstet Gynecol* 1985;66:89–92.

38   Lam CS, Wong SF, Chow KM, Ho LC. Women with placenta praevia and antepartum haemorrhage have a worse outcome than those who do not bleed before delivery. *J Obstet Gynaecol* 2000;20:27–31.

39   Lydon-Rochelle M, Holt VL, Easterling TR, Martin DP. Risk of uterine rupture during labor among women with a prior caesarean delivery. *N Engl J Med* 2001;345:3–8.

40   Greene MF. Vaginal delivery after cesarean section – is the risk acceptable? *N Engl J Med* 2001;345:54–5.

41   Hall MH, Campbell DM, Fraser C, Lemon J. Mode of delivery and future fertility. *Br J Obstet Gynaecol* 1989;96:1297–1303.

42   Jolly J, Walker J, Bhabra K. Subsequent obstetric performance related to primary mode of delivery. *Br J Obstet Gynaecol* 1999;106:227–32.

43   Hemminki E, Meriläinen J. Long term effects of caesarean sections: ectopic pregnancies and placental problems. *Am J Obstet Gynecol* 1996;174:1569–74.

44   Hilder L, Costeloe K, Thilaganathan B. Prolonged pregnancy: evaluating gestation-specific

risks of fetal and infant mortality. *Br J Obstet Gynaecol* 1998;105:169–73.

45   Cotzias CS, Paterson-Brown S, Fisk NM. Prospective risk of unexplained stillbirth in singleton pregnancies at term: population based analysis. *BMJ* 1999;319:287–9.

46   Confidential Enquiry into Stillbirths and Deaths in Infancy. *4th Annual Report*. London: Maternal and Child Health Research Consortium; 1997.

47   Confidential Enquiry into Stillbirths and Deaths in Infancy. *8th Annual Report*. London: Maternal and Child Health Research Consortium; 2001.

48   Adamson SJ, Alessandri LM, Burton PR, Pemberton PJ, Stanley F. Predictors of neonatal encephalopathy in full term infants. *BMJ* 1995;311:598–602.

49   Smith J, Wells L, Dodd K. The continuing fall in incidence of hypoxic–ischaemic encephalopathy in term infants. *Br J Obstet Gynaecol* 2000;107:461–6.

50   Morrison JJ, Rennie JM, Milton PJ. Neonatal respiratory morbidity and mode of delivery at term: influence of timing of elective caesarean section. *Br J Obstet Gynaecol* 1995;102:101–6.

51   Smith JF, Hernandez C, Wax JR. Fetal laceration injury at cesarean delivery. *Obstet Gynecol* 1997;90:344–6.

52   Towner D, Ames Castro M, Eby-Wilkens E, Gilbert WM. Effect of mode of delivery in nulliparous women on neonatal intracranial injury. *N Engl J Med* 1999;341:1709–14.

53   Hankins GDV, Leicht T, Van Hook J, Uckan EM. The role of forceps rotation in maternal and neonatal injury. *Am J Obstet Gynecol* 1999;180:231–4.

54   Hannah ME, Hannah WJ, Hewson SA, Hodnett ED, Saigal S, Willan AR. Planned caesarean section versus planned vaginal birth for breech presentation at term: a randomised multicentre trial. *Lancet* 2000;356:1375–83.

55   Hofmeyr GJ, Kulier R. External cephalic version for breech presentation at term. *Cochrane Database Syst Rev* 2000;(2):CD 000166.

56   Shennan AH, Bewley S. How to manage term breech deliveries. *BMJ* 2001;323:244–5.

57   McMahon MJ, Luther ER, Bowes WA Jr, Olshan AF. Comparison of a trial of labour with an elective second cesarean section. *N Engl J Med* 1996;335:689–95.

58   Jackson NV, Irvine NM. The influence of maternal request on the elective cesarean section rate. *Obstet Gynecol* 1998;18:115–9.

59   Groom KM, Paterson-Brown S, Fisk NM. Temporal and geographical variation in UK obstetricians' personal preference regarding mode of delivery. *Eur J Obstet Gynecol Reprod Biol* 2002;100:185–8.

60   Al-Mufti R, McCarthy A, Fisk NM. Survey of obstetricians' personal preference and discretionary practice. *Eur J Obstet Gynecol Reprod Biol* 1997;73:1–4.

61   Wright JB, Wright AL, Simpson NAB, Bryce FC. A survey of trainee obstetricians preferences for childbirth. *Eur J Obstet Gynecol Reprod Biol* 2001;97:23–5.

62   McGurgan P, Coulter-Smith S, O'Donovan PJ. A national confidential survey of obstetricians' personal preferences regarding mode of delivery. *Eur J Obstet Gynecol* 2001;97:17–19.

63   Gabbe SG, Holzman GB. Obstetricians' choice of delivery. *Lancet* 2001;357:722.

64   Dickson MJ, Willett M. Midwives would prefer a vaginal delivery. *BMJ* 1999;319:1008.

17

Morbidity of postpartum haemorrhage

Neelima Deshpande

OBSTETRIC HAEMORRHAGE AND MORTALITY

Obstetric haemorrhage continues to account for significant mortality and morbidity, both in developing and developed countries. Each year approximately 600 000 women die of pregnancy-related causes and 98% of these occur in developing countries. For every woman who dies, at least 30 suffer injuries and, often, permanent disability.[1] Considering that postpartum haemorrhage (PPH) accounts for around 28% of maternal deaths in developing countries (about one death in 1000 deliveries),[2,3] the extent of the morbidity it causes can only be guessed at. The speed and skill with which patients are managed affect the mortality and morbidity rates. Mortality rates are significantly lower where there are facilities for intensive care and blood transfusion. Maternal morbidity is highly prevalent but remains under-reported in both developing and developed countries.

According to the Confidential Enquiries into Maternal Deaths (CEMD) in the UK 1994–1996 report,[4] 12 *direct* deaths from haemorrhage were recorded. The reasons for these were placenta praevia (three), placental abruption (four) and PPH (five). It is, however, a well-known fact that placenta praevia and placental abruption are associated with a high postpartum blood loss, as well as postpartum morbidity. The latest report (1997–1999) found seven deaths directly related to haemorrhage, both ante- and postpartum. The causes were placenta praevia (three), placental abruption (three) and PPH (one). There was a total of 14 deaths in which haemorrhage played a substantial part.

The data on PPH from the last four CEMD reports are summarised in Table 1. It is obvious that, although maternal mortality has decreased over the years, the proportion of women dying from PPH is relatively similar. In the reports the various factors identified as being responsible were:

- inadequate resuscitation (under transfusion and excessive use of isotonic crystalloid fluid, inadequate central venous pressure monitoring and failure to anticipate and treat disseminated intravascular coagulation)

- failure to anticipate obstetric risk, including anaemia

- treatment by insufficiently experienced obstetric and anaesthetic staff

- delay in major surgical intervention.

The last point is a combination of the earlier mentioned factors. A major surgical intervention such as peripartum hysterectomy is a decision made at consultant level and this will inevitably be delayed if the consultant is not involved early enough.

The morbidity due to PPH itself might be five times the number of deaths if all accounts of 'near-miss mortality' were to be collated.[5] Considering that massive PPH itself occurs in about 1%

Table 1 *Summary of data on maternal mortality relating to postpartum haemorrhage (PPH) in the UK since 1985*[4]

Triennium	Total maternal deaths from all causes	Maternal deaths from haemorrhage (n)	Maternal deaths from PPH	Proportion of deaths from PPH (%)
1985–87	249	10	6	60.00
1988–90	325	22	11	50.00
1991–93	321	15	8	53.30
1994–96	376	12	5	41.66
1997–99	378	7	1	14.28

of all deliveries and life-threatening haemorrhage occurs in about one in a thousand deliveries, there would be an estimated 600 cases of 'near-miss mortality' due to PPH each year.[3,6] An incidence of 12/1000 deliveries was identified in a study of severe obstetric morbidity in the South East Thames Region in the UK. The disease-specific morbidity for severe haemorrhage was 6.7/1000 deliveries. Thus, two-thirds of the cases were related to severe haemorrhage. Caesarean section (CS) quadrupled the risk of morbidity.[7] PPH occurs with frightening speed and a decision about major surgical intervention is life-saving – both anaesthetic and obstetric consultants must be available and blood-bank facilities on site are essential if deaths are to be prevented.

METHODS ADVOCATED FOR CONTROL OF HAEMORRHAGE AND PREVENTION OF HYSTERECTOMY

The morbidity of PPH is related to the obstetric catastrophe that caused it, as well as to the various measures undertaken to save the patient's life.

Although peripartum hysterectomy remains a valuable life-saving operation, various operative procedures have been described that can control blood loss and possibly avoid hysterectomy. These are:

- internal iliac artery ligation[8]
- uterine artery ligation and ovarian artery ligation[9]
- O'Leary suture[10]
- B-Lynch technique for PPH[11]
- uterine packing or balloon tamponade[12]
- radiographic arterial embolisation.[13,14]

Individual surgical skills and experience often determine the choice of surgery and the lack of adequate training limits the use of these procedures. In the event of an emergency, it is difficult to use an operative procedure that one is not trained to perform.[15] The frequency with which an internal iliac artery ligation will need to be performed is directly related to the number of cases of massive obstetric haemorrhage in the relevant unit. This often means that obstetricians are unlikely to be able to perform such a procedure frequently during their training years. It is even more difficult to resort to all the different techniques described by various other obstetricians in order to arrest bleeding, especially when faced by a rapidly exsanguinating patient.[8,10,11,16–18]

A variety of medical methods has been advocated in the prevention of third-stage haemorrhage. These include the use of 'active' management with the help of oxytocin, with or without ergometrine,[19] and prostaglandins administered by various routes.[20] The use of prostaglandins to prevent massive haemorrhage is restricted by delay in diagnosis, lack of availability, unsuitability or simply a perceived delay in action.[21] Misoprostol and gemeprost have been used successfully in managing haemorrhage refractory to other medical methods.[22-26] There are few data on how secondary PPH should be managed.[27] The presentation and causes of haemorrhage are not always well-defined[28,29] and management poses a dilemma when conventional methods fail to arrest haemorrhage.

Peripartum hysterectomy is undertaken as a life-saving operation in approximately 1/2500 deliveries. This varies between 1/1400 and 1/4000 across world literature and includes data for a variety of elective indications rather than just haemorrhage.[30] Most obstetricians would perform the operation as a last resort when all other measures have failed. However, it must not be left too late, and there must be a balance between aggressive and conservative treatment. Where a hysterectomy has been performed for haemorrhage, there may be problems with coagulopathy, abnormal hepatic and renal function and massive blood and blood-product transfusion, which may all contribute to a difficult recovery period. These patients often have multi-organ dysfunction as a consequence of massive haemorrhage and need care on an intensive therapy unit (ITU). They suffer additional morbidity secondary to invasive monitoring and additional life-saving therapeutic procedures.[5,6]

SOURCES OF DATA ON MORBIDITY DUE TO POSTPARTUM HAEMORRHAGE

In order to understand the morbidity of massive PPH better, an audit with emphasis on peripartum hysterectomy as a life-saving operation was conducted at a district general hospital in the West Midlands in the UK (approximately 2500 deliveries per annum).[25] In addition, data on peripartum hysterectomy and its related postoperative morbidity were identified by a literature search.

Results[31]

In order to identify those cases in which significant haemorrhage had occurred, the case notes of all patients undergoing peripartum hysterectomy, all cases of PPH discussed in 'critical incident' meetings and all cases with PPH of more than 500 ml (from labour ward records) were reviewed for the period June 1995 to April 2000.

During the period June 1995 to April 2000 there were 10 800 total deliveries. During this time there were 94 'critical incident' reported cases of PPH (8.7/1000 deliveries); 81 cases needed blood transfusion (7.5/1000 deliveries), 12 cases needed admission to ITU (1.1/1000 deliveries) and eight cases needed hysterectomy (0.7/1000). Of the 94 patients reviewed, 22 had a previous history of PPH and 15 had previous blood transfusions. Of the 17 cases with a previous CS, four were diagnosed with placenta praevia. There were 11 cases of placental abruption.

The number of patients suffering from PPH of more than 1500 ml has always been high in the group undergoing caesarean delivery. This may, in part, be due to the nature of the indication for the operative delivery (placenta praevia). Figure 1 shows the frequency distribution of cases, with PPH identified as greater than 500 ml on labour ward records in relation to the mode of delivery for each year since 1995.

The age distribution of the 94 cases of PPH is shown in Figure 2. Four patients from the 30–39-years age group needed a hysterectomy, possibly because the actual number of parturient women is higher in this age group in this area. However, it appears that the older women (over 40 years) have a greater chance of having a hysterectomy as a life-saving procedure should they suffer massive obstetric haemorrhage. Data from the Confidential Enquiries into Maternal Deaths in the UK,[4] as well as data from the study on 'near miss' mortality in the South East Thames Region,[7] have identified age over 34 years as a risk factor for mortality and morbidity.

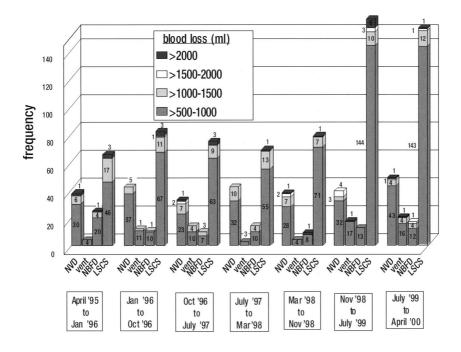

Figure 1 *Blood loss versus mode of delivery; period distribution June 1995–April 2000[31]; NVD = normal vaginal delivery; NBFD = Neville Barnes forceps delivery; Vent = Ventouse delivery; LSCS = lower segment caesarean section*

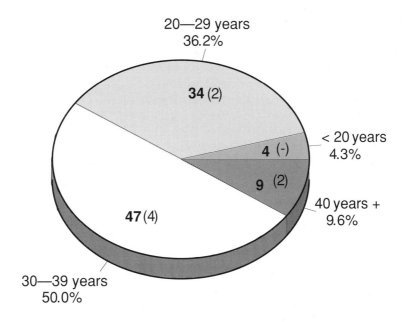

Figure 2 *Age distribution (n=94) of women having postpartum haemorrhage[31]*

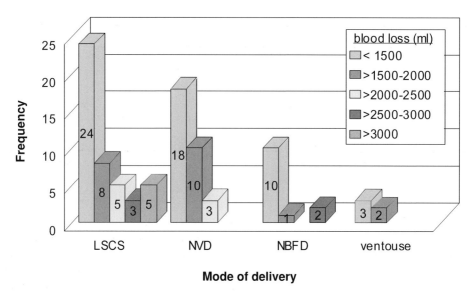

Figure 3 *Mode of delivery versus blood loss (n=94)[31]; LSCS = lower segment caesarean section; NVD = normal vaginal delivery; NBFD = Neville Barnes forceps delivery*

In the audit report, massive haemorrhage (greater than 1500 ml) did not seem to be related to high birthweight. For blood loss exceeding 2000 ml there were two peaks – one at 2500–3000 g and the other at 3500–4000 g. There was no correlation between blood loss and birthweight, duration of the first stage of labour or duration of the second stage. However, blood loss was significantly greater if a manual removal of placenta was required.

CS was associated with the highest number of women suffering massive haemorrhage (Figure 3). In contrast, only three women who had normal vaginal deliveries had haemorrhage exceeding 2000 ml.

With increasing parity, the likelihood of massive obstetric haemorrhage and the risk of undergoing a hysterectomy increased. Table 2 shows the number of women who suffered PPH in previous deliveries and the number who had previous deliveries by CS. Among these, four had a placenta praevia. Two of these patients needed hysterectomy for uncontrolled haemorrhage.

Eight women underwent hysterectomy for massive PPH (Table 3). The mean age for hysterectomy was 35.4 years, the youngest patient being 26 years and the oldest 45 years. Three of these women had placenta praevia (cases 1–3 in Table 3). These three cases all suffered massive PPH

Table 2 *Cases of postpartum haemorrhage in previous deliveries and previous delivery by caesarean section*

Parity	Number	Hysterectomy		Previous PPH		Previous LSCS	
		n	%	*n*	%	*n*	%
P1	37	2	5.4				
P2	37	1	2.7	15.0	40.5	13.0	35.1
P3	11	2	18.2	2.0	18.2	2.0	18.2
P4	2	1	50.0	1.0	50.0	1.0	50.0
> P4	7	2	28.6	4.0	57.1	1.0	14.3
Total	94	8	8.5	22.0	23.4	17.0	18.1

PPH= postpartum haemorrhage; LSCS = lower segment caesarean section

Table 3 *Reasons for hysterectomy*

	Parity	Cause
1	P3	Placenta praevia Gr III (subtotal)
2	P5	Placenta praevia Gr IV (prev. 2 LSCS) massive PPH
3	P2	Placenta praevia Gr 3 ant, massive PPH – return to theatre (subtotal)
4	P4	Postpartum haemorrhage after LSCS (failed kiellands)
5	P1	Failed forceps – cervical/vaginal tear – TAH – hydronephrosis, nephrostomy
6	P5	Rupture uterus at 2nd stage, grande multiparae, dinoprostone IOL
7	P3	Atonic PPH – subtotal hysterectomy
8	P1	Subinvolution of placental bed – secondary PPH 10 days

IOL = induction of labour; LSCS = lower segment caesarean section; PPH = postpartum haemorrhage; TAH = total abdominal hysterectomy

following CS for placenta praevia. Two of these returned to theatre for subtotal hysterectomy in the immediate postoperative period and one had placenta increta at histology. One of these cases returned to theatre for resuturing of wound dehiscence at eight days postoperatively. Two cases occurred after failed instrumental deliveries, and these cases (4 and 5 in Table 3) demonstrate the effects of obstetric trauma leading to massive PPH. One woman suffered a ruptured uterus following a prostaglandin induction of labour; this patient was a grande multipara who had a rapid labour with ruptured uterus during the second stage. The fetus was stillborn. This case illustrates the problem of using prostaglandins for induction of labour in grande multiparae. There was one case of placental abruption associated with uterine atomy, disseminated intravascular coagulation (DIC) and massive haemorrhage that resulted in hysterectomy. There was one case of delayed secondary PPH requiring hysterectomy. Rapid onset of massive PPH with inability to arrest bleeding with dilatation and curettage, uterine packing and impending DIC. This led to a decision for a subtotal hysterectomy as a life-saving procedure. Histology showed 'subinvolution of the placental bed'.

The mode of delivery and proportion of cases from each group who needed admission to ITU with or without a hysterectomy is shown in Table 4. The patient in the normal delivery group who had a hysterectomy was the patient with secondary PPH and 'subinvolution of the placental bed'.

The morbidity at delivery and following delivery is shown in Figures 4 and 5. The problems encountered at CS that led to massive obstetric haemorrhage are illustrated in Figure 4. These include uterine torsion, scar dehiscence and trauma. Uterine atony, trauma at delivery (vaginal and abdominal), and hysterectomy were expected causes of haemorrhage (Figure 5). An unusual finding was of two cases of uterine torsion diagnosed at CS. Here, the incision was made on the posterior surface of the uterus, and haemorrhage was an accompanying problem.

Table 4 *Mode of delivery and proportion of cases needing admission to intensive care with or without hysterectomy*

	Cases (*n*)	Induced	Augmented	Spontaneous onset	ITU	Hysterectomy
LSCS	45	12	4	9	9	7
NVD	31	13	18	17	3	1
NBFD	13	7	9	6		
Ventouse	5	4	3	1		
Total	94	36	34	33	12	8

ITU = intensive care unit; LSCS = lower segment caesarean section; NVD = normal vaginal delivery; NBFD = Neville Barnes forceps delivery

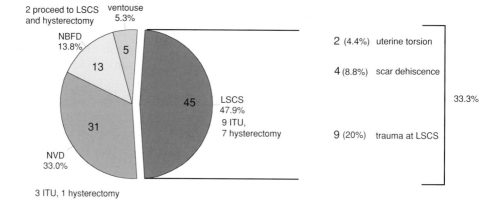

2 proceed to LSCS and hysterectomy

ventouse 5.3%

NBFD 13.8%

LSCS 47.9%
9 ITU,
7 hysterectomy

NVD 33.0%

3 ITU, 1 hysterectomy

2 (4.4%) uterine torsion

4 (8.8%) scar dehiscence

9 (20%) trauma at LSCS

33.3%

Figure 4 *Morbidity at lower segment caesarean section[11]; ITU = intensive care unit; LSCS = lower segment caesarean section; NBFD = Neville Barnes forceps delivery*

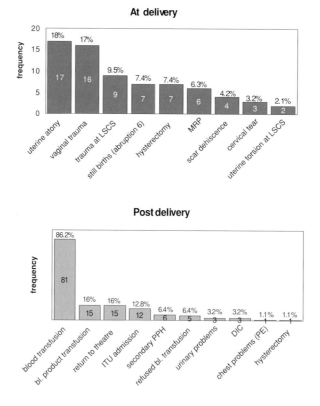

At delivery

frequency

18% 17
17% 16
9.5% 9
7.4% 7
7.4% 7
6.3% 6
4.2% 4
3.2% 3
2.1% 2

uterine atony | vaginal trauma | trauma at LSCS | still births (abruption 6) | hysterectomy | MRP | scar dehiscence | cervical tear | uterine torsion at LSCS

Post delivery

frequency

86.2% 81
16% 15
16% 15
12.8% 12
6.4% 6
6.4% 5
3.2% 3
3.2% 3
1.1% 1
1.1% 1

blood transfusion | bl. product transfusion | return to theatre | ITU admission | secondary PPH | refused bl. transfusion | urinary problems | DIC | chest problems (PE) | hysterectomy

Figure 5 *Morbidity at delivery and post-delivery[11]; DIC = disseminated intravascular coagulation; ITU = intensive care unit; LSCS = lower segment caesarean section; MRP = manual removal of placenta*

The morbidity for the postpartum period is illustrated in Figure 5. This shows that 86.2% of cases required blood transfusion and 16% returned to theatre for further operative intervention, i.e. hysterectomy, resuturing of vaginal tears, retained placental cotyledons. Four of the eight cases needing hysterectomy needed to return to theatre following their hysterectomy (50%). Three (37.5%) required relaparotomy (two for subtotal hysterectomy and a third for nephrostomy). Two of these patients had a wound dehiscence and needed resuturing in theatre. Four cases required exploration and repair of vaginal trauma in theatre and four cases underwent an evacuation of retained products of conception for secondary PPH.

Summary of the audit results

During the five-year period studied:

- eight cases needed hysterectomy (0.7/1000), i.e. approximately 1/1500 deliveries
- 94 critical incident reported cases of PPH needing special care (8.7/1000 deliveries)
- 81 cases needed blood transfusion (7.5/1000 deliveries)
- 12 cases needed admission to ITU (1.1/1000 deliveries).

Additional findings

There was a high incidence of massive PPH following CS, related to the mode of delivery.

A high proportion (19%) of women who suffered massive PPH (1500 ml or more) at CS returned to theatre.

A high proportion (50%) of women who went on to have a hysterectomy for massive PPH returned to theatre for postoperative complications.

The number of women undergoing hysterectomy is higher than one would expect in a district general hospital in the UK. There is a lack of published reports on peripartum hysterectomy rates within the UK from other similar hospitals. A report from a larger teaching hospital shows a similar rate for peripartum hysterectomy for massive obstetric haemorrhage.[32] The rates for blood transfusion are similar to those quoted for other parts of the country.[33] However, there is little information about the morbidity relating to various interventions required to manage the exsanguinated critically ill patient following massive haemorrhage.

MORBIDITY AND POSTOPERATIVE COMPLICATION RATES IN RELATION TO PERIPARTUM HYSTERECTOMY FOR HAEMORRHAGE

Maternal morbidity relating to peripartum hysterectomy serves as an indicator of the overall morbidity experienced by patients with massive PPH. Table 5 summarises various studies that looked at peripartum hysterectomy and highlights the causes relating to haemorrhage and its morbidity. It is obvious that morbidly adherent placentas, rupture uterus and uterine atony are major causes identified. Table 6 summarises the various groups of complications identified in the postoperative period following hysterectomy for haemorrhage. The main categories are those of infection, haemorrhage, urinary tract injuries, need for reoperation and thromboembolic diseases.

Febrile morbidity

The incidence of febrile morbidity following peripartum hysterectomy ranges from 20% to 60%. This postoperative complication is not reported with consistency, and it is therefore difficult to

Table 5 *Indications for peripartum hysterectomy*

Authors	Cases (n)	Adherent placenta (%)	Rupture uterus (%)	Haemorrhage and uterine atony (%)
Abu Heija[38]	21	38.1	33.30	14.30 (each)
Al Sibai[39]	117	7.7	53.80	20.55 (atony) 4.30 (at caesarean)
Hill DJ[40]	34	15.0	18.00 all 9.00 after vaginal delivery	9.00 (after caesarean) 15.00 (secondary PPH)
Sturdee[32]	47	6.38	8.51	59.50
Haynes[41]	149 (26 emergency 123 elective)	–	–	–
Rachagan[42]	21	13.3	38.10	28.60
Chew[36]	14	50.0	–	28.00 (placenta praevia) 43.00 (after vaginal delivery)
Clark[43]	70	30.0	13.00	43.00 (atony) 10.00 (extended incision)
Gupta[44]	140	23.0	42.00	34.00 (atony) 18.00 (placenta praevia)

Table 6 *Postoperative complications and morbidity relating to peripartum hysterectomy for haemorrhage*

Complication	Abu Heija[38]	Al Sibai[39]	Sturdee[32]	Rachagan[42]	Chew and Biswas[36]	Haynes and Martin[41]
Cases (n)	21.00	117.00	47.00	21.00	14.00	149.00
Infections (%)						
Febrile morbidity	19.04	17.10	NR	NR	28.50	34.00
Wound infection	4.70	13.70	6.38	NR	NR	4.70
Pelvic/cuff cellulitis/ vault infection		1.70	NR	4.76		7.40
Vault haematoma	4.70	NR	4.20	4.70	NR	NR
Pelvic abscess	NR	1.70	NR	NR	NR	NR
Respiratory infection	NR	5.10	19.10	NR	21.00	3.40
Urinary tract infection	9.40	4.30	NR	47.60	21.00	7.40
Endotoxic shock	NR	2.60	NR	NR	NR	NR
Urological injuries (%)						
Bladder laceration	NR	4.30	2.15	4.70	7.00	7.40
Ureteric injury	NR	3.40	2.10	4.70	NR	NR
DVT/pulmonary embolism	NR	2.60	2.10	NR	NR	2.00
Re exploration for haemorrhage	4.70	NR	NR	9.50	14.00	NR
Coagulopathy	4.70	NR	2.10	4.70	57.00	NR
Paralytic ileus	NR	NR	NR	9.50	NR	NR
Puerperal psychosis	NR	NR	NR	4.70	NR	NR

NR = Not recorded/not reported; DVT = deep vein thrombosis assess the exact causes for it as well as identify the measures taken to manage it. There are no clear-cut definitions for diagnosis or management. In the audit, rates for postoperative febrile morbidity were difficult to assess accurately because of the way in which nursing records are filed. The most accurate estimation of febrile morbidity is from data recorded on high dependency unit (HDU) or ITU charts. Nearly all patients who had invasive monitoring on ITU had raised white-cell counts and pyrexia more than 24 hours postoperatively. In addition, those patients suffering urinary tract infections, vault abscesses and haematomas had postoperative pyrexia. However, these may not account for all patients who suffered febrile morbidity on the postnatal ward due to sepsis following PPH. Some of these may have presented as secondary PPH. Only those cases that underwent an operative procedure for secondary PPH during their inpatient stay following delivery would have been identified from the records. Currently, there are problems with identifying records from the way they are indexed, as well as with retrieval of data from theatre records of operative procedures and their coding.

Infections and related complications

Wound infections, urinary tract infections, respiratory infections, vault abscesses and pelvic abscesses constitute some of the range of infective processes to which patients suffering massive haemorrhage are subject. Those associated with peripartum hysterectomy seem to be most susceptible because of the increased surgical and medical intervention. It may be noted that the number of cases reported with vaginal cuff cellulites or urinary tract infection is probably lower than the actual number, as many patients attend their general practitioner's surgery for antibiotics after they are discharged from hospital. There appears to be wide variation in complication rates for elective procedures versus emergency procedures and this is to be anticipated from the morbidity that haemorrhage causes.[9]

Urological injuries

The incidence of urological injuries following peripartum hysterectomy ranges from 0.3–6.0% or more. The range reflects the differences in urological injuries following planned peripartum hysterectomies as opposed to emergency peripartum hysterectomies, which are fraught with complications and surgical challenges.[9] Attempted haemostasis during emergency peripartum hysterectomy is the main cause of ureteric damage. In the audit report, trauma at CS following a rotational forceps delivery was the main complicating factor leading to ureteric damage. Obstetric catastrophes requiring hysterectomy are at greatest risk of ureteric and bladder damage. There are mixed data on the advantages of performing a subtotal hysterectomy and this is partly due to the differences observed in individual cases. Where there are tears extending deep into the vagina and cervix, it is all the more difficult to assess whether a total or subtotal hysterectomy is being carried out.

Inadvertent cystotomy is another complication that is often encountered during obstetric hysterectomies. This is related to adhesions from previous CS, dissection of the bladder in completing a total hysterectomy and as a result of necrosis from sutures and clamps at the bladder pillars presenting as vesicovaginal fistulas at a later date. In a study by Plauche *et al.*[9,14,34,35] that included both elective and emergency peripartum hysterectomies there were 39 cystotomies, 28 cases of ureteral injuries and five fistulas per 1000 hysterectomies at the Louisiana State University Service Charity hospital of New Orleans. These data seem to be the most comprehensive on intraoperative as well as postoperative complication rates relating to peripartum hysterectomies. However, not all data relate to emergency procedures.

Relaparotomy/re-exploration

Some patients who suffer haemorrhage at CS need to return to theatre. In cases of CS for placenta praevia, this may be for surgical methods to control haemorrhage, including internal iliac artery ligation or a hysterectomy. In some cases, patients who undergo a peripartum hysterectomy for haemorrhage need to return to theatre for continued blood loss. Nearly 50% of the cases in the audit group returned to theatre for control of haemorrhage, nephrostomy and repair of wound dehiscence. One of the patients in the audit group needed reoperation for a nephrostomy for ureteric occlusion.

Blood and blood product transfusion

The reported transfusion rate in obstetrics varies from 0.16% to 2.6% with rates up to 50% in cases with placenta praevia.[33] The rates of transfusion in cases with peripartum hysterectomy for haemorrhage are 100% (excluding Jehovah's witnesses). The volumes of blood transfused ranged from 680–7820 ml in the study by Chew and Biswas.[36] Patients needing repeat laparotomy or peripartum hysterectomy had much larger volumes of blood and blood product transfusion, especially in the face of coagulopathy. In the study by Chew and Biswas nearly 50% of cases with massive haemorrhage suffered some form of coagulopathy. Where large amounts of blood and blood products are transfused, the risk of multisystem dysfunction is markedly increased.

Admission to ITU

A variety of authors have looked at admission to ITU as a criterion for near-miss mortality.[6,37] Significant proportions are cases with massive haemorrhage. Often when patients need monitoring on ITU, they have multisystem dysfunction.

CONCLUSIONS AND RECOMMENDATIONS

PPH contributes two-thirds of the cases of severe obstetric morbidity in the UK.[7] Morbidity of PPH is high and needs accurate estimation through well-designed audits on 'near-miss mortality' to identify failures in the system that can be changed to reduce it.

The general ill health and debility resulting from massive haemorrhage can be seen from the incidence of wound infection, wound dehiscence, resuturing and cases returning to theatre for evacuation of retained placental tissue. Admission to ITU involves invasive monitoring and strict fluid balance control. Large volumes of blood and blood-product transfusion also require intensive monitoring as well as frequent blood parameter testing until the patient is on the way to full recovery. There is a paucity of data on long-term follow-up of patients' health, both physical and psychological, following such procedures. With the introduction of critical incident meetings and risk management, as well as introduction of consultant cover on labour ward, we can anticipate a reduction in this morbidity. Audits of 'near-miss mortality' on all delivery suites will give a more accurate estimate of these numbers.[5,7] This would help to improve the quality of care being provided at all levels and thus reduce the economic, physical and psychological cost of massive PPH.

Cost

The cost of managing a case with massive PPH is difficult to estimate. This would include the medical costs of admission to an HDU or ITU as well as materials costs. Additional costs would be those borne by society in terms of psychological damage, costs of single parenthood in cases of mortality, costs of long-term medical care in cases with urological injuries and continuing problems with body image and premature menopause. It appears that the costs of preventing or managing PPH aggressively will be lower than costs of managing patients suffering morbidity as a result of substandard care. Considerable effort has gone into setting up training and teaching courses on managing obstetric emergencies. Data on 'near-miss mortality' in units where staff are regularly trained in dealing with obstetric emergencies will indicate whether such courses are achieving the objectives in reducing morbidity in addition to mortality.

Need for further research

The studies by Waterstone and Bewley[7] and Mantel et al.[6] have highlighted the need for studies on 'near-miss mortality' in other regions within the UK. They have also provided a framework for the collection and interpretation of a wide range of data. The impact of training and teaching workshops in obstetric emergencies may also be assessed using the data on mortality and morbidity. This may also help in designing a cost–benefit analysis so that such programmes may be modified and included in the teaching programmes for health workers in developing countries.

Acknowledgement

I would like to thank Marian Benjamin from the Department of Clinical Effectiveness, Warwick Hospital, UK, for her help in analysing and presenting the audit data.

References

1   Donnay F. Maternal survival in developing countries: what has been done, what can be achieved in the next decade. *Int J Gynaecol Obstet* 2000;70:89–97.

2   Chamberlain GVP. The clinical aspects of massive haemorrhage. In: Patel N, editor. *Maternal Mortality - The Way Forward*. London: RCOG Press; 1992. p. 54–62.

3   Drife, J. Management of primary postpartum haemorrhage. *Br J Obstet Gynaecol* 1997;104:275–7.

4   Lewis G, Drife J, editors. *Why Mothers Die. Report on Confidential Enquiries into Maternal Deaths in the United Kingdom 1997–1999*. London: RCOG Press; 2001.

5   Baskett TF, Sternadel J. Maternal intensive care and near-miss mortality in obstetrics. *Br J Obstet Gynaecol* 1998;105:981–4.

6   Mantel GD, Buchmann E, Rees H, Pattinson RC. Severe acute maternal morbidity: a pilot study of a definition for a near-miss. *Br J Obstet Gynaecol* 1998;105:985–90.

7   Waterstone M, Bewley S, Wolfe C. Incidence and predictors of severe obstetric morbidity: case-control study. *BMJ* 2001;322:1089–93.

8   Floyd RC, Morrison JC. Postpartum hemorrhage. In: Plauche WC, Morrison JC, O'Sullivan MJ, editors. *Surgical Obstetrics*. Philadelphia: WB Saunders; 1992. p. 373-82.

9   Plauche WC. Peripartal hysterectomy. In: Plauche WC, Morrison JC, O'Sullivan MJ, editors. *Surgical Obstetrics*. Philadelphia: WB Saunders; 1992. p. 447–65.

10   O'Leary JA. Uterine artery ligation in the control of postcesarean hemorrhage. *J Reprod Med* 1995;40:189–93.

11   Goddard R, Stafford M, Smith JR. The B-Lynch surgical technique for the control of massive

postpartum haemorrhage: an alternative to hysterectomy? Five cases reported. *Br J Obstet Gynaecol* 1998;105:126.

12 Johanson R, Kumar M, Obhrai M, Young P. Management of massive postpartum haemorrhage: use of a hydrostatic balloon catheter to avoid laparotomy. *BJOG* 2001;108:420–2.

13 Oei PL, Chua S, Tan L, Ratnam SS, Arulkumaran S. Arterial embolization for bleeding following hysterectomy for intractable postpartum hemorrhage. *Int J Gynaecol Obstet* 1998;62:83–6.

14 Pelage JP, Le Dref O, Jacob D, Soyer P, Herbreteau D, Rymer R. Selective arterial embolization of the uterine arteries in the management of intractable post-partum hemorrhage. *Acta Obstet Gynecol Scand* 1999;78:698–703.

15 Plauche WC. Peripartal hysterectomy. *Obstet Gynecol Clin North Am* 1988;15:783–95.

16 Vedantham S, Goodwin SC, McLucas B, Mohr G. Uterine artery embolization: an underused method of controlling pelvic hemorrhage. *Am J Obstet Gynecol* 1997;176:938–48.

17 Das BN, Biswas AK. Ligation of internal iliac arteries in pelvic haemorrhage. *J Obstet Gynaecol Res* 1998;24:251–4.

18 Fahmy K. Internal iliac artery ligation and its efficiency in controlling pelvic hemorrhage. *Int Surg* 1969;51:244–5.

19 Choy CM, Lau WC, Tam WH, Yuen PM. A randomised controlled trial of intramuscular syntometrine and intravenous oxytocin in the management of the third stage of labour. *BJOG* 2002;109:173–7.

20 Gulmezoglu AM, Forna F, Villar J, Hofmeyr GJ. Prostaglandins for prevention of postpartum haemorrhage. *Cochrane Database Syst Rev* 2001;(4):CD000494.

21 Gulmezoglu AM. Prostaglandins for prevention of postpartum haemorrhage. *Cochrane Syst Database Rev* 2000;(2):CD000494.

22 Ramsey PS, Ramin KD. Rectally administered misoprostol for the treatment of postpartum hemorrhage unresponsive to oxytocin and ergometrine: a descriptive study *Obstet Gynecol* 1999;93:157–8.

23 Bamigboye AA, Hofmeyr GJ, Merrell DA. Rectal misoprostol in the prevention of postpartum hemorrhage: a placebo-controlled trial. *Am J Obstet Gynecol* 1998;179:1043–6.

24 O'Brien P, El Refaey H, Gordon A, Geary M, Rodeck CH. Rectally administered misoprostol for the treatment of postpartum hemorrhage unresponsive to oxytocin and ergometrine: a descriptive study. *Obstet Gynecol* 1998;92:212–14.

25 Bamigboye AA, Merrell DA, Hofmeyr GJ, Mitchell R. Randomized comparison of rectal misoprostol with Syntometrine for management of third stage of labor. *Acta Obstet Gynecol Scand* 1998;77:178–81.

26 Bennett BB. Uterine rupture during induction of labor at term with intravaginal misoprostol. *Obstet Gynecol* 1997;89:832–3.

27 Alexander J, Thomas P, Sanghera J. Treatments for secondary postpartum haemorrhage. *Cochrane Database Syst Rev* 2002;(1):CD002867.

28 Khong TY, Khong TK. Delayed postpartum hemorrhage: a morphologic study of causes and their relation to other pregnancy disorders. *Obstet Gynecol* 1993; 82:17–22.

29 Deshpande N, Oláh KS. Subinvolution of the placental bed: a rare cause of secondary postpartum haemorrhage. *J Obstet Gynecol* 2001; 21:633.

30 Park RC, Duff WP. Role of cesarean hysterectomy in modern obstetric practice. *Clin Obstet Gynecol* 1980;23:601–20.

31 Deshpande N, Oláh KS. Audit of massive postpartum haemorrhage. 2000. Warwick Hospital, Department of Clinical Effectiveness. Audit report (unpublished).

DIAGNOSIS AND ASSESSMENT

It is important that there should be a careful confirmation of the diagnosis; as with all medical conditions, the first step is to take a careful history. Typically this would include the pattern of symptoms, the predominant symptoms of a typical attack medication used and the response. A contraceptive and menstrual history and a history of atopic symptoms should also be elicited. In particular, the patient should be asked if she has any nasal symptoms suggestive of allergy.

The differential diagnosis includes infection with *Herpes genitalis*, *Trichomonas vaginalis*, bacterial vaginosis and other causes of a vaginal discharge. Vulval disease, especially vulval eczema, dermatitis, lichen sclerosus and vulval vestibulitis, are also important to consider.[60]

Clinical signs and symptoms include vulvovaginal pruritis, irritation, soreness, dyspareunia, burning on micturition and a discharge ranging from a thick 'cottage cheese' substance to a thin watery liquid. None of these symptoms is individually or collectively pathognomic.[61] Itching is the only symptom with any predictive value for VVC.[62] A diagnosis cannot be established on the basis of history, symptomatology or physical examination alone; laboratory confirmation is essential.

Tests at presentation should include microscopy to identify fungal hyphae and spores, trichomonas and bacterial vaginosis. Any yeasts grown from a vaginal swab must be differentiated to species level to exclude chronic non-albicans yeast infection. This may be suggested by a history of persistently positive vaginal swabs for 'candida species' with a poor response to treatment. Non-albicans infection cannot reliably be differentiated from *C. albicans* on symptoms or signs alone.[60,63] Unfortunately, speciation is not routine practice in many laboratories.

The nature of recurrent VVC dictates that vaginal swabs are often only transiently positive at the beginning of symptomatic recurrences. Our clinical practice is to ask women with possible recurrent VVC to keep a symptom diary and take swabs when they are symptomatic. Self-taken swabs are equivalent to those taken by medical/nursing staff for the diagnosis of vaginitis.[64] Recurrent VVC cannot be diagnosed on the basis of a single vaginal swab. Candida may be present in asymptomatic women and as an 'innocent bystander' and can therefore be falsely accused of causing symptoms.

Examination should look for any vulval disease. This can often be easily demonstrated by asking the patient to identify the itchy area. If there are symptoms of dyspareunia, the 'Q-tip' test for the vulval vestibulitis syndrome should be performed,[65] although this is only diagnostic in the absence of VVC.

It is arguable that there is little point in performing blood tests on otherwise healthy women presenting with complicated VVC. Although iron deficiency has been suggested as a a cause of recurrent VVC, there is no evidence to support this.[66] Diabetes is rarely newly diagnosed, but many physicians would still send blood samples for a full blood count and random blood sugar test. An HIV test need only be considered if there are other risk factors, signs or symptoms, such as oral candidiasis.

TREATMENT

Various licensed topical and oral anti-fungal treatments of proven clinical and mycological effectiveness are available. All of these except for nystatin are azoles. Topical azoles have minimal adverse effects; systemic absorption is minimal and they are safe to use in pregnancy. Occasionally local burning, discomfort and itching may occur. Oral agents have few adverse effects[67] but may be associated with nausea, abdominal discomfort and headaches. Both azoles and nystatin are fungistatic rather than fungicidal.

Uncomplicated vulvovaginal candiasis

There has been a trend towards shorter and more cosmetically acceptable treatments, which has culminated in the current market leaders of intravaginal clotrimazole and oral fluconazole 150 mg single-dose treatments; both have been made available over the counter. Overall, there are few differences between the various oral and topical preparations in effectiveness, although patients often prefer oral preparations. Nystatin is less effective than azole treatment. It needs to be given for 14 days, but is indicated if there is a possibility of non-albicans yeast infection.

Severe candidiasis

Symptoms of VVC have been shown to correlate with the amount of yeast present in the vagina.[7,68] This greater yeast burden means that severe attacks respond less well to therapy[12] and might be expected to require more prolonged therapy. Studies specifically analysing the effects of therapy in women with severe VVC have shown that, in comparison with a single 150 mg dose of fluconazole, vaginal clotrimazole 100 mg daily for seven days is no more effective,[12] but a second dose of fluconazole 150 mg repeated after three days gave an improved response.[69]

Non-albicans yeast infection

Evidence to guide treatment of non-albicans yeast infection is mostly based on case reports of *C. glabrata* infection. Other yeasts may show differing anti-fungal sensitivity patterns. Unfortunately, *in vitro* sensitivity does not reliably predict a clinical response. Standard-dose azole treatments should be avoided, as these may induce greater resistance. The first-line treatment for all non-albicans yeasts is nystatin pessaries once or twice nightly for 14 days. Nystatin is the only licensed non-azole treatment available and resistance is rare *in vitro*.[18,19]

For *C. glabrata*, boric acid 600 mg at night in gelatine capsules for 14 nights is usually second-line treatment.[70] This will need to be made up by a pharmacy. There is a theoretical risk of boron toxicity and this should be discussed.[71] Most isolates of *C. glabrata* retain relative sensitivity to itraconazole and miconazole or clotrimazole.[18,19] If boric acid fails, it is sometimes possible to overcome relative azole insensitivity by combining itraconazole 200 mg daily for 14 days with intravaginal anti-fungals, either nystatin or miconazole, e.g. miconazole nitrate 1.2 g on alternate nights.[72] Since this is non-licensed, the patient will need to be informed of the potential adverse effects and this should be documented in the notes. Intravaginal painting with gentian violet and oral progesterone supplements have also been tried, although there is little information available.[72] The final resort is flucytosine, the only fungicidal agent currently available, and amphotericin B in lubricating jelly for 14 nights.[73] Preparation will need to be arranged with a manufacturing pharmacy.

Treatment response should be guided by the results of speciated vaginal swabs taken two or more weeks after cessation of therapy. Vulval symptoms can sometimes be slow to settle and reinfection with other, usually anti-fungal sensitive, species of yeasts sometimes occurs. Once two or more negative swabs have been obtained, relapse is unlikely.

TREATMENT OF RECURRENT VULVOVAGINAL CANDIASIS

Individual attacks

Anti-fungal resistance is currently not an issue in recurrent VVC due to *C. albicans*.[74,75] The evidence for vaginal persistence of infection, i.e. 'vaginal relapse',[28–31] suggests that more intensive and prolonged therapy might reduce the chances of recurrence. Since azole anti-fungals are fungistatic rather than fungicidal, it is unclear whether eradication of a predominant strain of *C. albicans* from the vagina is possible with these agents. In contrast to severe VVC, increasing the length of therapy by up to a week, for example by adding a second dose of fluconazole, does not improve response.[13,69]

Approaches to long-term treatment

Patients are often frustrated by what they perceive as a failure of the medical profession to take their recurrent symptoms seriously. Reassurance is needed that their problem will be managed as a chronic medical condition. It may be helpful to draw parallels with allergic rhinitis/hayfever, which may be immunologically linked with recurrent VVC. A wry smile is often produced when it is pointed out that both cause itching and a discharge. Like hay fever, recurrent VVC can resolve spontaneously but may also require long-term management. Once the diagnosis is confirmed and these issues are discussed, the following approaches to long-term treatment can be addressed.

Suppressive anti-fungals

Whether long-term suppressive treatment is justified depends on the distress caused. Many affected women prefer to keep a course of anti-fungals 'in the bathroom cabinet'.[76] For suppression, various oral and vaginal regimens, ranging from daily to monthly dosing,[56,77–84] have been found to be effective in open label non-comparative studies. As a general rule, increased frequency of dosing is more effective but this needs to be set against increased cost and inconvenience. When considering suppression, the most important choice is between pessaries and oral anti-fungals, neither of which is licensed for this indication. Pessaries are absorbed minimally and it is therefore unlikely that there are any long-term systemic adverse effects. They are, however, 'messy' and can cause failure of latex barrier contraceptives. Some women develop local irritation to certain pessaries but this usually responds to a change of preparation. Although oral treatment with itraconazole or fluconazole is more acceptable to patients, this has to be set against the increased cost and some slight uncertainty about their long-term safety. Post-marketing surveillance has shown both drugs to be safe for episodic use,[67] but the same cannot be stated with absolute certainty for long-term use. Neither drug is licensed for use in pregnancy. Although ketoconazole is effective and cheap, it should not be used because of the concerns over hepatic toxicity.

Once the choice between oral versus vaginal anti-fungals has been made, the frequency of administration needs to be discussed. If more than one attack per month occurs, weekly doses are usually needed. If there is a clear cyclical pattern to recurrences, twice-monthly doses are usually adequate. Monthly administration is occasionally effective in women with a clear pattern of premenstrual recurrences. A symptom diary can be used to guide timing. Our usual practice is to start with day 8 and day 18 of the cycle, i.e. just before the hormonal peaks. The patient is then asked to keep a symptom diary, which is reviewed three months later when adjustments to the timing and/or frequency of doses are made. Suppression is then continued for six months to a year. After this time, suppressive therapy is usually stopped. Relapse occurs in 50–60% of women.[85] If relapse occurs, the cycle of suppressive therapy can be continued indefinitely.

Medroxyprogesterone acetate (MPA)

Studies are contradictory as to whether the combined contraceptive pill causes recurrent VVC.[56,86–89] In women who might otherwise consider this, parenteral MPA should be specifically discussed. A small retrospective study has shown MPA to be an effective treatment for recurrent VVC.[90] A prospective study has shown a reduction in vaginal candida isolation on commencing

MPA.[91] Its effects are probably mediated by the reduction in oestrogen that accompanies the induced anovulation.[92] If breakthrough symptoms occur, increasing the frequency of injections or using an anti-fungal prophylactically a week before the injection is due is an option. Other progesterone-only methods of contraception cannot be assumed to have the same effects on recurrent VVC, although the levonorgestrel-releasing implant system has been associated with a reduced incidence of vaginitis compared with intrauterine contraceptive device users.[93]

Other treatments

Although suppressive anti-fungal therapy and MPA are useful, there is a need for new approaches to treating recurrent VVC. In particular, there is a need for properly designed studies of intensive therapy of individual recurrences aiming to break the cycle of 'vaginal relapse'. Ideally, these should be with fungicidal agents when these become available.

Other approaches are likely to reflect improved understanding of the immune processes involved in recurrent VVC. Allergen desensitisation has been reported in two open studies[94] but this is unlikely to be widely used without further studies and standardisation of antigens. A pilot study of zafirlukast in recurrent VVC is nearing completion. Zafirlukast, which inhibits leukotriene-mediated allergic inflammation, is currently licensed as add-in therapy for mild to moderate asthma. Preliminary results have been promising[95] and the study will be completed soon. Zafirlukast may be particularly indicated for patients with allergic rhinitis and/or asthma.

General advice

There is little doubt that antibiotics can precipitate attacks of VVC due to disturbances in vaginal flora. The association is particularly with broad-spectrum antibiotics,[96] including metronidazole,[87] for the treatment of bacterial vaginosis and occurs mostly in the first few days of a course.[96] There is less likely to be a problem with long-term antibiotic use. Women with recurrent VVC should avoid antibiotics if possible. If antibiotics are unavoidable, these should preferably be narrow-spectrum. Nitrofurantoin and nalidixic acid are recommended for urinary tract infections, since they give low tissue levels.

Psychosexual problems are common in women with recurrent VVC. Mechanical damage to vaginal mucosa may precipitate VVC by exposing intermediate squames.[97] Psychosexual advice, including a recommendation to use vaginal lubricants, is important. Epidemiological studies[98–100] and partner treatment studies do not support a major role for sexual transmission in uncomplicated and recurrent VVC.[82,101,102] Some[103] show an association with frequency of intercourse[62,88,98] and cunnilingus.[85,103] Most women with recurrent VVC continue to have attacks whether or not they are having intercourse. Witkin has suggested that IgE in semen can precipitate VVC.[104]

If a patient is convinced that intercourse precipitates attacks, a pragmatic approach is to recommend a trial of non-latex condoms and abstention from cunnilingus rather than treating her partner. Whether spermicides are associated with VVC is not clear.[105,106]

'Alternative' treatments

Many patients will have read one or more of the many self-help books or websites on 'Candida'.[107] Their suggested rationale, for example of overgrowth of candida in the bowel, may seem far-fetched, but physicians dealing with women with recurrent VVC need to be aware of some of the treatments that are tried. Some of the more common suggestions include yoghurt and *Lactobacillus acidophilus* and diet manipulation.

that high-risk HPV DNA was present in 95% of all cervical cancers.[6] In addition, women infected with oncogenic HPV types have relative risks of 40 to 180 for the development of high-grade precancerous cervical abnormalities.[6,7] HPV types are also detected in 50–80% of vaginal, 50% of vulval and almost all penile and anal carcinomas.

MECHANISM OF CARCINOGENESIS

Most HPV types exist in the episomal (circular) DNA form as seen in Figure 1. The genome can be divided into three regions: the upstream regulatory region (URR), the early region (E) and the late region (L). The URR is responsible for the control of viral replication and controls transcription of sequences in the early region, in particular the E6 and E7 sequences that are discussed below. Thus, the genes in the early region are involved with events that occur early in the viral life cycle, hence the nomenclature. The *L1* and *L2* genes code for structural proteins that make up the viral capsid, which occurs late in the viral life cycle. The capsid surrounds and protects the viral genome and also mediates entry into the host cell. Animal studies have shown that an immune response is generated to these capsid proteins and it is this host antigenic response that is being targeted in current trials of HPV therapeutic vaccines where the *L1* capsid protein is being employed as an immunogen to try and prevent HPV infections.

The E6 and E7 regions of the viral genome code respectively for the E6 and E7 viral proteins that are responsible for the oncogenic potential of the virus.[8] The E6 and E7 proteins of high-risk HPVs bind to and inactivate host cellular proteins that are the guardians of the cell cycle (E6 inactivates p53 and E7 inactivates pRb). In the normal course of events, when damage to DNA occurs, these cellular proteins act as brakes on the cell cycle, allowing the cell time to repair the damaged DNA (Figure 2) or drive the cell towards apoptosis (programmed cell death). The inactivation of these proteins (tumour suppressor proteins) by E6 and E7 impairs the ability of the

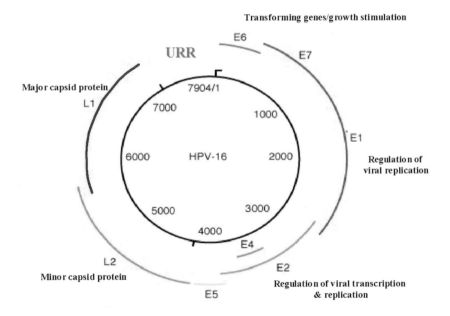

Figure 1 *Schematic drawing of the human papillomavirus 16 genome; E = early region; HPV16 = human papillomavirus type 16; L = late region; URR = upstream regulatory region*

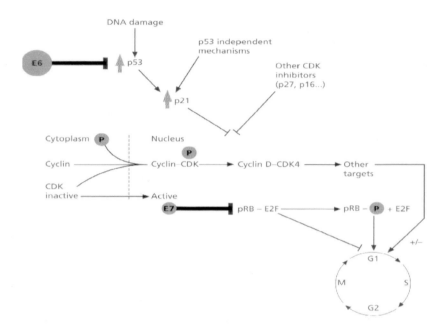

Figure 2 *E6 and E7 viral protein involvement in cell cycle regulation; CDK = cyclin-dependent kinase; URR = upstream regulatory region*

cell to repair its DNA and thus leads to genetic instability and the accumulation of genetic mutations. These additional spontaneous mutations are required prior to the development of any cancer. Low–risk types of HPV are much less able to induce malignant transformation than high-risk types due to functional differences between their E6 and E7 proteins. This results in the proteins being able to bind p53 and pRb only weakly and hence being less likely to disrupt cell regulatory mechanisms. In addition, it appears that low–risk viral types are unable to integrate their DNA into the host cell genome. This process of integration into the host genome is crucial to the final step in the transformation of the host cell into an immortalised cell capable of invasion. When integration occurs, the break in the viral DNA tends to occur at the junction of the E1/E2 region. This is important because E2 plays a role in the regulation of both the E6 and E7 oncogenes (Figure 2).

MANIFESTATIONS OF HUMAN PAPILLOMAVIRUS INFECTION

The ability of the virus to spread is dependent on its ability to infect epithelial cells capable of cell division. The only cells present in the cervical squamous epithelium that are capable of this reside in the basal layer of the epithelium. Minor traumas such as those which could easily occur during sexual intercourse would allow HPV to reach these cells and infect them. Once this has occurred, the possible consequences of infection include the HPV genome in a latent form and an active infection of the parabasal cells. The HPV genome persists in a latent form in the basal and parabasal cells without causing any noticeable changes in the architecture of the epithelium. Latent HPV infection represents cases where the viral genome is present in an otherwise normal target tissue, where normal is specified as having no cytological, morphological or colposcopic evidence of disease. A number of prospective studies have demonstrated that around 80% of young women who acquire a high-risk HPV type will typically clear the virus in around six to eight months without subsequently developing a precancerous cervical abnormality. Many of the more recently published studies conducted in women with cytologically normal smears have used sensitive tests such as polymerase chain reaction (PCR) and the Hybrid Capture® II test (Digene Corp.)[9] for the detection of HPV DNA.

In an active infection of the parabasal cells, HPV proliferates independently of host cell division, in contrast to latent infection, where HPV replicates only when the host cell divides. Indeed, HPV stimulates proliferation of the basal cells and may lead to the formation of a visible lesion such as a genital wart (Figure 3 – Plate 5). Histological manifestations include acanthosis, koliocytosis, nuclear atypia and multinucleation. In most cases of active infection, a subclinical lesion develops that requires magnification and the application of acetic acid for identification. Many of these lesions exhibit only minor cytological atypia and are designated as low-grade lesions. Most are transient and will be missed by infrequent screening intervals. Of those low-grade abnormalities that are detected by cytological screening, more than 60% will regress with approximately 20–30% remaining unchanged. Of those 10% that do progress to high-grade lesions during follow-up, almost all are HPV DNA high-risk positive. A large meta-analysis, drawn from studies between 1952 and 1992, assessed rates of progression, regression and persistence of cervical intraepithelial neoplasia (CIN) and gave us our best evidence of the natural history of CIN.[10]

The visible clinical lesions, i.e. genital warts, have a variety of appearances ranging from flat to papillary. The appearance of such lesions coincides with a substantial quantity of complete virions being exfoliated at the epithelial surface. Cells at the surface have a high number of copies of the HPV genome and it is the accumulation of HPV-induced proteins, as well as of complete HPV virions in the upper epithelium, that is responsible for the cytopathic effect of HPV known as koliocytosis (Figure 4 – Plate 5). Koss and Durfee[11] first described this in 1956, although it had been described as 'perinuclear cavitation' by Papanicolaou two years earlier.[12]

NATURAL HISTORY OF HPV INFECTION

The natural history of HPV infection has received considerable attention, with numerous epidemiological studies conducted in differing populations and age groups worldwide. HPV infections are among the most common sexually transmitted diseases (STDs) in most countries. They may be latent infections, as described above, or subclinical, as in Figure 5 (Plate 6), being noted only at the time of colposcopic examination of the cervix after the application of 3–5% acetic acid. Clinical infection usually manifests itself in subjects infected with HPV types 6 or 11 who develop genital warts (Figure 3 – Plate 5).

Cervical HPV infections are mostly sexually transmitted,[13,14] affecting in a lifetime at least 50–80% of sexually active adults, with an annual incidence of 10–15%. The peak incidence of HPV occurs in women between the ages of 20–24 years, with a gradual decline up to about the age of 40–45 years. Most infections are transient,[15,16] with a median duration of eight to ten months,[17,18] and pose no risk of cervical neoplasia.[19] Only the 10–20% of infections that remain persistent are of concern. Of those women with persistent infection, 5–10% may develop high-grade CIN within two to four years,[19–21] with approximately one-third of cases progressing to cancer if left untreated.[10] Among women over the age of 35 years, the prevalence of HPV infection with high-risk types varies from 1–8%[22,23] and within this group the presence of HPV is likely to be indicative of persistent infection. It has been shown from a number of studies that viral persistence is associated with an increased risk of neoplastic progression.[21,24,25]

EPIDEMIOLOGY

It has been over a hundred years since the first report proposing an association between sexual behaviour and cervical cancer. In the ensuing years, the elusive agent has been intensively sought and for a long time it was thought that the herpes simplex virus (HSV) was the culprit, an opinion formed on the basis of serological studies. In 1976, zur Hausen[26] proposed an association between HPV and cervical neoplasia and since then there has been a wealth of epidemiological and biological data to support this view.

There are no universally accepted criteria to establish causation of cancer by infectious agents but several were proposed by Sir Austin Bradford Hill.[27] These include the strength of the association and its consistency among different groups of women, the temporal relation between infection and disease, and the degree to which interruption of infection is associated with disease elimination.

In order to establish causation, a number of epidemiological approaches have been used, including:

- case reports and case series
- cohort studies
- case–control studies.

Case reports and case series

Initially, the data linking high-risk HPV types and cervical cancer were suggestive but certainly not conclusive. However, with the advances in DNA hybridisation technology and more specifically PCR, the evidence of causality has grown stronger. In 1995, in a reported case series of over 30 studies, the prevalence rate of HPV DNA in CIN and cervical cancer varied from 22% to 100%.[6] The broad range in HPV prevalence was due to variation in the hybridisation technique used, the different tumour specimens (cervical swabs, lavages, biopsies or surgical specimens) and tissue preservation (fresh, frozen or fixed). In response to these studies, the IARC coordinated an international prevalence survey of HPV in cervical cancer. Over 1000 frozen biopsies from histologically confirmed cervical cancers were collected from 22 countries worldwide and tested in a central laboratory using a PCR-based assay capable of detecting more than 25 HPV types. HPV DNA was detected in 93% of tumours and the use of additional HPV detection methods suggested that less than 5% of those cervical cancer specimens were HPV DNA negative. The most common HPV types detected were HPV 16 (49.2%), HPV 18 (11.7%), HPV 45 (8%) and HPV 31 (5%). HPV 16 was the predominant type in all countries except Indonesia, where HPV 18 was more common. HPV 16 was the most common type detected in squamous carcinomas, whereas HPV 18 predominated in adenocarcinomas.[5] In 1999, Walboomers et al.[28] reanalysed the HPV negative cases from the previous study as well as controls from the HPV positive group. After combining their data with the previous study and excluding inadequate specimens, the worldwide HPV prevalence in cervical carcinomas was 99.7%. This represents the highest worldwide attributable fraction so far reported for a specific cause of any major human cancer.

Cohort studies

There are now a significant number of studies reported from a number of centres worldwide. One of the earliest studies came from Koutsky et al.,[19] where 241 cytologically normal women were recruited from a sexual health clinic. These women were followed every four months for an average of 25 months with cytological and colposcopy examinations. HPV DNA was detected using dot blot and Southern blot hybridisation. HPV DNA positivity increased the risk of developing CIN grades II/III with an adjusted relative risk of 11 for HPV 16 and 18. All 24 cases of CIN grade II or III among HPV-positive women were detected within 24 months after the first positive test for HPV. In another study from the USA, 70 women with a histological diagnosis of CIN were followed up at three-monthly intervals for a period of 15 months. Persistent cervical disease was associated with persistent HPV infection and especially with a persistent high viral load with an odds ratio of 4:1.[20] In a Dutch study, 353 women were recruited with smears reported as showing mild to moderate and severe dyskaryosis. The median follow-up time was 33 months with biopsies only being taken at the last visit. The primary endpoint was clinical progression, defined as CIN III, covering three or more cervical quadrants on colposcopy, or a cervical-smear result of suspected cervical cancer. Thirty-three women reached clinical progression, all of whom had persistent infection with high-risk HPV DNA. The cumulative six-year incidence of clinical progression among these women was 40% (95% CI 21–59). In the women with an endpoint of CIN III, 98 (95%) of 103 had had persistent infection with high-risk HPV from entry into the study.[29]

Case–control studies

In a number of case–control studies, the odds ratios for both CIN and cervical cancer in women with oncogenic HPV, and in particular HPV 16, have been shown to be higher than those observed for cigarette smoking and lung cancer. In particular, when women with the disease are compared with population-based controls, the odds ratios observed have been in excess of 200.[30] A recent prospective study investigated the risk of CIN in a group of initially cytologically normal women; 17 654 women were recruited into the study and 380 incident cases were identified during follow-up and matched with 1037 control subjects. HPV DNA was detected using a PCR-based method. In comparison with initially HPV-negative women, women who tested positive for HPV DNA at enrolment into the study were 3.8 times (95% CI 2.6–5.5) more likely to have low-grade CIN subsequently diagnosed for the first time during follow-up and 12.7 times more likely (95% CI 6.2–25.9) to develop CIN 2/3. At the time of diagnosis, the odds ratio for low-grade CIN was 44.4 (95% CI 24.2–81.5) and 67.1 (95% CI 19.3–233.7) for high-grade CIN. HPV type 16 was most predictive of CIN, even for low-grade disease.[31]

In a retrospective study of archival material from women in a population-based cervical screening programme in Sweden (1969–95), a comparison was made between the number of normal cervical smears that were positive for HPV DNA among 118 women in whom invasive cervical cancer developed an average of 5.6 years later (0.5 months to 26.2 years) with the number of HPV DNA-positive smears from 118 women who remained healthy during a similar period of follow-up (control group). The control group was matched for age and had had two normal Pap smears obtained at time points that were similar to the times of the baseline smear and the diagnosis of cancer confirmed by biopsy in the women with cancer. At baseline, 35 of the women with cancer (30%) and three of the control women (3%) were positive for HPV DNA (OR 16.4) At the time of diagnosis, 80 of the 104 women with cancer for whom tissue samples were available (77%) and four of the 104 matched control women (4%) were positive for HPV DNA. Interestingly, the HPV DNA type was the same in the baseline smear and the biopsy specimen in all of the women with cancer in whom HPV DNA was detected at baseline. None of the control women had the same type of HPV in both smears.[32]

In another Swedish study, the archival smears of women who developed carcinoma *in situ* (CIS) were analysed for HPV DNA; 484 women were recruited and their archival smears were compared with those from 619 individually matched controls. After DNA extraction, a highly sensitive PCR system was used to detect HPV 16. In the case group, the prevalence of HPV 16 was 56% at the time of diagnosis. The relative risk of cervical CIS increased from 3.6 at 13 years before diagnosis to 11.1 at one year prior to diagnosis. Having a positive smear at entry to the cohort increased a woman's risk greater than five-fold, whereas persistent infection with HPV in two subsequent smears increased risk more than thirty-fold. It was estimated that among HPV 16 positive women, the median incubation period from infection to carcinoma *in situ* was between seven and twelve years.[33]

It has been suggested by a number of authors that viral load is an important determinant for the development of high-grade cervical disease.[34,35] Ylitalo *et al.*[34] used a sensitive quantitative PCR assay to estimate the viral load of HPV 16 in multiple smears, taken during a period up to 26 years prior to the diagnosis of CIS for each woman in the study. They found that among 478 cases, a consistently increased load of HPV 16 was detectable 13 years or more prior to the histological diagnosis, even when many smears were still cytologically normal. Women with high HPV 16 viral loads had a relative risk at least 30 times greater than HPV 16 negative women for the development of CIS more than a decade before diagnosis. The increase in relative risk was constant over time. About 25% of women (95% CI 0.12–0.32) infected with a high viral load before the age of 25 years developed cervical CIS within 15 years. These data suggest that women at high risk of progression of disease could be identified by use of a quantitative HPV test.[34]

A consistent criticism levelled at many of the earlier epidemiological studies of HPV infection and cervical cancer and precancerous disease cites the fact that cervical tissue was submitted for viral testing at or after the diagnosis of disease had been made. This provides no information on the temporal order of events and, furthermore, results might be biased in their risk estimation, since the very disease process itself might have increased the detectability of the virus. An unbiased estimate of the risk of cervical cancer associated with HPV, HPV DNA prevalence rates and the time interval from initial HPV infection to progression to invasive cancer can only come from prospective studies in women who are cytologically normal at enrolment. To date, these studies support the concept that CIN is preceded by the persistence of detectable high-risk HPV DNA in healthy women.

A study has recently been published whereby a cohort of young women who had only just become sexually active were followed up at regular intervals both cytologically and with HPV DNA testing in a bid to investigate the time interval from exposure to initial HPV infection to development of high-grade disease.[36] A cervical smear was taken every six months and samples were stored for virological analysis. The endpoint of the study was taken to be progression to high grade CIN. In 1075 women who were cytologically normal and HPV negative at recruitment, the cumulative risk at three years of any HPV infection was 44% (95% CI 40–48). Within the group of 246 women with abnormal smears, 40% were negative for HPV and a further 33% only tested positive for the first time at the same visit as the abnormal smear was reported. In only 21% of women was a positive HPV test predictive of abnormal cytology at a subsequent visit. Of the 28 women who developed high-grade CIN during the study, 82% became HPV-positive. The risk of a smear showing moderate or severe dyskaryosis was significantly greater in those women who were HPV positive; the risk was maximal at six months after the first positive HPV test, but declined rapidly thereafter. These findings suggest that, in contrast to a large USA study,[31] persistence of an HPV infection does not appear to confer the greatest risk of an abnormal smear.

HUMAN PAPILLOMAVIRUS TESTS

There are three major HPV tests that could potentially be useful in a population screening programme:

- general primer PCR based on the primer pair GP5+/GP6+

  This test operates by amplifying a 140bp region in the *L1* gene of papillomaviruses and has shown a very high sensitivity and specificity for the prediction of high-grade CIN.[21] The test has been developed into a simple, rapid enzyme immunoassay PCR format able to process large volumes of samples.

- Hybrid Capture® II

  This is a commercially available system and consists of an *in vitro*, solution hybridisation, signal-amplified test able to detect 18 types of HPV DNA in cervical specimens. It consists of RNA probes that hybridise with the denatured DNA target. Specific monoclonal antibodies then bind to the RNA/DNA hybrid and the complex is captured on to microtitre plates. A second monoclonal antibody conjugated to an enzyme, alkaline phosphatase is then reacted with the captured hybrids followed by the addition of a chemiluminescent substrate. Cleavage of the substrate by the alkaline phosphatase yields a light reaction that can be measured. The amount of light emitted is proportional to the amount of target DNA in the sample and hence it is possible to obtain a quantitative result.

  Hybrid Capture® II can differentiate between two HPV DNA groups: low-risk HPV types: 6, 11, 42, 43, and 44; high-/intermediate-risk HPV types: 16, 18, 31, 33, 35, 39, 45, 51, 52, 56, 58, 59 and 68.

  The test can detect the presence of HPV DNA in concentrations as low as 0.2 pg/ml. However, in order to optimise sensitivity and specificity for management, particularly in the triage of women with minor smear abnormalities, it is usually set to give a positive result at concentrations of 1.0 pg/ml (corresponding to 5000 copies of the HPV genome) and above. The test has been used in numerous studies and has good sensitivities for the detection of high-grade disease. A potential disadvantage of the test is that it does not allow specific HPV typing of the sample since a cocktail of probes is used for detection of the oncogenic HPV types. It has also been reported that the test has been found to detect additional HPV types that cross-hybridise with the probe mixture. The great advantage of this test is that it is easy to process and involves simply taking a sample from the cervix in much the same way as a conventional smear.

- general primer MY09/11 system

  This PCR test amplifies a 450bp region of the *L1* gene. Recent developments including an improved primer design (PGMY09/11) have resulted in better consistency and sensitivity for a broad range of HPV types.

POSSIBLE ROLES OF ONCOGENIC HPV DETECTION IN THE PREVENTION OF LOWER GENITAL TRACT PRECANCER

In the light of the available epidemiological data, it would seem logical to incorporate testing for high-risk HPV types as part of a comprehensive cervical screening programme. In terms of possible screening applications, HPV DNA testing could play a number of possible roles:

- in primary screening, either alone or in combination with cytology

- in the triage of patients with borderline or low-grade cervical smears.

Primary screening

As discussed previously, the prevalence of HPV declines with age, being relatively high in young women of less than 25 years old and falling to less than 5% in women over the age of 30 years.[19,37,38] In view of the high prevalence of HPV infection in young women, the issue of in which age group of women to use HPV as a primary screening test is of critical importance,[39] to reduce the number of false positive results and over-referral for colposcopy. In a study of a well-screened population over the age of 35 years, Cuzick et al.[23] have reported a 95.5% sensitivity for CIN II/III using Hybrid Capture® II using a cut-off point of 4 pg/ml of viral load. Others have reported sensitivities of 88–95% for the detection of high-grade disease (CIN 2/3).[40,41]

In women under the age of 30 years the significance of a positive HPV DNA test is more likely to signify transient infection than the presence of CIN II/III. It has become clear that it is persistence of HPV that is predictive of the development of CIN II/III.[20] Women over the age of 30 years with normal cytology but who are positive for high-risk HPV have an 116-fold risk of developing high-grade lesions compared with similar women who are HPV-negative.[42] In the light of the existing epidemiological data, it seems unlikely that as a primary screening test HPV DNA would be useful in the younger population and its place is likely to be in screening women over the age of 35 years where its positive predictive value for high-grade disease is much higher.

Using HPV in triaging patients with minor cytological abnormalities

About 7% of the 4.5 million Pap smear tests performed each year in the UK are reported as showing minor cytological abnormalities (borderline and mild dyskaryosis). Under current guidelines these women are kept under cytological surveillance and are only referred for colposcopy if a repeat smear is abnormal. The majority of these minor abnormalities are likely to represent the transient effects of HPV infection. Most will revert back to normal and 20% will not present with any visible lesion at colposcopy. There are increased cost implications if implementing a policy of immediate referral for colposcopy and this may result in overtreatment of women with mildly abnormal smears. Indeed, in one study, half the women referred with a mildly abnormal smear treated by loop diathermy in a 'see and treat' clinic had no CIN in the biopsy specimen.[43]

However, there are some who would argue for a policy of immediate referral for colposcopy given that a number of studies have shown that up to 30% of women with minor smear abnormalities will in fact have high-grade disease, CIN II/III.[44] This has been demonstrated in both retrospective analyses and in prospective trials.[45–47] In addition, Flannelly et al.[46] reported that only one-quarter of the women with an initial mildly abnormal Pap smear avoided colposcopy after two years of cytological surveillance and they pointed out that this management policy was not cost-effective.

HPV testing has been proposed as an ideal method of triaging those women with minor cytological abnormalities in view of its pivotal role in cervical carcinogenesis. Thus, those women who are positive for high-risk HPV DNA would be referred immediately, whereas those women who are HPV DNA-negative could safely be followed cytologically. A number of studies have looked at the role of HPV in identifying those women with high-grade CIN within a population with borderline smears.[48–51] This policy has now been implemented in a managed healthcare programme in Northern California. Data published by Manos et al.[52] provide convincing evidence for the use of HPV DNA testing in triaging women with atypical squamous cells of undetermined significance (ASCUS) smears. In their study, they estimate an overall combined sensitivity for HPV as an adjunct to cytology of 97% for the detection of high-grade CIN. The negative predictive value for high-grade CIN was greater than 99% for an HPV test performed at the time of the

20

Lower urinary tract damage during gynaecological surgery

Michael Brudenell

INTRODUCTION

'I do not see any mode of certainty providing against the mischance of dividing one or both ureters. I fear that, with all possible care, it is an accident which may occasionally prove unavoidable' (Spencer Wells, 1882).

The lower urinary tract may be injured during any gynaecological operation. Historically, it was accepted that such injuries were sometimes unavoidable, especially when the operation was complicated by pelvic pathology, and that this could happen without negligence on the part of the operator. With the growth of the compensation culture, the 'victim' in such cases will seek someone to blame and will allege negligence in the carrying out of the operation that resulted in her injury. The law is increasingly likely to be sympathetic to the victim and award her damages. Although most gynaecologists believe that the ureter and bladder may be damaged without operator negligence, a successful defence against the allegation is hard to mount when the operation has been apparently straightforward. The defence difficulties are compounded by a small number of 'experts' who believe that all cases of urinary tract injury are due to negligence. Such experts are popular with the legal profession, who seek support for a ruling of *res ipsa loquitur* ('the thing itself speaks') in these cases.

There is no doubt that lower urinary tract damage is a considerable cause of morbidity, especially when the diagnosis is delayed. It is therefore important that all gynaecological surgeons take every possible precaution against inflicting such damage and equally important from a medico-legal point of view that they write clear clinical notes indicating that they have done so. If the proper precautions are taken and a correct technique is used, the incidence of lower urinary tract injury will be low and when it does occur in these circumstances it will be reasonable to claim that the operator was not negligent. No operative technique is 100% successful and to argue that it is, as some experts do, is to go against clinical experience.

INCIDENCE

The quoted incidence of ureteric and bladder damage varies with different authors and with different operative procedures. In the USA, the American College of Obstetricians and Gynecologists[1] gives an incidence of 1% of major gynaecological procedures and caesarean deliveries. Seventy-five percent are associated with hysterectomy. An estimated 500 000–600 000 hysterectomies are performed in America each year, so that there will be 5000–6000 women who would experience an injury each year. The incidence of injury for various operations quoted by other authors is shown in Table 1. Both ureter and bladder are at risk, the ureter being more commonly damaged during abdominal hysterectomy and the bladder during colposuspension.

Table 1 *Lower urinary tract injury in surgery*

Author	Cases (*n*)	Incidence (*n*)	Incidence (%)	Operation
Takamizawa 1999[2]	923	10	1.10	Abdominal hysterectomy for fibroids; all ureters
Mann 1991[3]	4195	16	0.38	Major gynaecological surgery; all ureters
Stevenson 1999[4]	109	10	9.00	Burch colposuspension; 8 bladder, 2 ureter
Gilmour 1999[5]	22[a]		1.60 ureter 2.60 bladder	Major gynaecological surgery
Goodno 1995[6]	4665	19	0.40	Major gynaecological surgery; all ureters
Tamussino 1998[7]	790	4	0.50	Laparoscopic operations; all ureter; 3 out of the 4 during LAVH (4.3%)
Demirci 1999[8]	360	11	3.00	Burch colposuspension; 10 bladder, 1 ureter

[a] *Medline search reports; LAVH = laparoscopically assisted vaginal hysterectomy*

Both organs may be damaged at the same operation. Ureteric injury is usually unilateral but rarely may be bilateral. None of the authors of the above papers attempts to assess the part that negligence plays in the injury. The same applies to gynaecological surgery textbooks, which are full of helpful hints on how to avoid injury to the ureter and bladder but do not say when, and if, such measures may fail. Neither do they express an opinion on the part that operator negligence may play in such a failure.

LITIGATION AND LOWER URINARY TRACT INJURY

In England and Wales, litigation about these injuries occurring in NHS hospitals is dealt with by the NHS Litigation Authority, where the amount of damages involved is likely to exceed £50,000. Claims for lesser sums are dealt with by the trust involved. The Authority does not separately identify ureteric injury, but does list post-gynaecological surgery/injury to the bladder, fistula and incontinence. It seems reasonable to use these three categories to estimate the frequency with which gynaecologists face litigation over lower urinary tract injury under the clinical negligence scheme for trusts. Table 2 shows the incidence of these injuries and the legal outcome over a period of six years ending on 31.5.01 dealt with under the Clinical Negligence Scheme for Trusts (CNST).

The NHS Litigation Authority have dealt with 58 cases, i.e. just over ten cases per annum. Taken together, the three categories of injury constitute 13% of all gynaecological surgical claims, second only to failed sterilisation. Since this figure does not include claims dealt with by the trusts, it is certain to be an underestimate. The Medical Defence Union (MDU) has kindly provided me with the cases of lower urinary tract damage they have dealt with outside the NHS over the ten years from 1990 to 2000. These figures are shown in Table 3. There were 69 cases of ureteric damage, 24 of bladder damage and three where the ureteric damage and the bladder damage were combined.

The operation associated with ureteric injury in the 69 cases in the MDU series is shown in Table 4. In three of the 69 cases, the lesion was bilateral and in five the bladder was also damaged. A fistula developed in eight cases. With regard to bladder damage, the MDU dealt with 24 cases. Of these, 15 were associated with hysterectomy, one with hysterectomy and colposuspension, one

Table 2 *Clinical Negligence Scheme for Trusts claims for gynaecological surgery as at 31.5.01*

Injury	Cases (n)	Withdrawn or statute-barred (n)	Outcome pending (n)	Settled; damages paid (n)	Settled; no damages paid (n)	Proportion of all gynaecology surgery (%)
Incontinence	24	3	18	3	0	5.40
Fistula	11	2	11	2	0	3.28
Bladder damage	18	1	18	0	0	4.15
Total	58	6	47	5	0	12.80

with colposuspension, two with laparoscopy and one each for colposuspension, endometrial resection, salpingectomy, insertion of an intrauterine contraceptive device and transvaginal egg collection. It is clear from these figures that any gynaecological surgical procedure can cause these injuries and this possibility must always be borne in mind. The legal situation with regard to negligence is far from clear. Fifty-three of the total of 154 cases listed in Tables 2 and 3 are still pending. Damages have been paid in 39 cases of ureteric damage; the average of these payments made by the MDU was £40,000, with a range from £400 to £230,000. Payments for the five cases of bladder damage by the MDU were in the range of £4 000 to £240,000, with the majority of cases being settled in excess of £100,000. Although 27 have been withdrawn or have been statute-barred, in all but one of the ureter and bladder cases that have been settled, damages have been paid. The only successful defence was in a case in which the bladder was damaged during egg collection. Until more cases have come to Court and been argued out in front of a judge, the question of negligence cannot be clearly defined, but if anything the available figures suggest that a successful defence of ureteric injury is hard to achieve as the Hendy case (see below) illustrates.

Two cases where the defence was successful give some slight grounds for optimism. The first reported in the *Journal of the MDU* in 1996[9] is a case where a ureterovaginal fistula developed 18 days after a hysterectomy complicated by multiple pelvic adhesions and increased vascularity leading to troublesome bleeding. The case came to Court in Dublin and the defence expert said that ureteric damage was a well-recognised complication of hysterectomy, especially when the operation was complicated. The plaintiff's expert took the view that with proper care, specifically by palpation of the ureter, or in certain circumstances surgical dissection of it, the ureter should not be damaged and to do so was 'a major cardinal error'. When asked if the ureter could still be damaged even if the operation was done competently, he agreed that it could and quoted an incidence of about one in 200 cases. The judge found for the defence and as a fact that the consultant's technique, which did not involve palpation of the ureter, was perfectly acceptable. The MDU's cost for defending the case was just under IR£37,500, none of which could be recovered from the plaintiff. The second case[10] involved obstruction of a left ureter during the course of a hysterectomy complicated by endometriosis that caused excessive bleeding. Although the exact cause of the obstruction was not found, when a urologist was called in to reimplant the ureter two

Table 3 *Lower urinary tract cases dealt with by Medical Defence Union 1990–2000*

Injury	Cases (n)	Pending (n)	Withdrawn or statute-barred (n)	Outcome settled; damages paid (n)	Settled; no damages paid (n)
Ureteric damage	69	38	13	18	0
Ureter and bladder	3	0	0	3	0
Bladder damage	24	8	8	5	1

Table 4 *69 operations causing ureteric damage 1990–2000 (Medical Defence Union)*

Operation	Injuries (*n*)
Hysterectomy	
Abdominal	17
Vaginal	9
Vaginal, laparoscopically assisted	4
Unspecified	24
Total hysterectomies	54
Colposuspension	3
Abdominal	3
Laparoscopic	2
Total colposuspensions	5
Laparoscopic surgery	
Division of uterosacral ligaments	1
Laparoscopic ablation	3
Total laparoscopic surgeries	4
Other operations	
Oophorectomy	2
Sacro–colpopexy	1
Lower segment caesarean section	1
Endometrial resection	2

weeks later, the judge, Lord MacLean, found that the ureter was most likely to have been obstructed by a suture inserted close to it to stop the bleeding. He further found that the insertion of the suture so that it encircled the ureter was a misjudgement but that, because the operator's technique was otherwise correct, the misjudgement did not amount to negligence. The additional interest in this case was that the operation was performed by a registrar (post-MRCOG) assisted by a senior registrar. The judge did not find fault with this arrangement, in striking contrast to the Bouchta case,[11] where the operation was also complicated by bleeding, but the judge found for the plaintiff because the operation was performed by a senior registrar assisted by his consultant and not the other way round.

HOW TO AVOID BEING SUED

There is no easy way to avoid being sued but mitigating factors and a well-written contemporaneous account of the clinical course of events will allow a stout defence to be mounted.

ABDOMINAL HYSTERECTOMY

Injury to the ureter

The ureter may be obstructed by an encircling suture or be kinked by an adjacent stitch put in to control bleeding. It may be cut or crushed by a clamp, leading to a leakage of urine. The ureter may undergo avascular necrosis due to interference with its blood supply. This is a well-recognised complication of radical surgery for cervical cancer but may also occur whenever pelvic pathology, such as endometriosis, is so extensive that the ureter has to be dissected completely free from its surrounding structures.

Of the three ureteric injuries, the last is unlikely to be the subject of a negligence claim but obstruction of the ureter by kinking has been used successfully by the defence (Hooper versus Young).[12] This latter judgement in the Court of Appeal overturned an earlier judgement and is important in those cases where the exact cause of the obstruction is not established (as is most

Table 5 *24 operations causing bladder damage (Medical Defence Union 1990–2000)*

Operation	Injuries (*n*)
Hysterectomy	15
Hysterectomy and colposuspension	1
Colposuspension	2
Laparoscopy	2
Endometrial resection	1
Salpingectomy	1
Insertion of intrauterine contraceptive device	1
Transvaginal egg collection	1

colleagues, must be started. The patient must be kept fully informed and reassured that every effort will be made to put things right as quickly as possible. In explaining to the patient why the damage happened, it is fair to point out to her the difficulties of gynaecological surgery and how close any affected structures are to the operative field. Patients and their lawyers will eventually show the judge clear anatomical diagrams that bear no relation to the scene at operation, but which make it difficult for them, and him, to believe that any damage could have occurred without operator negligence.

CONCLUSION

Because it is hard, in the present climate of excessive patient expectation and the victim and blame culture, to defend an allegation of negligence when lower urinary tract damage occurs, and with the high cost of going to court, health authorities will be tempted to accept liability as the cheapest way out. Only if a gynaecologist can show in such a case that he was aware of the danger of causing such damage and that his technique as fully described was designed to minimise the risk is there much chance of a successful defence. When the diagnosis is made postoperatively, the notes must indicate that the patient was seen and examined always with the possibility of lower urinary tract damage in mind, and that immediate and appropriate investigations and treatment were carried out. Fortunately, from the patient's point of view, even when the diagnosis is made postoperatively, a skilled urologist will be able to repair ureteric and bladder damage with a good chance of success in restoring the urinary tract to normal function. When a case comes to court, the support of experienced gynaecological surgeons, in active practice, is essential. They will underline for the court's benefit the difficulties of gynaecological surgery in general and when appropriate the particular difficulties of the operation in question. It is to be hoped that the precedent that acknowledges what most gynaecologists believe, i.e. that lower urinary tract damage can occur during pelvic surgery without negligence on the part of the operator, can be set. For the moment, however, the best advice to a gynaecologist in relation to causing lower urinary tract damage is that given by *Punch* to the man about to be married – DON'T!

References

1   American College of Obstetricians and Gynaecologists. Lower urinary tract operative injuries. Educational Bulletin of the ACOG. No. 238. Washington DC: ACOG;1997.

2   Takamizawa S, Minakami H, Usui R, Noguchi S, Ohwada M, Suzuki M, *et al.* Risk of complications and uterine malignancies in women undergoing hysterectomy for presumed

benign leiomyomas. *Gynecol Obstet Invest* 1999;48:193–6.

3   Mann WJ. Intentional and unintentional urethral surgical treatment in gynaecologic procedures. *Surgery, Gynaecology & Obstetrics* 1991;172: 453–6.

4   Stevenson KR, Cholhan HJ, Hartmann DM, Buchsbaum GM, Guzick DS. Lower urinary tract injury during the Burch procedure: is there a role for routine cystoscopy? *Am J Obstet Gynecol* 1999;181:35–8.

5   Gilmour DT, Dwyer PL, Carey MP. Lower urinary tract injury during gynaecologic surgery and its detection by intra-operative cystoscopy. *Obstet Gynecol* 1999;94:883–9.

6   Goodno JA, Powers TW, Harris VD. Ureteral injury in gynaecologic surgery: a ten year review in a community hospital. *Am J Obstet Gynaecol* 1995;172:1817–20.

7   Tamussino KF, Lang PF, Breinl E. Ureteral complications with operative gynaecological laparoscopy. *Am J Obstet Gynecol* 1998;178:967–70.

8   Demirci F, Yucel N, Ozden S, Delikara N, Yalti S, Demirci E. A retrospective review of perioperative complications in 360 patients who had Burch colposuspension. *Austr N Z J Obstet Gynaecol* 1999;39:472–5.

9   Irish Case History - Ureteric damage not negligent. *Journal of the MDU* 1996;12:44–5.

10   Loughran. The Lanarkshire Acute Hospitals NHS Trust Outer House Court of Session of Edinburgh. Lord MacLean's Opinion 2001 (unpublished).

11   Brudenell, M. Medico-legal aspects of ureteric damage during abdominal hysterectomy. *Br J Obstet Gynaecol* 1996;103:1180–3.

12   Hooper V. Young Royal Courts of Justice Judgement by Sir Michael Davies 1994; Court of Appeal Judgement by Lords Justice Stewart Smith Waite and Otton 1996.

13   Piscitelli JT, Simnel DL, Addison WA. Who should have intravenous pyelograms before benign disease? *Obstet Gynecol* 1987;69:541–5.

14   Phipps JH, Tyrrell NJ. Transilluminating ureteric stents for preventing operative ureteric damage. *Br J Obstet Gynaecol* 1992;99:81.

15   Hendy versus Milton Keynes H. A. (No. 2) (QBD Mr. Justice Jowett) *Medical Law Reports* 1992;3:119–27.

21

Tension-free vaginal tape: the minimalist approach to continence surgery

Paul Hilton

INTRODUCTION

The tension-free vaginal tape (TVT™)* procedure was conceived from the researches of Petros and Ulmsten into the pathophysiology of urinary incontinence and expounded in their publications on the so-called 'integral theory'.[1,2] Its gestation period might be characterised as the series of surgical experiments described in the second of their publications,[2] culminating in the description of the intravaginal slingplasty (IVS).[3] Its eventual delivery was in the description by Ulmsten *et al.*[4] from Uppsala in 1996 of 'an ambulatory surgical procedure under local anaesthesia for treatment of female urinary incontinence' – which we have since come to know as the TVT.

The procedure represents a significant departure from our traditional approaches to surgery for stress incontinence in several respects. First, the TVT tape is placed suburethrally using an introduction needle, and hence the dissection required is limited. This reduces the postoperative analgesic requirements and also enhances recovery. In contrast to other needle suspension procedures, however, it is carried out under local anaesthesia, which not only allows patient cooperation, but shortens the recovery and the period of hospitalisation. In contrast to traditional sling procedures, where the support is provided at the bladder-neck level, the TVT tape is placed under the mid-urethra under minimal or no tension; this reduces the degree of obstruction produced and thereby limits the need for catheterisation in the postoperative period.

These various advantages have been seen as making the procedure attractive to patients and surgeons alike, and have led to its widespread introduction throughout mainland Europe, then the UK, Australasia and most recently the Americas, over the last five years. Some 16 000 procedures have now been undertaken in the UK, 250 000 worldwide, and this is now the most frequently undertaken procedure for the treatment of stress incontinence. This development has, of course, been based on the perceived immediate advantages of rapid recovery, with limited operative complications, and encouraging short-term outcome data. Long-term results and morbidity data are awaited with interest.

---

* The term TVT™ is a trademark of *Gynecare*, a division of Ethicon Inc., a Johnson and Johnson company. It is difficult to find an appropriate generic term for such procedures, although the Safety and Efficacy Register of New Interventional Procedures (SERNIP) uses the term 'tension free urethropexy'. Nevertheless, TVT is already so built into our terminology that it is used throughout this chapter to imply the procedure described by Ulmsten and colleagues,[4] and the device most commonly used in that procedure.

PROCEDURE

Instruments

The TVT comes packaged with its introducing needles swaged in position on either end of the tape; the tape itself is housed within a removable polyurethane sheath, which is split at the mid-point and overlapped in the central 4 cm, to aid removal (Figure 1). A reusable handle introducer and rigid catheter guide are also available from the manufacturers. Otherwise, no special instruments are required for the procedure.

Current anticoagulant therapy should be looked on as a contraindication to the procedure; since patients are generally fully mobile within a few hours of surgery, they are not at high risk of thromboembolic complications and prophylactic heparin is usually not required. Where a TVT procedure is carried out under regional block, or concurrently with other procedures, it is my practice to administer heparin only after tape insertion. Although infective complications are rare, conventional single-dose antibiotic prophylaxis using co-amoxiclav or cephalosporin and metronidazole is advised.

Anaesthesia

The original reference to the TVT procedure describes it as an ambulatory procedure carried out under local anaesthesia.[4] Many surgeons continue to use this approach, where TVT is carried out as an isolated procedure. Others prefer to use regional or general anaesthesia. The benefits of the local anaesthetic technique include more rapid recovery and earlier discharge from hospital. By maintaining patient cooperation, the tape tension can be adjusted by the 'cough test', in an effort to achieve optimal cure of incontinence with the minimum voiding difficulty. In the one randomised trial that has looked at different anaesthetic techniques, the cure rate was not found to be any better where local anaesthesia was used, although the need for catheterisation in the postoperative period was reduced.[5]

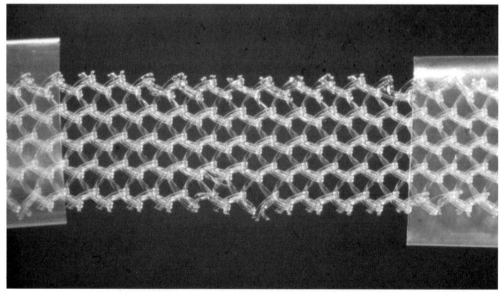

Figure 1 *Close-up view of TVT tape and its investing polyurethane sheath; the sheath is initially overlapped in the mid-portion of the tape by some 4 cm; this is best eased apart slightly prior to insertion but should not be completely removed until adjustment of the tape is completed*

Detrusor overactivity

Detrusor overactivity following incontinence surgery in patients with a stable bladder preoperatively is well recognised.[56] In a systematic review, this has been reported to average between 1% and 16% for different procedures,[25] and individual series give incidences of up to 25%.[46] The incidence parallels to a degree the incidence of voiding difficulty, i.e. those procedures with the highest incidence of voiding difficulty tend to be associated with a higher incidence of detrusor overactivity.[25,46] In one series, symptomatic detrusor overactivity was found postoperatively in 15% of patients.[53] In the UK randomised trial of TVT and colposuspension, although 9% of patients showed urodynamic evidence of detrusor overactivity postoperatively, there was no difference between the two procedures,[6] and in the latter trial few patients developed new symptoms of urgency or urge incontinence postoperatively.

Pain

Chronic pain has been reported in up to 12% of patients following colposuspension,[57–59] and 10% following needle-suspension procedures. This is characteristically described in the site of the suspensory sutures, and may be due to traction on muscle, nerve entrapment or local inflammatory change.[46,59] This phenomenon has not previously been reported in association with the TVT, although anecdotally cases have been associated with perforation of the urinary tract at TVT. This seems likely to be a different mechanism from the pain associated with the so-called 'post-colposuspension syndrome'.[57]

Prolapse

Prolapse, particularly of the uterus, vaginal vault or posterior wall, is reported in up to 26% of patients following colposuspension.[46] This is thought to be due to the redistribution of intra-abdominal pressure changes having stabilised the anterior vaginal wall, in patients who inevitably have deficient endopelvic fascia. The UK randomised trial of TVT and colposuspension offers a unique opportunity to investigate this phenomenon.[19] There was a reduction in the clinical findings of cystocele at six months following both procedures, although this was significantly more apparent following colposuspension. There were more findings of both rectocele and enterocele at each assessment period up to two years postoperatively; in each case the increase was significantly greater for colposuspension. Seven patients underwent further surgery for prolapse during the two years following incontinence surgery; all of these were in the colposuspension arm of the study. These findings suggest that while TVT has minimal impact on prolapse up to two years, colposuspension may specifically exacerbate vault and posterior wall descent.

OTHER MINIMAL-ACCESS PROCEDURES

There have of course been a number of moves towards minimal-access surgery for incontinence before TVT, including laparoscopic colposuspension and periurethral injectables. Initial results with these have not been entirely encouraging, nor have they had the applicability or popularity of TVT. There have also been a number of 'TVT-like' devices that have entered the market since TVT.

Laparoscopic colposuspension

Laparoscopic colposuspension was first described by Vancaillie in 1991 in an effort to reproduce the good results from the open Burch procedure with the benefits of minimal-access surgery.[60]

While there have been almost 200 papers reporting results from the procedure, most are small and short-term, and demonstrate little other than the feasibility of the approach. Four randomised controlled trials have been undertaken comparing the open and laparoscopic approaches,[61–64] and at least one other large multicentre study is under way. Unfortunately the results in these studies do not allow consistent conclusions to be drawn, two showing comparable results between the procedures, and two indicating inferior results from the laparoscopic approach. It does seem clear that there is a considerable 'learning curve' associated with laparoscopic colposuspension, which means that optimal results might not be expected until an experience of perhaps 50 cases has accrued.[65]

Periurethral injections

The concept of periurethral injection of paste was first applied to the treatment of stress incontinence by Berg in 1973.[66] Since that time polytetrafluoroethylene (PTFE),[66] microparticulate silicone,[67] glutaraldehyde cross-linked collagen,[68] hydroxyapatite[69] and autologous fat[70] have all been used in an attempt to better appose the urothelium at the bladderneck, to correct stress incontinence. Although individual reports have often indicated good short-term results, systematic review suggests less than 50% cure in either primary or secondary surgery.[25] In one long-term study, the subjective cure rate was only 26% and the objective cure rate less than 10% at four years following the last injection.[71] Periurethral injectables certainly have the advantage of being the least invasive surgical procedures available and are appropriate for local anaesthetic application. Nevertheless, the currently available data suggest that they have only potential advantage in those women with a rigidly fixed urethra in whom other procedures are not feasible.

Other 'TVT-like' procedures

Several 'TVT-like' devices have recently entered the market, as alternatives for use in tension-free urethropexy. These include the 'IVS Tunneller'® (Tyco Healthcare, Pembroke, Bermuda) and the 'SPARC sling'® system (American Medical Systems, Minnetonka, MN). The former, like the TVT, is developed from the original IVS procedure,[7] although it now employs a different material for the tape. Petros reports an 81% cure rate from his series of 85 cases,[72] and results from across Australia have been presented as an internal report by the Australian Association of Vaginal and Incontinence Surgeons.[73] It is difficult to judge how far this material relates to the original device and how far to the currently available product.

The 'SPARC sling' system has a similar but not identical woven polypropylene tape to the TVT, but employs a different insertion needle in a 'top–down approach', as distinct from that of the TVT. No clinical studies on this device have been published to date.

CONCLUSIONS

The TVT procedure represents a significant departure from traditional approaches to surgery for stress incontinence. The reported cure rates both in primary stress incontinence and in other patient groups are comparable to more conventional procedures, although the speed of recovery is significantly more rapid. Operative complications are generally minor, although a small number of extremely serious morbidities have been reported. It should be noted, however, that there has probably been greater scrutiny of this procedure than of any other to date, and these complications are almost certainly no more frequent following TVT than other operations. The rate of tape erosion into the urinary tract or vagina remains to be clarified with longer-term follow-up.

The TVT has been marketed as a simple minimal-access ambulatory procedure. The presumption is therefore often made that it is an easy procedure for the generalist gynaecologist or urologist to adopt. While the procedure is indeed relatively simple for those surgeons with experience of sling or needle suspension and with skills in cystourethroscopy, this should not be taken to imply safety and efficacy for those without these skills. The new 'TVT-like' devices are promoted as having an improved safety profile over the original device. This has not yet been shown in comparative studies and, even if it were, this should not be taken to indicate that they are any more appropriate for use by the unskilled surgeon.

Guidance from the National Institute for Clinical Excellence in the form of a Health Technology Appraisal of TVT is awaited. The procedure does, however, seem to have wide application and is perhaps appropriate for a greater range of patients than other procedures to date. If the short- to medium-term results currently available are borne out in the longer term and the feared complication of tape erosion does not materialise in significant numbers, TVT could potentially replace colposuspension, sling, needle suspension and periurethral injectables. What a boring surgical life the urogynaecologists may be in for!

References

1   Petros PE, Ulmsten UI. An integral theory of female urinary incontinence. Experimental and clinical considerations. *Acta Obstet Gynecol Scand Suppl* 1990;153:7–31.

2   Petros PE, Ulmsten UI. An integral theory and its method for the diagnosis and management of female urinary incontinence. *Scand J Urol Nephrol Suppl* 1993;153:1–93.

3   Ulmsten U, Petros P. Intravaginal slingplasty (IVS): an ambulatory surgical procedure for treatment of female urinary incontinence. *Scand J Urol Nephrol* 1995;29:75–82.

4   Ulmsten U, Henriksson L, Johnson P, Varhos G. An ambulatory surgical procedure under local anesthesia for treatment of female urinary incontinence. *Int Urogynecol J Pelvic Floor Dysfunct* 1996;7:81–6.

5   Wang AC, Chen MC. Randomized comparison of local versus epidural anesthesia for tension-free vaginal tape operation. *J Urol* 2001;165:1177–80.

6   Ward K, Hilton P, Browning J. A randomised trial of colposuspension and tension-free vaginal tape (TVT) for primary genuine stress incontinence. *Neurourol Urodyn* 2000;19:386–8.

7   Ulmsten U, Petros P. Intravaginal slingplasty (IVS): an ambulatory surgical procedure for treatment of female urinary incontinence. *Scand J Urol Nephrol* 1993;29:75–82.

8   DeLancey J. Pubovesical ligament: a separate structure from the urethral supports ('pubo-urethral ligaments'). *Neurourol Urodyn* 1989;8:53–62.

9   DeLancey J. Structural support of the urethra as it relates to stress urinary incontinence: the hammock hypothesis. *Am J Obstet Gynecol* 1994;170:1713–23.

10   Falconer C, Ekman-Ordeberg G, Malmstrom A, Ulmsten U. Clinical outcome and changes in connective tissue metabolism after intravaginal slingplasty in stress incontinent women. *Int Urogynecol J Pelvic Floor Dysfunct* 1996;7:133–7.

11   Ward K, Hilton P. Tension-free vaginal tape (TVT) – early experience. *Int Urogynecol J Pelvic Floor Dysfunct* 1998;9:320.

12   Jacquetin B. 'TVT procedure' for surgical treatment of female urinary incontinence. *Journal de Gynécologie, Obstétrique et Biologie de la Réproduction* 2000;29:242–7.

13   Adam E, Fischer A. Anaesthesiological aspects of tension-free vaginal tape (TVT)-procedure:

an experience report [German]. *Anästhesiologie und Intensivmedizin* 1998;39:584–6.

14 Cervigni M, Vittori G, Natale F, Panei M, Sbiroli C. Tension free vaginal tape (TVT) a new mini-invasive technique in the treatment of stress urinary incontinence [Italian]. *Urogynaecologia International Journal* 1998;12:71–6.

15 Jimenez Calvo J, Hualde Alfaro A, Santiago Gonzalez de Garibay A, Lozano Urunuela F, de Pablo Cardenas A, Pinos Paul M, *et al.* T. V. T. (tension-free vaginal tape). New surgical technique in the treatment of stress urinary incontinence. *Archivos Españoles de Urología* 2000;53:9–13.

16 Maltau JM, Verelst M, Holtedahl KA, Due J. A new minimally invasive surgical method for stress incontinence in women. *Tidsskr Nor Laegeforen* 1999;119:2342–5.

17 Nilsson CG. The tensionfree vaginal tape procedure (TVT) for treatment of female urinary incontinence. A minimal invasive surgical procedure. *Acta Obstet Gynecol Scand Suppl* 1998;168:34–7.

18 Olsson I, Kroon UB. A three-year postoperative evaluation of tension-free vaginal tape. *Gynecol Obstet Invest* 1999;48:267–9.

19 Ward KL, Hilton P. A randomised trial of colposuspension and tension-free vaginal tape (TVT) for primary genuine stress incontinence – 2 year follow-up. *Int Urogynecol J Pelvic Floor Dysfunct* 2001;12 Suppl 1:S7.

20 Nilsson C, Kuuva N, Falconer C, Rezapour M, Ulmsten U. Long-term results of the tension-free vaginal tape (TVT) procedure for surgical treatment of female stress urinary incontinence. *Int Urogynecol J Pelvic Floor Dysfunct* 2001;12 Suppl 2:S5–S8.

21 Rezapour M, Falconer C, Ulmsten U. Tension-free vaginal tape (TVT) in stress incontinence women with intrinsic sphincter deficiency – a long-term follow up. *Int Urogynecol J Pelvic Floor Dysfunct* 2001;12 Suppl 2:S12–S14.

22 Rezapour M, Ulmsten U. Tension-free vaginal tape (TVT) in women with recurrent stress urinary incontinence – a long-term follow up. *Int Urogynecol J Pelvic Floor Dysfunct* 2001;12 Suppl 2:S9–S11.

23 Rezapour M, Ulmsten U. Tension-free vaginal tape (TVT) in women with mixed urinary incontinence – a long-term follow-up. *Int Urogynecol J Pelvic Floor Dysfunct* 2001;12 Suppl 2:S15–S18.

24 Nilsson CG. The effect of age and time on the outcome of TVT surgery. 31st Annual Meeting of the International Continence Society, 18–21 August 2001, Seoul, Korea.

25 Jarvis GJ. Surgery for genuine stress incontinence. *Br J Obstet Gynaecol* 1994;101:371–4.

26 Azam U, Frazer MI, Kozman EL, Ward K, Hilton P, Rane A. The tension-free vaginal tape procedure in women with previous failed stress incontinence surgery. *J Urol* 2001;166:554–6.

27 Behr J, Winkler M, Schwiersch U. Urodynamic observations on the Marshall-Marchetti-Krantz operation. *Geburtshilfe Frauenheilkd* 1986;46:649–53.

28 Francis LN, Sand PK, Hamrang K, Ostergard DR. A urodynamic appraisal of success and failure after retropubic urethropexy. *J Reprod Med* 1987;32:693–6.

29 Hilton P. A clinical and urodynamic study comparing the Stamey bladder neck suspension and suburethral sling procedures in the treatment of genuine stress incontinence. *Br J Obstet Gynaecol* 1989;96:213–20.

30 Hilton P, Mayne CJ. The Stamey endoscopic bladder neck suspension: a clinical and urodynamic investigation, including actuarial follow-up over four years. *Br J Obstet Gynaecol* 1991;98:1141–9.

31 Hilton P, Stanton SL. A clinical and urodynamic assessment of the Burch colposuspension for genuine stress incontinence. *Br J Obstet Gynaecol* 1983;90:934–9.

Table 1 *Published articles on transabdominal cerclage*

Authors	Year	Patients (n)	Pregnancies (n)	Indications for cerclage	Fetal survival before cerclage (%)	Fetal survival after cerclage (%)
Benson and Durfee[4]	1965	10	13	Shape of cervix, cervicitis	11.0	82.0
Mahran[5]	1978	10	10	Shape of cervix and history of failed transvaginal cerclage	10.0	70.0
Novy[6]	1982	16	22	Shape of cervix	24.0	95.0
Olsen and Tobiassen[7]	1982	17	17	Past obstetric history and shape of cervix	12.0	88.0
Herron and Parer[8]	1988	8	13	Shape of cervix and failed cerclage	15.0	85.0
Gibb and Salaria[9]	1995	50	61	Shape of cervix, or previous failed vaginal cerclage	6.1	85.0
Cammarano et al.[10]	1995	23	29	Shape of cervix, or history of failed vaginal cerclage	18.0	93.0
Craig, Fliegner[11]	1997	12	14	History and failed vaginal cerclage	17.8	69.0
Anthony et al.[12]	1997	13	13	Previous failed cerclage or shape of cervix	16.0	86.6
Turnquest et al.[13]	1999	11	12	Prior failed vaginal cerclage or anatomical defect	N/A	83.0
Davis et al.[19]	2000	82	96	Prior failed vaginal cerclage	N/A	82.0

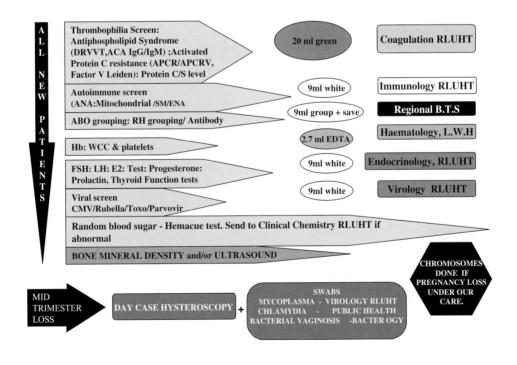

Figure 1 *List of investigations for midtrimester loss history, Liverpool Women's Hospital, 2001*

for chlamydia, mycoplasma and bacterial vaginosis. A hysteroscopy was performed as a day case under general anaesthetic or in an outpatient clinic, noting resistance to Hegar dilators, cervical length and exclusion of uterine anomaly. Blood was screened for chromosome abnormalities (both partners): full blood count, thyroid function, diabetes and autoimmune disease. A thrombophilia screen including antiphospholipid syndrome (APS) and, more recently, activated protein C resistance (APCR) was taken (Figure 1).[14] Because of the lack of consensus regarding the definition of cervical weakness, we used strict criteria for diagnosis. These are (1) painless dilatation of the cervix resulting in ruptured membranes and second-trimester miscarriage after 12 weeks or extreme preterm delivery and (2) passage of size-nine Hegar dilator, without resistance, through the cervix in the non-pregnant state.

Those patients in whom cervical weakness was diagnosed and who had previously experienced a failed vaginal cerclage, or in whom the cervix was so severely damaged that vaginal cerclage was considered impossible, were offered transabdominal cerclage. Prepregnancy counselling requires careful handling and considerable explanation regarding risks of failure, complications of insertion following previous surgery, e.g. classical caesarean section delivery, hourglass constriction of cervix and adjacent major vessels and the need for two major operations. All factors need to be addressed so that the patient has all the relevant information before proceeding to conception.

The procedure

Laparotomy for insertion of a transabdominal cerclage is performed between nine and 13 weeks. Viability is confirmed prior to the procedure by ultrasound. The procedure is performed under general anaesthesia. The bladder is emptied and the catheter left *in situ* during the procedure. We have found that packing the vagina before laparotomy can elevate the uterus with improved access to the cervico-isthmic region. The patient is placed in Trendelenburg position. A low transverse abdominal incision is made and packs used to keep bowel away from operative field. The peritoneum of the vesicocervical fold is incised transversely in the midline. Often it is not necessary to reflect the bladder inferiorly as the bladder reflection lies at the level of the isthmus. The uterine vessels and isthmus are identified digitally.

Double-stranded two-gauge Ethilon™ (Ethicon, UK, type 186) is mounted onto a loose 40-mm round-bodied Mayo needle. The isthmus is grasped between the thumb and forefinger to stabilise the uterus. The suture is inserted postero-anteriorly through the substance of the cervix lateral to the canal but medial to the vessels, at the level of the uterine isthmus above the insertion of the uterosacral ligaments. The needle is remounted and the procedure repeated again postero-anteriorly on the opposite side. The knot is tied anteriorly and covered by a loose peritoneal fold and the abdomen closed. There were no cases of severe haemorrhage in our series, although several cases required the knot to be tightly closed to achieve adequate haemostasis (Figure 2 – Plate 12).

A single dose of intraoperative antibiotics was given. Nonsteroidal anti-inflammatory agents (diclofenac sodium suppositories 100 mg) were given for pain relief and uterine quiescence over the following 72 hours. Preoperative thromboprophylaxis was recommenced on the first postoperative day using dalteparin 5000 units subcutaneously daily and low-dose aspirin 75mg orally daily. Women remained in hospital for five to seven days until removal of the skin sutures; fetal viability was confirmed on scan prior to discharge. Follow-up included serial growth scans, appropriate treatment was continued for coexisting pathologies, such as low molecular weight heparin (LMWH) and low-dose aspirin for APS and clindamycin cream for bacterial vaginosis.

Prophylactic antenatal steroid treatment was prescribed once only at 24 weeks of gestation where dual pathology was present and the mother consented to the administration. Transvaginal ultrasound measurement of cervical length in several cases has shown little more change than would be expected with physiological shortening seen with advancing gestation. Prophylactic bed-rest was not used. Pregnancies progressing beyond viability were delivered by caesarean section; the suture was left in place if the woman wished to consider another pregnancy.

RESULTS OF TRANSABDOMINAL CERCLAGE

Of 30 patients who underwent transabdominal cervical cerclage, 23 resulted in successful outcome (defined as a live birth with no ensuing neonatal death) and three resulted in midtrimester loss or extreme preterm delivery and neonatal death. Four pregnancies are continuing (all beyond 29 weeks). The success rate was 88%.

Five pregnancies ended prior to 30 weeks of gestation (Figure 3). The three recorded failures showed a mixed pattern of presentation. One aborted at 12 weeks of gestation and this was associated with APS. A second had spontaneous rupture of the membranes at 17 weeks followed by chorioamnionitis and intrauterine death, requiring hysterotomy. The third pregnancy failure was delivered by caesarean section at 25 weeks following preterm rupture of the membranes and labour. The infant died at three days of age from acute pulmonary haemorrhage and extreme prematurity. Two further deliveries occurred before 30 weeks, progressing to 27 and 29 weeks respectively and both infants subsequently did well. Eight babies were delivered at a gestation of 30–36 weeks. This was for a variety of reasons including preterm rupture of the membranes, preterm labour and intrauterine growth restriction. All infants are now doing well.

As 50% of pregnancies progressed to near term, we looked at the presence of other pathologies found on initial screening at the miscarriage clinic (Table 2). This demonstrated that 62% (16/26) of delivered patients had another pathology in conjunction with the cervical weakness and that the presence of more than one pathology increased the risk of preterm delivery. In the four patients who had two pathologies, as well as cervical weakness, three delivered prior to 30 weeks and only one of these survived.

DISCUSSION

There is little doubt that transabdominal cervical cerclage is an effective surgical technique in reducing fetal loss in a highly selective group of patients with true cervical weakness and/or a past history of failed vaginal cerclage.[15]

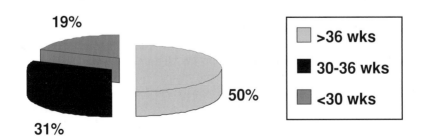

Figure 3 *Gestation at delivery following transabdominal cerclage*

Table 2 *Gestations of patients at delivery according to the number of pathologies that can lead to midtrimester miscarriage identified during screening*

Pathology	Delivery						
	< 30 weeks		30–36 weeks		> 36 weeks		Total
	(n)	(%)	(n)	(%)	(n)	(%)	
Cervical weakness alone	0		3	30.0	7	70.0	10
Cervical weakness and one other pathology	2	17	5	41.5	5	41.5	12
Cervical weakness with two other pathologies	3	75	0		1	25.0	4
Total	5		8		13		26

Examination of published series fails to highlight the coexistence of further pathology, especially the presence of thrombophilia. The data from Liverpool suggest that the presence of coexisting pathology increases the risk of preterm delivery to 45% (12/26), which increases to 75% when there are two or more coexisting pathologies. It is important that women are aware of this confounding variable, as the patient will require laparotomy to insert the suture and abdominal delivery irrespective of gestation.

The presence of coexisting pathology in 60% of patients stresses the need for a full preconceptual screen for dual pathology that can be treated in all patients with cervical weakness. The most common cofactor was APS, found in 33% of cases. All were treated with low-dose aspirin and LMWH. Bacterial vaginosis was treated with oral erythromycin throughout pregnancy combined with a weekly course of clindamycin cream *per vaginam* every month. Two cases of uterine anomaly were untreated by surgery and both had successful outcomes.

There is no study comparing insertion of transabdominal cervical cerclage during pregnancy with insertion prepregnancy. In the non-pregnant state, more manipulation of the tissues is possible, as well as improved access. To counterbalance this advantage, there is the problem of early pregnancy loss before ten weeks of gestation, where spontaneous miscarriage may allow the suture to tear through the substance of the pregnant cervix. In addition, fetal loss rates are higher in the presence of the most common thrombophilia, APS, where suction evacuation may pose a considerable threat to the integrity of a preconceptual abdominal cerclage. Furthermore, in the non-pregnant state, the uterine vessels are not as easily identified and it is more difficult to ensure that they are not caught within the suture. Also, cervical tissue is not as soft and it is difficult to pass the round-bodied needle through the substance of the cervix.

Preconceptual transabdominal cerclage was performed in two of 30 cases. One patient was homozygous for factor V Leiden and at high risk of thrombosis, having suffered two previous episodes of venous thromboembolic disease. The second patient had laboured at 25 weeks after insertion of her first transabdominal cerclage, and had an emergency classical caesarean section when the suture was removed and subsequent access to the lower segment was poor.

There are case reports describing insertion and removal of transabdominal cerclage laparoscopically;[16,17] there is as yet no series published using the laparoscopic approach. Clinical experience with transabdominal cerclage in the UK is limited to a few centres.[9,12,18] Selection criteria vary between centres and often include patients with preterm delivery histories and bad outcome, as well as classical midtrimester loss due to true cervical weakness. Our series contains only patients suffering midtrimester loss.

There are as yet no randomised trials comparing the use of transabdominal cerclage with the transvaginal approach. A highly selective retrospective study[19] looked at the outcome of a group of patients with previous failed vaginal cerclage who were assigned either repeat vaginal cerclage or transabdominal cerclage. Assignment to either group was at the discretion of the authors and no randomisation occurred. They found that delivery at less than 35 weeks occurred significantly less frequently in the transabdominal group (18% versus 42%) and that preterm premature rupture of the membranes also occurred less commonly (8% versus 29%). Extrapolation from these data should be viewed with caution, as no prospective analysis has been made available and many performed cases were excluded from the report.

It is unlikely that a randomised controlled trial will be feasible; women referred for this procedure often perceive it as their last chance and are unlikely to accept randomisation. We are also looking at a small number of patients and the possibility of recruiting sufficient numbers to satisfy a credible power calculation is unlikely.

References

1   Emmett TA. Laceration of the cervix uteri as a frequent and unrecognised cause of disease. *Am J Obstet Gynecol* 1874;7:44–6.

2   Shirodkar VN. A new method of operative treatment for habitual abortion in the second trimester. *Antiseptic* 1955;52:299–300.

3   McDonald IA. Suture of the cervix for inevitable miscarriage. *J Obstet Gynaecol Br Emp* 1957;64:346–50.

4   Benson RC, Durfee RB. Transabdominal cervico-uterine cerclage during pregnancy for the treatment of cervical incompetence. *Obstet Gynecol* 1965;25:145–55.

5   Mahran M. Transabdominal cerclage during pregnancy, a modified technique. *Obstet Gynecol* 1978;52:502–6.

6   Novy MJ. Transabdominal cervicoisthmic cerclage for the management of repetitive abortion and preterm delivery. *Am J Obstet Gynecol* 1982;143:44–54.

7   Olsen S, Tobiassen T. Transabdominal isthmic cerclage for the treatment of incompetent cervix. *Acta Obstet Gynecol Scand* 1982;61:473–5.

8   Herron MA, Parer JT. Transabdominal cerclage for fetal wastage due to cervical incompetence. *Obstet Gynecol* 1988;71:865–8.

9   Gibb DMF, Salaria DA. Transabdominal cervicoisthmic cerclage in the management of recurrent second trimester miscarriage and preterm delivery. *Br J Obstet Gynaecol* 1995;102:802–6.

10   Cammarano CL, Herron MA, Parer JT. Validity of indications for transabdominal cervicoisthmic cerclage for cervical incompetence. *Am J Obstet Gynecol* 1995;172:1871–5.

11   Craig S, Fliegner JRH. Treatment of cervical incompetence by transabdominal cervicoisthmic cerclage. *Aust N Z J Obstet Gynaecol* 1997;37:407–11.

12   Anthony GS, Walker RG, Cameron AD, Price JL, Walker JJ, Calder AA. Transabdominal cervico-isthmic cerclage in the management of cervical incompetence. *Eur J Obstet Gynecol Reprod Biol* 1997;72:127–30.

13   Turnquest MA, Britton KA, Brown HL. Outcome of patients undergoing transabdominal cerclage: a descriptive study. *J Matern Fetal Med* 1999;8:225–7.

14   Drakeley AJ, Quenby S, Farquharson RG. Midtrimester loss – appraisal of a screening protocol. *Hum Reprod* 1998;13:1975–80.

15   Novy MJ. Transabdominal cervicoisthmic cerclage: a reappraisal 25 years after its introduction. *Am J Obstet Gynecol* 1991;164:1635–42.

16   Scibetta JJ, Sanko SR, Phipps WR. Laparoscopic transabdominal cervicoisthmic cerclage. *Fertil Steril* 1998;69:161–3.

17   Lesser KB, Childers JM, Surwit EA. Transabdominal cerclage: a laparoscopic approach. *Obstet Gynecol* 1998;991:855–6.

18   Topping J, Farquharson RG. Transabdominal cervical cerclage. *Br J Hosp Med* 1995;54:510–12.

19   Davis G, Berghella V, Talucci M, Wapner RJ. Patients with a prior failed transvaginal cerclage: a comparison of obstetric outcomes either transabdominal or transvaginal cerclage. *Am J Obstet Gynecol* 2000;183:836–9.

23

Converting abdominal hysterectomies into vaginal hysterectomies

Nicholas J Wood and Derek J Tuffnell

INTRODUCTION

When deciding on the management of a patient's condition, doctors are usually confronted with various options from which they have to recommend the most appropriate. This is determined by clinical effectiveness, safety to the patient and cost-effectiveness. When a decision has been made to perform a hysterectomy for benign indications, a surgeon has three options: abdominal hysterectomy (AH), vaginal hysterectomy (VH) or laparoscopy-assisted vaginal hysterectomy (LAVH). The available evidence shows that VH has less morbidity and reduces hospital stay, as compared with AH, and that LAVH is far more expensive in terms of operating time and cost, with no added benefits in reducing morbidity. This clearly implies that vaginal hysterectomy should be the first option. Other options should be considered only if vaginal hysterectomy is not possible. So why is it that experienced vaginal surgeons can achieve a 70–90% vaginal hysterectomy rate for benign indications, while nationally over two-thirds are performed abdominally? This must be doing a disservice to our patients, so we need to find ways to encourage the vaginal route. This chapter aims to offer such encouragement by exploring the evidence available.

BACKGROUND

Despite recent advances in the management of menstrual disorders, hysterectomy is one of the most common major operations performed, with 66 137 procedures performed in the National Health Service in England from 1998–99.[1] This rate is reflected in other western countries and is even higher in the USA, where there were 645 000 hysterectomies in 1998.[2] Around the world, the rate varies dramatically, and it is especially low in Muslim countries. The first recorded abdominal hysterectomy (AH) was performed by Charles Clay in his consulting rooms in Piccadilly, Manchester, UK in 1843. Unfortunately his patient died from massive haemorrhage. The first successful procedure was performed by Ellis Burnham in Lowell, Massachusetts, USA, in 1853.[3] This was a time before anaesthesia and antisepsis and the mortality from the series described by Burnham was 80%. In fact, even after the introduction of anaesthesia in 1846, Charles Clay felt that it interfered with his results, which for 'ovariotomy' were relatively good (mortality 25/395). He was sure that the type of patient who had the character to undergo an operation without anaesthesia did well because of it, stating that 'I would infinitely prefer to operate without it, as the patient would bring to bear on her case a nerve and determination which would assist beyond value the after-treatment'.[3] AH has remained the basis of general gynaecological surgery ever since. After caesarean section, it is the first major surgical procedure that trainees aim to learn to perform independently and, in appraising a trainee's experience, the question 'How many hysterectomies have you performed?' invariably refers to AH. It has become the 'default' major operation in gynaecology.

Vaginal hysterectomy was first described by Conrad Langenbeck in 1817.[3] He had performed the first operation in 1813. At the time he was ridiculed and, in fact, his colleagues and peers did not believe him. His patient was demented and was therefore deemed an unreliable witness, and his assistant had died two weeks after the procedure. It was not until after the patient's death 26 years later that postmortem findings confirmed his story. As the 19th century progressed, the technique was refined and standardised. The advantage over the abdominal approach seemed obvious at the time, and data from individual series suggest that in the 1880s mortality from AH was 70%, whereas mortality from VH was much lower at 15%. The safety and efficacy of VH over AH was re-emphasised in the 1930s by both Babcock and Heaney.[4,5] They both published large series of VH, suggesting lower mortality than AH. This led to the latter stating at the end of his paper: 'It is the purpose of this paper to show again how low the mortality and morbidity of vaginal hysterectomy may be, with the hope that this operation may find a place in the operative armamentarium of every gynaecologist'.[5] Until relatively recently in the history of the operative techniques, the differences in morbidity between AH and VH had not been tested in robust studies. Evidence now clearly implies the advantage of VH over AH in terms of a reduction in febrile morbidity, less bleeding necessitating transfusion, shorter hospital stay and faster recovery. This comes in the form of both a prospective observational study and a randomised controlled trial.[6,7] The observational study involved 1851 women of whom 568 (30.7%) were listed for a VH.[6] Overall, the complication rate was 24.5% for the VH group and 42.8% for the AH group. Among women who received prophylactic antibiotics intraoperatively the complication rates were 20.9% for VH and 50.5% for AH (relative risk 2.4). Women who underwent AH had longer postoperative hospital stays and convalescence periods, experienced more febrile morbidity and received more blood transfusions than women who underwent VH. The indication for hysterectomy varied between the VH and AH group as would be expected. However, a sub-analysis of a group of women for whom either surgical approach would have been appropriate (parous women with menorrhagia or dysplasia) showed an increased overall complication rate in the AH group (relative risk 2.1). The only adverse observation was that the unintended laparotomy and intraoperative procedure rate was higher in the VH group (5.1–1.7%). However, of the VH group, 1.1% of this was accounted for by laparotomy to complete the hysterectomy abdominally. All three of the women who required postoperative laparotomy for ureteral transection had undergone AH. There was one mortality in each group in the study period. In the AH group, a patient was admitted with a postoperative deep vein thrombosis and died from complications related to pelvic venography. In the VH group, a women who was known to be depressed took an overdose and died one week after discharge.

The randomised controlled trial assesses short-term outcome only.[7] It was designed and powered to assess time in hospital after surgery as a primary outcome. This showed that theatre time was the same for VH and AH but patients were discharged home on average one day sooner and had a shorter convalescence by one week in the VH group compared with AH. The study was not large enough to comment upon complication rates. From this evidence, VH is the superior operation and thus if we return to the basis of our decision making in patient management (effectiveness, safety and cost) VH should be the default operation for removing the uterus. The advantages of vaginal over abdominal hysterectomy are:

- overall reduced complication rate

- less febrile morbidity

- less haemorrhage requiring transfusion

- shorter postoperative hospital stay

had a caesarean delivery. Interestingly, the same study did demonstrate that previous vaginal delivery in women who had caesarean sections reduced the rate of complications compared with women who had never had a vaginal delivery.[47] The morbidity was not affected by the number of previous caesarean deliveries; however, earlier studies did suggest that VH should be avoided in women who had more than two caesarean deliveries.[48] There are no prospective randomised controlled trials to assess the safety of VH compared with AH with a history of previous abdominal or pelvic surgery.

The main concern with a history of previous caesarean section is of bladder injury. Many methods have been described as a way of avoiding any renal tract trauma, including the use of a finger or probe to define the limit of the uterovesical pouch during sharp dissection. The integrity of the bladder may be assessed by instilling methylene blue solution if there is concern about occult laceration during dissection. Unger and Meeks[47] state in their paper that:

'With the vaginal approach the distal vesicouterine space, that part closest to the original vaginal dissection, is unaffected by the previous operation on the lower uterine segment. This enables one to begin the dissection in the correct surgical plane and aids in the location of the bladder and the caesarean scar. Once this area is encountered, sharp dissection helps to prevent tearing into the bladder, as may occur with blunt dissection'.

This confirms personal observation that it can sometimes be easier to reflect the bladder at VH rather than AH after previous caesarean section. It also emphasises the importance of using sharp dissection rather than blunt dissection if there is any previous scarring.

NULLIPARITY

There is no evidence that nulliparity is a risk factor for increased morbidity at VH. The principle of the fear of performing VH in nulliparous women is a lack of uterine descent. Therefore, the same arguments as used in that case apply here. All the studies showing the safety of VH include women who have not had children. Interestingly, in the study by Davies et al.,[13] which retrospectively analysed the notes of patients who had undergone hysterectomy (by any route) to assess their suitability for VH, a greater proportion of the women in the 'not suitable group' were nulliparous (34.7%) compared with the women deemed suitable for VH (16.5%). The only reasons for exclusion from suitability for VH that were used in that study were uterine size of more than 20 weeks, known endometriosis, adnexal masses, cancer and those undergoing abdominal procedures such as colposuspension. The greater proportion of nulliparous women in the 'not suitable' group may therefore be there because of the association between large fibroids and endometriosis, with infertility and nulliparity being a risk factor for endometrial cancer. Lack of uterovaginal prolapse needing repair was not a reason to avoid VH in this study. In fact, it suggested that if the criteria for VH were extended to women without clinically significant prolapse, it would increase the proportion of vaginal hysterectomies by a factor of six.

PELVIC PAIN AND TENDERNESS

A history of pelvic pain and pelvic tenderness or uterine immobility at examination are also stated by some surgeons to be a contraindication to VH.[49,50] The unreliability of history and examination to predict the presence and extent of pelvic disease is well-documented in relation to pelvic inflammatory disease and endometriosis.[51,52] In a prospective study by Kovac[16] of 617 women who were listed for hysterectomy, only 63 had risk factors from history or examination that might contraindicate VH. These women underwent laparoscopy before hysterectomy (LAVH). Laparoscopic surgery was necessary to permit a transvaginal operation in only 12 of 63 cases. Two women had AH after laparoscopic assessment because LAVH was not felt to be feasible. Thus, from this study it would appear that when there is concern regarding endometriosis, pelvic inflammatory disease or other benign adnexal pathology, history and examination alone have a poor positive predictive value for patients for whom VH is unsuitable. Therefore, even if a surgeon is not trained to perform LAVH, an assessment with the laparoscope will increase the proportion of hysterectomies that can be performed vaginally.

GUIDELINES TO DETERMINE THE ROUTE OF HYSTERECTOMY

There is no clear guidance from formal bodies about decision of route of hysterectomy. The American College of Obstetricians and Gynaecologists suggests that the choice 'depends upon the patient's anatomy and the surgeon's experience' but adds that VH is usually performed in women with mobile uteri no larger than one at 12 weeks of gestation (i.e. 280 g).[53] The guideline does accept that larger uteri can also be removed by experienced surgeons. There are three studies that assess the prospective use of guidelines in determining the appropriate method of hysterectomy.[10,16,54] Their exclusions vary, but the VH rate ranges from 77–94%. In the French study that gave a VH rate of 77%, those women with uterovaginal prolapse were excluded. Thus, given all indications, the prospective use of guidelines to determine the route of hysterectomy would appear to be able to achieve a 90% VH rate in experienced hands. This is in stark contrast to the approximate ratio of VH to AH in the UK of one to three,[1] but one series has shown that this may be as high as one in five.[20]

The guidelines devised by Kovac involve a decision-making tree that is shown in Figure 4.[18,55] In those cases in which the history or examination raise the possibility of serious pelvic disease (risk factors), a laparoscopy is performed and a scoring system is used to assess the feasibility of VH, LAVH or AH (Table 1).[56] Using these guidelines, the study achieved a VH rate of 89%. Of the 617 patients in his study, only six required AH because of uterine immobility or inaccessibility. A further two patients required AH after initial laparoscopic assessment, i.e. scored more than 20 on laparoscopic assessment. In only one patient was the vaginal operation abandoned in favour of an abdominal one; that woman had had five previous caesarean sections and had extensive anterior abdominal wall adhesions. Sixty-three patients required LAVH because of 'risk factors'; apart from the two requiring AH, only 12 patients required any operative laparoscopy to allow VH. In assessing the complication rates between the three procedures, the numbers of the AH and LAVH are too small to show any significant difference in specific injuries, but there were bladder injuries in the LAVH and VH group and bowel injury in the VH group. When summing up complications as a marker of morbidity, AH had significantly more complications (16%) than the LAVH (5%) or VH (7%) group.[16]

Authors of these guidelines accept that surgical skill will play a role in the VH rate that is achievable. However, if the decision-making process is clarified and made more objective by the use of guidelines, a significant increase in VH rate could be achieved by a surgeon without having to consider particularly different surgical techniques from a routine VH, for example, including those patients without uterovaginal prolapse requiring repair, with pelvic pain, with previous pelvic surgery, could achieve a 40% VH rate that could be even greater if GnRH analogues were used preoperatively to shrink enlarged uteri.[13]

PRACTICAL EXPERIENCE

Most of the series of cases have examined a particular concern or relative contraindication to vaginal hysterectomy and examined the impact of changing practice with regard to that risk factor. Often this is within the context of a tertiary referral centre.

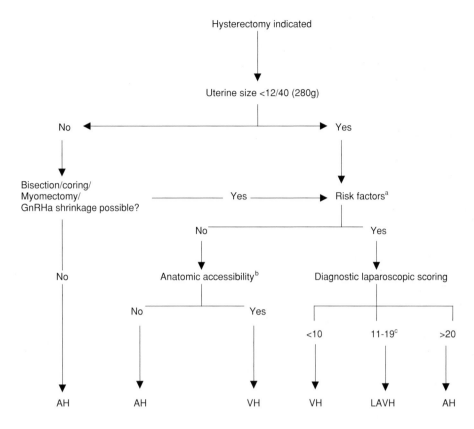

Figure 4 *Guidelines for determining route of hysterectomy; AH = abdominal hysterectomy, LAVH = laparoscopic abdominal hypsterectomy, VH = vaginal hysterectomy; reproduced with permission from* Postgraduate Medicine *and ECRI*[18,55]

This published experience often allows gynaecologists in district general hospitals to suggest that it is not relevant to their case mix, surgical experience or availability of resources or theatre time. From 1994–99, 323 hysterectomies for benign disease were performed by a single consultant team in Bradford Hospitals NHS Trust. The case mix reflected the women commonly referred across the whole unit. The primary indications for the hysterectomies were: menstrual dysfunction 218, prolapse 59, pelvic mass 25, pain and endometriosis 21. In total 253 (78.3%) were performed vaginally. In four cases (1.5%), the operation was commenced vaginally but converted to an abdominal approach. The reason for the abdominal approach in the remaining 66 cases is set out in Table 2. When the published evidence described above is considered, it could be argued that more than half of these could have been removed vaginally, possibly with the help of the laparoscope. Even so the proportion of cases removed vaginally is much higher than the national average; 146 of the cases (45%) were performed by trainees with a similar overall rate of VH.

In all 59 cases with prolapse, the procedure was VH; 186 of 218 (85.3%) of cases for menstrual problems were VH. With pain only three of 21 and with a pelvic mass five of 25 were VH. With previous caesarean section 21 of 29 (72%) were VH and in six of 13 nullipara (46%). Overall in the presence of endometriosis 13 of 35 (37%) were VH.

Table 1 *Laparoscopic scoring system for determining operative approach;[56] reproduced with permission from Liebert Publishers*

Parameter	Points
Uterine size	
Grade I: 8 weeks or less	1
Grade II: 8–12 weeks	3
Grade III: 12–16 weeks	5
Mobility of adnexa as judged by stretched length of infundibulo pelvic ligament	
Good: > 5cm	1
Moderate: 2–5cm	3
Poor: < 2cm	5
Adhesion of adnexa	
None/mild: peritubal or periovarian adhesions	1
Moderate: periovarian and/or peritubal adhesions without fixation, minimal cul-de-sac adhesions	3
Severe: dense pelvic or adnexal adhesions with fixation of ovary and tube to either broad ligament, pelvic wall, omentum and/or bowel, severe cul-de-sac adhesions	5
Status of cul-de-sac	
Accessible	0
Obliterated	5
Total	20
Endometriosis (American Fertility Society classification)	
Stage I	1
Stage II	2
Stage III	3
Stage IV	4
Total	24

The rate of VH of 80% was maintained until the uterus was 12-week-size and over this size it dropped to 42%. With trainees, operating complications were greater. In two cases, bladder injury occurred at VH and five cases of primary haemorrhage requiring return to theatre occurred (3 VH 2 AH). Three women had haematoma that prolonged stay by over seven days (2 AH 1 VH). In only one of these ten cases was the primary surgeon a consultant; 15 patients were transfused (4/178 [2.2%] consultant and 11 of 145 [7.6%] trainee); 13 readmissions occurred, nine after VH (3.5%) and four after AH (5.7%). Trainees had ten readmissions (6.9%) and the consultant four (2.2%).

Table 2 *Reason for decision to perform abdominal hysterectomy in audit series*

Indication	Cases (*n*)
Uterus over 10 weeks	23 (17 over 16 weeks)
Ovarian cysts	13
Previous caesarean section	2
Adhesions /pelvic inflammatory disease	10
Endometriosis	10
Patient choice	3
Other	5
Total	66

No specialised instruments or advanced techniques were used and the consultant had had only a general gynaecological training, with no specialised training that would influence the rate of VH. The major difference in this series of cases was the mind-set with which the operation of hysterectomy was approached. The cases were assessed with the view that the operation should be a VH unless particular reasons were present to suggest otherwise. A number of the AH cases were undertaken when the consultant was on leave – the trainee reverting to the 'default' operation when left without direct supervision. This emphasises the necessity of ensuring that trainees feel comfortable with VH and, ideally, that they prefer it. It is, after all, the most minimally invasive form of major gynaecological surgery.

PRIORITY OF SURGICAL TRAINING IN THE UK

This section considers the training in the UK but may be as relevant to other countries. While individual surgeons can personally influence the proportion of hysterectomies they perform vaginally, it is unlikely that this will have a significant impact. Unfortunately, a high proportion of gynaecologists must hardly ever be performing VH. It is unlikely that a widespread change will occur in the practice of those who are already consultants. The change must therefore come from those who are either in training or still open to change in practice. In order to facilitate this, training in gynaecological surgery should be targeted at VH. Currently trainees will be taught AH, as it is easier to supervise and only when competent at this will they be taught VH. This reinforces the vicious circle of gynaecologists feeling more comfortable with AH and then performing less VH than is easily achievable. This circle of training and experience needs to be interrupted.

There must also be a concern that laparoscopic procedures are getting a much greater emphasis than VH. There are huge numbers of courses in relative terms. This may in part be due to the fact that sponsorship is easy for a course that will teach a skill requiring sophisticated and expensive equipment. These courses would be better aimed at skilled vaginal surgeons, to allow them to tackle the small proportion of cases that cannot be tackled with the straightforward VH. LAVH should not be seen as the alternative to AH for most procedures.

There is no direct guidance to trainees and trainers from the Royal College of Obstetricians and Gynaecologists about specifics in surgical training. A logbook of surgical procedures is no longer required to be kept by trainees as proof of surgical training, although in our experience some trainees continue to keep a personal record of their surgical experience. The Royal College of Obstetricians and Gynaecologists is piloting an electronic database for trainees (PATREC) that documents both gynaecological and obstetric cases and allows the recording of fairly detailed patient and operative information. At present it is not available on 'palm' or 'hand-held' devices, which restricts the flexibility of its use. The surgical logbook has been replaced by a personal development file that includes a 'logbook' of experience. This contains a module for surgical procedures in which VH is a single entry with no reference to the ability to perform oophorectomy at vaginal hysterectomy or procedures to allow VH of enlarged uteri. In contrast, laparotomy, oophorectomy and adhesiolysis are listed as individual targets to achieve. The ability of a trainee to perform VH will depend upon their exposure and experience. These will be limited by their trainers. If a trainer is not an exponent of VH and is unfamiliar with techniques of uterine reduction and oophorectomy, then the current rate of VH will be perpetuated despite the evidence that it is the superior operation.

While changes in training are needed, the mechanisms to facilitate this may not be easy to achieve. There are several possible ways of making changes but these would need to gain wide acceptance. It would be possible to set trainees targets not just for numbers of cases but also for what proportion are VH rather than AH. If a trainee 'fails', however, whose failure is it – supervisor or trainee? This is not greatly different from situations that arise now when some consultants allow trainees more operative experience than others and some provide too much or too little supervision. Therefore, as these 'inequalities' in training are ironed out, the issue of balance of VH and AH could be addressed.

Alternatively, supervising consultants could be accredited. Case mix would need to be considered, but evidence of a certain proportion of cases being performed vaginally could be required. Currently the number of trainees is still close to the number of consultants, so this is not possible but, as trainee numbers reduce and consultant numbers increase, it may be that accreditation for training could be required. All of these measures are in the future and will take time, but consideration of ways to change training is the method most likely to increase the proportion of hysterectomies performed vaginally.

CONCLUSION

The variation in the VH rate reflects a variation in surgical expertise, as well as unjustified preconceptions about contraindications to VH. By more open-minded selection of cases with the use of guidelines and by using preoperative GnRH analogues to shrink uteri enlarged by fibroids, a greater proportion of hysterectomies could be performed vaginally without employing any new surgical techniques. Evidence would suggest that in skilled hands, a VH rate of 90% can be achieved. It is clearly unrealistic to expect all surgeons to achieve this. However, it is unacceptable that patients are not offered a safer operation that will return them to normal activities more quickly just because the surgeon has had inadequate training and feels more comfortable with an abdominal operation. The operation should be chosen to suit the patient rather than the surgeon.

In an environment where our surgical performance is to be more closely scrutinised, we should accept standards, especially when evidence-based, and question ourselves when they are not achieved. There is firm evidence that VH has many advantages over AH. There is also firm evidence that many abdominal hysterectomies may have easily been performed vaginally. We should therefore be happy to accept an achievable VH rate and audit ourselves against it. Those who have difficulty with vaginal surgery should address this with further training or accept that hysterectomy should only be offered by those with the adequate skills. To encourage the development of the appropriate skills in trainees, the targets in the personal development file should be more specific when describing vaginal hysterectomy. This will encourage supervisors of the training programme to recognise that not all consultants and trainers can offer the appropriate surgical training for what is 'general' gynaecology.

References

1   Main Operations, NHS Hospitals, England, 1998–99. London: Department of Health, Government Statistics Service; 2001.

2   Inpatient discharges from non-Federal hospitals, United States, 1998. National Centre for Health Statistics, US Department of Health and Human Services; 2001.

3   Sutton C. Hysterectomy: a historical perspective. *Bailliere's Clin Obstet Gynaecol* 1997;11:1–22.

4   Babcock WW. A technique for vaginal hysterectomy. *Surg Gynecol Obstet* 1932;34:193–9.

5   Heaney NS. A report of 565 vaginal hysterectomies performed for benign pelvic disease. *Am J Obstet Gynecol* 1934;28:751–5.

6   Dicker RC, Greenspan JR, Strauss LT, Cowart MR, Scally MJ, Peterson HB, *et al.* Complications of abdominal and vaginal hysterectomy among women of reproductive age in the United States. The Collaborative Review of Sterilisation. *Am J Obstet Gynecol* 1982;144:841–8.

7   Ottosen C, Lingman G, Ottosen L. Three methods for hysterectomy: a randomized, prospective study of short term outcome. *Br J Obstet Gynaecol* 2000;107:1380–5.

8   Reich H, DeCaprio J, McGlynn F. Laparoscopic hysterectomy. *J Gynecol Surg* 1989;5:213–16.

9   Munro MG, Parker WH. A classification system for laparoscopic hysterectomy. *Obstet Gynecol* 1993;82:624–9.

10   Richardson RE, Bournas N, Magos A. Is laparoscopic hysterectomy a waste of time? *Lancet* 1995;345:36–41.

11   Meikle SF, Nugent EW, Orleans M. Complications and recovery from laparoscopy-assisted vaginal hysterectomy compared with abdominal and vaginal hysterectomy. *Obstet Gynecol* 1997;89:304–11.

12   Dorsey JH, Steinberg EP, Holtz PM. Clinical indications for hysterectomy route: patient characteristics or physician preference? *Am J Obstet Gynecol* 1995;173;1452–60.

13   Davies A, Vizza E, Bournas N, O'Connor H, Magos A. How to increase the proportion of hysterectomies performed vaginally. *Am J Obstet Gynecol* 1998;179:1008–12.

14   Magos A, Bournas N, Sinha R, Richardson RE, O'Connor H. Vaginal hysterectomy for the large uterus. *Br J Obstet Gynaecol* 1996;103:246–51.

15   Davies A, O'Connor H, Magos A. A prospective study to evaluate oophorectomy at the time of vaginal hysterectomy. *Br J Obstet Gynaecol* 1996;103:915–20.

16   Kovac SR. Guidelines to determine the route of hysterectomy. *Obstet Gynecol* 1995;85:18–23.

17   Sheth SS, Malpani A. Vaginal hysterectomy for the management of menstruation in mentally retarded women. *Int J Gynaecol Obstet* 1991;35:319–21.

18   Kovac SR. Which route for hysterectomy? Evidence-based outcomes guide selection. *Postgraduate Medicine* 1997;102:153–8.

19   Amirikia H, Evans TN. Ten year review of hysterectomies: trends, indications and risks. *Am J Obstet Gynecol* 1979;134:431–7.

20   Vessey MP, Villard-Mackintosh L, McPherson K, Coulter A, Yeates D. The epidemiology of hysterectomy: findings in a large cohort study. *Br J Obstet Gynaecol* 1992;99:402–7.

21   Kovac SR. Intramyometrial coring as an adjunct to vaginal hysterectomy. *Obstet Gynecol* 1986;67:131–6.

22   Babcock WW. A technique for vaginal hysterectomy. *Surg Gynecol Obstet* 1932;35:193–9.

23   Heaney NP. A report of 565 vaginal hysterectomies performed for benign pelvic disease. *Am J Obstet Gynecol* 1934;28:751–5.

24   Grody MHT. Vaginal hysterectomy: the large uterus. *J Gynecol Surg* 1989;5:301–12.

25   Unger JB. Vaginal hysterectomy for the woman with a moderately enlarged uterus weighing 200 to 700 grams. *Am J Obstet Gynecol* 1999;180:1337–44.

26   Mazdisnian F, Kurzel RB, Coe S, Bosuk M, Montz F. Vaginal hysterectomy by uterine morcellation: an efficient non-morbid procedure. *Obstet Gynecol* 1995;86:60–64.

27   Hoffman MS, DeCesare S, Kalter C. Abdominal hysterectomy versus transvaginal morcellation for the removal of enlarged uteri. *Am J Obstet Gynecol* 1994;171:309–13.

28   Stovall TG, Ling FW, Henry LC, Woodruff MR. A randomized trial evaluating leuprolide acetate before hysterectomy as treatment for leiomyomas. *Am J Obstet Gynecol* 1991;164:1420–23.

29 Stovall TG, Summit RL, Washburn SA, Ling FW. Gonadotrophin-releasing hormone agonist before hysterectomy. *Am J Obstet Gynecol* 1994;170:1744–8.

30 Vercellini P, Crosignani PG, Mangioni C, Imparato E, Ferrari A, De Giorgi O. Treatment with gonadotrophin releasing hormone agonist before hysterectomy for leiomyomas: results of a multicentre randomised controlled trial. *Br J Obstet Gynaecol* 1998;105:1148–54.

31 Bradham DD, Stovall TG, Thompson CD. Use of GnRH agonist before hysterectomy: a cost simulation. *Obstet Gynecol* 1995;85:401–6.

32 Wilcox LS, Koonin LM, Pokras R, Strauss LT, Zhisen X, Peterson HB. Hysterectomy in the United States, 1988–1990. *Obstet Gynecol* 1994;83:549–55.

33 Gross CP, Nicholson W, Powe NR. Factors affecting prophylactic oophorectomy in postmenopausal women. *Obstet Gynecol* 1999;94:962–8.

34 Jacobs I, Oram D. Prevention of ovarian cancer: a survey of the practice of prophylactic oophorectomy by fellows and members of the Royal College of Obstetricians and Gynaecologists. *Br J Obstet Gynaecol* 1989;96:510–15.

35 Kovac SR, Christie SJ, Bindbeutel GA. Abdominal versus vaginal hysterectomy: a statistical model for determining physician decision making and patient outcome. *Med Decis Making* 1991;11:19–28.

36 Davies A, O'Connor H, Magos AL. A prospective study to evaluate oophorectomy at the time of vaginal hysterectomy. *Br J Obstet Gynaecol* 1996;103:915–20.

37 Kovac SR, Cruikshank SH. Guidelines to determine the route of oophorectomy with hysterectomy. *Am J Obstet Gynecol* 1996;175:1483–8.

38 Sheth SS. The place of oophorectomy at vaginal hysterectomy. *Br J Obstet Gynaecol* 1991;98:662–6.

39 Smale LE, Smale ML, Wilkening RL, Mundy CF, Ewing TL. Salpingo-oophorectomy at the time of vaginal hysterectomy. *Am J Obstet Gynecol* 1978;131:122–8.

40 Wright RC. Vaginal oophorectomy. *Am J Obstet Gynecol* 1974;120:759–63.

41 Magos AL, Bournas N, Sinha R, Lo L, Richardson RE. Transvaginal endoscopic oophorectomy. *Am J Obstet Gynecol* 1995;172:123–4.

42 Heaney NS. Vaginal hysterectomy – its indications and technique. *Am J Surg* 1940;48:284–8.

43 Ingram JM, Withers RW, Wright HL. Vaginal hysterectomy after previous pelvic surgery. *Am J Obstet Gynecol* 1957;74:1181–6.

44 Jacobs WM, Adels MJ, Rogers SF. Vaginal hysterectomy after previous pelvic surgery. *Obstet Gynecol* 1958;12:572–4.

45 Carpenter RJ, Silva P. Vaginal hysterectomy following pelvic operation. *Obstet Gynecol* 1967;30:394–7.

46 Coulam CB, Pratt JH. Vaginal hysterectomy: is previous pelvic operation a contraindication? *Am J Obstet Gynecol* 1973;116:252–60.

47 Unger JB, Meeks GR. Vaginal hysterectomy in women with history of previous cesarean delivery. *Am J Obstet Gynecol* 1998;179:1473–8.

48 Sheth SS, Malpani AN. Vaginal hysterectomy following previous caesarean section. *Int J Gynecol Obstet* 1995;50:165–9.

49 Gupta JK, Frank TG, Nwosu CR. The Gupta-Frank clamp for salpingo-oophorectomy at vaginal hysterectomy. *Obstet Gynecol* 1998;92:144–7.

50 Kovac SR. Vaginal hysterectomy. *Bailliere's Clin Obstet Gynaecol* 1997;11:95–110.

51 Lee NC, Dicker RC, Rubin GL. Confirmation of the pre-operative diagnosis for hysterectomy. *Am J Obstet Gynecol* 1984;150:283–7.

52 Lundberg WI, Wall JE, Mathers JE. Laparoscopy in evaluation of pelvic pain. *Obstet Gynecol* 1973;42:872–6.

53   American College of Obstetricians and Gynecologists. *Precis IV. An Update in Obstetrics and Gynecology*. Washington, DC: ACOG; 1990. p. 197.

54   Querleu D, Cosson M, Parmentier D, Debodinance P. The impact of laparoscopic surgery on vaginal hysterectomy. *Gynaecological Endoscopy* 1993;2:89–91.

55   Emergency Care Research Institute. *Laparoscopy in hysterectomy for benign conditions*. Plymouth Meeting, PA: ECRI, 1995; Technology Assessment Custom Report Level 2:1–117.

56   Kovak SR, Cruikshank SH, Retto HF. Laparoscopy-assisted vaginal hysterectomy. *J Gynecol Surgery* 1990;6:185–93.

24

Postoperative adhesions: the extent and impact of the problem

Adrian Lower

INTRODUCTION

Adhesion formation is an almost inevitable consequence of abdominal and pelvic surgery, with almost 95% of patients who have undergone laparotomy being shown to have adhesions at subsequent surgery.[1] Adhesions are the body's response to trauma, effectively an internal 'scar' formed through complex processes involving injured tissues and peritoneum. For the majority of patients, adhesion formation has few consequences. However, for a small proportion, the consequences can be serious, resulting in infertility, pain, small-bowel obstruction and even death.

CLINICAL CONSEQUENCES

Intestinal obstruction is the most severe consequence of adhesions. Between 30% and 41% of patients with intestinal obstruction that requires surgery have adhesion-related disease.[2] For small-bowel obstruction, this figure rises to 65–75%.[2,3] Adhesions are a leading cause of secondary infertility in women,[4,5] either by blocking or kinking the fallopian tubes and interfering with the tubal transport mechanism or by preventing oocyte release due to the ovaries being adherent to the pelvic side wall or bowel. Adhesions can also cause significant abdominal and pelvic pain and may complicate future surgery. A study looking at workload in a consecutive series of 120 patients undergoing reoperative laparotomy estimated a mean increase of 18 minutes in total theatre time as a result of intra-abdominal adhesions from previous surgery.[6] Van Goor *et al.*[7] have identified a 21% risk of adhesion-related bowel perforation in a series of 274 patients undergoing relaparotomy. This risk increases in proportion to the patient's age and the number of previous laparotomies.

Until recently, few data existed on the basic epidemiology of adhesions on a population basis. The Surgical and Clinical Adhesion Research (SCAR) study group used validated data from the Scottish NHS Medical Record Linkage Database to define a cohort of patients undergoing open abdominal or pelvic surgery in 1986 who had no record of abdominal or pelvic surgery in the preceding five years.[8] This cohort was followed for ten years and subsequent readmissions were intensively reviewed and allocated to outcome categories according to the degree of adhesion involvement. The prevalence of adhesion-related admissions in a single year (1994) was also assessed for the entire population of five million people. Overall, one in three (34.6%) of the 29 790 patients who underwent open abdominal or pelvic surgery in 1986 were readmitted a mean of 2.1 times in the subsequent ten years for a problem directly or possibly related to adhesions, or for abdominal/pelvic surgery potentially complicated by adhesions; 5.7% (1209) of all readmissions (21 347) were categorised as directly related to adhesions, with 3.8% (1169) managed operatively; 22.1% of all outcome readmissions occurred in the first year after initial surgery, but readmissions

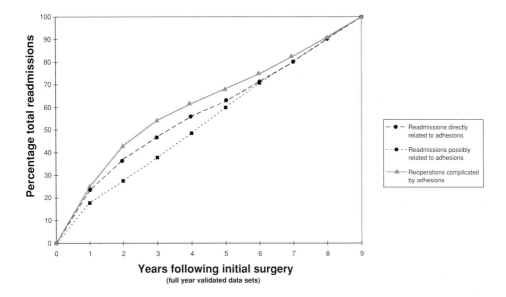

Figure 1 *Readmissions over time*

continued steadily throughout the ten-year period (Figure 1). In 1994, there were 4199 admissions directly due to adhesions, a figure comparable to the total numbers of hip replacements (4394) and appendix operations (4846) in the same year and population.

A subset of this study involving 8489 patients undergoing gynaecological procedures was reported separately.[9] A similar proportion of readmissions due to adhesions was identified; 2931 (34.5%) patients had a total of 5433 readmissions over the next ten years, a mean of 1.9 per patient. The majority of patients were readmitted on one occasion, although a significant number had between two and five readmissions for a complication that was directly related to adhesions, 'possibly related' or for further surgery that would be complicated by adhesions (Table 1). One hundred and sixty-four abdominal surgical interventions for direct adhesion-related disease were identified over the ten-year study, of which 26 cases had small-bowel obstruction. A further 57 non-operative readmissions directly associated with adhesions were identified. In addition, there were 24 readmissions for gynaecological adhesiolysis. This represents 4.5% of all readmissions following open surgery on the female reproductive tract.

Table 1 *Patient readmissions by site of surgery*

Site of initial open surgery	Patients undergoing initial open surgery (n)	Patients readmitted (n)	Hospital readmissions (n)	Readmitted patients (%)	Average per patient
Ovary	624	300	664	48.1	2.2
Fallopian tubes	1171	482	943	41.2	2.0
Uterus	6616	2122	3759	32.1	1.8
Vagina	78	27	67	34.6	2.5
Total	8489	2931	5433	34.5	1.9

ECONOMIC BURDEN

The economic burden to the healthcare system is substantial. The SCAR data from 1994 showed 4199 admissions for surgery due to adhesions: 4060 surgical admissions with an average length of stay of 5.4 days and 139 gynaecological admissions with an average length of stay of 3.4 days. The inpatient costs per day were conservatively estimated at £271 for general surgery and £322 for gynaecology.[10] The cost for Scotland alone for one year was therefore £6,093,581, equivalent to a cost of more than £72 million if extrapolated to the whole of the UK; similar costs have been estimated elsewhere.

An attributable-risk, cost-of-illness study was recently carried out in the USA.[4] A hospital discharge database was used to identify all abdominal adhesion procedures performed in 1994 and the costs were calculated from Medicare records. The results were compared with data from 1988. Adhesiolysis accounted for 303 836 hospital admissions in 1994 and US$1.3 billion in hospitalisation and surgical costs.

ECONOMIC MODEL OF A SUCCESSFUL ANTI-ADHESION STRATEGY

Postoperative adhesions clearly have an important impact on successful clinical outcomes of surgery and impose a significant cost burden. In considering the implementation of an anti-adhesion strategy, as well as considering the clinical efficacy of an adhesion-reduction agent, there are important economic considerations – particularly if the implementation of routine prophylactic adhesion-reduction strategies is considered.

Epidemiological data from the SCAR study in open lower abdominal surgery[11] can be used to model the cumulative costs over time of adhesion-related ('directly' or 'possibly related') readmissions, with or without surgery.

Adhesion-related readmissions usually present as small bowel obstruction[12] and cost data from an audit of adhesion-related SBO (readmissions without surgery £1370.53, mean hospital stay seven days and with surgery £4231.00, mean hospital stay 14 days)[13] can be applied to the SCAR incidence data over the ten years of the study.

This model can be used to compare the 'control' costs for 100 patients undergoing lower abdominal surgery where no adhesion-reduction strategy is implemented with the costs of treating 100 patients with an adhesion-reduction agent. For the purposes of the model, the costs of such treatments have been hypothetically priced at either £50 or £200 per patient treatment. It is then possible to estimate the level of clinical efficacy required to reduce the costs of adhesion-related readmissions such that the costs of using an adhesion-reduction agent will be repaid at perhaps one or three years after use in surgery.

Applying this model to a low-cost adhesion-reduction agent (hypothetically priced at £50 per patient) it is estimated that a 36.9% reduction in readmissions will be required to repay the £50 cost of the product within the first year, and up to an 18.1% reduction in readmissions will be required to repay the £50 spent after three years. Thereafter for each patient cost savings will occur (Figure 2).

An adhesion-reduction agent hypothetically costing £200 per patient will not return the initial costs per patient within the first year even if it results in a 100% reduction in readmissions, but the product would return the initial costs only if a reduction in adhesion-related readmissions of 72.5% could be demonstrated after three years (Figure 3). It is clear from this that in considering the choice of adhesion-reduction strategy the cost of the product versus the clinical impact of the agent needs to be carefully considered.

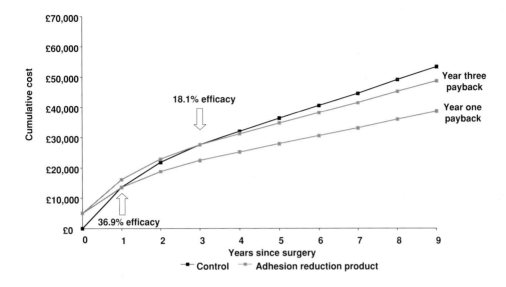

Figure 2 *Cumulative costs of adhesion-related readmissions since surgery for 100 patients, without treatment (control) or with an adhesion reduction product priced at £50 per treatment patient; modelled on efficacy required to pay back cost of treatment after one or three years*

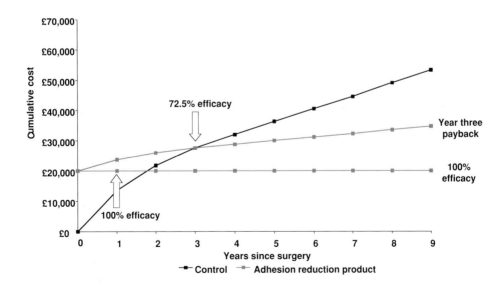

Figure 3 *Cumulative costs of adhesion-related readmissions since surgery for 100 patients, without treatment (control) or with an adhesion reduction product priced at £200 per patient; modelled on efficacy required to payback cost of treatment after one or three years*

HOW ARE ADHESIONS FORMED?

Abdominal postoperative adhesions develop following trauma to the mesothelium, which is often damaged by surgical handling and instrument contact, foreign materials such as sutures and glove-dusting powder, desiccation and overheating. Although understanding of the pathogenesis of adhesions has been improving, the molecular mechanisms involved continue to be delineated. Adhesions develop as part of the normal wound-healing response to trauma and form in the first five to seven days after injury. A cascade of events begins with coagulation at the site of trauma, leading to the build-up of a fibrin gel matrix. This fibrin gel matrix forms a band or bridge when two peritoneal surfaces coated with it are apposed and become the basis for the organisation of an adhesion, unless it is removed. Protective fibrinolytic enzyme systems of the peritoneum, such as the plasmin system, can remove the fibrin gel matrix, leading to adhesion-free recovery. However, surgery, infection and hypoxia dramatically diminish fibrinolytic activity. The most important events determining whether the pathway taken is adhesion formation or re-epithelialisation are therefore the apposition of two damaged surfaces and the extent of fibrinolysis.

There has been a wide range of avenues of investigation into research in postoperative adhesion formation, including:

- identification on a molecular level of the components involved in adhesiogenesis and their interactions

- clarification of the role of fibrin and fibrinolysis in adhesion formation

- standardisation of design in preclinical and clinical studies of adhesion formation and reduction

- delineation of the relationship between adhesion formation and adhesive complications

- elucidation of efficient, site-specific methods of prophylactic drug delivery.

Currently, it seems logical to focus preventive research on development of agents that keep tissue surfaces apart, fibrinolytic drugs and selected agents such as phospholipids.

STRATEGIES FOR ADHESION REDUCTION

The most important factor in bringing about a reduction in the consequences of adhesion-related disease is education. Key points are:

- awareness of adhesions

- careful tissue handling

- minimal-access surgery

- avoidance of desiccation

- avoidance of foreign-body introduction.

Surgeons must be aware of the potential adhesive complications of a procedure. The single most important factor in adhesion avoidance is careful surgical technique.[14] Tissue should be handled as little as possible. Desiccation can be kept to a minimum by the use of minimal-access techniques and the use of irrigation fluids during the course of open surgery. Abdominal packs should be used sparingly, as these cause significant desiccation and peritoneal abrasions. Where packing is required, the packs must be soaked in an irrigation fluid such as Hartmann's solution or, potentially, an adhesion reduction solution such as 4% icodextrin.

Excessive diathermy should be avoided and monofilament sutures should be used where possible to avoid large avascular pedicles. Talc- or starch-containing gloves should never be used.

Infection should be kept to a minimum by avoiding spillage of intestinal contents and appropriate use of prophylactic antibiotics.

A number of adjuvants have been developed to help to further reduce adhesion complications. These fall into the categories of physical barriers (films and gels) to keep tissue surfaces apart during the healing process, use of fluids for hydroflotation and enhancement of the fibrinolytic enzyme system by factors such as tissue plasminogen activator (TPA).

Physical barriers

Physical barriers have been used for some time, initially in the form of omental or peritoneal grafting and, more recently, in the form of inert barriers such as polytetrafluoroethylene (Preclude®, Gore-tex®). These barriers are introduced at the site of trauma, for instance over a suture line, for procedures such as myomectomy. Preclude has the disadvantage that it must be sutured in place and then removed at a second-look laparoscopy. Subsequently absorbable barriers were introduced. Interceed® (Johnson & Johnson) is an absorbable mesh of oxidised regenerated cellulose. There is a substantial literature on Interceed and it has been shown to reduce adhesion formation while not affecting wound healing.[15] It is, however, relatively difficult to handle and its efficacy is reduced by the presence of blood, so meticulous haemostasis must be achieved before it can be applied. It can be used laparoscopically but is not easy to apply. It is also relatively expensive. Seprafilm® (Genzyme, Cambridge, MA) is another barrier composed of hyaluronic acid cross-linked with carboxymethylcellulose.[16,17] This is presented as a rather brittle sheet or film that is placed over a suture line. It also persists during the period of re-epithelialisation and is spontaneously absorbed. It does not conform to the shape of the pelvic organs as well as Interceed and is more useful as a barrier placed between the bowel or omentum and the anterior abdominal wall at the time of wound closure where it can prevent adherence, reducing the risk of enterotomy at subsequent laparotomy. All physical barrier methods suffer from the disadvantage that they are effective only at the site of application.

Hydroflotation

Hydroflotation has long been suggested as a technique that may be efficacious both at the site of application and elsewhere in the abdominal cavity. This involves the instillation of a fluid into the peritoneal cavity at the end of the procedure to provide a physical, fluid barrier preventing apposition of damaged peritoneal surfaces. Saline, Ringer Lactate and Hartmann's solution have all been (and still are) widely used. However, these crystalloids are rapidly absorbed and do not work to reduce adhesions.[18] These solutions are absorbed from the peritoneal cavity at the rate of 30–60 ml per hour, so that by 10–12 hours after surgery, little, if any, crystalloid solution would be left in the pelvic or abdominal cavity.[19,20]

A further strategy in adhesion reduction has been the intraperitoneal instillation of macromolecular solutions. The investigation of such solutions was led by 32% dextran 70. Dextran 70 is an α-1,6-linked dextrose polymer, originally used (at 6%) as a plasma expander, which is absorbed systemically but metabolised slowly. In clinical practice, it can produce undesirable local and systemic adverse effects because of its osmotic and anaphylactic properties.[21] Dextran 70 is indicated for use as an aid to hysteroscopy and not as an adhesions barrier. Clinical trials did not find it to be an effective adhesion reduction device.[22]

A dilute solution of 0.04% hyaluronic acid-phosphate-buffered saline, Sepracoat® (Genzyme, Cambridge, MA) was developed for 'tissue precoating'. Intraoperative application protects the peritoneal surfaces from indirect surgical trauma and, when left as an instillate at the end of surgery, this low-viscosity solution has been shown to reduce *de novo* adhesions at non-surgical sites.[23] Marketing of Sepracoat has, however, been discontinued.

Hyaluronic acid has been used in a number of other different preparations. It is a major constituent of the extracellular matrix, physiologically inert and as synovial fluid has lubricant properties. It is fairly readily absorbed from the peritoneal cavity, but the intraperitoneal residence can be increased by cross-linking either with carboxymethyl cellulose (as in the physical barrier Seprafilm®), with ferric chloride as a gel formulation such as Intergel,® (Johnson & Johnson) or with itself as Hyalobarrier Gel™ (Baxter). Intergel is the most widely available of these two gel products and initial experience was favourable.[24,25] It is certainly easier to apply either at open surgery or laparoscopy. Widespread acceptance has not been forthcoming, however, partly because of the cost.

Since then, 4% icodextrin (Adept,® Shire Pharmaceuticals) has been approved for adhesion reduction. Icodextrin was originally developed as a peritoneal dialysate and has been marketed and used as such for a number of years in 7.5% solution. More than 10 000 patient years of safety data exist. In a 4% solution, it has a long enough intraperitoneal residence to provide hydroflotation during the crucial period of adhesion formation (Figure 4).[26] Icodextrin looks and handles like normal saline or Hartmann's, is isosmolar and does not potentiate infection.[27] As well as being easy to use, requiring no change to routine surgical practice, or any special training, it is inexpensive.

Preclinical studies confirmed that, when used as an intraoperative wash and postoperative instillate, Icodextrin significantly reduced the incidence, severity and extent of postoperative adhesions.[27] No differences have been demonstrated between icodextrin and Ringer Lactate in the healing and strength of midline incisions and bowel anastamoses.[28] Initial clinical studies are encouraging. A multicentre US study of 60 patients undergoing laparoscopic gynaecological surgery, powered to confirm safety, has shown a net 30% improvement in adhesion reduction in

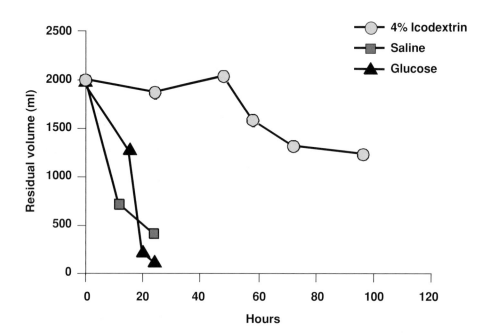

Figure 4 *Four percent icodextrin – residual peritoneal volume over 96 hours*

patients treated with 4% icodextrin compared with a net 16% increase in adhesions in patients in whom Ringer Lactate was used.[29] The results of a larger pivotal study powered to demonstrate efficacy are awaited.

An audit of icodextrin use in laparoscopic and open surgery was conducted in the UK last year.[30] The resulting patient register (ARIEL) reported the experience of 162 gynaecological procedures, of which 117 were laparoscopic, 38 open and seven combined. There were no intraoperative adverse events thought likely to be due to icodextrin and only eight cases in which adverse events were reported after laparoscopy and three after laparotomy. Five adverse events following laparoscopy were considered as possibly, probably or definitely related to icodextrin. These included minor nausea and bloating, slight discharge from the wound and minor leakage from the port site in one case. With these experiences, we have started to advise patients that they may experience some leakage at the port sites and that they may have a feeling of fluid moving around in their abdomen for up to five days. After laparotomy, a slight increase in bruising around the wound was reported in one case and in one patient delayed wound healing and scar breakdown was reported. This is not thought to be of great clinical significance; however, the author now tends to leave wound staples in place a day or two longer than previously. In one further patient it appeared that the icodextrin escaped beneath the rectus sheath and tracked inferiorly. The patient recovered well and no similar problems have been reported in laparotomy patients in a similar general surgery audit.

Icodextrin is a satisfactory vehicle for drug administration and is approved in the UK and other European countries as a pharmacological agent for the administration of intraperitoneal drug therapy. Heparin has been successfully added for irrigation purposes by some surgeons who previously had used heparinised Hartmann's solution for irrigation purposes. Antibiotics have also been added. An interesting area of future research would be to consider the addition of TPA to icodextrin. TPA has been shown to significantly reduce adhesion formation in the rabbit model without affecting haemostasis, bowel anastamosis or wound strength.[31] Its use has not been reported in human studies.

CONCLUSION

Postoperative adhesions are an important cause of morbidity and constitute a significant burden on the health service. Careful surgical technique and limited use of physical barriers have been the mainstays adopted to date among surgeons who recognise the problems of adhesions. There is increasing evidence of the impact of postoperative adhesions on successful surgical outcome. As surgeons we need to be aware of the potential for litigation if we do not actively consider the impact of postoperative adhesions.[32,33] At present, in the absence of other credible and economically viable adhesion reduction strategies, the author recommends the use of icodextrin for perioperative irrigation and postoperative instillation of up to one litre pending the outcome of further studies.

References

1   Menzies D, Ellis H. Intestinal obstruction from adhesions – how big is the problem? *Ann R Coll Surg Engl* 1990;72:60–3.

2   Menzies D. Postoperative adhesions: their treatment and relevance in clinical practice. *Ann R Coll Surg Eng* 1993;75:147–53.

3   Ellis H. The magnitude of adhesion-related problems. *Ann Chir Gynaecol* 1998;87:9–11.

4   Fox-Ray N, Denton WG, Tharner M, Henderson SC, Perry S. Abdominal adhesiolysis: inpatient care and expenditure in the United States in 1994. *Am Coll Surg* 1998;186:1–9.

5   Hershlag A, Diamond MP, DeCherney AH. Adhesiolysis. *Clin Obstet Gynecol* 1991;34:395–401.

6   Coleman MG, McLain AD, Moran BJ. Impact of previous surgery on time taken for incision and division of adhesions during laparotomy. *Dis Colon Rectum* 2000;43:1297–9.

7   Van Der Krabben AA, Dijkstra FR, Nieuwenhuijzen M, Reijnen MM, Schaapveld M, Van Goor H. Morbidity and mortality of inadvertent enterotomy during adhesiotomy. *Br J Surg* 2000;87:467–71.

8   Ellis H, Moran BJ, Thompson JN, Parker MC, Wilson MS, Menzies D, *et al.* Adhesion-related hospital readmissions after abdominal and pelvic surgery: a retrospective cohort study. *Lancet* 1999;353:1476–80.

9   Lower AM, Hawthorn RJS, Ellis H, O'Brien F, Buchan S, Crowe AM. The impact of adhesions on hospital readmissions over ten years after 8849 open gynaecological operations: an assessment from Surgical and Clinical Adhesions Research Study. *BJOG* 2000;107:855–62.

10   Parker MC. The economic and practical implications of adhesive small bowel disease. ASCRS and Tripartite Meeting Symposium: Adhesive Small Bowel Obstruction Following Colon and Rectal Surgery: Can we do better? 1–6 May 1999, Washington DC.

11   Parker MC, Ellis H, Moran BJ, Thompson JN, Wilson MS, Menzies D, *et al.* Post operative adhesions: ten-year follow-up of 12,584 patients undergoing lower abdominal surgery. *Dis Col Rectum* 2001;44:822–9.

12   Ellis H. The magnitude of adhesion-related problems. *Ann Chir Gynaecol* 1998;87:9–11.

13   Menzies D, Parker M, Hoare R, Knight A. Small bowel obstruction due to postoperative adhesions: treatment patterns and associated costs in 110 hospital admissions. *Ann R Coll Surg Engl* 2001;83:40–6.

14   Monk BJ, Berman ML, Monitz FJ. Adhesions after extensive gynaecological surgery: clinical significance, etiology and prevention. *Am J Obstet Gynecol* 1994;170:1396–403.

15   Interceed (TC7) Adhesion Barrier Study Group. Prevention of postsurgical adhesions by Interceed, an absorbable adhesion barrier: a prospective randomised multicentre clinical study. *Fertil Steril* 1989;51:933–8.

16   Diamond MP and the Seprafilm Study Group. Reduction of adhesions after uterine myomectomy by Seprafilm membrane (HAL-F): a blinded, prospective, randomised, multicentre clinical study. *Fertil Steril* 1996;66:904–10.

17   Becker JM, Dayton MT, Fazio VW, Beck DE, Stryker SJ, Wexner SD, *et al.* Prevention of postoperative abdominal adhesions by a sodium hyaluronate-based bioresorbable membrane: a prospective, randomized, double-blind multicenter study. *J Am Coll Surg* 1996;183:297–306.

18   Wiseman DM, Trout JR, Diamond MP. The rates of adhesion development and the effects of crystalloid solutions on adhesion development in pelvic surgery. *Fertil Steril* 1998;70:702–11.

19   Shear L, Swartz C, Shinaberger J, Barry KG. Kinetics of peritoneal fluid absorption in adult man. *N Engl J Med* 1965;272:123–7.

20   Hart R, Magos A. Laparoscopically instilled fluid: the rate of absorption and the effects on patient discomfort and fluid balance. *Gynaecological Endoscopy* 1996;5:287–91.

21   Gauwerky JFH, Heinrich D, Kubli F. Complications of intraperitoneal dextran application for prevention of adhesions. *Biol Res Pregnancy Perinatol* 1986;7:93–7.

22   Rosenberg SM, Board JA. High molecular weight dextran in human infertility surgery. *Am J Obstet Gynecol* 1984;148:380–5.

23   Diamond MP and the Sepracoat Adhesion Study Group. Reduction of de novo postsurgical adhesions by intraoperative precoating with Sepracoat (HAL-C) TM solution: a prospective, randomised, blinded, placebo-controlled multicentre study. *Fertil Steril* 1998;69:1067–74.

24   Johns DB, Keyport GM, Hoehler F, diZerega GS. Intergel Adhesions Prevention Study Group. Reduction of postsurgical adhesions with Intergel adhesion prevention solution: a multicenter study of safety and efficacy after conservative gynecologic surgery. *Fertil Steril* 2001;76:595–604.

25   Lundorff P, van Geldorp H, Tronstad SE, Othon L, Larsson B, Johns DB, *et al.* Reduction of post-surgical adhesions with ferric hyaluronate gel: a European study. *Hum Reprod* 2001;16:1982–8.

26   Hosie K, Gilbert JA, Kerr D, Brown CB, Peers EM. Fluid dynamics in man of an intraperitoneal drug delivery solution: 4% icodextrin. *Drug Deliv* 2001;8:9–12.

27   Verco SJS, Peers EM, Brown CB, Rodgers KE, Roda N, diZerega GS. Development of a novel glucose polymer solution (icodextrin) for adhesion prevention: pre-clinical studies. *Hum Reprod* 2000;15:1764–72.

28   Data on file. ML Laboratories plc, Blaby, Leicestershire LE8 4FA, UK (unpublished).

29   DiZerega GA, Verco SJS, Young P, Kettel M, Kobak W, Martin D, *et al.* A randomized, controlled pilot study of the safety and efficacy of 4% icodextrin solution (Adept®) in the reduction of adhesions following laparoscopic gynaecological surgery. *Hum Reprod* 2002;17:1031–8.

30   Sutton C. Practical experience of Adept. Adhesions workshop on 'Practical issues and solutions to peritoneal adhesions', 29th British Congress of Obstetrics and Gynaecology, Birmingham, 10–13 July 2001.

31   Menzies D, Ellis H. The role of plasminogen activator in adhesion prevention. *Surg Gynecol Obstet* 1991;172:362–6.

32   Ellis H. Medico-legal consequences of postoperative intra-abdominal adhesions. *J R Soc Med* 2001;94:331–2.

33   Skene L, Smallwood R. Informed consent: lessons from Australia. *BMJ* 2002;324:39–41.

25

Microwave endometrial ablation for menorrhagia: a second-generation endometrial ablation technique

Michael Milligan

INTRODUCTION

Menorrhagia remains a common reason for referral to a gynaecologist[1] and accounts for 12% of all gynaecology referrals; 60% of these women will have had a hysterectomy within five years[2] or, viewed differently, by the age of 43 years, 10% of women will have undergone major surgery in the UK.[3]

Over 70 000 hysterectomies are still performed annually in the UK and more than half of these are for menorrhagia.[4] In up to 30% of these patients, the uterus is found to be structurally normal and the diagnosis is dysfunctional uterine bleeding.[5] The morbidity of hysterectomy is well-documented[6,7] and gynaecologists have therefore continued to explore other surgical treatments of a less radical nature to treat menorrhagia. Improved medical treatments (e.g. tranexamic acid, mefenamic acid) can help up to 50% of patients,[8] but these do not appear to have reduced the number of women who ask gynaecologists for a surgical solution.

A number of ablative surgical techniques (transcervical resection of endometrium, TCRE, and laser ablation) are more effective than medical treatment in the management of menorrhagia[9,10] and the MISTLETOE study has helped to establish more firmly the role for these surgical techniques in treating menorrhagia by demonstrating their safety.[11] These first-generation endometrial ablation techniques have still been shown to have significant morbidity and, in the same study, two patients died as a direct consequence of the procedure (one from a combined loop excision with rollerball procedure and the other from loop excision alone). This study showed that 1.2% required emergency surgery and other intermediate complications ranged from 4% to 8%. Further details of these complications are well set out by Hodgson *et al.*[12] These techniques require considerable hysteroscopic skills with a relatively long learning curve. For the most part, they are carried out under general anaesthesia and, apart from the need to visualise the endometrium, there is the coexistent problem of excessive fluid absorption, which can cause anything from mild electrolyte disturbance to pulmonary oedema and encephalopathy.[13] For this reason, they tend to require the facilities of a main theatre and are therefore not ideal for a free-standing day surgery setting or outpatient use. Research has therefore continued into more effective and safer techniques that are easier to learn and have less morbidity but similar patient outcome satisfaction.

An ideal second-generation ablation technique (SEAT) should:

- constitute a complication-free surgical method of treating dysfunctional uterine bleeding with a short surgical learning curve and duration of treatment

- provide a high patient satisfaction rate and demonstrate a significant improvement in quality of life

- demonstrate significant changes in menorrhagia by menstrual scores or validated pictorial diary systems

- treat successfully the 'irregular cavity' due to fibroids

- perform the procedure in a non-acute day surgery setting or gynaecological investigations suite

- perform the majority of the procedures under local anaesthesia

- provide the patient with a rapid return to normal activities.

Microwave endometrial ablation (MEA) has been developed since 1992 as one of a number of SEATs that have been reported. It was developed at the University of Bath Microphysics department in conjunction with the Royal United Hospital department of Gynaecology and Medical Physics. Clinical trials started in October 1994 in Bath and, following a successful outcome,[14] proceeded to a multicentre trial at Southampton and Canterbury, which resulted in Medical Devices Agency (MDA) approval for safety.

The purpose of this chapter is to give the gynaecologist a working understanding of the physics of MEA, patient selection, preparation of the endometrium, surgical procedure, outcome assessment, clinical effectiveness and, finally, potential complications and safety.

THE PHYSICS OF MICROWAVE ENDOMETRIAL ABLATION

It is important for the gynaecologist to have a working knowledge of the principles of MEA. Patients more familiar with its domestic use can conjure up somewhat alarming scenarios of what might be happening to their uterus. All ablation techniques rely on the application of energy in order to destroy the tissue of the endometrium.

The microwave spectrum ranges from 1 GHz to 100 GHz. Figure 1 displays the other uses of the microwave spectrum, ranging from the use of mobile phones to microwave ovens and military and satellite imaging. The wavelength determines the depth of penetration of the microwaves. The commercial microwave oven at 2.5 GHz achieves a penetration of 20 mm using 750 watts. The chosen wavelength of MEA (9.2 GHz) gives a penetration of 3 mm at 22 watts, providing 3% of the power of a commercial microwave oven.

The actual depth of thermal necrosis was found to be 5–6 mm around the applicator's tip from initial *in vitro* tests.[12] This confirmed the initial assumption that, according to the electromagnetic theory, the depth of penetration was due to the high water content of endometrial tissue. Further tests demonstrated that the depth of cell enzyme inactivity was consistent with 5–6 mm (average 3.8 mm), with a further *circa* 1 mm zone of transitional cell necrosis to cell death.[12]

The microwave energy released from the tip causes the endometrium to heat rapidly while the applicator itself remains cool, albeit with some reabsorption of conducted heat into the applicator. The ideal temperature range of 70–80°C is constantly monitored on a real-time display. The precise depth of microwave penetration in terms of cell necrosis is 6 mm, similar to laser treatment, and other *in vitro* tests showed little heat conduction through the myometrium to the serosa. Uterine bloodflow is therefore not important, as with radio frequency ablation. Earlier experiences showing the microwave wave guide in egg white clearly demonstrate the precise distance of energy penetration.[12]

The microwave wave guide is a metal tube through which the energy passes. If this were air-filled, the diameter would have to be in excess of 20 mm and this would be too wide to pass through the cervix. A dielectric material therefore fills the wave guide, which therefore reduces the wavelength as it passes through, allowing 9.2 GHz to pass along an 8 mm wave guide. This dielectric material also acts as a 'heat sink', which is constantly monitored by the thermocouple at the tip.

The wave guide itself is covered in a fluoroplastic sheath in order to allow it to be autoclaved

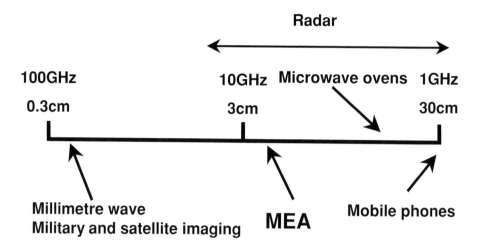

Figure 1 *Microwave spectrum; MEA = microwave endometrial ablation*

or chemically cleaned, and this has been shown to give good surgical 'feel' at the time of the procedure. The microwave wave guide or endometrial ablation applicator is a rigid structure with a graduated scale and a yellow band at 5 cm to warn the surgeon when the tip is reaching the endocervix. It is connected to a microwave generator by a cable while a second data cable and thermocouple connector provide the real-time temperature print-out. Within each applicator is a microchip that records the number of times and the patients with whom it has been used. Each applicator is used approximately 30 times before being returned to the manufacturer (Microsulis Plc, Denmead, Hants). For any individual treatment the applicator can be identified immediately, which is excellent for risk-management purposes.

PATIENT SELECTION

Patients should be suffering from intractable menorrhagia that has failed to respond to clinically effective medical treatments. They should have a current negative cervical smear and normal endometrial histology. For patients wishing to maintain their potential fertility this procedure is contraindicated and an intrauterine progestogen-releasing system such as Mirena® may be the treatment of choice.[15] The presence of fibroids does not exclude the patient from MEA. At the present time, most users offer MEA if the fibroids are less than 4 cm in diameter and are not protruding by more than 40% into the cavity. However, patients with bigger fibroids have been treated successfully. The above criteria can be achieved with an ultrasound scan and outpatient endometrial aspiration biopsy, e.g. Pipelle™ but, in the case of fibroids or any other concurrent abnormal bleeding, a hysteroscopy should be carried out prior to MEA treatment. Other special circumstances that ought to be considered include the acutely retroverted uterus, the fixed uterus, previous caesarean section, known connective tissue disorders and corticosteroid therapy. In my unit we continue to carry out pre-ablation scanning with particular reference to those patients with previous caesarean sections and measurement of the thickness of the lower segment.

PATIENT PREPARATION

The majority of patients undergoing MEA have their endometrium prepared either with a single injection of a gonadotrophin-releasing hormone (GnRH) such as goserelin 3.6 mg or with danazol 400 mg twice daily for four to six weeks. The beneficial effect of this priming of the endometrium in terms of thickness has been demonstrated by many workers. This brings the endometrial thickness well within the 5–6 mm depth of penetration of the microwaves. Few patients have been found to have inadequate preparation of the endometrium with this regimen, although compliance with danazol can be a problem. This is eliminated by the use of GnRH. There is no doubt that the hypo-oestrogenic effect of the latter does cause greater cervical resistance and the gynaecologist has to be aware that dilation following preparation is more difficult than that experienced at normal hysteroscopies. History of previous surgery to the cervix (e.g. large loop excision of the transformation zone – LLETZ – or cone biopsy) should also be considered and, in these cases, danazol is the preparation of choice.

In East Kent, primary care services undertake to deliver the endometrial primer, thus preventing the patient further visits to the main unit. Patients are written to and asked to visit their general practitioner five weeks prior to their date of admission. Patients should be warned that they will experience some symptoms of oestrogen deficiency (e.g. hot flushes and night sweats), which are short-lived. The MEA treatment is carried out in a free-standing day surgical unit with no facilities for overnight stay using a non-acute surgical unit. This prevents the problem of late cancellation due to emergencies.

THE PROCEDURE OF MICROWAVE ENDOMETRIAL ABLATION

Patients are admitted to the Menorrhagia Day Unit, where they undergo preoperative transvaginal scanning for endometrial thickness. A single dose of rectal diclofenac 100 mg is given preoperatively for analgesia.

The choice of anaesthesia is dictated by the inclusion criteria for local anaesthesia following thorough counselling:

- patient's choice

- obesity

- medical conditions that could complicate general anaesthesia (patients not conforming to the criteria of the American Society of Anesthesiologists).

We have found the addition of sedation to local anaesthesia to be exceedingly effective, and more than 80% of the patients currently treated undergo this regimen. Following the administration of midazolam 100 μg and fentanyl 5 mg, the patient undergoes a similar four quadrant local anaesthetic to that used for LLETZ. The patient also receives one dose of intravenous antibiotics (e.g. augmentin 1.25 mg).

THE SURGICAL TECHNIQUE

The patient is examined and prepared similar to a routine hysteroscopy. The distance from the ectocervix to the fundus is measured with the sound and checked against a metal rule. The cervix is then dilated to 9 mm and the canal length is again checked with a steel rule marked in millimetres. If there is any significant difference between the two measurements or if there is any doubt in the surgeon's mind at this point, then a hysteroscopy using CO_2 should be carried out

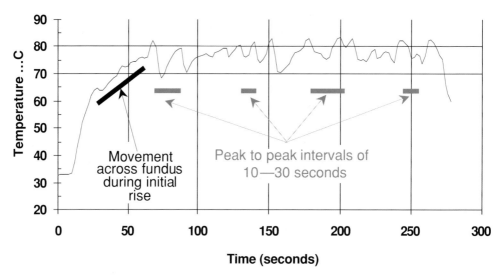

Figure 2 *Treatment temperature profile*

prior to MEA being attempted. Hysteroscopy with saline cannot be used if the operator still wishes to proceed with treatment, because of concerns as to the potential effect on microwave propagation. Some users routinely carry out hysteroscopy with CO_2 pretreatment and others rely on the use of ultrasound. Since this is probably the only major source of morbidity throughout the whole procedure, one cannot overemphasise the importance of the discipline of cervical dilatation coupled with the position of the uterus. If, however, there is no discrepancy then the MEA applicator is inserted into the uterus up to the fundus and the length on the wave guide should be consistent with the initial sounding (the operator will be asked this question on screen in order to continue). This triple measure rule is of fundamental importance to the safety of MEA.

The surgeon is now ready to initiate MEA via a foot pedal. In our unit an extra safety procedure has been instituted, which empowers the nurse overseeing the microwave generator not to proceed to the treatment screen until the triple measurement has been established. Following the start of treatment (once the probe has reached a temperature of 30°C) the temperature profile should show a fairly steep linear increase to 60°C (Figure 2). The recognition of this 'gate' to the experienced MEA user is a significant safety factor. As soon as 60°C is reached, the probe is moved from side to side across the fundus of the uterus, 'painting the endometrium'. Each movement will create a drop in temperature and the user should attempt to stay out of the temperature range (as indicated on the screen) as long as possible. This is important in order to achieve full treatment of the cornu and fundus.

The technique is quite different for the rest of the procedure. Once the user is unable to stay out of the temperature range (indicating that the fundal endometrium has been treated) a second and different technique is used for the remaining endometrium. The applicator is held in position and moved only once the temperature exceeds the upper limit. At this point, the applicator is moved to a different area, each time slowly withdrawing. Every time the tip comes into contact with untreated endometrium, the temperature falls and then rises again when treatment has finished. Experience will provide a smooth temperature profile and it is indeed one of the few gynaecological procedures where experience will lengthen the treatment rather than shorten it. Slow withdrawal of the applicator continues until the yellow warning band is seen, indicating that the tip of the applicator is coming towards the endocervix. As soon as all of the yellow band is visualised, the treatment should be stopped. In a patient with multiple caesarean section scars and a thin lower segment, it is advisable to stop the treatment immediately when the yellow band appears.

Users will notice occasionally that as the energy of the MEA increases there is a tendency for the applicator to be 'pushed' out of the cavity, causing a continuing drop in the recorded temperature. For this reason it is important for the surgeon to keep as close an eye as possible on both the treatment screen and the applicator. The temperature will return into the treatment zone as long as the probe is held steady. An occasional 'pop' might be heard, similar to that heard in a commercial microwave oven; this does not indicate any problem and slow withdrawal should continue. It is essential that the applicator is not at any time pushed into the uterus and, again, experience will lengthen this part of the procedure.

Once the applicator has been turned off and withdrawn, it should be realised that the tip is still cool. The cables are now disconnected once the appropriate treatment display has been achieved. The temperature profile is printed and added to the patient's notes. The duration of treatment (average three minutes) directly relates to the length of the uterus, the measurement of which has already been described.

Patients are discharged two hours following treatment with suitable analgesia. Only 5% of our patients require analgesia in excess of oral administration and either buscopan or pethidine is used intramuscularly. Patients are advised to expect vaginal discharge for up to three weeks following the procedure and occasional bleeding. Nurses in the unit record the pain scores at the time of discharge and routinely contact the patients the following day by telephone to check for immediate postoperative problems. An emergency contact line is also provided for the patients. For those patients undergoing local sedation anaesthesia, one should never underestimate the importance of supportive nursing staff, both in the theatre and in the recovery area, and this is one of the main reasons why these types of procedures are best carried out in dedicated units on a regular basis.

OUTCOME ASSESSMENT

Unfortunately, the outcome measures reported in trials concerning surgical treatment of menorrhagia are not uniform. Indeed, it must be remembered that menorrhagia is defined as a blood loss at each menstrual cycle of more than 80 ml[16] and a large proportion of women presenting with menorrhagia will be found to lose less than this when accurate blood measurements are carried out.[17]

Different methodologies have therefore been developed, first, in the assessment of menorrhagia and, second, in outcome measures related to patient satisfaction. A validated pictorial diary system has a reasonable correlation with actual menstrual loss.[18] Sharp et al.[12] produced a menstrual scoring system based on a range of specific symptoms. Other workers have used an assessment of satisfaction assessed by the patient.[19]

Finally, other workers have used an amenorrhoea/oligomenorrhoea/no change outcome assessment. However, since menorrhagia directly affects quality of life, most workers are using a measurement of this parameter as an appropriate outcome measure. Quality-of-life scores using the Short-Form Questionnaire (SF-36)[20,21] or the work of Shaw et al.[22] appear to provide a greater insight into the impact on patients' lives.

CLINICAL EFFECTIVENESS

The lack of appropriately designed prospective randomised trials measuring clinical effectiveness of new ablation procedures has made it difficult for the gynaecologist to make the appropriate choice for his patients.

Cooper et al.[23] carried out a randomised trial comparing MEA (129 patients) to TCRE (134 patients), based on what was then the gold standard in endometrial ablation. Only 23 patients were lost to follow-up, 116 completed follow-up for MEA at 12 months and 124 completed the follow-up for TCRE. A large majority of the procedures were carried out by two senior specialist registrars, although it is notable that they had carried out 50 TCRE procedures compared with only five MEA procedures before the trial started.

The results of this excellent trial were reported. Entry was based on subjective complaint of intolerable menstrual loss. The treatment groups had similar characteristics and irregular cavities with submucous fibroids were present in 32 women. The main difference between the two procedures was that the operating times for MEA were significantly shorter than those for TCRE. Two patients in the TCRE group were readmitted with abdominal and pelvic pain two weeks after the procedure and underwent hysterectomy for problems with bleeding; there was no such occurrence in the MEA group.

Both techniques led to a highly significant reduction in bleeding, and amenorrhoea rates in the region of 40% were obtained. More importantly, patients reported a high satisfaction rate of 90% in each group and were prepared to recommend it to others. A questionnaire on health-related quality of life (SF-36)[20,21] showed changes in all eight health scores after MEA (significant for six items; $P < 0.001$). Seven items showed significant improvements after TCRE ($P < 0.05–0.001$). It was concluded that on the basis of general health items, the improvements were significantly greater after MEA than after TCRE. Finally, it was noted that nine women in the MEA arm and 12 women in the TCRE arm had undergone further surgery in the form of hysterectomy.

Cooper et al.[24] concluded that MEA was as good as TCRE, based on what was then the gold standard of endometrial ablation, in respect of patient outcome and satisfaction. The procedure avoided the problems of primary haemorrhage and emergency hysterectomy and had a similar effect on quality-of-life scores, sexual function and improvement of dyspareunia, although MEA led to a significantly larger improvement in physical role limitation scores. Both techniques also demonstrated significant improvement in the ability to undertake leisure pursuits. They concluded that the main advantage of MEA over TCRE was in the operative technique, which was easy to learn and did not require hysteroscopic surgical skills, taking considerably less time then TCRE and appearing to be safe to use for outpatient management.

Hodgson et al.[12] reported further clinical experience. They reported on 43 women having completed three years of follow-up in a non-randomised trial. Using a menstrual score questionnaire preoperatively, the median menstrual score was 15. Ten women in this group were noted to have intramural fibroids but were not excluded.

This study confirms the effectiveness of MEA with a primary satisfaction rate at three years of 84% with a 33% amenorrhoea rate. They also reported that the learning curve for surgeons to be trained in this procedure was comparatively short and that the speed and simplicity of the procedure combined with local anaesthesia makes it ideal for high-risk patients suffering from menorrhagia.

This paper also included patients who were retreated. One patient was found to have a haematometra at transvaginal scanning but hysteroscopy and dilatation and curettage did not confirm this. She was successfully re-treated, with her menstrual score falling to three, and she remained satisfied. Other apparent failures included a patient who, despite having failed to improve initially with MEA, requested a repeat procedure and became amenorrhoeic. However, six months later her periods worsened with pain. She opted for a hysterectomy and the histology showed fibroids and diffuse adenomyosis. Residual secretory endometrium was present.

Two further papers by Milligan *et al.*[19,25] confirmed the clinical experience elsewhere. The first paper (part of the multicentre trial) showed a patient satisfaction rate of 87.5% and there was a significant reduction in the frequency of high menstrual scores at three months, compared with preoperative scores ($P < 0.001$). This group went on to investigate patients' experience in the first three months following MEA for menorrhagia and to assess the suitability of local anaesthesia versus general anaesthesia. A cross-sectional questionnaire survey of 173 patients at three months after treatment of MEA was carried out between September 1997 and December 1999. All patients were treated in a free-standing day hospital equipped with a minor operating theatre. Of the 173 women treated (aged 26 years to 54 years), 87.3% returned their questionnaires, 98 (57%) were treated using general anaesthesia (GA) and 63 (43%) underwent local anaesthetic with sedation (LA). In 71%, the postoperative pain was either absent or mild and only 5% had pain requiring a single dose of opiate analgesia. Both the GA and LA groups had similar results and 70% of all patients showed a return to normal daily activity within one week and 95% by three weeks.

Commonly reported symptoms in the immediate postoperative period were abdominal pain (75%), vaginal discharge (87%), vaginal bleeding (74%) and occasional vaginal dryness (21%). However, these symptoms were mild and did not require medical intervention. More importantly, there was no requirement for either blood transfusion or hysterectomy within the first three months of treatment. The paper concluded that MEA was well tolerated by patients, and the adverse effects were minor without requiring medical intervention. In terms of the patient's experience, LA is comparable to GA and obviously has potential benefits.

Our experience of 320 patients treated at the menorrhagia day unit in Herne Bay has shown a consistent patient satisfaction over the first three years in the region of 95% with amenorrhoea rates above 40% (Figure 3). The overall hysterectomy rate during this time was 5% and more than

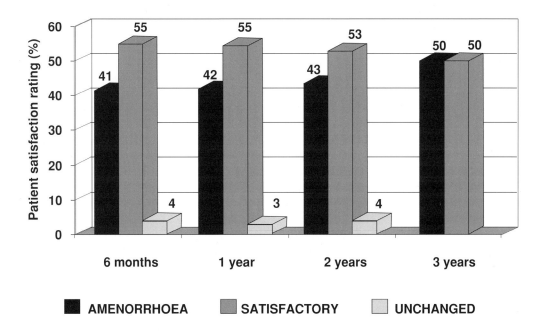

Figure 3 *Menstrual results from 320 patients treated at the menorrhagia day unit in Herne Bay, Kent*

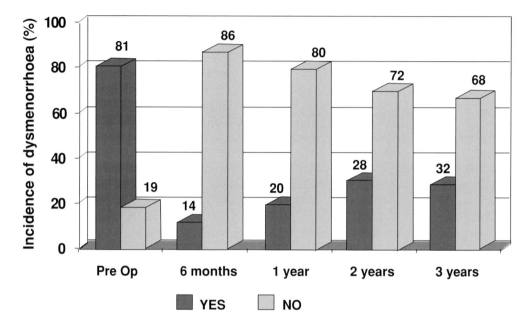

Figure 4 *Incidence of dysmenorrhoea among 320 patients treated at the menorrhagia day unit in Herne Bay, Kent*

half of this patients had surgery primarily for pelvic pain rather than menorrhagia. Indeed, breakdown of the 16 patients undergoing hysterectomy following MEA show that two were carried out following patient request due to a general 'unwell' feeling. A further five were carried out where the primary reason was persistent dysmenorrhoea and pelvic pain, leaving only nine patients undergoing hysterectomy for persistent intractable menorrhagia. Histological examination showed these patients to have persistent or regenerative endometrium near the endocervix or in the fundal area and is similar to the experience reported by Tulandi *et al.*[22] As with other groups, patients have been treated a second time with a successful outcome in terms of menstrual scores.

We used a different quality-of-life score, developed by Shaw *et al.*[23], and this showed a significant improvement at six months when compared with preoperative scores. Many patients have independently reported a feeling of improved wellbeing.

DYSMENORRHOEA

As with other ablative techniques, there was a noticeable reduction in the incidence of dysmenorrhoea (Figure 4). In our experience, the preoperative incidence of dysmenorrhoea (83%) was greatly reduced when reviewed at six months (18%). Figure 4 also demonstrates the slow increase in the incidence of dysmenorrhoea over the three-year period of audit, reaching a level of 38%, which is still 50% less than the preoperative incidence. The cause for this remains unexplained at present. These figures exclude the patients undergoing hysterectomy for dysmenorrhoea and pelvic pain. Other users have reported the occasional case of haematometra, although we have not experienced it at our menorrhagia day unit. Two patients undergoing hysteroscopy prior to the possibility of retreatment failed to have their endometrial cavity examined and a provisional diagnosis of Asherman syndrome was made.

LONG-TERM MINOR COMPLICATIONS

We have had patients presenting with vaginal bleeding after more than one year of amenorrhoea following treatment with MEA. Such patients should be investigated in a similar way to other patients presenting with possible abnormal bleeding from the endometrium, with a combination of ultrasound, endometrial biopsy and hysteroscopy. On the relatively few tests carried out, residual endometrium appears to be more accurately determined by magnetic resonance imaging (MRI) and appears to be better than a routine transvaginal scan, which can still demonstrate endometrial thickness in spite of amenorrhoea, cervical stenosis having been excluded. We have yet to find abnormal uterine pathology. If the investigator is unable to obtain evidence of endometrial pathology, a hysterectomy should be considered. Patients requesting hormone replacement therapy at a later date should be advised of the need for progesterone protection of the endometrium and we also prefer to use continuous combined preparations for these patients because of its well-established safety in endometrial pathology.

SCHEDULING

In order to avoid the need for endometrial priming, the possibility of scheduling treatment on and around the seventh day of the cycle has been attempted.[26] Initial results suggest that patient satisfaction is not affected and that the clinical outcomes are similar. However, the author prefers to continue with endometrial priming, particularly within the confines of the National Health Service. As long as the patients are treated in a unit not affected by acute emergencies, endometrial priming affords the ability to be cost-effective and, coupled with local sedation, results in few patients ever being cancelled. Sharp *et al.*[27] have also developed a technique of endometrial aspiration prior to treatment without the need for endometrial priming. Initial results suggest that patient satisfaction is unaffected but the amenorrhoea rate is slightly reduced.

SAFETY

The safety of the procedure was assessed by Parkin[28] for the MEA Users Group 2000, who looked at the complication data from a prospective series of 1400 cases. This showed that there had been only four blunt perforations (2.6/1000).

Only one of these was caused by insertion of the MEA probe, and this was in a retroverted uterus where dilatation was difficult. This was easily recognised, since it was inserted at a longer distance than the original sounding. It was confirmed by hysteroscopy and the procedure was abandoned. Two further perforations occurred during cervical dilation, one of which was recognised at a routine pretreatment hysteroscopy. In a further case, a false passage was suspected during a difficult dilatation and after ultrasound scanning the procedure was abandoned.

However, there was one major complication in the series, which resulted in visceral damage in a woman with a history of two lower segment caesarean sections who underwent MEA under general anaesthesia. There was no discrepancy in the measurements of the cavity length and a scan appeared to show that the probe was within the uterus. MEA was carried out, although it was noticed in retrospect that the time taken to reach the treatment temperature was prolonged. She was admitted the following day with increasing abdominal pain. At laparotomy the anterior uterine surface was blanched, as was the uterocervical fold; there was no uterine perforation. However, a small defect was found in the bowel, a small bowel resection and primary anastomosis were carried out, and she made a satisfactory recovery. This gives an overall visceral damage rate of 0.7/1000, which is similar to that expected with other hysteroscopic methods.

Parkin concluded that MEA is at least as safe as hysteroscopic methods with regard to bowel damage and it completely avoids the risk of excessive fluid absorption. There were no cases of primary haemorrhage leading to emergency hysterectomy and only a single uterine perforation with the probe was reported.

CONCLUSION

On reviewing the ideal criteria for a SEAT, MEA appears to come close to satisfying nearly all of the conditions. To date, no complication-free surgical method of ablation, or indeed any other surgical technique for the treatment of dysfunctional uterine bleeding, has been either developed or reported.

All such procedures carry the risk of uterine perforation and it is important for the gynaecologist to be particularly careful in the accurate measurement of uterine length. Steel rulers should be a mandatory piece of equipment in the hysteroscopy tray and the user should not rely on measurements taken from old irregular uterine sounds. In spite of this, uterine perforation will never be totally eliminated but it should be diagnosed prior to the procedure and before any form of energy is applied to the endometrium. Whether hysteroscopy should be routine prior to the treatment has yet to be established.

A major advance with MEA is the absence of perioperative emergency hysterectomy for haemorrhage, thus making it safe for 'low-tech' surgical areas or free-standing surgical units. The author feels that the presence of an anaesthetist is still essential and prefers local sedation techniques to local anaesthesia on its own. Its other main advantage over TCRE/rollerball techniques is the short learning curve required for the experienced gynaecologist and the lack of increased morbidity during this learning phase. Being a non-hysteroscopic method of ablation, MEA removes any risk of excessive fluid absorption and subsequent pulmonary oedema.

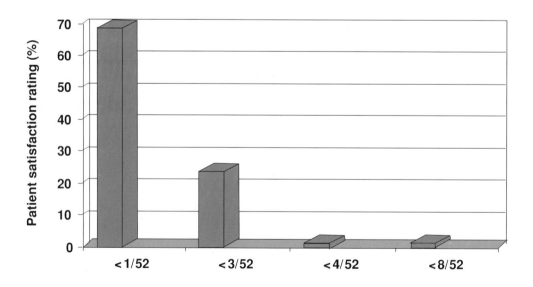

Figure 5 *Return to normal activities following microwave endometrial ablation; results from 320 patients treated at the memorrhagia day unit in Herne Bay, Kent*

With an average treatment length of three minutes (related to the length of the uterus), MEA provides the opportunity of treating a considerable number of patients at a time and we are able to treat six to eight patients in an afternoon surgical session. With the hysterectomy rate for failed treatments being so low (5%), there should be a subsequent reduction in the need for main theatre time for the surgical treatment of menorrhagia.

MEA provides a high patient satisfaction rate, whether judged by menorrhagia scores, patient satisfaction surveys or quality-of-life scores. It is also associated with a significant improvement in the quality of life and can provide the patient with a rapid return to normal activities (71%) within seven days (Figure 5). The ability to use the technique under local sedation broadens the patient selection to those who are medically unfit for major surgery; it also enables patients to be treated in relatively simple surgical settings, which would not be suitable for acute surgery and thus not vulnerable to last minute cancellations due to emergencies.

The ability to treat irregular uterine cavities with or without fibroids does not exclude a relatively large group of patients from this type of treatment. Cavities of up to 100 mm have been successfully treated and, indeed, larger ones have also been treated with relative success. The technique therefore provides a successful minimal invasive surgical treatment for the treatment of menorrhagia. It has been demonstrated to be cost-effective and in randomised controlled trials to be as clinically effective as TCRE, the present gold standard. It should therefore become an essential part of the hysteroscopic surgeon's armamentarium. The techniques of TCRE, however, should still be retained in the hands of surgeons with special skills to deal with those few patients that fall outside the criteria for MEA.

References

1   Bradlow J, Coulter A, Brooks P. *Patterns of Referral*. Oxford: Oxford Health Services Research Unit; 1992.

2   Coulter A, Bradlow J, Agass M, Martin-Bates C, Tulloch A. Outcomes of referrals to gynaecology outpatients clinics for menstrual problems: an audit of general practice records. *Br J Obstet Gynaecol* 1991;98:789–96.

3   Kuh D, Stirling S. Socio-economic variation in admission for diseases of the female genital system and breast in a national cohort aged 15-43. *BMJ* 1995;311:840–3.

4   Coulter A, McPherson K, Vessey M. Do British women undergo too many or too few hysterectomies? *Soc Sci Med* 1998;27: 987–94.

5   Vessey MP, Villard-Mackintosh L, McPherson K, Coulter A, Yeates D. The epidemiology of hysterectomy: findings in a large cohort study. *Br J Obstet Gynaecol* 1992;99:402–7.

6   Lalonde A. Evaluation of surgical options in menorrhagia. *Br J Obstet Gynaecol* 1994;101 Suppl:8–14.

7   Harkki-Siren P, Sjoberg J. Evaluation and the learning curve of the first one hundred laparoscopic hysterectomies. *Acta Obstet Gynecol Scand* 1995;74:638–41.

8   Coulter A, Kelland J, Peto V, Rees MC. Treating menorhaggia in primary care. An overview of drug trials and a survey of prescribing practice. *Int J Technol Assess Health Care* 1995;11:456–71.

9   Cooper KG, Parkin DE, Garratt AM, Grant AM. A randomised comparison of medical versus hysteroscopic management in women consulting a gynaecologist for treatment of heavy menstrual loss. *Br J Obstet Gynaecol* 1997;104:1360–6.

10   Coulter A, Peto V, Jenkinson C. Quality of life and patient satisfaction following treatment

for menorrhagia. *Fam Pract* 1994;11: 394–401.

11   Overton C, Hargreaves J, Maresh M. A national survey of the complications of endometrial destruction for menstrual disorders: the MISTLETOE study. Minimally Invasive Surgical Techniques-Laser, Endothermal or Endoresection. *Br J Obstet Gynaecol* 1997;104:1351–9.

12   Hodgson DA, Feldberg IB, Sharp N, Cronin N, Evans M, Hirschowitz L. Microwave endometrial ablation: development, clinical trials and outcomes at three years. *Br J Obstet Gynaecol* 1999;106:684–94.

13   Allen I, Arieff AI, Ayus JC. Endometrial ablation complicated by fatal hyponatraemic encephalopathy. *JAMA* 1993;270:1230–2.

14   Sharp NC, Cronin N, Feldberg I, Evans M, Hodgson DA, Ellis S. Microwaves for menorrhagia: a new fast technique for endometrial ablation. *Lancet* 1995;346:1003–4.

15   Crosignani PG, Vercellini P, Mosconi P, Oldani S, Cortesi I, De Giorgi O. Levonorgestrel releasing intrauterine device versus hysteroscopic endometrial resection in the treatment of dysfunctional uterine bleeding. *Obstet Gynecol* 1997;90:257–63.

16   Hallberg L, Hogdahl AM, Nilsson L, Rybo G. Menstrual blood loss – a population study. Variation at different ages and attempts to define normality. *Acta Obstet Gynecol Scand* 1966;45:320–51.

17   Chimbira TH, Anderson ABM, Turnbull AC. Relation between measured menstrual blood loss and patient's subjective assessment of loss, duration of bleeding, number of sanitary towels used, uterine weight and endometrial surface area. *Br J Obstet Gynaecol* 1980;87:603–9.

18   Higham JM, O'Brien PMS, Shaw RW. Assessment of menstrual blood loss using a pictorial chart. *Br J Obstet Gynaecol* 1990;9:734–9.

19   Milligan MP, Etokowo GA. Microwave endometrial ablation for menorrhagia. *J Obstet Gynaecol* 1999;19:496–9.

20   Ware JE Jr, Sherbourne CD. The MOS 36-item short-form healthy survey (SF-36) – I: conceptual framework and item selection. *Med Care* 1992;30:473–83.

21   Ware JE. Measuring patients' views: the optimum outcome measure. *BMJ* 1993;306:1429–30.

22   Tulandi T, Felemban A. Hysteroscopic appearance of the uterine cavity before and after microwave endometrial ablation. *Journal of the American Association of Gynecologic Laparoscopists* 2001;8:83–6.

23   Shaw RW, Brickley MR, Evans L, Edwards MJ. Perceptions of women on the impact of menorragia on their health, using multi-attribute utility assessment. *Br J Obstet Gynaecol* 1998;105:1155–9.

24   Cooper KG, Bain C, Parkin DE. Comparison of microwave endometrial ablation and transcervical resection of the endometrium for treatment of heavy menstrual loss: a randomised trial. *Lancet* 1999;354:1859–63.

25   Milligan MP, Etokowo GA, Kanumuru S, Mannifold N. Microwave endometrial ablation: patients' views in the first three months following treatment. *J Obstet Gynecol* 2002;2:201–4.

26   A Alfrestein, personal communication.

27   N Sharp, personal communication.

28   Parkin DE for the MEA™ Users' Group. Microwave endometrial ablation (MEA™): a safe technique? Complication data from a prospective series of 1400 cases. *Gynaecological Endoscopy* 2000;9:385–8.

26

Hair today: the modern management of hirsutism

Karl S Oláh

INTRODUCTION

The portrayal of 'femininity' by most media sources is an ideal to which few women can aspire. The ideal woman is slim and certainly not hirsute. With this in mind, the psychological distress caused by the onset of hirsutism must be immense.[1-3] Although the problem is not new, the degree of hirsutism that is tolerated by women before they consult their doctor is likely to be much smaller today. In addition, there is a large racial variation in the degree of hirsutism, and in the past a marked degree of hirsutism was largely ignored by some racial groups. However, with the adoption of westernised culture by second- and third-generation immigrants, these women may also indicate a desire to reduce their degree of hirsutism.

Hirsutism is not a disease but, rather, a cutaneous manifestation of hyperandrogenism. Polycystic ovary syndrome (PCOS) is a cause of hyperandrogenism in women and, since other features of this syndrome include menstrual disturbance and infertility, hirsutism frequently presents to gynaecologists. Although the most common causes of hirsutism are 'idiopathic' and secondary to chronic anovulation with PCOS, an increase in the production of androgens from the adrenal gland and ovary must be considered in order to exclude such diseases as Cushing syndrome, congenital adrenal hyperplasia (CAH) and adrenal or ovarian tumours.

THE HAIR-GROWTH CYCLE

Hair follicles are present over all of the body except the lips, soles of the feet and palms of the hands.[4,5] In animals, during the process of moulting, the individual hair follicles go through a cyclical process of growth, degeneration and regeneration in a more or less synchronous manner. This same hair cycle apparently continued in higher mammals through evolution, but in humans, it has been replaced by a more asynchronous or mosaic pattern. The hair cycle (Figure 1) consists of an active phase (anagen), during which growth occurs, followed by a short transition phase (catagen) and, finally, a resting phase (telogen).[6] The more prolonged the growth phase, the longer the hair. An understanding of the hair cycle is necessary to optimise treatment of hirsutism.

The duration of anagen varies at different sites and is influenced by hormonal and environmental factors. Oestrogen and thyroxine change the duration of the hair-growth cycle by altering the length of the telogen/anagen phase. Oestrogen shortens the resting phase and thyroid hormones lengthen it.[7] Women with untreated Turner syndrome have sparse body hair that increases during oestrogen replacement. This effect is also demonstrated by the high oestrogen state of pregnancy. In the normal physiological state, 85% of scalp hair is in the anagen phase. In the second and third trimesters of pregnancy, this figure exceeds 90%. The situation creates a heavier than normal growth of scalp hair in the latter part of pregnancy, followed by a noticeable shedding

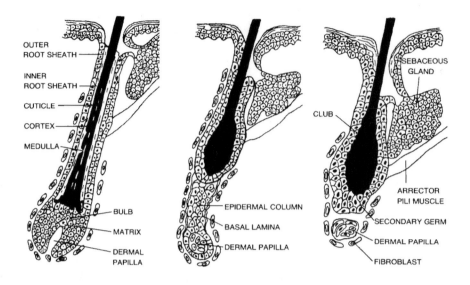

Figure 1 *The hair cycle*

of hair in the first three months postpartum when the normal physiological hormonal state is re-established.[8]

Androgens lengthen the growth phase at the expense of the resting phase. Androgens also stimulate follicles to promote the conversion of vellus hair, which is fine and lightly pigmented, to terminal hair, which is coarse and darkly pigmented. Non-sexual terminal hair occurs in both men and women in the scalp, eyebrows and eyelashes. During puberty in both sexes, vellus hair is converted to terminal hair in the axillae, lower legs, arms and lower pubic triangle (ambosexual hair). In adult men, androgens cause terminal hair growth in other areas such as the upper lip, chin and intergluteal region. In women, male-pattern hair growth occurs under the influence of excessive amounts of androgens. Hirsutism is diagnosed when there is increased growth of terminal hair in a male pattern of distribution. Although androgens increase the growth rate of hair on the trunk, they play an instrumental role in the balding of susceptible men, and women exposed to androgenic stimuli. Experimental evidence indicates that the uptake, 5-α reduction and metabolism of testosterone are increased in the scalp hair follicles of balding men compared with non-balding controls.[9]

ANDROGEN SECRETION

Hirsutism results from an excess of circulating androgens, an increase in the sensitivity of hair follicles to normal androgen concentrations or a combination of these factors.[10,11] In women, androgens are secreted both by the ovaries and by the adrenal glands and also arise from peripheral conversion of androstenedione and dehydroepiandrosterone (DHEA). The major androgens of biological importance are testosterone and its metabolite dihydrotestosterone (DHT); this metabolite is the more potent and is produced in the skin by conversion of testosterone by the enzyme 5-α reductase. Ovarian secretion of testosterone is stimulated by luteinising hormone (LH). Testosterone does not control LH secretion, so there is no long-loop inhibitory feedback mechanism and excess ovarian production can readily occur. Adrenal androgen secretion is stimulated by adrenocorticotrophin (ACTH) release but, in an analogous manner, androgens do not control ACTH secretion. Testosterone circulates bound predominantly to sex hormone binding globulin (SHBG), which is produced by the liver. It is the free, unbound testosterone that is biologically active.

ANDROGEN PRODUCTION: THE OVARIAN COMPARTMENT

Polycystic ovarian syndrome

The classic description of women with this syndrome is well-known. However, PCOS may present in a variety of women, and it is not essential for the sufferer to be obese or hirsute. Enlarged polycystic ovaries (Figure 2 – Plate 13) are a feature, although it is not certain where the pathology originates. A heterogeneous clinical disorder, PCOS has an unclear pathophysiology. Although it is difficult to find agreement on a common definition, PCOS is characterised by chronic anovulation with evidence of hyperandrogenaemia, which is usually perimenarchal in onset. Furthermore, in any patient with chronic anovulation, hirsutism may be progressive. Patients with late-onset CAH can be clinically indistinguishable from patients with PCOS.[12] Laboratory findings in patients with PCOS include high serum LH levels with normal or low follicle-stimulating hormone (FSH) concentrations on day three of the cycle, resulting in elevated LH:FSH ratios. In addition, testosterone, androstenedione and DHEA all may be mildly elevated.[13] Classically, testosterone concentrations in patients with PCOS are not usually greater than 200 ng/dl (Table 1). Other endocrine abnormalities described in patients with PCOS include hyperinsulinaemia, altered oestrone to oestradiol ratios, abnormalities in LH pulse patterns and elevated prolactin levels. A subset of PCOS characterised by hirsutism, hyperandrogenism (HA), insulin resistance (IR) and acanthosis nigricans (AN) has been termed the HAIR-AN syndrome.[14] However, determination of levels of 17-hydroxyprogesterone will aid in excluding 21-hydroxylase deficiency that is similar clinically to PCOS, and the determination of dehydroepiandrosterone sulphate (DHEAS) and testosterone may be useful in planning an ovulation induction regimen in patients with PCOS.[15]

Hyperthecosis

This histological diagnosis is characterised by ovarian stromal hyperplasia and an excess of testosterone production from luteinised theca cells. In contrast to typical patients with PCOS, signs of virilisation are more common, and testosterone levels may exceed 150–200 ng/dl. In addition, levels of LH and FSH are either normal or lower than in normal women.

Table 1 *Levels of hormones generally associated with various clinical conditions causing hirsutism*

	Testosterone	DHEAS	17-OH Progesterone
Mildly elevated	PCOS CAH Idiopathic	PCOS CAH Idiopathic	21-OH deficiency 11β-OH deficiency 3β-HSD deficiency
Markedly elevated	Ovarian tumour Adrenal tumour Hyperthecosis	Adrenal adenoma Adrenal carcinoma Phaeochromocytoma	21-OH deficiency

CAH = congenital adrenal hyperplasia; DHEAS = dehydroepiandrosterone sulphate; HSD = hydroxysteroid dehydrogenase; OH = hydroxylase; PCOS = polycystic ovary syndrome

Ovarian tumours

Ovarian neoplasms are capable of excess ovarian androgen production, including non-hormonally active neoplasms such as primary ovarian epithelial tumours (Figure 3 – Plate 13). It is believed that these non-hormone-secreting tumours cause androgen production by stimulation of adjacent theca and stromal tissues. Other rare ovarian tumours can produce sex steroids directly and include oestrogen and/or androgen production by sex cord stromal tumours, including granulosa theca cell and Sertoli–Leydig cell (androblastoma), the hilar and lipoid cell tumours and gonadoblastomas.

It has been suggested that ovarian androgen-secreting tumours are associated with serum total testosterone concentrations greater than 200 ng/dl. However, some ovarian neoplasms have been found to have levels below 200 ng/dl and, in addition, patients with levels higher than 200 ng/dl may have benign ovarian disease.[16] In those patients with elevated testosterone, the ovaries often can be imaged satisfactorily by transvaginal ultrasonography and the adrenal glands with computed tomography or magnetic resonance imaging (MRI). In cases where the source of the hyperandrogenaemia is unclear and the index of suspicion for neoplasm remains high, selective venous catheterisation may be helpful.[17] Although the use of gonadotrophin-releasing hormone (GnRH) agonists as a probe for determining an ovarian versus adrenal source of androgens appears useful, this approach cannot discriminate a benign from a malignant ovarian testosterone-secreting tumour. The GnRH agonists have been reported to decrease testosterone levels in a patient with a Leydig cell tumour.[18]

ANDROGEN PRODUCTION: THE ADRENAL COMPARTMENT

Cushing syndrome

Cushing's disease (hypercortisolism secondary to pituitary adrenocorticotrophic hormone, ACTH-secreting adenoma) and Cushing syndrome (hypercortisolism from a pituitary-independent source) are uncommon final diagnoses in a patient with hirsutism. However, the morbidity and mortality associated with untreated cases warrants evaluation in patients with the clinical stigmas. An appropriate screening test is a 24-hour urine analysis for free cortisol or an overnight dexamethasone-suppression test. In patients with documented hypercortisolism, a combination of endocrine and radiological evaluation can distinguish pituitary-dependent from nonpituitary-dependent disease.[19] Endocrine evaluation includes measurement of basal ACTH, measurement of ACTH after corticotrophin-releasing hormone (CRH) administration if available, and formal low- and high-dose dexamethasone-suppression testing. In pituitary Cushing's disease and ectopic ACTH production, ACTH measurements will be normal or elevated, whereas ACTH will be low or undetectable in adrenal neoplasms and micronodular disease. Administration of CRH will give a positive response in pituitary Cushing's, and high-dose dexamethasone (2 mg every six hours for 48 hours) will show a greater than 50% suppression of urinary 17-hydroxycortosteroids in these patients. In patients with pituitary Cushing's, computed tomography and MRI of the sella can aid in localisation of the ACTH-secreting pituitary microadenoma. In patients with an adrenal source of hypercortisolism, ACTH will be low or undetectable, and there will be no significant response to CRH or dexamethasone suppression.

Hyperprolactinaemia

DHEAS levels are elevated in a subset of patients with mild hyperprolactinaemia. Furthermore, treatment with bromocriptine results in a decrease in both DHEAS and prolactin levels. Although the mechanism of hyperandrogenaemia in hyperprolactinaemic patients is not clear and many do not have hirsutism, in associated cases measurement of serum prolactin is indicated.

variations may occur in association with PCOS and an elevated morning basal follicular phase serum 17-hydroxyprogesterone concentration warrants further endocrine investigation.[1]

Pelvic ultrasound – transvaginal or transabdominal – not only allows ovarian size and morphology to be assessed, but permits measurement of the endometrial thickness, which is of particular significance in the amenorrhoeic woman at risk of hyperplasia. Polycystic ovaries are commonly diagnosed on the basis of stromal thickening, together with ten or more cysts per ovary, usually arranged in a 'necklace' around the periphery.[30] The overall dimensions of the ovary are increased (> 5 ml), although polycystic ovaries of normal size may be found, particularly during treatment with the combined oral contraceptive pill and in women with hypogonadotrophism. Further diagnostic imaging is essential when a neoplastic cause is suspected and may include spiral computerised tomography or MRI of the adrenal glands.

MANAGEMENT

Patients need a realistic idea of what to expect. The goal of therapy is to decrease the rate of hair growth or, practically speaking, decrease the frequency of the need for physical removal of undesired hair. Patients must be told that mechanical means of hair removal will be required for hair already present despite successful medical therapy. Only hair responsive to sex hormones will be affected by medical therapy. This includes hair on the face, chest, abdomen and upper thighs. Hair around the nipples on the arms, back and lower limbs is unresponsive to medical therapy. Hair growth increases during the summer months, which may help explain the apparent decreased therapeutic benefit during this time. A period of at least six months is necessary to judge the success of medical therapy. Discontinuation of treatment usually is associated with the return of symptoms. Patients should be told that most medications used to treat hirsutism cannot be taken during pregnancy, making simultaneous treatment for infertility and hirsutism difficult. The adverse effects of therapy should be explained and used to individualise therapeutic selection.

Cosmetic measures and indirect treatment

Cosmetic measures play an important role in the management of hirsutism. In milder cases, they usually represent the mainstay of treatment.

Bleaching

Bleaching removes the hair pigment. The active ingredient in most preparations is hydrogen peroxide, ideally in a 6% solution. This is often combined with ammonia. The hydrogen peroxide will bleach, soften and oxidise the hair. Disadvantages include skin irritation, hair discoloration and lack of effectiveness.[31] Several commercial preparations are available that are relatively inexpensive and easy to use. Bleaching is often used in conjunction with other methods; for example, patients will bleach the hair while it is growing to a length adequate for waxing.

Depilation

Shaving is effective and does not change the quality, quantity or texture of hair.[32] There is a significant initial resistance in women towards shaving. This resistance may be due to shaving being perceived as unfeminine and causing increased hair coarseness and growth. However, once these concerns are addressed, shaving is a popular choice of treatment. In a large survey of women using physical methods of hair removal, one-third shaved, one-third used electrolysis and one-third used nothing or other methods.[31] Shaving can improve electrolysis results. Disadvantages include need to shave daily, skin irritation, cuts and beard stubble. Cosmetics are useful in disguising beard stubble. Chemical depilatories break down and dissolve hair by hydrolysing disulfide bonds.[31] The hair shaft contains much more of the disulfide-containing amino acid cysteine than the keratin found in the epidermis. A major disadvantage is skin irritation. As few as 1–4% of women can tolerate depilatories on their face.

Epilation

Plucking is used for areas where little hair is present, such as the eyebrows and nipples. Disadvantages include pain, which some people cannot tolerate, and skin irritation. Post-inflammatory pigmentation, folliculitis, ingrown hairs and scarring can occur. Repeated plucking often damages the hair follicle and can make subsequent electrolysis difficult. Waxing is a grouped even method of plucking. The results of waxing last longer (up to six weeks) than shaving or depilatory creams because the hairs are plucked out from under the skin surface.[31] Patients often feel waxing makes hair become finer. This perceived effect is secondary to the growth of fine hairs in anagen phase that were just below the skin surface during waxing. Disadvantages of waxing include considerable discomfort, expense, time required, irritation, folliculitis and possible thermal burn from applying the wax when too hot.

Electrolysis

Electrolysis is the only form of permanent hair removal. Treatment involves inserting a needle into the hair follicle, using current to destroy the follicle, removing the needle and using a forceps to remove the hair.[33] Hair regrowth rates are variable and range from 15–50%. The drawbacks of electrolysis include pain, scarring, pigmentation, cost and frequent visits for electrolysis. Herpes simplex may be reactivated by electrolysis. Patients at high risk for bacterial endocarditis and those with artificial joints should receive prophylactic antibiotics. Initiating medical therapy before electrolysis will decrease the frequency of visits.

Laser therapy has been known to induce a prolonged telogen phase and delay hair growth.[34] It may offer an alternative method for permanent hair removal but at present is an expensive option and its role remains to be defined.

Weight loss

Weight reduction in obese hirsute women may correct gonadotrophin and sex steroid secretion, hyperinsulinaemia and insulin resistance. These changes improve menstrual patterns, decrease hirsutism and enhance the efficacy of other medical therapies while improving the patient's overall health. Successful weight reduction usually requires professional counselling and should be directed at permanent dietary changes for lasting benefits.

Metformin

Preliminary evidence suggests that, in lean or overweight women with PCOS, metformin (1500–1700 mg daily) reduces serum insulin and testosterone concentrations and may improve menstrual regularity and, when used in conjunction with a hypocalorific diet in obese women, may also reduce weight and hirsutism.[35,36]

Orlistat

Orlistat (Xenical®, Roche) has been introduced to aid weight loss in women motivated to diet. The dietary absorption of fat is reduced but, where fat intake is high, severe gastrointestinal adverse effects may ensue.

Acupuncture

Many patients are experimenting with acupuncture as an alternative to standard therapies. In an uncontrolled clinical trial, acupuncture decreased density and length of hair in ectopic hypertrichosis and decreased plasma testosterone, urinary 17-hydroxycorticosteroid and 17-hydroxycorticosterone concentrations.[37] Twenty women were treated with two courses of therapy; each course consisted of 15 20-minute sessions given every other day. Plasma testosterone concentrations decreased 70% ($P < 0.001$), falling into the normal range. There was a trend towards resumption of regular menses and ovulation in those women with irregular menses.

Specific pharmacological treatment

Pharmacological intervention slows the growth of new hair but does not lead to loss of established hair. It is a preventive measure and is thus most effective when initiated in the younger patient and combined with cosmetic measures. Most therapies fall into two major categories. One group of drugs acts by suppressing androgen production from either the ovaries or the adrenal glands. The other group acts peripherally to reduce the effect of androgens on the skin. The selection of a pharmacological agent depends on the severity of the hirsutism, patient preference and the need to treat associated conditions such as hypertension or oligomenorrhoea. The latter will require correction either because of the development of endometrial hyperplasia or because induction of ovulation is needed to treat infertility. The dosage of drugs used to treat hirsutism should be the lowest that is effective, although high doses of medication may be required initially to induce remission of hair growth.

SUPPRESSION OF OVARIAN ANDROGEN PRODUCTION

Progestins

Synthetic progestins alone were used to treat hirsutism with moderate success. Medroxyprogesterone acetate (MPA) and megestrol are weak anti-androgens and they suppress gonadotrophin secretion mildly. By decreasing testosterone production, MPA reduces free testosterone concentrations despite lower SHBG levels.[38] It is administered continuously at doses of 20–40 mg per day orally or 150 mg intramuscularly every six weeks to three months in the depot form. A few cases of hirsutism were reported after MPA therapy. Treatment must be discontinued if the patient becomes pregnant because sexual ambiguity of male and female fetuses has occurred during therapy. The drug may be associated with disorders of thrombosis, fluid retention, changes in body weight, hepatic dysfunction, depression and other adverse effects associated with progestins.

Oral contraceptives

The oral contraceptive pill is the drug of first choice for most women and has been shown to be effective in the treatment of hirsutism. It suppresses LH secretion and hence LH-mediated androgen secretion by the ovary. The oestrogen component increases the concentration of SHBG by slowing its clearance rate and so decreases the amount of free testosterone available.[39] The progestogen component of the contraceptive pill also has therapeutic benefit because it confers cycle control and so prevents endometrial hyperplasia. Together with oestrogen, it provides contraception, an essential requirement when anti-androgen medication is administered. Dianette® (Schering Health) is an oral contraceptive pill that contains the progestogen cyproterone acetate, which has specific anti-androgen activity. It has been licensed for the treatment of acne but has also been shown to be beneficial in the treatment of hirsutism.[1] Adverse effects of the pill include weight gain, nausea, emotional lability and breast tenderness.[40] A past history of venous thrombosis constitutes an absolute contraindication to the oral contraceptive pill and its use is cautioned in those with family history of spontaneous thrombosis. Unfortunately, many women with hirsutism caused by PCOS are obese, which in itself increases the risk of a thrombotic event. Other features of the PCOS may form relative contraindications to the use of the oral contraceptive oral pill. Hypertension is a common accompaniment to the syndrome and when severe constitutes an absolute contraindication. Synthetic oestrogen should be avoided in the woman with diabetes mellitus in the presence of microvascular complications.

Gonadotrophin-releasing hormone

GnRH agonists initially stimulate the secretion of gonadotrophins but with continuous administration, desensitisation of GnRH receptors on the gonadotropes occurs. Consequently, gonadotrophin secretion is decreased and ovarian steroid secretion suppressed.

GnRH agonists require parenteral administration and are too cumbersome and expensive to find a role as first-line therapy in the treatment of hirsutism. They may, however, be indicated when other gynaecological conditions exist that merit their use, such as menorrhagia, severe premenstrual syndrome or endometriosis. With continuous administration, superactive GnRH analogues suppress LH and FSH secretion and thus reduce LH-mediated androgen secretion.[41–46] GnRH analogues suppress ovarian hormone secretion to a greater degree than the oral contraceptive pill alone and would therefore be expected to be more effective.[41] The oestrogen in the pill, however, has the added advantage of increasing the concentration of SHBG and thus decreasing the concentration of unbound testosterone. A GnRH analogue combined with a low-dose oral contraceptive pill or with a postmenopausal oestrogen regimen has been shown to be more effective than either alone,[46] although another study did not confirm this result.[47] Because it is mildly androgenic, tibolone is not a suitable form of hormone replacement in combination with GnRH analogues in the treatment of hirsutism. Use of GnRH analogues can be complicated by adverse effects such as headache, depression, breast tenderness and fatigue.[40] Use as a single agent risks the sequelae of a hypo-oestrogenic state, including hot flushes, urogenital dryness and bone resorption. Given the risk of osteoporosis, long term use of GnRH analogues as monotherapy cannot be justified for a benign condition.

SUPPRESSION OF ADRENAL ANDROGEN PRODUCTION

Steroids

Glucocorticoid therapy decreases serum androgen concentrations by suppressing ACTH-mediated adrenal secretion. Since many women with hirsutism caused by PCOS have a degree of adrenal hyperandrogenism;[48] therapy targeted at reducing this source might at first sight seem a logical option. However, judging the optimal dose that suppresses adrenal androgen production without

normal-mode ruby laser pulses. *J Am Acad Dermatol* 1996;35:889–94.

35   Moghetti P, Castello R, Negri C, Tosi F, Perrone F, Capputo M, *et al.* Metformin effects on clinical features, endocrine and metabolic profiles and insulin sensitivity in polycystic ovary syndrome: a randomized double-blind, placebo controlled 6-month trial, followed by open, long-term clinical evaluation. *J Clin Endocrinol Metab* 2000;85:139–46.

36   Pasquali R, Gambineri A, Biscotti D, Vicennati V, Gagliardi L, Colitta D, *et al.* Effects of long term treatment with metformin added to hypocaloric diet on body composition, fat distribution, and androgen and insulin levels in abdominally obese women with and without the polycystic ovary syndrome. *J Clin Endocrinol Metab* 2000:85;2767–74.

37   Wu ZS, Cai XA. Acupuncture treatment of hirsutism and its effect on the endocrinosity. *J Tradit Chin Med* 1989;9:207–9.

38   Wortsman J, Khan MS, Rosner W. Suppression of testosterone-estradiol binding globulin by medroxyprogesterone acetate in polycystic ovarian syndrome. *Obstet Gynecol* 1986;67:705–9.

39   Murphy AA, Cropp CS, Smith BS, Burkman RT, Zacar HA. Effect of low-dose oral contraceptive on gonadotrophins, androgens, and sex hormone binding globulin in non-hirsute women. *Fertil Steril* 1990;53:35–9.

40   Prelevic GM. Hirsutism and the polycystic ovary syndrome. In: Ginsberg J, editor. *Drug Therapy in Reproductive Endocrinology*. London: Arnold; 1996. p. 67–85.

41   Rittmaster RS. Gonadotrophin-releasing hormone (GnRH) agonists and estrogen/progestin replacement for the treatment of hirsutism: evaluating the results. *J Clin Endocrinol Metab* 1995;80:3403–5.

42   Azziz R, Ochon TM, Bradley EL Jr, Potter HD, Boots LR. Leuprolide and estrogen versus oral contraceptive pills for the treatment of hirsutism: a prospective randomized study. *J Clin Endocrinol Metab* 1995;80:3406–11.

43   Heiner JS, Greendale GA, Kawakami AK, Lapolt PS, Fisher M, Young D, *et al.* Comparison of a gonadotrophin-releasing hormone agonist and a low dose oral contraceptive given alone or together in the treatment of hirsutism. *Clin Endocrinol Metab* 1995;80:3412–8.

44   Andreyko JL, Monroe SE, Jaffe RB. Treatment of hirsutism with a gonadotrophin-releasing hormone agonist (nafarelin). *J Clin Endocrinol Metab* 1986;63:854–9.

45   Carr BR, Breslau NA, Givens C, Byrd W, Barnett-Hamm C, Marshburn PB. Oral contraceptive pills, gonadotrophin-releasing hormone agonists or use in combination for the treatment of hirsutism: a clinical research center study. *J Clin Endocrinol Metab* 1995;80:1169–78.

46   Carmina F, Janni A, Loho RA. Physiological estrogen replacement may enhance effectiveness of the gonadotrophin-releasing hormone agonist in the treatment of hirsutism. *J Clin Endocrinol Metab* 1994;78:126–30.

47   Tiitinen A, Simberg N, Stenman UH, Olavi Y. Estrogen replacement does not potentiate gonadotrophin-releasing hormone agonist-induced androgen suppression in treatment of hirsutism. *J Clin Endocrinol Metab* 1994;79:447–51.

48   Carmina E, Lobo RA. Peripheral androgen blockade versus glandular androgen suppression in the treatment of hirsutism. *Obstet Gynecol* 1991;78:845–9.

49   Spritzer P, Billaud L, Thalabard JC, Birman P, Mowsowicz I, Raux-Demay MC, *et al.* Cyproterone acetate versus hydrocortisone treatment in late-onset adrenal hyperplasia. *J Clin Endocrinol Metab* 1990;70:642–6.

50   Pepper GM, Poretsky L, Gabrilove JL, Ariton MM. Ketoconazole reverses hyperandrogenism in a patient with insulin resistance and acanthosis nigricans. *J Clin Endocrinol Metab* 1987;65:1047–52.

51   Verhelst JA, Druwe P, van Erps P, Denis U, Mahler C. Use of ketoconazole in the treatment

of a virilizing adrenocortical carcinoma. *Acta Endocrinol (Copenh)* 1989;121:229–34.

52 Weber MM, Luppa P, Engelhardt D. Inhibition of human adrenal androgen secretion by ketoconazole. *Klin Wochenschr* 1989;67:707–12.

53 Sonino N, Scaroni C, Biason A, Boscaro M, Mantero F. Low-dose ketoconazole treatment in hirsute women. *J Endocrinol Invest* 1990;13:35–40.

54 Venturoli S, Fabbri R, Dal Prato L, Mantovani B, Capelli M, Magrini O, *et al.* Ketoconazole therapy for women with acne and/or hirsutism. *J Clin Endocrinol Metab* 1990;71:335.

55 Miller JA, Jacobs HS. Treatment of hirsutism and acne with cyproterone acetate. *Clin Endocrinol Metab* 1986;15:373–89.

56 Jasonni VM, Bulletti C, Naldi S, Di Cosmo E, Cappuccini F, Flamigni C. Treatment of hirsutism by an association of oral cyproterone acetate and transdermal beta estradiol. *Fertil Steril* 1991;55:742–5.

57 O'Brien RC, Cooper ME, Murray RML, Seeman E, Thomas AK, Jerums G. Comparison of sequential cyproterone acetate/estrogen versus spironolactone/oral contraceptive in the treatment of hirsutism. *J Clin Endocrinol Metab* 1991;72:1008–13.

58 Lobo RA, Shoupe D, Serafini P, Brinton D, Horton R. The effects of two doses of spironolactone on serum androgens and anagen hair in hirsute women. *Fertil Steril* 1985;43:200–5.

59 Chapman MG, Dowsett M, Dewhurst CJ, Jeffcoate SL. Spironolactone in combination with an oral contraceptive: an alternative treatment for hirsutism. *Br J Obstet Gynaecol* 1985;92:983–5.

60 Shaw JC. Spironolactone in dermatologic therapy. *J Am Acad Dermatol* 1991;24:236–43.

61 Committee on Safety of Medicines. *Monitoring Safety and Quality of Medicines: Current Problems in Pharmacovigilance.* London: CSM; 1988 [www.mca.gov.uk/aboutagency/ regframework/csm/csmhome.htm].

62 Vigersky RA, Mehlman I, Glass AR, Smith CE. Treatment of hirsute women with cimetidine. *N Engl J Med* 1980;303:1042.

63 Lissak A, Sorokin Y, Calderon I, Dirnfeld M, Lioz H, Abramovici H. Treatment of hirsutism with cimetidine: a prospective randomized controlled trial. *Fertil Steril* 1989;51:247–50.

64 Rittmaster RS. Finasteride. *N Engl J Med* 1994;330:120–25.

65 Fruzzetti F, de Lorenzo D, Parrini D, Ricci C. Effects of finasteride, a 5α-reductase inhibitor, on circulating androgens and gonadotrophin secretion in hirsute women. *J Clin Endocrinol Metab* 1994;79:831–5.

66 Wong IL, Morris RS, Chang L, Spahn MA, Stanczyk FZ, Lobo RA. A prospective randomized trial comparing finasteride to spironolactone in the treatment of hirsute women. *J Clin Endocrinol Metab* 1995;80:233–8.

67 Ciotta L, Cianci A, Calogero AE, Palumbo MA, Marletta E, Sciuto A, *et al.* Clinical and endocrine effects of finasteride, a 5a-reductase inhibitor, in women with idiopathic hirsutism. *Fertil Steril* 1995;64:299–306.

68 Marcondes JAM, Minnani SL, Luthold WW, Wajchenberg BL, Samojlik E, Kirschner MA. Treatment of hirsutism in women with flutamide. *Fertil Steril* 1992;57:543–7.

69 Gomez JL, Dupont A, Cusan L, Tremblay M, Suburu R, Lemay M, *et al.* Incidence of liver toxicity associated with the use of flutamide in prostate cancer patients. *Am J Med* 1992;92:465–70.

70 Dollery C, editor. *Therapeutic Drugs.* Edinburgh: Churchill Livingstone; 1991.

71 Donesky BW, Adashi EY. Surgically induced ovulation in the polycystic ovary syndrome: wedge resection revisited in the age of laparoscopy. *Fertil Steril* 1995;63:439–63.

72 Tiitinen A, Tenhunen A, Seppala M. Ovarian electrocauterization causes LH-regulated hut

not insulin-regulated endocrine changes. *Clin Endocrinol* 1993;39:181–4.

73   Campo S, Felli A, Lamanna MA, Barini A, Garcea N. Endocrine changes and clinical outcome after laparoscopic ovarian resection in women with polycystic ovaries. *Hum Reprod* 1993;8:359–63.

74   Judd HL, Rigg LA, Anderson DC, Yen SSC. The effect of ovarian wedge resection on circulating gonadotrophin and ovarian steroid levels in patients with polycystic ovary syndrome. *J Clin Endocrinol Metab* 1976;43:347–55.

75   Greenblatt F, Casper R. Endocrine changes after laparoscopic ovarian cautery in polycystic ovary syndrome. *Am J Obstet Gynecol* 1987;156:279–85.

76   Gjonnaess H, Norman N. Endocrine effects of ovarian electracautery in patients with polycystic ovarian disease. *Br J Obstet Gynaecol* 1987;94:779–83.

27

Alternative medicine for hormone replacement therapy

Jan Brockie

In the western world, the current medical view of the menopause could be interpreted as a pathological event with its own distinct set of symptoms and diseases. There is an increase in cardiovascular disease, stroke, Alzheimer's disease and osteoporosis because of the decline of oestrogen and the clinical literature would lead us to believe that there is a need to replace oestrogen in menopausal women. However, there are huge individual differences in the experience of menopause symptoms and long-term health risks and indeed what women would consider as treatment options.

Many women are choosing to avoid oestrogen therapy in the form of hormone replacement therapy (HRT), despite the wealth of medical literature showing benefits. Instead, they are opting for non-conventional therapies and lifestyle changes rather than HRT or other pharmacological treatments (Table 1). Alternative therapies can offer treatment options to women who either have a contraindication to oestrogen or who, through choice, would prefer to avoid it, for both symptomatic relief and long-term protection, for one or more of the following reasons:

- contraindication to HRT
- belief that HRT interferes with nature
- desire to be in control
- dislike of continued menstruation
- fear of long-term effects of HRT
- fear of adverse effects
- lack of information about HRT.

Just as HRT is given under medical supervision, women using alternative approaches need to understand that there is also the potential for harm, either because of a lack of efficacy or possible risks in the treatment itself. In many of the non-conventional approaches, there is a lack of evidence to confirm benefits or to highlight possible adverse effects because sufficient trials have not been done. Complementary and alternative medicine lacks a research tradition and also the research infrastructure. It fails to attract experienced researchers and most alternative practitioners are self-employed, without access to large numbers of patients. Orthodox medicine generally remains highly sceptical of alternative and complementary medicine and as a consequence funding is minimal.[1]

Generally, women have to be motivated to use alternative therapies. A single HRT preparation can effectively reverse all the effects of the menopause. However, when considering alternative therapies, most only treat a single problem and so women with multiple symptoms may need to try several approaches. Some alternatives will not be as effective as HRT but a reduction in symptoms in many cases is sufficient. Pursuing alternative therapies can be costly, so women on low incomes are disadvantaged.

Table 1 *Alternatives to HRT; reproduced from the Oxford Menopause Distance Learning Course with permission from the Oxford Menopause Clinic*

	Dietary changes and supplements	Lifestyle changes	Complementary therapies	Pharmacological alternatives, over-the-counter products
Vasomotor symptoms	Phytoestrogens, multivitamins, minerals, reduction of caffeine, alcohol, spicy food	Stress reduction, avoidance of trigger factors, exercise, smoking reduction, heat avoidance	Stress-reducing therapies, acupuncture, herbalism	Clonidine, progestogens, antidepressants
Mood swings	Oil of evening primrose (premenstrual syndrome)	Exercise, support groups	Stress-reducing and nutritional therapies, herbalism	Antidepressants
Vaginal/urinary symptoms	Phytoestrogens, caffeine reduction	Pelvic exercises, regular intercourse	Aromatherapy, herbalism	Long-acting vaginal moisturisers, simple lubricants
Insomnia	Caffeine reduction	Exercise, relaxation techniques	Stress-reducing therapies, herbalism	Night sedation
Heart disease	Cholesterol reduction, moderation of alcohol intake, vitamin and mineral supplements	Exercise, reduction of weight, smoking, stress	Therapies to help with lifestyle changes, nutritional therapies	Blood-pressure- and cholesterol-reducing medication
Osteoporosis	Calcium, vitamin D, reduction of sodium, animal protein, alcohol, caffeine	Exercise, smoking reduction	Therapies to help with lifestyle changes, nutritional therapies	Bisphosphonates, raloxifene

MENOPAUSE ACROSS CULTURES

The severity and reporting of menopause symptoms vary enormously worldwide.[2,3] The diversity in the menopause experience is apparent not only from the frequency with which symptoms are reported but in their relative rankings compared with other symptoms. In some cultures there is only a weak association between vasomotor symptoms (the most commonly reported symptom in the UK) and the menopause. In Japan, the principal symptom reported is shoulder stiffness; in Taiwan, it is backache and tiredness; in Lebanon, it is fatigue and irritability. In many countries, fatigue is the most frequently reported symptom, but not every culture associates symptoms with the menopause at all.[4] The association between the hormonal changes at the menopause and symptoms is complex and influenced by many factors such as social environment, support networks, children, diet, affluence, frailty, exercise, education, smoking, the environment, attitudes and beliefs.

There may be lessons to learn from other cultures. Traditional women from ethnic groups are more likely to view the menopause as a normal part of ageing and not to associate it with illness.[2] This raises the possibility that our western society, which favours youth, discriminates against the elderly and concentrates on problems associated with the menopause, may be contributing to a negative attitude towards it. Demedicalisation of the menopause might actually improve a woman's experience of this event and reduce the need for treatment.

COMPLEMENTARY THERAPIES

Complementary therapies have become a popular alternative in the treatment of menopausal symptoms and many women continue to use them despite the limited evidence to support their efficacy or indeed their safety. In a recent survey into the use of complementary medicine in an orthodox menopause clinic where 93% of women were taking HRT, 45% were also regularly using complementary medicine.[5] Another study reported that 32% of menopausal women used complementary medicine alone but 16% used a combination of complementary medicine and HRT.[6] Although complementary medicine may help with the short-term (and possibly the medium-term) problems, they are unlikely to have any effect on the long-term consequences, except through helping with lifestyle changes.

Complementary medicine is confusing; there are over 100 therapies in existence. Those that have been reported as helpful include massage, aromatherapy, reflexology, herbalism, homeopathy, nutritional therapy and acupuncture.[7] Most people investigate the different therapies and find one that seems suitable for them and their health condition. Finding a practitioner with appropriate qualifications and experience needs care. The more common and established therapies have governing bodies that set qualifications and standards and can advise on local practitioners. Any person embarking on complementary therapy should check a practitioner's qualifications, experience and success in treating a complaint, the cost and number of treatments, insurance and whether they keep the general practitioner informed.

There is no scientific evidence to show any benefits of aromatherapy, massage and reflexology on menopause symptoms. However, they are helpful in stress reduction and this may have a domino effect on other symptoms. Homoeopathy has many sceptics, although as an alternative treatment it is safe, relying on the use of infinitely small doses of a substance. Randomised, placebo-controlled studies are needed to clarify its value in the menopause.

Herbalism

For historical reasons, herbalism is much more widely available in this country than in other countries, without any effective method of reporting adverse effects or monitoring quality control. An attempt was made in the 1960s to control over-the-counter products but about 80% are still unlicensed. As a result, there is no manufacturing control or quality guarantee on many products. There is a widespread belief among the public that 'natural' means harmless, but herbs may contain potent chemicals and should be used with caution. This has been highlighted in a study in Belgium when a Chinese herb was contaminated by a carcinogen.[8] As the active ingredient in most preparations is unknown, women with a contraindication to HRT, such as breast cancer, should be discouraged from using them. There is a number of known drug–herb interactions and practitioners should caution patients against mixing herbs and pharmaceutical drugs.[9] Women should always be encouraged to buy reputable, well-known brands and to tell their practitioners what they are taking.

From the great number of herbs available, there are a few that have research to support their use at the menopause. In Germany, herbs are classified as drugs and are regulated by Commission E, which provides accurate information on the therapeutic value of individual herbs, including adverse effects, dosing and pharmacology.[10]

Black cohosh (Cimicifugae racemosae)

A native herb in eastern North America, black cohosh is traditionally used by native Americans for a variety of conditions including vasomotor symptoms, menopausal anxiety and depression. A review of a number of clinical studies of a standardised extract of black cohosh has demonstrated efficacy for the alleviation of vasomotor symptoms, insomnia and low mood.[11] The safety profile is good, with low toxicity, few and mild adverse effects and good tolerability.[12] Commission E recommends its use for 'menopausal ailments', at a daily dose of 40 mg, with a recommended duration of treatment no longer than six months.[10] No drug interactions with black cohosh are known.

St John's Wort (Hypericum)

There is an abundance of evidence to support the use of St John's Wort for the treatment of depression.[13,14] In a trial of menopausal women taking 900 μg daily, the incidence and severity symptoms, including flushes, low mood, insomnia and sexual wellbeing were reduced by at least 75%.[15] However, known drug interactions with St John's Wort include parotetine, trazodone, sertraline, nefazodone, theophylline, digoxin, phenprocoumon, cyclosporin and the combined oral contraceptive.[9] Commission E recommends its use for depression, anxiety and nervous unrest.

Other herbal remedies often recommended by alternative practitioners at the menopause include valerian, sage, chaste tree, dong quai, ginseng, gingko biloba, kava, garlic and feverfew. Commission E does not recommend them for use at the menopause. There are either limited scientific data on these or there is concern about adverse effects or drug interactions.

A number of studies have shown the effect of valerian on insomnia.[14] Taken orally at night, 60 mg daily, it was not shown to result in reduced performance the following morning.[16] The only known drug reaction is with alcohol, to reduce its effect on concentration.[9]

Sage, when used in combination with alfalfa, was shown in one small study significantly to reduce vasomotor symptoms.[17] Chaste tree has some data to show an effect in premenstrual tension and this is the use that Commission E recommends, not for menopausal symptoms.[10] Ginkgo biloba has been shown to stabilise and even improve cognitive and social functioning. Commission E approves this herb for improving memory performance; there is no evidence that it protects against Alzheimer's disease.[10] Kava is effective for reducing anxiety[10] but has been reported as causing hepatotoxicity and is being reviewed by the US Food and Drugs Administration (FDA).[18] Dong quai is frequently included in the selection of herbs for menopausal women but in a placebo-controlled trial it was no more effective than placebo.[19] Patients with clotting disorders, awaiting surgery or on anticoagulants, should be warned against using dong quai, gingko biloba and garlic, as they are likely to interfere with prothrombin times.[9]

Chinese medicinal herbs were not shown to be more effective than placebo in a randomised controlled trial in Australia.[20] But Chinese traditional medicine incorporates lifestyle changes, physical activity, nutrition and acupuncture.[21] It is worthy of more research as it aims to give targeted treatment to reduce symptoms and provide long-term protection. Oil of evening primrose in a double-blind placebo-controlled study was not shown to have any effect.[22]

Acupuncture

Two studies have shown significant reduction in vasomotor symptoms using acupuncture and the benefits continued for three weeks after the last treatment.[23,24]

Stress reduction

Encouraging women to reassess their priorities in life, to reduce unnecessary stress that in turn may help alleviate some symptoms. A pilot study highlighted the value of support groups for menopausal women, helping women to overcome the feeling of isolation or alienation.[25] With a number of menopausal women meeting together, a group can help normalise the experience. They can serve an educational and support function.

Lifestyle and dietary changes

Many of the lifestyle and dietary changes ideally need to be adopted in early life to create good habits and maximise the benefits later in life. It is well recognised that there are trigger factors for vasomotor symptoms. These include alcohol, caffeine, smoking, hot or spicy food or drinks, together with a hot environment and stress. Women may need to review the way they dress, with layers that can easily be removed and then replaced. Good ventilation, minimal heating and light bed-linen may help symptoms to become more bearable but unpopular with partners, family and colleagues.

Studies looking at the effect of vitamins since the 1940s have conflicting results.[25] Some work suggested that vitamin E reduced vasomotor symptoms and supplementation of vitamin E 400-1200 iu daily is a fairly common recommendation of some alternative practitioners, with apparent success.[26] Some anecdotal evidence suggests that multivitamin and mineral supplements can reduce flushes but its effect may be partly dependent on the quality of the woman's diet.

Certainly, dietary habits are strongly implicated in disease and a varied diet with fresh fruits, vegetables and wholemeal products is likely to provide the daily requirements of vitamins and minerals that are significant for optimising cardiac health. Some alternative practitioners recommend vitamin and mineral supplements but there is debate concerning the supplements needed and the dosages. One argument for supplementation is that it serves as a 'nutritional insurance' in the face of environmental pollutants that increase exposure to free radicals and the poor quality of fruit and vegetables due to nutrient deficient soil and their loss during food processing. In the Nurses' Health Study, the risk of coronary artery disease decreased by approximately 46% among women who had consumed 100 iu of vitamin E for more than two years.[27] Oily fish eaten at least twice a week was significant in reducing mortality from coronary heart disease.[28] The evidence for garlic in reducing cholesterol is unconvincing, yet it remains a popular over-the-counter product.

Adolescent nutrition can influence lifelong bone health. About 40% of bone mass is accumulated during the adolescent years.[29] The acquisition of bone during these years is affected within the genetic potential by diet, exercise and smoking. Although precise requirements may not be known, insufficient nutrients, particularly calcium, vitamin D, phosphorus and magnesium, will hinder bone mass potential. Other studies have shown the association of eating disorders such as anorexia nervosa with bone loss or failure to gain bone. Poor calcium nutrition in early life may account for as much as 50% of the difference in hip-fracture rates in postmenopausal women.[30] Milk consumption generally has declined dramatically in the past 20 years, with the possibility that a generation has failed to gain its maximum bone mass potential.

Maintaining an adequate calcium intake throughout adulthood into the postmenopause should be encouraged. As calcium is absorbed with more difficulty from the gut with increasing age, more is needed to maintain a positive calcium balance. In a meta-analysis, a calcium intake of at least 1000 mg daily reduced hip fracture by 22%.[31] Calcium alone is not sufficient to prevent either the hormone or ageing-related bone loss in postmenopausal women but avoiding a negative calcium balance will prevent accelerating this loss. In the postmenopause, women not on HRT are recommended to include 1500 mg of calcium daily. In an elderly population, calcium and vitamin D supplementation significantly reduced fracture risk.[32] Some clinicians would recommend adding vitamin D 400 iu daily to the calcium. As they grow older, women have less exposure to sunlight, and food in the UK is not fortified with vitamin D as in some other countries. Several other nutritional deficiencies have been linked with osteoporosis, such as magnesium and other minerals, vitamins and trace elements. Studies are limited but some would recommend a calcium supplement that has added nutrients,[33] although there is concern that oversupplementation could have negative physiological effects.

Dehydroepiandrosterone

Dehydroepiandrosterone (DHEA) is an androgen, whose exact physiological role is unknown. The levels decline with age, independently of menopausal status. It is available as a food supplement, although there are limited data to support its use or safety. A number of small studies suggest that DHEA improved mood, sleep, tiredness and ability to cope.[34] Adverse effects include lowering high density lipoprotein, increasing insulin resistance and raising blood pressure.

Natural progestogen creams

Skin creams containing natural progesterone have been available over the counter and via mail order for about 20 years. They are unlicensed. Their use has been promoted by Dr John Lee, who claims that it is a progesterone deficiency rather than an oestrogen deficiency that causes all menopause-related problems, including osteoporosis. This 'natural' progesterone is extracted from plant sources, mainly yams and soya, and is structurally identical to the body's own progesterone. There is limited evidence to support their use, although one study did report an improvement in vasomotor symptoms but no effect on bone. They should not be promoted or used for the prevention or treatment of osteoporosis. The plasma levels achieved using the creams appear inadequate to offer endometrial protection when used in conjunction with oestrogen.[35] However, some women have reported dramatic improvements in menopause symptoms and wellbeing when using the cream and a trial currently in progress will show whether this is a placebo response.

Phytoestrogens

In recent years, soy and phytoestrogens have stimulated much interest in the public and pharmaceutical industry, in an attempt to identify effective alternatives to HRT. Diet is thought to be one factor that helps to explain the cultural differences in the menopause experience. Asian women experience fewer menopausal symptoms than western women and their traditional diets contain high levels of phytoestrogens, about 200 mg daily compared with less than 5 mg daily in a western diet.[2]

The Japanese also have a lower incidence of cardiovascular disease, osteoporosis; breast, colon, endometrial and ovarian cancers. Furthermore, women with breast cancer in Japan have a better prognosis than those with breast cancer in the USA or Great Britain. Phytoestrogens have a variety of activities: oestrogenic, anti-oestrogenic, antiviral, anti-carcinogenic, bactericidal, antifungal, antioxidant, antimutagenic, antihypertensive, anti-inflammatory and antiproliferative effects.

Phytoestrogens are compounds that are found in plants to differing degrees. They are structurally similar to oestradiol and may mimic its action in the body. However, they are much weaker than the body's own natural oestrogen. There are many different types of phytoestrogens. It is the isoflavones, e.g. genistein and lignans, that may be significant at the menopause. Isoflavones are found in legumes and the soya bean is the richest source. Lignans are found in seed oils, cereals, fruit and vegetables.

The evidence that phytoestrogens reduce menopause symptoms is conflicting and in one short study soy seems to be no more effective than placebo.[36] A number of other studies have examined the effect of isoflavones on menopausal hot flushes. In a double-blind study comparing the effects of an isoflavone-rich to an isoflavone-poor treatment in 69 women over 24 weeks, there was no difference in the severity or frequency of vasomotor symptoms.[37] In another placebo-controlled study of 177 women, there was significant reduction in frequency and severity of vasomotor symptoms in the active group.[38] Small studies on vaginal epithelium have shown that isoflavones have a mild oestrogenic effect on the vagina.[38,39] Similarly, there are also debates about the effects on lipoproteins, endothelial function and blood pressure.[40–42]

In the USA, the FDA has approved food or food substances containing specific amounts of soy protein to reduce the risk of heart disease. Benefits of soy on cardiovascular risk factors have been demonstrated. In a meta-analysis of 38 clinical studies comparing soy protein and a placebo, the active group showed a 9.3% reduction in total cholesterol concentrations, with a 12.9% reduction in the more harmful low density lipoproteins and 10.5% reduction in triglycerides.[43] The results of this meta-analysis have stimulated further research and the FDA has now permitted soy-based foods to state that they can lower cholesterol. Although there are preliminary data to suggest that isoflavone dietary supplements have a number of potential benefits, such as an improvement in the lipoprotein profile, reduction in atherosclerosis and improving arterial function, randomised placebo-controlled trials are still required to demonstrate a reduction in cardiovascular disease.[44,45] With regard to osteoporosis, data showing the ability of genistein and the synthetic isoflavone, ipriflavone, to maintain bone mass are conflicting.[46,47]

Some clinicians would argue that it is not possible to draw absolute conclusions about the benefits of phytoestrogens without large long-term randomised trials. However, early lifetime exposure to phytoestrogens may offer the greatest benefits of phytoestrogens. Phytoestrogen supplements as part of a westernised diet may not offer the same benefits as food high in phytoestrogens as part of a traditional diet.

There remain many gaps in the knowledge, scepticism and understanding of the effects of these compounds, but they are certainly worthy of more research. Studies have not shown any adverse effects from phytoestrogens; they are well tolerated and, despite their cost, they remain a highly popular supplement.

Other dietary and lifestyle changes

Lifestyle risk factors associated with osteoporosis include smoking, alcohol misuse and inactivity. Although caffeine has been thought to be detrimental to bone density, some recent studies do not support this, except that with the highest caffeine intake there was a modest increase in fracture risk.[48] It has been known for many years that there is a correlation between urinary calcium and sodium levels, so that high sodium intake increases calcium loss. This may be significant if calcium intake is limited; however, an average salt intake of 9g/day was not shown to constitute a risk factor for osteoporosis.[49] A high protein intake, generally in the form of animal protein, also raises urinary calcium and is probably additive to the sodium effect.[50] In postmenopausal women, protein levels need to be sufficient to maintain the microarchitecture of the bone without increasing urinary loss. High phosphorus intake has been linked to increased urinary calcium loss, is present in soft drinks such as cola and may be damaging for young people's bones.[33]

The effect of alcohol on fracture risk is puzzling: moderate alcohol intake appears to increase bone density but there is a weak positive association with fracture risk.[51] However, heavy drinkers are more likely to smoke and have poor diets; these in turn will increase osteoporotic risk. Smoking is associated with reduced bone formation. This may be the result of a toxic effect of nicotine on osteoblasts or the increased hepatic clearance of oestrogen, which in turn will increase bone resorption.[52]

Exercise throughout life is important to bone, in early life to maximise bone mass potential and later to help conserve it. During the hormone-related, rapid period of bone loss immediately after the menopause, frequent high-impact exercise can slow bone loss, but many women would not be able to achieve this.[53] However, exercise is effective in slowing the gradual long-term ageing-related bone loss. Exercise needs to be geared to a woman's physical ability, regular and weight-bearing. The safest exercise to recommend to women is walking. Optimum levels of exercise needed are not known but are probably in the region of 30 minutes, four or five times per week. Exercise will only offer protection as long as it is continued.

Exercise is also extremely important to cardiac health, helping to reduce weight, blood pressure and cholesterol levels. A recent study investigated the relationship between physical activity and coronary heart disease (CHD).[54] Physical activity, including walking pace and distances, was recorded in almost 40 000 health professionals, mean age 54 years, over five years. More active women had a lower body mass index (BMI), were less likely to smoke, more likely to consume alcohol, less saturated fat, more fibre and more fruit and vegetables and were more likely to use HRT. More active women had less hypertension, lower cholesterol and diabetes. When the results were adjusted for smoking, diet, alcohol use, menopausal status and HRT use, active women were at significantly lower risk of developing CHD than less active women. These results are probably predictable but the amount of exercise needed to reduce CHD was surprising. Women who walked for at least one hour per week experienced about half the CHD risk of women who did not walk regularly. This study indicated that physical activity easily within the ability of almost all women is associated with lower CHD rates.

A study suggested that women who exercised regularly were less likely to suffer severe hot flushes.[55] Exercise can also reduce depression and improve insomnia, together with providing a greater feeling of wellbeing.[56] Recently, physical activity has also been reported to protect elderly women from cognitive decline.[57]

Pharmacological alternatives and 'over-the-counter' products

Many of the pharmacological alternatives offer effective alternatives but only for the treatment of a single problem. Bisphosphonates and raloxifene are licensed for the prevention and treatment of osteoporosis and are discussed elsewhere.

It was noticed that progestogens given to women as treatment for endometrial cancer led to a reduction in vasomotor symptoms. Historically, medroxyprogesterone acetate was used. More recently, megestrol acetate 40 mg has been used in the treatment of hot flushes, mainly in women with a history of breast cancer, as it is sometimes also used in the treatment of the disease. It reduces flushes by 80% of women after two months of treatment. However, the long-term effects of megestrol acetate on the 'at-risk' breast and blood lipids are not known.[58] Progestogens need to be used with caution in women with a history of venous thromboembolism.

The aetiology of vasomotor symptoms remains unclear, which hinders the development of alternative treatments. However, recent studies have shown the potential of antidepressants.[59,60] These studies have been done in women with a history of breast cancer and trials are now needed in other women. An uncontrolled study using paroxetine, increasing to 20mg daily, showed a 67% reduction in flushes,[59] while a larger placebo-controlled study of venlafaxine 75 mg reduced flushes by 61%.[60] The benefits were seen within a couple of weeks and were unaffected by the use of tamoxifen or the depression rating. Antidepressants also offer a possible positive effect on mood and libido but adverse effects include dry mouth, nausea, constipation and reduced appetite. Venlafaxine 37.5 mg daily resulted in fewer adverse effects but reduced flushes by only 37%. Occasionally, it may be appropriate to treat menopausal mood swings and insomnia with antidepressants or night sedation.

A small, uncontrolled study showed a reduction in flushes with gabapentin[61] but more studies are needed. Clonidine is rarely used now; it is effective in only about 30% of women in reducing the severity of vasomotor symptoms,[62] which is little different from a placebo response. Propanalol has traditionally been used in the treatment of vasomotor symptoms, but there are no data to support its use.

Simple vaginal lubricants will help prevent some discomfort during intercourse. However, a longer-acting bioadhesive vaginal moisturiser can provide symptomatic relief from atrophic vaginitis,[63] which is comparable to a vaginal oestrogen preparation. Available over the counter, it is a gel containing water and a polycarbophil that adheres to the vaginal wall, encouraging water back into the dehydrated cells. Each application lasts for about three days.

Oestriol or oestradiol vaginal preparations provide local therapy for atrophic symptoms of the vagina and the lower urinary tract, without being absorbed systemically to any significant degree. They can be used safely in women with a contraindication to systemic oestrogen and in the long term without any effect on the breast or endometrium.

The menopause often occurs in a woman's life when there are other stressful circumstances, such as difficulties with elderly parents or adolescent children, financial worries, job stresses or marital problems. These may well exacerbate the menopausal symptoms. Some women present at the menopause with issues that are confused with menopausal symptoms. It is valuable to identify those symptoms are menopausal in origin. Other problems cannot be dealt with either by hormone replacement therapy or by the alternatives to it.

References

1   Ernst E. The role of complementary and alternative medicine. *BMJ* 2000;321:1133–5.

2   Lock M, Kaufert P. Menopause, local biologies and cultures of ageing. *Am J Human Biol* 2001;13:494–504.

3   Hewner SJ. Postmenopausal function in context: biocultural observations on Amish, neighbouring Non-Amish and Ifugao household health. *Am J Human Biol* 2001;13:521–30.

4   Obermeyer CM. Menopause across cultures: a review of the evidence. *Menopause* 2000;7:184–92.

5   Vashisht A, Domoney C, Wirth KA, Studd JWW. Unorthodox versus conventional therapies for the treatment of menopausal symptoms. *J Br Meno Soc* 2000;6 Suppl 3:34.

6   Ernst E. Herbalism and the menopause. *J Br Meno Soc* 2002. In press.

7   Brockie J. Complementary and non medical approaches. In: Singer D, Hunter M, editors. *Premature Menopause: A Multidisciplinary Approach.* London: Whurr Publishers; 2000.

8   Nortier JL, Muniz Martinez MC, Schmeiser HH, Arlt VM, Bieler CA, Petein M, *et al.* Urothelial carcinoma associated with the use of a Chinese herb (Aristolochia fangchi). *N Engl J Med* 2000:342:1686–92.

9   Fugh-Berman H. Herb–drug interactions. *Lancet* 2000;355:134–8.

10   Blumenthal M, editor. *The Complete German Commission E Monographs.* Boston, MA: Integrative Medicine Communications; 1998.

11   Lieberman S. Evidence-based natural medicine. A review of the effectiveness of Cimicifuga racemosa (Black cohosh) for the symptoms of menopause. *J Women's Health* 1998;7:525–9.

12   McKenna DJ, Jones K, Humphrey S, Hughes K. Black cohosh: efficacy, safety and use in clinical and preclinical applications. *Altern Ther Health Med* 2001;7:93–100.

13   Woelk H. Comparison of St John's Wort and imipramine for treating depression: randomised

number and the physiological range of steroids can be seen among the vertebrates, with the invertebrate *Mollusca* (octopus and squid) and the *Echinodermata* (starfish) possessing the enzymatic capability to elaborate androgens, progesterone and oestrogens from the basic cholesterol. The advent of glucocorticoids came with the vertebrates in the elasmobranchs (sharks and rays) while the final steroid development, aldosterone, first appeared with the teleosts, the bony fishes. *Homo sapiens,* belonging to the primate order of the mammalian class of vertebrates, possesses a full set of some 30 steroid hormones known as the three sex-steroid groups, glucocorticoids and mineral corticoids. These, together with the elaborate receptor and transcriptional apparatus, translate their presence in a tissue into gene transcription, protein production and, ultimately, modified biological activity.

The most primitive living entity shown to elaborate oestradiol is the fungus *Saccharomyces cerevisiae.*[2] This organism evolved around 1.2 billion years ago and it is testament to the utility of the original fungal steroid that is molecularly identical to the central human oestrogen 17β-oestradiol.

Nature is parsimonious. Evolution generally conserves biological systems and molecules that confer adaptation to the current environment, provided that these systems or molecules do not themselves interfere with survival and hence reproductive capacity. Thus, over evolutionary time, a molecule such as oestradiol, which possesses a useful set of physicochemical characteristics, may have conferred upon it one function after another in one system after another. These functions operate today and all are subject to modification by the midlife ovarian failure that sooner or later proves inevitable.

THE SKELETON

In his classic paper of 1941, Fuller Albright[3] of Boston proposed that oestrogen deficiency consequent on natural or artificial menopause was causally related to osteoporosis and related fracture. The truth of that proposal is now beyond scientific dispute, although the mechanism was to prove more complex than a simple failure of osteoblastic bone formation, as Albright originally suggested.

Oestrogen is an essential ingredient in the metabolism of bone in both sexes. Adult women lose bone if the plasma oestrogen declines below a threshold value of around 200 pmol/l. Bone health, by which is meant the maintenance of a normal density of bone tissue and hence strength, is dependent on a dynamic balance between bone resorption and bone formation. The bone remodelling cycle operates at the level of the microscopic bone remodelling unit (BRU) of which there are around 0.5 million always in operation in the adult skeleton, and which are more frequent in the trabecular bone of spine, hip and distal radius than in the compact bone of the diaphyses of the long bones. Trabecular or cancellous bone, with its high surface area, is thus at greater exposure to bone loss if the amount of bone resorbed at each microscopic site by the multinucleate osteoclasts exceeds the amount of refill provided by osteoblasts whose function is the production of new bone. This is the problem provoked by oestrogen deficiency and is compounded by the fact that lack of oestrogen releases the brakes on the recruitment of new remodelling sites. Hence a multiplier effect comes into play, with the abnormal rapid bone turnover accentuating the discrepancy between bone removal and inadequate replacement (Figure 2 – Plate 16).

In the face of this decoupling of bone removal and replacement, the skeleton begins to deplete. This would be of little consequence if life normally ended around the time of menopause, as it does in nearly all species save *Homo sapiens.* Nor would it matter if, as at present, life continued for some 30 years thereafter, provided that the menopausal skeleton contained sufficient bone reserves to sustain normal function until death. Among European women, however, this is seldom the case.

The bone mineral density (BMD) that women bring to menopause is often far from sufficient to sustain three decades of continuous loss and the result may be a progressive descent from normality, through osteopenia or low bone mass, to osteoporosis and consequent fracture after moderate or even minimal trauma.

The causation of oestrogen deficiency is of little moment. Whether by natural, medical or surgical menopause, by hyperprolactinaemic ovarian suppression or anorexia nervosa, if ovarian output fails to sustain a plasma oestrogen level above the bone-loss threshold, depletion of the skeleton will commence.

For the first ten years after menopause, bone loss is relatively rapid but thereafter increased physical strain on the surviving trabeculae stimulates bone formation. Consequently bone loss slows and proceeds at a rate comparable to that seen in older men. By this time, however, BMD may have declined to the osteopenic range, defined as 1.0–2.5 standard deviations (SD) below the young normal mean. From here it is but a short slip to full osteoporosis, reached when the BMD declines to more than 2.5 SD below the mean. In men, by contrast, although trabeculae become thinner, the three-dimensional honeycombed trellis that gives the bone of both sexes its shock-absorbing power remains intact. In women, however, there is not only a thinning of trabeculae but a progressive dismantling of the all-important network of these tiny spars of bone, significantly reducing the ability of the network to contribute to absorb shock without fracture.

At the cellular level, progressive layers of complexity have been discovered as the hunt continues for the ultimate site or sites of oestrogen action. The hormone is involved in a complex modulatory role in marshalling the array of cytokines, growth factors and hormones that cooperate in managing bone turnover and the all-important balance between resorption and formation.

It is known, for example, that oestrogen receptors are present in both osteoblasts and osteoclasts, and the osteocyte network – buried as it is in the matrix of bone tissue – is also sensitive to oestrogen.[4] The latter may yet prove to be highly significant, since the maintenance of osteocyte reactivity by oestrogen permits these cells to function as the cellular strain gauge that signals to osteoblasts to maintain their bone conservation mode. Oestrogen lack may encourage their switch to disuse mode, which encourages the decoupling of bone formation and resorption and leads to bone loss. Finally, the ability of the osteoblasts to respond to strain can be significantly inhibited by the use of selective oestrogen receptor modulators (SERMs), another potential mechanism for the use of oestrogens and their substitutes in the preservation of bone mass.

With regard to the calcitrophic hormones, oestrogen appears to have a restraining influence on the action of parathyroid hormone (PTH) on bone. PTH is responsible for inhibition of calcium from gut and bone in order to protect the all-important plasma level of ionised plasma calcium. Initial postmenopausal oestrogen lack leads to rapid calcium efflux into the plasma, which suppresses PTH. Later, when the skeleton is depleted and the increased strain on the surviving trabeculae brings the first phase of bone loss to an end, the second phase of bone loss begins. In this phase – usually known as the age-related phase – it is believed that the extraskeletal results of oestrogen deficiency, reduced gut calcium absorption and higher renal calcium loss, conspire to reduce plasma calcium – not outwith the normal range, but sufficiently to provoke an increase in PTH production. This overrides the strain-induced bone problems and raids the skeleton for the calcium required to re-elevate store the sagging plasma calcium into its tight band. This hypothesis, proposed by Riggs and Melton[5] in 1997, assigns a central role to oestrogen in both early and late postmenopausal bone loss and encourages the long-term use of bone-active oestrogens or SERMs backed up with adequate calcium, vitamin D and exercise provision in the management of the disease. Thinned trabeculae can be augmented by physical or pharmacological means but once the trabeculum itself is lost there is simply no template upon which to rebuild it.

Although there are numerous reports attesting the ability of oestrogens to restrain bone loss after menopause and to stabilise BMD, the critical question has always been: do oestrogens reduce the risk of fracture? Two recent meta-analyses suggest that they do: Torgerson and Bell-Syer[6] at York evaluated 12 randomised trials involving 6726 women examining the effect of oestrogen on vertebral fracture and found that, overall, the relative risk of such a fracture fell, on the point estimate by 33%, the full relative risk being 0.67 (95% CI: 0.43–0.98). When the randomised 22 trials involving 6776 women looking at oestrogen on non-vertebral fracture were analysed, again there was apparent protection by oestrogen, the reduction in risk this time being 28% with the relative risk 0.72 (95% CI: 0.56–0.93).

Other interesting features of these data were that, in general, protection by oestrogen again was best when the hormone replacement therapy (HRT) was started below the age of 60 years. Ideally, in patients at risk the HRT or a SERM should be continued long-term, as the protective effect is most potent when oestrogen is current and perhaps for five years maximum after treatment is stopped.

In practical terms, all women at significant risk of osteoporosis, such as those with premature menopause, family history, steroid enforcement, a suspicious radiograph or a suspiciously easy fracture should undergo assessment by bone densitometry. If classed at risk, the patient should be offered oestrogen initially, with a cyclic regimen at perimenopause, followed by an amenorrhoeic HRT regimen – or tibolone – from age 55 years, and thereafter a SERM – raloxifene – from age 60–75 years. At any age, a bisphosphonate such as alendronate or risedronate can be deployed if the patient cannot or will not accept or tolerate oestrogen.

Osteoporosis costs the National Health Service £1.7 billion in expenditure per annum. Much can be done to mitigate this by the judicious use of bone scanning for detecting and oestrogen for arresting the bone loss that appears to be otherwise obligatory after climacteric ovarian failure withdraws the native protection afforded by oestradiol.

CARDIOVASCULAR SYSTEM

The second important network, which is both oestrogen-reliant and compromised by oestrogen withdrawal, is the cardiovascular system. Indeed, it may be argued that it is the most important, since the most prevalent cause of death among postmenopausal women in Western Europe and the USA is cardiovascular and cerebrovascular disease. The precise relationship between oestrogen and the pathological processes – principally atheroma – that underpins vascular disease is a matter of much current controversy. Some ten years ago Grady et al.[7] concluded that the evidence of observational studies was consistent in showing that oestrogen use brought down the incidence of cardiovascular disease by about one-third. There have been literally scores of observational, i.e. case–control and cohort, studies that have reached this conclusion, but all of them suffer from an intractable disability – they are observational. No matter how large or well-conducted such a study may be, it simply cannot account for all potential sources of bias or confounding. These can only be eliminated to a degree by randomised controlled trials (RCTs). However, that said, the observational evidence looked strong and internally consistent save for one critical caveat. It could be that women who embark on and continue with HRT are themselves inherently less likely to develop cardiovascular problems. In other words, do they constitute a selected sample who, by virtue of their genetic background and lifestyle behaviours – or a combination of both – are intrinsically at lower risk of myocardial infarction or stroke?

Against this background the medical world awaited with great interest the publication in 1998 of the Heart Estrogen/Progestin Replacement Study (HERS),[8] the first large RCT with predetermined cardiovascular endpoints in women with established cardiovascular disease. The results were disappointing. Of the over 1300 women randomised to continuous conjugated equine oestrogens (CEE) plus medroxyprogesterone acetate (MPA), there was an excess of cardiovascular disease or cardiovascular system events in the first year of study compared with the placebo-treated control group. This did not recur in years two, three and four of the study and overall there was an excess of deaths in the treated group. However, the damage was done. The first-year excess of events was strongly reminiscent of the excess of venous thromboembolic events that have been well described – in RCTs – as being associated with HRT and SERM therapy – particularly in the first six months of treatment. What had been observed in the venous side of the circulation seemed to be true of the arterial side as well. In consequence of this study, the American Heart Association in the summer of 2001 issued a set of guidelines for clinical practice[9] recommending that HRT should not be used solely for the prevention of events in women with established cardiovascular disease – and also that until further evidence accrued it should not be used solely for primary prevention either. These guidelines, almost entirely conditioned by the HERS study, drew criticism from other workers in the field – and rightly so. Mendelsohn and Karas[10] pointed out that the guidelines should only have applied to the population studied in the HERS trial, who were neither perimenopausal nor immediately postmenopausal but were in fact much older women, on average some 20 years after menopause. HERS had nothing to say about the use of oestradiol, any progestogen other than MPA or the prevention of cardiovascular disease, or indeed treatment of it, in younger women. Hence the question must remain open until further RCT observations on this younger cohort are available. All the HERS data suggest is that the addition of CEE plus MPA to the regimen of women 20 years postmenopause who are suffering from cardiovascular disease may result in an excess of events in the first year – although not over a four-year period. However, few British gynaecologists would, in any event, pursue such a strategy.

Thus, for the moment, the gynaecologist faced with a patient at perimenopause who has a primary indication for HRT use through her menopausal symptoms or through the risk of osteoporosis should not be disbarred from using such treatment by the presence of cardiovascular disease risk factors. She should, of course, be advised to stop smoking, lose weight, take more exercise, have hypertension therapy as appropriate, but the HRT should be deployed if indicated. With regard to risk factors, patients should be told the straightforward facts that HRT does not in general elevate blood pressure – indeed it often lowers it – and is likely to be associated with a lowering of total and low density lipoprotein (LDL) cholesterol in the plasma. Women discerned to be hypertensive at the obligatory blood pressure check before receiving HRT should be rendered normotensive before starting oestrogen in accordance with accepted good practice. With regard to blood pressure, the recent findings[11] are of considerable interest. In a prospective randomised study of postmenopausal women with a mean age of 64 years at entry, they reviewed the effects of HRT on blood pressure over a follow-up period of up to a decade. Women taking HRT exhibited an increase of 7.6 mmHg in systolic pressure over ten years, while matched women not taking oestrogen showed a rise of 18.7 mmHg. Diastolic pressure was unchanged in both groups. The interpretation of these data is that HRT maintained a healthy suppressant effect on peripheral vascular resistance, the effect being most pronounced in those at higher risk of cardiovascular events, the older and more obese among the study group.

One frequent problem that many gynaecologists face is the patient with a definite past history of myocardial infarction. A recent study by Shlipak et al.[12] has addressed this issue. In a large group of 114 724 survivors of myocardial infarction aged 55 years and over, these investigators found that a history of current HRT exposure was associated with an improved survival, the adjusted point estimate of reduction in risk of death being 35% with a 95% CI of 28–50. This figure is, interestingly, close to the mean reduction in cardiovascular mortality noted by Grady et al.[7] in their meta-analysis of observational studies. Several large RCTs with cardiovascular disease endpoints are due to report in the next two to three years. While we await their analysis it is fair to say that, in summary, a large body of *in vitro* evidence supports the notion that the oestrogen receptors in endothelium and in vascular smooth muscle are functionally important. They appear to be associated with a reduction in vascular resistance, maintenance of the plasticity of small vessels and an inhibition of thrombogenesis.[13] Oestrogen, acting through nitrogen oxidase synthetase to promote prostacydin production, is felt to be a significant player in the restraint of atherogenesis. In addition, the effects of oestrogen on lipid profile, although less potent than the direct vascular effects, are also probably of importance and point towards a lowering of cardiovascular risk with a lowering of total and LDL cholesterol and elevation of high-density lipoprotein (HDL) cholesterol.

Thus, the observational data point to risk reduction, as do the acute myocardial infarction figures. In deference to the HERS study, it should be agreed that the initiation of CEE and MPA 20 years after menopause in women with established cardiovascular disease is probably not a good idea.

CENTRAL NERVOUS SYSTEM

The third great network that is oestrogen-sensitive and responds adversely to oestrogen deprivation is the central nervous system (CNS). That oestrogens have specific areas of action in the brain has long been known and was first suspected through the symptoms of tiredness, irritability, mood swings, loss of short-term memory and depression that often accompany natural or surgical menopause. Conversely, it has long been appreciated that these psychological symptoms of menopause are often ameliorated by HRT in varying degrees. Indeed, a frequent tactic of physicians faced with a postmenopausal woman who has a spectrum of psychological complaints is to use HRT initially for the standard trial period of three months. This will subtract from the symptom load those which are truly oestrogen-sensitive and the residual, non-menopausal, complaints can then be seen in isolation and the appropriate management, or referral, can be instituted.

One acute CNS-based symptom that frequently confronts practitioners is migraine. Many women who suffer from this condition experience an exacerbation in the perimenopause with, in some cases, a reduction in attacks when amenorrhoea intervenes. The effects of oestrogen on CNS endorphin production shown by Fioretti *et al.*[14] are of relevance here. Restabilisation of endorphin production by HRT, especially if given continuously and by the transdermal route, may be the best means of stabilising the migrainous cycle of treated postmenopausal women.[15] Although migraine is an acute practical problem, the central long-term issue involving oestrogen on the CNS relates to the dementias. Although there is no evidence that oestrogen will modify the clinical course of established Alzheimer's disease, there is a substantial body of observational evidence that oestrogen, taken in the postmenopause, may reduce the incidence of the disease in later life. The best and most recent study to look at this issue is the Cache County Study, reported by Carlson *et al.*[16] from Johns Hopkins University, Baltimore. This group followed up 2073 neurologically normal females aged 65 years and over in Cache County, Utah. To assess cognitive decline over the three-year follow-up period, they used the Mini-Mental State Examination, sensitive to those indices such as verbal memory and global cognition that are abnormal in Alzheimer's or related dementias. The authors recorded HRT exposure and duration and were properly cautious in correcting their results for potential confounding by age, years of formal education, depression and the *APOEe4* genotype, all of which influence dementia. With these variables accounted for, the authors detected a clear superiority among HRT-exposed women both in terms of baseline assessment of cognition and in its subsequent decline. Indeed, the strongest influence of prior HRT appeared in the oldest cohort, those aged 85 years and over. Interestingly, the age at which HRT was started did not affect the results and the average duration of exposure was six years. Until the true association between the dementias and HRT is attested by RCT – it would be sensible for the practitioner, faced with a patient concerned about Alzheimer's or someone who has a relative with the problem – to consider HRT for a period of around five years – comparable to the first-instance exposure of patients who are at risk of osteoporosis. It should be remembered, however, that the HRT preparations are not, at present, licensed for this indication and that the prescription should be given primarily either for a licensed indication or on a named patient basis.

GASTROINTESTINAL SYSTEM

Oestrogen receptors are found at all levels of the bowel wall but their greatest concentrations, and indeed the greatest potential for therapeutic modification of bowel disorder, lie in the colon. Colorectal cancer is a common tumour and in the USA is the second leading cause of death from malignant disease. Over recent years, several observational studies have suggested that the use of HRT may be associated with a reduced incidence of colonic adenocarcinoma. The position has recently been admirably summarised by Grodstein *et al.*[17] from Harvard. Their meta-analysis of 18 studies detected an overall reduction of about one-fifth, the relative risk being 0.80 (95% CI: 0.74–0.86), together with a similar reduction in rectal cancers among ever-users of HRT versus non-ever-users. A significant segment of this reduction applied only to those currently on therapy. Separately examined, cancer rates in current users were lowered by one-third compared with rates in never-users. Further work is required to determine how these effects operate at the cellular level. This may involve secondary bile acid changes in HRT-treated women or a direct effect on the oestrogen receptor-rich colonic epithelium.

IMMUNE SYSTEM

The interaction between various steroid hormone groups, such as the oestrogens, and the immune response is complex. However, it may be said in general that there is a sexual dimorphism in the response, that certain cells of the immune system express oestrogen receptors and, as is well known, there is often a marked sex difference in the prevalence of autoimmune diseases. These include Hashimoto's thyroiditis, a prime forerunner of hypothyroidism, where the male–female ratio is 1:25–50, and rheumatoid arthritis, where the ratio is 1:5. This sex difference presents elsewhere in the animal kingdom,[18] but only in the human can the effect of menopause be assessed. In general, there is a decline in the rigour of the immune response with the ending of the reproductive years, during which there is great resistance to the induction of immune tolerance[19] and a speedier rejection of homografts.[20] In general, the incidence of autoimmune diseases falls in women after menopause and there is no hard evidence that HRT use promotes the appearance, or exacerbation, of such conditions.

CONCLUSIONS

The oestrogens are polyvalent. Their principal, and indeed primal, activity is command and control of the female reproductive cycle of ovulation, gestation, parturition and lactation. Outwith reproduction, the true extent of their scope and range is only now coming into sharp focus with our new-found ability to detect their receptors, tissue by tissue, and to assess their contributions to normal function. In general, it seems that evolution has found these ancient steroid bioregulators useful for the close – or remote – control of many systems, particularly in humans, the 'Big Three' – the vascular tree, the CNS and the trabecular skeleton. It is now for clinicians to capitalise on the observations available and to determine whether or not oestrogen withdrawal at menopause is singly or jointly responsible for the development of such conditions as osteoporosis, cardiovascular disease and Alzheimer's disease. If so, it will be necessary to perform randomised trials that will eliminate confounders and ultimately reveal the true utility of HRT. It has repeatedly been observed above that, in respect of several important chronic conditions, patients currently on HRT seem to do best. It is now for the research community to develop variants of the classic oestrogen molecule, which will confer tissue-specific benefit where and when it is required, while eliminating those adverse effects involving the reproductive tissues that affect breast and endometrium, the prime causes of patient rejection of this useful therapy. There will probably never be an ideal synthetic oestrogen, but there will be useful steps along the way.

References

1   Brzozowski AM, Pike ACW, Dauter Z, Hubbard RE, Bonn T, Engstrom O, et al. Molecular basis of agonism and antagonism in the oestrogen receptor. *Nature* 1997;389:753–8.

2   Miller C, Bottema CDK, Stathis PA, Tokes LG, Feldman D. Unexpected presence of estrogens in culture-medium supplements. *Endocrinol* 1986;119:1362–9.

3   Albright F, Burnett CH, Cope O, et al. Acute atrophy of bone (osteoporosis) simulating hyperparathyroidism. *J Clin Endocrinol Metab* 1941;1:711–16.

4   Pacifici R. Postmenopausal osteoporosis: how the hormonal changes of menopause cause bone loss. In: Marcus R, Feldman D, Kelsey J, editors. *Osteoporosis*. San Diego, CA: Academic Press; 1996. p. 727–43.

5   Riggs BL, Khosla S, Melton LJ, III. A unitary model for involutional osteoporosis: estrogen deficiency causes both type I and type II osteoporosis in postmenopausal women and contributes to bone loss in aging men. *J Bone Miner Res* 1998;13:763–73.

6   Torgerson DJ, Bell-Syer SE. HRT and the prevention of vertebral fractures. *Biomed Central; Musculoskeletal Disorders* 2001;2:7–11.

7   Grady D, Rubin SM, Petitti DB, Fox CS, Black D, Ettinger B, et al. Hormone therapy to prevent disease and prolong life in postmenopausal women. *Ann Intern Med* 1992;117:1016–37.

8   Hulley S, Grady D, Bush T, Furberg C, Herrington D, Riggs B, et al. Randomized trial of oestrogen plus progestin for secondary prevention of coronary heart disease in postmenopausal women. HERS Research Group. *JAMA* 1998;280:605–13.

9   Mosca L, Collins P, Herrington DM, Mendelsohn ME, Pasternak RC, Robertson RM, et al. Hormone replacement therapy and cardiovascular disease: a statement for healthcare professionals from the American Heart Association. *Circulation* 2001;104:499–503.

10   Mendelsohn ME, Karas RH. The time has come to stop letting the HERS tale wag the dogma. *Circulation* 2001;104:2256–9.

11   Scuteri A, Bos AJG, Brant LJ, Talbot L, Lakatta EG, Fleg JL. Hormone replacement therapy and longitudinal changes in blood pressure in postmenopausal women. *Ann Intern Med* 2001;135:229–38.

12   Shlipak MG, Angeja BG, Go AS, Frederick PD, Canto JG, Grady D. Hormone therapy and in-hospital survival after myocardial infarction in postmenopausal women. *Circulation* 2001;104:2300–4.

13   Vargas R, Wroblewska B, Rego A, Hatch J, Ramwell PW. Oestradiol inhibits smooth muscle cell proliferation of pig coronary artery. *Br J Pharmacol* 1993;109:612–7.

14   Fioretti P, Paoletti AM, Gambacciani M, et al. Neuroendocrine effects of opioids in postmenopausal women. In: Fioretti P, Flamigni C, Jassoni VM, Melis GB, editors.

Postmenopausal Hormonal Therapy Benefits and Risks. New York: Raven Press; 1987. p. 1–8.

15   Kudrow L. The relationship of headache frequency to hormone dose in migraine. *Headache* 1975;15:36–49.

16   Carlson MC, Zandi PP, Plassman JT, *et al*. Hormone replacement therapy and reduced cognitive therapy decline in older women. The Cache County Study. *Neurology* 2001;57:2210–16.

17   Grodstein F, Newcomb PA, Stampfer MJ. Postmenopausal hormone therapy and the risk of colorectal cancer: a review and meta-analysis. *Am J Med* 1999;106:574–82.

18   Ahmed S, Penhale W, Talal N. Sex hormones, immune response and autoimmune disease. *Am J Pathol* 1985;121:531–51.

19   Waltman S, Burde R, Berrios J. Prevention of corneal homograft rejection by estrogen. *Transplant* 1971;11:194–6.

20   Kalland T. Alteration of antibody response in female mice after neonatal exposure to diethylstilbestrol. *J Immunol* 1980;124:194–8.

29

Problems with hormone implants

Michael Savvas and Nicholas Panay

INTRODUCTION

Subcutaneous hormone implants have been used for the relief of climacteric symptoms for many years. Greenblatt and Suran[1] published a double-blind study on the use of oestrogen and testosterone implants for the control of menopausal symptoms. A number of studies have been carried out since that confirm the value of implants for the treatment of climacteric symptoms. Indeed, hormone implants are more effective than the oral route and are often helpful in women who present with persistent climacteric symptoms despite taking oral oestrogen replacement. Implants have also been shown to be more effective than oral oestrogen in the prevention of postmenopausal osteoporosis. The use of implants also results in improvement in lipid profiles, which may be associated with a reduction in the risk of cardiovascular disease. Furthermore, the subcutaneous route avoids a first-pass effect through the liver, resulting in physiological premenopausal levels of oestradiol and oestrone.

This mode of treatment is preferred by many women, as it is more convenient and avoids the problem of poor compliance that is often seen with other forms of hormone replacement therapy (HRT). However, hormone implants have failed to gain the same popularity as other modes of HRT because of a number of perceived problems:

(1)   Implantation is seen as a surgical procedure that is perhaps a little too involved for routine use or is associated with a number of complications and cannot easily be removed if it becomes necessary.

(2)   The procedure needs to be carried out within hospital-based clinics, thereby overwhelming what are already extremely busy hospital clinics.

(3)   There are concerns regarding the androgenic adverse effects of testosterone implants.

(4)   Supraphysiological levels of oestradiol and tachyphylaxis: concern has been expressed that the relatively high levels of oestradiol achieved may be associated with increased adverse effects. The term 'tachyphylaxis' has been used to describe the problem of increasingly frequent recurrence of symptoms that make the implants wear off soon after insertion despite relatively high levels of circulating oestradiol.

(5)   Some prefer to restrict the use of implants to women who have had a hysterectomy and do not need to take progestogens. Women with severe progestogenic adverse effects may be unable to take cyclical progestogens and may thus be at risk of endometrial cancer because the implant may be difficult to remove once it is inserted.

SURGICAL TECHNIQUES

Implants are usually inserted into the subcutaneous fat of the abdominal wall. The technique is simple. A small area is cleaned with antiseptic and anaesthetised with 1% lignocaine, which is injected intradermally and then subcutaneously. A 5 mm incision is then made into the skin using a pointed scalpel blade. The introducer is then inserted into the subcutaneous layer, the trocar is withdrawn and the hormone pellet is placed into the barrel of a cannula using a forceps. A blunt trocar or obturator is then inserted into the cannula, gently forcing the pellet into the subcutaneous fat. The trocar and cannula are then removed and pressure is applied over the wound for about a minute to aid haemostasis. Suturing is almost never necessary and the procedure takes between five and ten minutes.

Complications are rare, but the patient should be advised that bleeding may occur occasionally a few hours after the procedure and this can be controlled by gentle pressure over the implant site. Bruising may also occur around the implant site, but this is generally not troublesome. Infection of the implant site is uncommon. Occasionally the implants, particularly testosterone, may be rejected and it is important that the implants are inserted to an adequate depth. A recent study from Sydney[2] aimed to determine whether an alternative implantation site (hip) and/or track geometry would reduce extrusion rates, compared with the standard abdominal site. Additionally, the study aimed to evaluate the effects of site and track geometry on other adverse effects (bruising, infection) and the pharmacology of testosterone release from the implants. The extrusion rate was significantly higher (OR 2.6; 95% CI 1.1–7.1) for the hip site (15/125, 12%) than for the abdominal site (6/121, 5%). Track geometry made no significant difference (OR 1.05; 95% CI 0.2–5.4) to the extrusion rate. No secondary end-points (bruising, infection) were significantly different according either to site or to track geometry. Neither implantation site nor track geometry influenced pharmacokinetics.

Removing hormone implants

Some doctors and patients are reluctant to undertake this form of HRT because the implant cannot easily be removed should it prove necessary. In the extremely rare instance that the implant requires removal it is possible to localise the implant with magnetic resonance imaging to facilitate removal.

HOSPITAL-BASED CLINICS

Many units are reluctant to initiate implant therapy because women will need to return on a six-monthly basis for repeat treatment. Treatment with oral or transdermal preparations is often preferred, because such treatment can be continued by the GP. However, as already described, the technique of hormonal implantation is simple and can quite easily be carried out in general practice. It can also be carried out by nurse practitioners either in a hospital-based clinic or in the community. Hormone implants are a cheap mode of HRT, even taking into account the cost of the insertion.

Prepackaged sterile disposable trocars and cannulae are now available, which further facilitate the use of this technique in the community. The 25 mg oestradiol implant is also available in a simple injectable form in some European countries (not in the UK yet), further simplifying the insertion procedure (Riselle®, Organon Laboratories Ltd).

TESTOSTERONE IMPLANTS

Testosterone can also be implanted at the same time as oestradiol pellets. The usual dose of 50–100 mg every six months should be considered in women who have persistent symptoms, such as tiredness or loss of libido, despite oestrogen therapy alone, and in those women who have undergone an iatrogenic menopause; 25 mg testosterone pellets are now available on a named patient basis in those situations in which either the clinician or the patient has concerns regarding potential androgenic adverse effects.

Testosterone should be considered, particularly in women who have undergone surgical menopause, as the ovaries are one source of up to 50% of a woman's androgen requirements. Excessive hair growth is rarely seen after long-term testosterone and will regress when the treatment is stopped. There is no evidence of an adverse effect of testosterone on lipids, lipoproteins or insulin resistance. In fact, there appears to be a beneficial effect on arterial vasodilatation, even in relieving the symptoms of myocardial ischaemia.[3]

Effect on menopausal libido

Determination of libido is multifactorial, being dependent on emotional and environmental influences as well as the hormonal milieu. Oestrogens are undoubtedly vital in the determination and maintenance of an individual's level of sexual desire but it appears that the balance of oestrogen and androgens is the pivotal factor. Studies of premenopausal women on the combined contraceptive pill have demonstrated a loss of libido mid-cycle due to a blunting of the testosterone surge that would normally occur with ovulation.[4] Also, in normal postmenopausal women sexual interest and coital frequency have been shown to correlate with testosterone, not with oestrone or oestradiol levels.[5]

Studies of women who have undergone hysterectomy and bilateral oophorectomy provide further evidence that, although exogenous oestrogens alone can produce some improvement in libido, the combination of oestrogen and testosterone usually produces a superior response.[6–8] It is also clear from these studies that some individuals will respond to oestrogen replacement alone but that most require testosterone, either alone or in combination with oestrogen (Figure 1).[9] The benefits are maintained even at long-term follow-up (Figure 2). Appropriate therapy with oestrogen and testosterone can increase the motivational aspects of sexual behaviour and has some effect on frequency of coitus and orgasmic response.

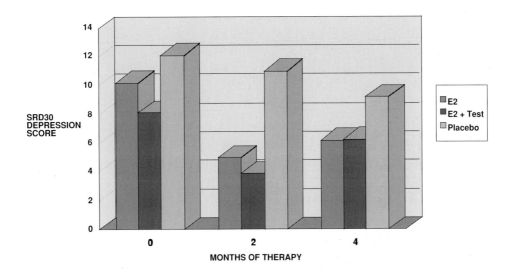

Figure 1 *Effect of oestradiol/testosterone implants on depression in perimenopausal women: 2-month results; E2 = oestradiol; Test = testosterone*[9]

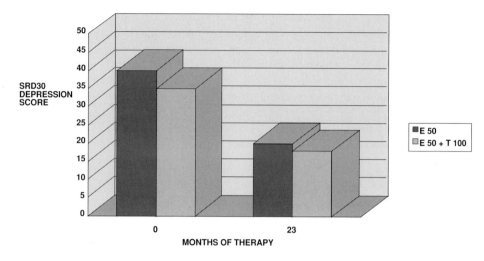

Figure 2 *Perimenopausal depression and hormone implants: 23-month results[9]; E = oestradiol; T = testosterone*

SUPRAPHYSIOLOGICAL LEVELS OF OESTRADIOL AND TACHYPHYLAXIS

The levels of serum oestradiol achieved with hormone implants are higher than those seen with oral or transdermal oestrogen preparations. Nevertheless, they remain within premenopausal range. Despite concern about these relatively high oestradiol levels, there is no evidence that this is associated with an increased incidence of thrombosis or breast cancer. Indeed, the higher levels of oestradiol are associated with better symptom control and better protection against osteoporosis. Savvas *et al.*[10] reported that the median oestradiol levels after 8.5 years of hormone implants at a dose of 50–100 mg every six months was 725 pmol/l and this was associated with a significantly higher bone density than that seen in women receiving oral oestrogen and a lower serum oestradiol.

Notelovitz *et al.*[11] reported that oestradiol implants given at six-monthly intervals result in premenopausal levels of serum oestradiol with a physiological ratio of oestradiol to oestrone. The carbohydrate metabolism and insulin was unaffected and no adverse effects were seen on the coagulation profiles, the coagulation inhibition and fibrinolysis assays.

The usual dose of oestradiol implant is 50 mg every six months but 25 mg may be used, which will result in lower serum oestradiol. Owen *et al.*[12] in an uncontrolled study reported that 25mg oestradiol may provide adequate symptom relief. Panay *et al.*,[13] in a randomised controlled study, demonstrated that 25 mg and 50 mg oestradiol resulted in similar symptom control for a similar duration, despite the fact that higher circulating oestradiol is seen following the use of the 50 mg dose. The 25 mg dose is also effective in the prevention of postmenopausal bone loss. Holland *et al.*[14] demonstrated that 25 mg oestradiol prevents postmenopausal bone loss and leads to a modest increase in bone density. However, higher doses have resulted in a greater increase in bone density. Studd *et al.*[15] have demonstrated that a 75mg implant given at six-monthly intervals resulted in an 8.3% increase in lumbar bone density and the increase was significantly correlated with the level of serum oestradiol.

Oestradiol implants at the dose of 25 mg may therefore be sufficient for the relief of climacteric symptoms in most women and this is sufficient to prevent postmenopausal osteoporosis. However, women who experience persistent symptoms or have already suffered significant bone loss may benefit from the higher dose. The implant frequency is just as important and, if this is kept to around six months, the oestradiol level is still within the premenopausal range.

Naessen et al.,[16] in a cross-sectional study of 35 women who received 20 mg oestradiol for a mean of 16 years, found that the median serum oestradiol in these women was 313 pmol/l (range 126–1711). All women, except one, who were reimplanted every six months had serum oestradiol levels less than 650 pmol/l. The higher levels were confined to the three women who were given higher doses or had an interval of less than six months between implants.

Barlow et al.[17] reported a randomised double-blind study comparing the use of 50 mg oestradiol implants with or without testosterone (100 mg). The implants were repeated six times at monthly intervals and the serum oestradiol was found to be 404 pmol/l (SD 132) at six months and 669 pmol/l (SD ± 211) at 36 months. Similar levels were seen in the women receiving testosterone together with oestradiol. The authors concluded that there was a degree of accumulation over the three-year study period, but the levels reported are similar to those seen in premenopausal women in the luteal phase. It was reassuring that these levels did not result in a significant increase in weight, blood pressure or liver function.

In a large study of 1388 women receiving implants at a dose of 50–100 mg, Garnett et al.[18] reported that only 3% had supraphysiological levels of oestradiol and, of these, 52% had a significant psychiatric history, suggesting that women with psychological symptoms require higher levels of circulating oestradiol to obtain symptom relief or that women with psychological symptoms return at an inappropriate frequency.

Tachyphylaxis

Tachyphylaxis is defined as reduced response to a standard dose of a drug. This term has been wrongly used to refer to the persistence of symptoms despite relatively high levels of oestradiol.[19] It is declining rather than absolute levels of oestradiol that result in symptom recurrence. Experience with this therapy has shown that it is impossible to correlate the return of symptoms with serum oestradiol. The timing of reimplantation should be determined by a combination of symptoms and the time elapsed since last insertion. Routine measurement of serum oestradiol is unhelpful and we would recommend that implants should not be repeated at less than four months. Women returning more frequently than this often complain of symptoms that are not due to oestrogen deficiency. Rather than repeat an implant prematurely, we would advise a detailed assessment of the woman's symptoms, which may reveal other – possibly psychological or social – causes. Inappropriate reimplantation in these circumstances may lead to some improvement through a placebo effect and lead to a pattern of learned behaviour in which the woman may misattribute a variety of problems to the implant wearing off and request reimplantation with increasing frequency.

In our practice we rarely see this problem because patients are given the right dose and we will not reimplant at less than four months. Women who request an implant sooner are carefully assessed and in many cases it can be established that their symptoms are not due to oestrogen deficiency. Sometimes oestrogen is given in the form of a patch or gel for a month or two, after which the implant can be repeated.

PROGESTOGEN INTOLERANCE: ENDOMETRIAL PROTECTION

Progestogens are necessary for non-hysterectomised women on oestrogen therapy if endometrial hyperplasia is to be prevented. However, progestogenic adverse effects and heavy, prolonged

Table 1 *Clinical management of progestogen intolerance*

Symptom/disturbance	Action
Heavy/prolonged bleeding	Increase dose/duration progestogen
	Use more androgenic progestogen
	Long-cycle/continuous combined HRT
	Progestogen/progesterone IUS
	Hysterectomy + unopposed oestrogen
Progestogenic adverse effects (physical/psychological)	Diuretics (fluid retention symptoms)
	Androgens (breast/headaches/libido)
	Decrease dose/duration progestogen
	Less androgenic progestogen (physical)
	More androgenic progestogen (psychological)
	Long-cycle HRT
	Progestogen/progesterone IUS
	Hysterectomy + unopposed oestrogen
	Unopposed oestrogen + endometrial sampling
Metabolic adverse effects (lipids/insulin resistance etc.)	Less androgenic progestogen
	?Long-cycle HRT
	?Progestogen/progesterone IUS

HRT = hormone replacement therapy; IUS = intrauterine system

withdrawal bleeds can be a significant problem in patients using HRT. This intolerance of progestogenic effects is one of the main reasons for poor compliance with HRT, leading to high discontinuation rates of prescribed HRT.

Oestradiol implants can produce relatively high levels of oestradiol. It is important that these high levels are opposed by an adequate duration and dosage of progestogen if endometrial hyperplasia is to be avoided. Unfortunately, this can lead to both psychological and physical progestogenic adverse effects, such as mood swings, irritability, migraines etc.[20] In addition, implanted pellets of oestradiol continue to deliver oestradiol for at least two years, which means that additional progestogen is required for some time after the last implant to protect the endometrium.[21] Occasionally women may request hysterectomy and bilateral oophorectomy, so that unopposed oestrogens may be used.

Attention now is focusing on how we can best avoid or improve the delivery of progestogens to minimise adverse effects, improve the benefit/risk ratio of HRT and thus maximise compliance. Recent developments in progestogens have provided greater scope for avoidance of adverse progestogenic effects (Table 1).

Dose and duration of sequential progestogen

Dealing with the adverse effects as they arise and manipulation of the dosage and duration of progestogen in sequential HRT is valuable and has been practised for many years. In the 'Consensus statement on progestin use in postmenopausal women' in Florida[22] it was deemed important to individualise the length of progestogen treatment (Table 1) because of potential metabolic effects and symptomatic complaints.

Continuous combined regimens

A smaller dosage of progestogen given on a daily basis should theoretically produce fewer

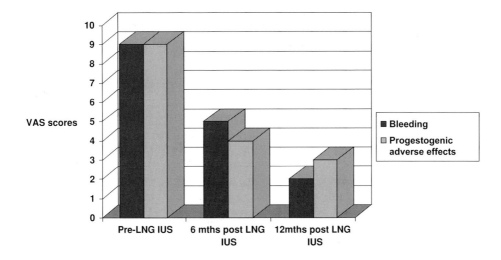

Figure 3 *Visual analogue scales (VAS) of global progestogenic adverse effects and bleeding severity in women using oestrogens with the levonorgestrel intrauterine system (LNG IUS) for progestogenic opposition*[24]

progestogenic adverse effects and amenorrhoea with an atrophic endometrium, which should be more acceptable to postmenopausal women.[23] Irregular vaginal bleeding in around 40% of women is common during the first three months of treatment, leading to high drop-out rates, but those who continue treatment over six to nine months can expect high rates of amenorrhoea with minimal adverse effects and good rates of compliance. Use of the 25 mg dosage oestradiol implant (with 1 mg of norethisterone) is more likely to achieve earlier amenorrhoea in view of the reduced endometrial stimulation by the lower serum levels.[24]

Local progestogenic opposition

In the authors' opinion, one of the best ways of opposing the relatively high oestradiol levels with implants is to use the 20 μg/day levonorgestrel-releasing intrauterine system (Mirena®; Schering). Adverse progestogenic effects and severity of bleeding can be reduced to a minimum when progestogen-intolerant patients using oestradiol implants, even with high serum oestradiol levels are switched from oral progestogens to Mirena. Endometrial suppression is uniform, with no cases of endometrial proliferation or hyperplasia at one year and a greater than 50% rate of amenorrhoea[25] (Figure 3). Although not licensed yet for this purpose in the UK, there is a great deal of data supporting its safety and efficacy for progestogenic opposition. A new system (the MLS; Schering), half the size and releasing half the dosage of levonorgestrel, is currently undergoing phase three trials and looks promising.[26]

It has been argued that oestradiol implant usage is not appropriate in non-hysterectomised women, especially if they are premenopausal and planning to have children. Premenopausal women using implants, e.g. for treatment of severe premenstrual syndrome, may continue to experience ovulation suppression long after therapy has ceased.[27] Also, endometrial stimulation can continue for up to two years following the last implantation, as a result of continued release of low levels of oestradiol from old implants. In order to avoid hyperplastic endometrial changes, a woman wishing to discontinue implants must still continue to use progestogens for up to two years (or at least until withdrawal bleeds have ceased in postmenopausal women).[21] Natural progesterone pessaries (Cyclogest®) also cause fewer progestogenic adverse effects. However, because natural progesterone is weaker at producing endometrial transformation, there may be problems with breakthrough bleeding with the high oestrogen levels produced by implants of 50 mg or greater.

CONCLUSIONS

Hormone implants have the benefit of ensuring good compliance with HRT; they avoid first-pass metabolic effects and are extremely effective in abolishing climacteric symptoms and increasing bone density. Testosterone can be added if there is any lack of energy or libido. They are not without drawbacks, such as the requirement for a minor surgical procedure for implantation, supraphysiological levels if used in inappropriately high doses, prolonged oestrogenic effects despite cessation of use and difficulty in removal if there is a problem. However, it is the authors' opinion that in appropriately selected cases (especially after hysterectomy) implants are extremely cost-effective and should be encouraged as a suitable and effective method of HRT.

References

1   Greenblatt RB, Suran RR. Indications for hormone pellets in the therapy of endocrine and gynecological disorders. *Am J Obstet Gynecol* 1949;47:294–301.

2   Kelleher S, Conway AJ, Handelsman DJ. Influence of implantation site and track geometry on the extrusion rate and pharmacology of testosterone implants. *Clin Endocrinol (Oxf)* 2001;55:531–6.

3   Webb CM, Adamson DL, de Zeigler D, Collins P. Effect of acute testosterone on myocardial ischemia in men with coronary artery disease. *Am J Cardiol* 1999;83:437–9.

4   Bancroft J, Sherwin BE, Alexander GN, Davidson HNC, Walker A. Oral contraceptive, androgens, and the sexuality of young women: 1. A comparison of sexual experience, sexual attitude and gender role in oral contraceptive users and non-users. *Arch Sex Behav* 1991;20:106.

5   McCoy N, Davidson JM. A longitudinal study of the effects of menopause on sexuality. *Maturitas* 1985;7:203–6.

6   Burger H, Hailes J, Nelson J, Menelaus M. Effect of combined implants of oestradiol and testosterone on libido in postmenopausal women. *BMJ* 1987;294:936–7.

7   Myers LS, Dixen J, Morrissette M, Carmichael M, Davidson JM. Effects of estrogen, androgen and progestin on sexual psychophysiology and behaviour in postmenopausal women. *J Clin Endocrinol Metab* 1990;70:1124–31.

8   Davis SR, McCloud P, Strauss BJG, Burger H. Testosterone enhances estradiol's effects on postmenopausal bone density and sexuality. *Maturitas* 1995;21:227–36.

9   Montgomery JC, Appleby L, Brincat M, Versi E, Tapp A, Fenwick PB, *et al*. Effect of oestrogen and testosterone implants on psychological disorders in the climacteric. *Lancet* 1987;i:297–99.

10   Savvas M, Studd JW, Fogelman I, Dooley M, Montgomery J, Murby B. Skeletal effects of oral oestrogen compared with subcutaneous oestrogen and testosterone in post-menopausal women. *BMJ* 1988;297:331–3.

11   Notelovitz M, Johnston M, Smith S, Kitchens C. Metabolic and hormonal effects of 25 mg

and 50 mg 17 beta estradiol implants in surgically menopausal women. *Obstet Gynecol* 1987;70:749–54.

12   Owen EJ, Siddle NC, McGarringle HT, Pugh MA. 5 mg oestradiol – the dosage of first choice for subcutaneous osterogen replacement therapy? *Br J Obstet Gynaecol* 1992;99:671–5.

13   Panay N, Versi E, Savvas M. A comparison of 25 mg and 50 mg oestradiol implants in the control of climacteric symptoms following hysterectomy and bilateral salpingo-oophorectomy. *Br J Obstet Gynaecol* 2000;107:1012–16.

14   Holland EF, Leather AT, Studd JW. The effect of 25 mg percutaneous oestradiol implants on the bone mass of postmenopausal women. *Obstet Gynecol* 1994;83:43–6.

15   Studd JW, Holland EF, Leather AT, Smith RN. The dose-response of percutaneous oestradiol implants on the skeletons of postmenopausal women. *Br J Obstet Gynaecol* 1994;101:787–91.

16   Naessen T, Persson I, Thor L, Mallmin H, Ljunghall S, Bergstrom R. Maintained bone density at advanced ages after long term treatment with low dose oestradiol implants. *Br J Obstet Gynaecol* 1993;100:454–9.

17   Barlow DH, Abdalla HI, Roberts AD, Al Azzawi F, Leggate I, Hart DM. Long term hormone implant therapy – hormonal and clinical effects. *Obstet Gynecol* 1986;67:321–5.

18   Garnett T, Studd JW, Henderson A, Watson N, Savvas M, Leather A. Hormone implants and tachyphylaxis. *Br J Obstet Gynaecol* 1990;97:917–21.

19   Gangar KF, Cust MP, Whitehead MI. Symptoms of oestrogen deficiency associated with supraphysiological plasma oestradiol concentrations in women with oestradiol implants. *BMJ* 1989;299:601–2.

20   Panay N, Studd JW. Progestogen intolerance and compliance with hormone replacement therapy in menopausal women. *Hum Reprod Update* 1997;3:159–71.

21   Gangar KF, Frazer D, Whitehead MI, Cust MP. Prolonged endometrial stimulation associated with oestradiol implants. *BMJ* 1990;300:436–8.

22   Utian WH. Consensus statement on progestin use in postmenopausal women. *Maturitas* 1989;11:175–7.

23   Magos AL, Brincat M, Studd JWW, Wardle P, Schlesinger P, O'Dowd T. Amenorrhoea and endometrial atrophy with continuous oral oestrogen and progestogen therapy in postmenopausal women. *Obstet Gynecol* 1985;65:496–9.

24   Panay N, Zamblera D, Sands RH, Jones J, Alaghband-Zadieh J, Studd JWW. Low-dose 25 mg oestradiol implants and 1 mg norethisterone as continuous combined hormone therapy. *BJOG* 2002;109:958–60.

25   Panay N, Studd J, Thomas A, Sands R, Khastgir G, Zakaria F, *et al.* Prospective study of menopausal women on subcutaneous oestradiol, switched to the levonorgestrel releasing intrauterine system because of oral progestogen intolerance. *Acta Obstet Gynecol Scand* 1997;76:56.

26   Raudaskoski T, Tapanainen J, Tomas E, Luotola H, Pekonen F, Ronni-Sivula H, *et al.* Intrauterine 10μg and 20 μg levonogesterel systems in postmenopausal women receiving oral oestrogen replacement therapy: clinical, endometrial and metabolic response. *Br J Obstet Gynaecol* 2002;109:136–44.

27   Magos AL, Collins WP, Studd JW. Effects of subcutaneous oestradiol implants on ovarian activity *Br J Obstet Gynaecol* 1987;94:1192–8.

30

How should we manage endometrial polyps?

Paul McGurgan, Peter O'Donovan and Sean Duffy

INTRODUCTION

In 1865, Pantaleoni reported the first case of diagnostic and therapeutic hysteroscopy when he happened to discover an endometrial polyp while investigating a woman with postmenopausal bleeding:[1] 'Having in such a way applied the endoscope … A polypous vegetation was easily discovered at the bottom of the cavity of the *fundus uteri* in my case. It was of a vivid red colour, unequal like a sponge, and of the largeness of a small strawberry'.

Pantaleoni's subsequent management to remove the polyp has since become the mainstay of treatment, with few data to guide clinicians as to why this should be effective.

Despite their great frequency, endometrial polyps have received relatively little attention, being largely regarded as mundane lesions of little significance. In recent years, however, several interesting aspects of endometrial polyps have begun to emerge, and this has awakened interest in the nature and significance of these common endometrial lesions.

The objectives of this chapter are to amalgamate the recent developments in our understanding of this common pathological entity and to review the available evidence on how to manage endometrial polyps most effectively.

DEFINITION

The term 'endometrial polyp' could be used to describe any polypoidal lesion protruding into the uterine cavity. By convention, however, the term is restricted to non-malignant pedunculated or sessile nodules composed of either functional or basal endometrium or a combination of the two.[2]

INCIDENCE

Although endometrial polyps are common, the true incidence in the female population is difficult to ascertain. The largest case series[3,4] report frequencies of approximately 10% in premenopausal women, doubling to over 20% in postmenopausal women. These figures are obtained from women presenting with symptoms; there are no published data for the incidence of endometrial polyps in the asymptomatic general population. Therefore, the true incidence may possibly be higher than the figures reported in the literature. Endometrial polyps are usually noted to be solitary (74%), with two polyps being diagnosed in 14% and three or more being present in 12% of cases.[4]

PRESENTATION

Endometrial polyps are diagnosed almost exclusively in women undergoing investigation for gynaecological problems. Most frequently, polyps are diagnosed in women presenting with abnormal uterine bleeding. This may either be postmenopausal bleeding, where polyps are found in 21.2% of women being investigated, or premenopausal, in women who present with intermenstrual/postcoital bleeding, where polyps are diagnosed in 16.8%, irregular periods (polyps found in 11.2%) or menorrhagia (polyps found in 10%).[3]

AETIOLOGY AND RISK FACTORS

Endometrial polyps are believed to develop as a consequence of focal stromal and glandular overgrowth.[2] The stimulus for this is unknown, but there is strong aetiological evidence for a hormonal basis. Polyps have never been reported before the menarche.[2] They are most commonly diagnosed in the fifth decade[5] – this is likely to be influenced by the different thresholds for investigating these two age groups of women.

Established risk factors for women with endometrial polyps are late menopause and the use of oestrogen-containing hormone replacement therapy or tamoxifen.[4] Women with symptomatic polyps also have increased rates of hypertension, obesity and anovulatory infertility (presumably secondary to hyperoestrogenism).[4] Obesity is believed to play a role through the increased aromatisation of androgens to oestrogens in adipose tissue.[6] Unlike endometrial cancer, there appears to be no association between endometrial polyps and either type 1 or type 2 diabetes mellitus.[4]

The role of oestrogen in the development of endometrial polyps is also supported at the cell receptor level. Studies have shown that there are relatively fewer receptors for progesterone compared with oestrogen in the stromal but not in the glandular component of polyps. This is believed to make polyps relatively insensitive to cyclic hormonal changes and it prevents the stroma from undergoing decidualisation and subsequent menstrual shedding.[7]

PATHOLOGY

Macroscopically, endometrial polyps vary greatly in size, and they may be sessile or pedunculated. In the reproductive years they are usually composed of what appears to be a non-functional basal endometrium or they have a central core of apparently basal type endometrium covered by a layer of functional endometrium of varying thickness.[2] The latter is usually out of step with the endometrium elsewhere in the uterine cavity, presumably as a result of the different hormone receptor expression in endometrial polyps.

The glands are usually inactive, weakly proliferative or weakly secretory, but simple hyperplasia, focal complex hyperplasia or focal atypical hyperplasia may also be seen. In postmenopausal women, polyps may be formed from either inactive basal-type endometrium or senile cystic endometrium, the latter probably reflecting more the tendency of foci of senile cystic change to become polypoid than the development of cystic change in the glands of an existing polyp.[2]

The stroma of a polyp always contains some fibrous tissue. In many, the stroma is predominantly fibrous; in others, the stroma is predominantly endometrial and, rarely, a mixed fibrous–endometrial stromal pattern may be seen.[8] The stromal cells not uncommonly show mild nuclear atypia[8] and, exceptionally, a fairly striking atypia can be seen in the stromal component.[9] Stromal mitotic figures are commonly either absent or sparse, but a modest number of mitoses may be seen in those polyps with an endometrial-type stroma.[8] The presence of stromal mitoses warrants a closer histological examination of the glandular pattern and degree of stromal condensation present in the endometrial polyp in order to distinguish benign from potentially malignant lesions.

A characteristic feature of polyps is the presence of a leash or cluster of small, thick-walled vessels in the base of the stalk. This can be a useful feature in differentiating endometrial polyps from polypoid endometrial hyperplasia.

Tamoxifen-associated endometrial polyps are unusually large, often exhibiting mitotic activity, periglandular stromal condensation and diverse, florid epithelial metaplasia.[10-13] The glands are often polarised to appear orientated along the long axis of the polyp and may have a staghorn morphology; in some series, foci of carcinoma within the polyps have been a not uncommon finding. There are no individual features present in tamoxifen-associated polyps that are not also found in non-tamoxifen-related polyps but nevertheless the particular combinations of features in tamoxifen-associated polyps are usually highly characteristic.

GENETICS

In common with other uterine pathologies such as leiomyoma, atypical endometrial hyperplasia and endometrial cancer, polyps have a monoclonal cell origin, shown by their non-random X-chromosome inactivation.[14]

Studies examining the patterns of X-chromosome inactivation support a premalignant potential for endometrial hyperplastic lesions. In contrast, endometrial polyps do not demonstrate the same patterns of positive X-chromosome inactivation demonstrated in coexistent carcinomas, supporting the hypothesis that endometrial polyps are benign with no obvious premalignant potential.[14]

Polyps are known to contain various karyotypic abnormalities. An inversion of chromosome 12 (p11.2q13) was found in 30% of endometrial polyp cells studied by Walter[15] in 1989. The same inversion also occurs in leiomyomas, salivary gland pleiomorphic adenomas and lipomas and is thought to contain a gene (or genes) that code for cellular proliferation rather than malignant transformation.[15] The twelfth chromosome in endometrial polyps is also known to contain a variety of other possible karyotypic abnormalities; these include t (12;13) (q14-15;q34) and inv (12) (p12-13q14-15). Since the 12q13-q15 locus is affected in different areas in the various studies, it is believed that this area contains important growth-regulation genes.[16]

Dal Cin and Speleman[17-19] have also reported abnormalities on chromosome 6 in endometrial polyps. Once again, these are similar to the changes seen on the short arm of chromosome 6 in other benign neoplasms such as leiomyomas, salivary gland pleiomorphic adenomas and lipomas. Fletcher et al.[20] have subsequently reported that the translocations on chromosome 6 are confined to mesenchymally derived tissue, with the presence of reactive epithelial populations (possibly stimulated in some way by the mesenchymal tissue). The most intensely investigated area on the short arm of chromosome 6 is the 6p21 site. This is thought to contain an oncogene, functioning either as an oncogene activator or a tumour suppressor gene. Genes that have been mapped to this area include the pim oncogene homologue gene (a factor in apoptosis),[21] and the genes for alpha and beta tumour necrosis factor (TNF, implicated in menstruation and implantation).[22,23]

It is now known that up to 60% of benign endometrial polyps studied have clonal rearrangements in three main areas: the 6p21-p22 region, the 12q13-15 region and the 7q22 region.

The two regions most commonly affected, 12q15 and 6p21, are the loci of the *HMGIC* (maps to 12q15) and *HMGIY* (maps to 6p21) genes. These genes code for 'architectural proteins' that influence chromatin structure and gene transcription. *HMGIC* is not usually expressed in adult cells (and is very rarely expressed by malignant cell lines).[24] These genes are commonly affected in other benign mesenchymal tumour cells.

There is a normal karyotype in approximately 40% of endometrial polyps, which suggests that there is a spectrum of cytogenetically different subgroups of endometrial polyps; a feature shared

factors for endometrial carcinoma. *Acta Obstet Gynecol Scand* 1985;64:653–9.

28   Armenia CS. Sequential relationship between endometrial polyps and carcinoma of the endometrium. *Obstet Gynecol* 1967;30:524–9.

29   Salm R. The incidence and significance of early carcinoma in endometrial polyps. *J Pathol* 1972;108:47–53.

30   Silva EG, Jenkins R. Serous carcinoma in endometrial polyps. *Mod Pathol* 1990;3:120–8.

31   Lee K, Belinson J. Recurrence in non-invasive endometrial carcinoma: relationship to uterine papillary serous carcinoma. *Am J Surg Pathol* 1991;15:965–73.

32   Sherman ME, Bitterman P, Rosenhein NB, Delgado G, Kurman RJ. Uterine serous carcinoma. A morphologically diverse neoplasm with unifying clinicopathologic features. *Am J Surg Pathol* 1992;16:600–10.

33   De Muldyer X, Neven P, De Somer M, Van Belle Y, Vanderick G, De Muylder E. Endometrial lesions in patients undergoing tamoxifen therapy. *Int J Gynecol Obstet* 1991;36:127–30.

34   Killackey MA, Hakes TB. Endometrial adenocarcinoma in breast cancer patients receiving antioestrogens. *Cancer Treat Rep* 1985;69:237–8.

35   IARC on tamoxifen. *Environ Health Perspect* 1996;104:688.

36   Neven P, Vergote I. Should tamoxifen users be screened for endometrial lesions. *Lancet* 1998;351:155–7.

37   Bandolier Evidence-Based Health Care [http://www.jr2.ox.ac.uk/bandolier/band54/b54-6. html].

38   Berliere M, Charles A, Galant C, Donnez J. Uterine side effects of tamoxifen: a need for a systematic pretreatment screening programme. *Obstet Gynecol* 1998;91;40–44.

39   Cohen I, Altaras MM, Shapira J, Tepper R, Beyth Y. Postmenopausal tamoxifen treatment and endometrial pathology. *Obstet Gynecol Surv* 1994;49:823–9.

40   Dal Cin P, Timmerman D, Van den Berghe I, Wanschura S, Kazmierczak B, Vergote I, *et al.* Genomic changes in endometrial polyps associated with tamoxifen show no evidence for its action as an external carcinogen. *Cancer Res* 1998;58:2278–81.

41   Varasteh NN, Neuwirth RS, Levin B, Keltz MD. Pregnancy rates after hysteroscopic polypectomy and myomectomy in infertile women. *Obstet Gynecol* 1999;94:168–71.

42   Mastrominas M, Pistofidis GA, Dimitropoulos K. Fertility outcome after out-patient hysteroscopic removal of endometrial polyps and submucous fibroids. *J Am Assoc Gynecol Laparosc* 1996;3 Suppl 4:S29.

43   Golan A, Halperin R, Herman A, Hadas E, Soffer Y, Bukovsky I, *et al.* Human decidua-associated protein 200 levels in uterine fluid at hysteroscopy. *Gynecol Obstet Invest* 1994;38:217–9.

44   Gebauer G, Hafner A, Siebzehnrubl E, Lang N. Role of hysteroscopy in detection and extraction of endometrial polyps: results of a prospective study. *Am J Obstet Gynecol* 2001;184:59–63.

45   Karlsson B, Granberg S, Wikland M, Ylostalo P, Torvid K, Marsal K, *et al.* Transvaginal ultrasonography of the endometrium in women with postmenopausal bleeding – a Nordic multicenter study. *Am J Obstet Gynecol* 1995;172:1488–94.

46   Ferrazzi E, Torri V, Trio D, Zannoni E, Filiberto S, Dordoni D. Sonographic endometrial thickness: a useful test to predict atrophy in patients with postmenopausal bleeding. An Italian multicenter study. *Ultrasound Obstet Gynecol* 1996;7:315–21.

47   Maia H Jr, Maltez A, Calmon LC, Marques D, Oliveira M, Coutinho E. Comparison between suction curettage, transvaginal sonography and hysteroscopy for the diagnosis of endometrial polyp. *Gynaecological Endoscopy* 1998;7:127–32.

48   La Torre R, De Felice C, De Angelis C, Coacci F, Mastrone M, Cosmi EV. Transvaginal

sonographic evaluation of endometrial polyps: a comparison with two dimensional and three dimensional contrast sonography. *Clin Exp Obstet Gynecol* 1999;26:171–3.

49   Kamel HS, Darwish AM, Mohamed SA. Comparison of transvaginal ultrasonography and vaginal sonohysterography in the detection of endometrial polyps. *Acta Obstet Gynecol Scand* 2000;79:60–4.

50   Heller DS. How accurate is the diagnosis of endometrial polyp? *Int J Gynecol Obstet* 1997;59:59–60.

51   Nagele F, Mane S, Chandrasekaran P, Rubinger T, Magos A. How successful is hysteroscopic polypectomy? *Gynaecological Endoscopy* 1996;5:137–40.

52   Porreca MR, Pansini N, Bettocchi S, Loverro G, Selvaggi L. Hysteroscopic polypectomy in the office without anaesthesia. *J Am Assoc Gynecol Laparosc* 1996;3 Suppl 4;S40.

53   O'Donovan, P, McGurgan P, Jones SE. *Versapoint: A Novel Technique for Operative Hysteroscopy in a Saline Medium.* Atlanta, GA: American Association of Gynecologic Laparoscopists; 1998.

31

New thoughts on the aetiology of cerebral palsy

Eve Blair and Fiona Stanley

INTRODUCTION

It is dangerous to commit to permanent record anything that bears the description 'new'. A term is then quickly required to denote what is even more up-to-date, as with 'postmodernism'. However, concepts concerning the aetiology of cerebral palsy may change in cycles rather than linearly. It is evidence to support or refute those concepts that accumulates over time. In order to set these 'new' thoughts in a more enduring context, this chapter gives a brief review of the history of ideas concerning the aetiology of cerebral palsy over the last 140 years.

THE CONCEPTS OF CEREBRAL PALSY AETIOLOGY

While the disabilities now included under the rubric of cerebral palsy have been recognised for millennia, it was not defined as an entity when WJ Little gave his seminal presentation in 1862 entitled 'On the incidence of the abnormal parturition, difficult labour, premature birth and asphyxia neonatorum on the mental and physical condition of the child, especially in relation to deformities'. [1] The deformities were contractures resulting from the progressive failure of muscle growth to keep pace with bone growth, typical of what we now call spastic cerebral palsy. The collective term 'cerebral palsy' was first employed in the 1930s and was defined as covering a variety of clinical entities, as in its most recent definition 'an umbrella term covering a group of non-progressive, but often changing, motor impairment syndromes secondary to lesions or anomalies of the brain arising in the early stages of its development'.[2] However, despite such constant reminders, there has been a recurring tendency in both lay and medical circles to act as though cerebral palsy were a single disease, rather than a diverse group with only an element of their clinical description in common. It is ironic that Little, in his report on children with spastic cerebral palsy, who constitute 80% of those now covered by the term 'cerebral palsy', should be accused of suggesting a single intrapartum cause. His report demonstrates both a belief in a multiplicity of possible causes and a belief that individual causes could be multifactorial: that intrapartum events could represent both the final straw in a series of events and only one among several possible causes. In answer to questions following his presentation, he tells us that in his day postneonatal acquisition, often a result of infection, was 20 times more common than was intrapartum acquisition. These concepts of multifactorial cause and multicausal aetiology were reiterated by Freud in 1897 and repeatedly during the 20th century,[3] yet the concept of one-to-one matching – one name for one disease resulting from one cause that consisted of one event – has doggedly persisted in the wider audience. That one cause sometimes remains the birth attendant and the one event, that ill-defined clinical entity, asphyxia, during labour and delivery.[4]

Multicausality and multifactorial cause are therefore old concepts, to which the current explosion of aetiological research brings additional support, as it sketches the diversity of causal paths and details possible factors within those paths.[5] 'What does cause cerebral palsy if not asphyxia at birth?' is a misframed question. Ask rather: 'What other causes are there in addition to asphyxia at birth?' and, when birth asphyxia is suspected, 'Why did it occur?' The interest in causal paths is not academic. If each causal route has many necessary factors, the possibilities for prevention are increased, allowing the most efficacious, acceptable and cost-effective to be chosen.

The aetiology of cerebral palsy may be considered under a series of broad headings: familial/genetic, multiple conception, early and late pregnancy factors, very preterm birth, intrapartum and neonatal factors, postneonatal acquisition and, of course, unknown. They are not mutually exclusive: a twin with cerebral palsy may be born very preterm and/or run into intrapartum difficulties or have no recognised cause of brain damage; a genetic variant may predispose to pregnancy complications or postneonatal acquisition. Much of the evidence concerning pathways to cerebral palsy published before 1998 was reviewed in our recent book.[5]

NEW EVIDENCE FOR CEREBRAL PALSY AETIOLOGY

This review concentrates on later publications. The immediate causes of postneonatally acquired cerebral palsy are well understood, but there are no recent reports concerning more distal causes, which tend to have their roots in social disadvantage.[6] Similarly, there has been little progress with the aetiology of cerebral palsy in multiple births despite reproductive technology ensuring that their contribution is increasing. It is appreciated that their risks are not limited to those born earlier and of lower birthweight, particularly in twins sharing a blood supply, but investigation of the hypothesis that the first-trimester loss of a co-twin predisposes to cerebral palsy[7] is hampered by the lack of any population data on twin conceptions.

The increasing survival of infants born very prematurely has created a well-defined group at relatively high risk of cerebral palsy that is routinely observed for a prolonged neonatal period and followed up to an age at which cerebral palsy can be recognised. Coupled with the fear that very preterm cerebral palsy may be an iatrogenic disease, arising from the unprecedented survival of very premature babies and/or the intensive neonatal care that they receive, it is not surprising that a large portion of the recent literature in cerebral palsy aetiology concerns this group. The role of chorioamnionitis and neonatal maintenance of blood gases is being explored, as are the effects of corticosteroids, administered either pre- or postnatally, indomethacin and magnesium. Neuroimaging is making technological progress, demonstrating a variety of neuropathological lesions and useful for predicting likely outcome, but as yet is of limited assistance in elucidating causal pathways. Gene-mapping has located genetic variants associated with familial cerebral palsy in isolated affected families, but these are likely to be relevant only to those families. Of wider applicability may be the hypothesis that more commonly occurring genetic variants associated with thrombophilia or thrombocytopenia predispose to cerebral insult. Birth asphyxia continues to be difficult to recognise clinically, which hampers investigation of strategies wishing to capitalise on the window of opportunity for neuronal rescue between the initial hypoxic insult and the onset of hypoxia-induced apoptosis. Across the spectrum of gestational age at delivery, there is the suggestion that the ability to preserve life in compromised neonates precedes the ability to ensure an intact outcome, whether at the borders of gestational viability or of intertwin transfused twins or of term infants compromised by a variety of factors.

FACTORS PRIMARILY OF IMPORTANCE FOR VERY PRETERM BIRTH

The risk of cerebral palsy in neonatal survivors born before 33 weeks of gestation in Western Australia 1980–94 was about 30 times that of a neonatal survivor born at term. As very preterm survival improved, its contribution to cerebral palsy increased. Infants born before 30 weeks of gestation contributed only 6.6% of all cerebral palsy born in Western Australia 1975–80, but 21% of those born in 1990–94. In 1980–84 the peak frequency of cerebral palsy was observed in infants born at 30 weeks of gestation, and infants born at shorter gestations had a lower risk of cerebral palsy. Explanations invoked an enhanced risk of germinal matrix haemorrhage around 29–31 gestational weeks. However, as survival among infants born before 30 weeks increased, so did their frequency of cerebral palsy. The gestation of peak cerebral palsy frequency declined from 30 weeks in 1980–84 to 29 weeks in 1985–89, to 27 weeks in 1990–94. Compared with Western Australian infants born 1980–84, the risk of cerebral palsy in births at 28–32 weeks in 1990–94 decreased[8] and similar decreases have been reported elsewhere.[9–11] However, the risk of cerebral palsy in Western Australian births at 20–27 weeks of gestation continued to increase.[8] The causes of cerebral palsy need not be the same as those of perinatal death, but perinatal survival is a prerequisite for acquiring a description of cerebral palsy.

The high risk of cerebral palsy in very preterm birth surprises nobody, but prematurity is not a sufficient cause of cerebral palsy. While there is a high frequency of abnormal outcomes, the majority do not have cerebral palsy.[12] Babies born very prematurely with cerebral palsy must therefore experience additional factors or constellations of factors that cause brain damage, increase cerebral vulnerability to postnatal hazards and/or protect a brain-damaged infant from perinatal death.

CORTICOSTEROIDS

Antenatal

Systematic review of a single course of antenatal corticosteroids administered shortly before delivery demonstrates unequivocal benefits in terms of survival, although the evidence suggesting protection against periventricular leukomalacia and long-term neurological morbidity is based on small numbers of births between one and three decades ago.[13] The evidence was sufficient in 1994 for the US National Institutes of Health (NIH) to recommend its use in all pregnancies threatening to deliver between 24 and 34 weeks and to launch a trial to investigate methods of encouraging its use.[14]

Their protective effects were believed to diminish after seven days, so corticosteroids were sometimes administered weekly for undelivered patients in whom the threat of preterm delivery persisted.[15] Since corticosteroids have been associated with impaired lung growth and function,[16] myelination,[17] adrenal function,[18] maternal and fetal immune function and reductions in fetal growth and numbers of neurones,[19] the NIH issued a consensus statement[20] on the use of repeat courses calling for further research, much of which is now in progress.[21] However, repeat doses may be unnecessary if the protective effects of corticosteroids last longer than seven days,[22–24] and the very limited available evidence concerning the long-term effects of multiple courses[25] suggests that it is not associated with cerebral palsy or other major disabilities.

Postnatal

The same cannot be said of corticosteroids administered postnatally to improve gas exchange and lung mechanics. Evidence of an association with adverse neurological outcome prompted a systematic review.[26] This review was hampered by frequent administration of corticosteroids to those allocated to placebo but, in those studies with less than 30% of controls receiving corticosteroids, the relative risk of cerebral palsy in the intervention group was almost three times that in the control group (RR 2.86; 95% CI 1.95–4.19). These same studies do not show any long-term benefits for mortality or lung function. Barrington estimated that about 12 800 infants received postnatal corticosteroids annually in North America and, on the basis of the systematic review, that there would be one additional case of cerebral palsy for every seven treated infants.[27] This suggests that 1727 cases of cerebral palsy could be prevented annually in North America if postnatal corticosteroids ceased to be administered.

The different effect of antenatal versus postnatal administration may be due to the tendency to use larger total doses postnatally and dexamethasone rather than betamethasone. Despite their molecular similarity, both animal and human observations suggest that the benefits of antenatally administered corticosteroids accrue exclusively from betamethasone.[28,29]

Indomethacin

Indomethacin is another drug commonly administered to very preterm infants, this time to prevent patent ductus arteriosus (PDA) and periventricular haemorrhage. In a randomised controlled trial of 1202 infants with birthweights between 500 g and 999 g, no clinical or statistical effect on rates of cerebral palsy, death or any other major impairment could be detected at 18 months, despite a significant reduction in PDA and grade III or IV periventricular or intraventricular haemorrhage.[30]

Magnesium sulphate

Retrospective studies reported in 1995–7 suggested that maternal administration of magnesium sulphate protected very preterm infants from cerebral palsy. While biologically plausible mechanisms existed, there was also considerable possibility for confounding and some workers failed to find similar effects. Another retrospective study of a more recent cohort of very preterm infants born to women without pre-eclampsia[31] failed to confirm the association and also demonstrated much higher rates of magnesium tocolysis than in the earlier cohort. The authors concluded that the original association arose because magnesium administration had previously been a marker for a protective factor but that, as a result of changing patterns of administration, it was no longer such a marker. Randomised controlled trials of magnesium prior to very preterm birth are in progress.[32,33]

Hypocapnia

Mechanical ventilation of very preterm babies enables carbon dioxide to be cleared extremely quickly, reducing pressure of carbon dioxide, which decreases cerebral bloodflow and hence oxygenation. In adults and newborn term infants hypocapnia is benign as the situation soon corrects itself automatically. However, several studies of very preterm babies have reported an association between measures of hypocapnia and neurodevelopmental deficits, particularly cystic periventricular leukomalacia and cerebral palsy.[34] Cumulative exposure to moderately low levels appears more dangerous than brief dramatic episodes.[35] Greisen and Vannucci[34] suggest that the peculiar vulnerability of very preterm infants may arise because hypocapnia and hypoxaemia act synergistically and hypoxaemia is less easy to detect in the very preterm, or because the mechanism for automatic correction is slower or does not occur in very preterm infants.

shown that there is a high prevalence (about 26%) of these antibodies in women receiving IVF.[84–86] Although it has been suggested that these antibodies are associated with infertility and implantation failure,[87–89] reports suggest that their presence does not adversely affect continuing pregnancy rates with IVF.[90] A further study, however, found that patients with autoantibodies, including antiphospholipid antibodies, had reduced chances of successful implantation that could be reversed by treatment with aspirin and oral steroids.[91] The effect of antiphospholipid antibodies on implantation does require further investigation.

EMBRYO FACTORS AFFECTING IMPLANTATION

One reason that human implantation rates may be much lower than those in other animals is that humans have a relatively high proportion of abnormal embryos.[92] Implantation may well be acting as a natural selection process in which only healthy embryos succeed.[43] The proportion of abnormal embryos increases with age, accounting for decreased pregnancy rates per embryo transfer with advancing age (Table 2).[61]

Number of embryos transferred

There is a continuing debate regarding the optimal number of embryos to transfer into the endometrial cavity. This debate centres on the fact that pregnancy rates increase with the number of embryos transferred, but so do multiple pregnancy rates and hence pregnancy complications.[73] If only one embryo is transferred, the livebirth rate is 7.3%, rising to 20.0% for two embryos and 22.5% for three embryos.

It has been shown that the most important factor for success is not the number of embryos transferred but the number of embryos available for transfer. HFEA data for 1997/98 illustrate that when four or more embryos are available for transfer the livebirth rates are the same whether two or three embryos are transferred. However, in this group the multiple pregnancy rate is much higher if three embryos are transferred (Table 5). For this reason, the current recommendations from Royal College of Obstetricians and Gynaecologists and British Fertility Society are that only two embryos should be transferred in women aged under 40 years.[93,94]

The true implantation rate is the number of implanted embryos per total embryos transferred. By this criterion, increasing the number of embryos transferred does not actually improve implantation rates. However, transferring a greater number of embryos increases the chances of multiple pregnancy and perinatal loss rate. Therefore it has been shown that electively transferring three rather than two embryos does not increase livebirth rates.[61] Embryo quality is affected by cryopreservation and this has a deleterious effect on implantation rates. The livebirth rate per embryo transfer for IVF and ICSI is 22.9% compared with 13.4% for frozen embryo replacements.[10]

Table 5 *Two and three embryo transfers for fresh stimulated in vitro fertilisation only (where more than four embryos were created)*[73]; *reproduced with permission from the Human Fertility and Embryology Authority*

Embryos transferred (*n*)	Cycles (*n*)	Livebirth rate (%)	Multiple birth rate (% of livebirths)
2	4650	26.4	26.0
3	8158	26.0	34.3

Assisted hatching

As laboratory techniques in assisted conception have improved, a number of techniques have emerged that enhance embryo implantation in certain circumstances. Embryo implantation rates can be improved by 'assisted hatching', a technique by which the zona pellucida is drilled or thinned by either mechanical[95] or chemical[96] methods. Cohen *et al.*[97] published a set of three studies in 1992, showing the beneficial effects of assisted hatching on implantation rates achieved by zona drilling with acid Tyrode's solution. They found that assisted hatching in patients with elevated follicle-stimulating hormone levels significantly increased clinical pregnancy rates (47% versus 13%) and implantation rates per embryo (26% versus 10%). Selective assisted hatching in embryos with thickened zonae also proved successful in increasing implantation rates (25% versus 18%). However, blanket use of assisted hatching was not recommended, as it was found to have a deleterious effect on healthy embryos with normal zonae. The same authors extended their work on embryo micromanipulation with a study examining the effect of embryo fragmentation on pregnancy and implantation.[98] The proportion and distribution of embryo fragmentation inversely affected implantation rates of embryos. Subsequent microsurgical removal of these fragments in conjunction with assisted hatching improved implantation rates.

Blastocyst culture

Blastocyst culture and transfer may hold the key to improving implantation rates in the future. It has been noted that embryos formed by IVF have a high *in vitro* attrition rate between days 2/3, when embryo transfer usually takes place, and days 5/6 at the blastocyst stage. Naturally this attrition can also take place *in vivo* after the embryos have been replaced and will therefore contribute to failed implantation rates. Embryo transfer on days 2/3 still has disappointingly low implantation rates of between 5% and 30%, leading to the preferred use of multiple embryo transfers. In contrast, the implantation rate for human blastocysts has been quoted as higher than 50 % whether developed *in vivo*[12] or *in vitro*.[99]

The rationale for culturing embryos to the blastocyst stage is that it allows selection of embryos with proven developmental potential. The idea is not new, as blastocyst transfer established the first clinical human pregnancy resulting from *in vitro* techniques.[100] Ultimately, the goal of blastocyst culture and transfer is to reduce the need for multiple embryo transfer, greatly reducing the risks of multiple pregnancy.[101] Recent studies have established improved blastocyst scoring systems and reported implantation rates and pregnancy rates of 70% and 87%, respectively, for two blastocyst transfers.[102]

Other potential benefits of blastocyst culture and transfer are that they increase the potential for pre-implantation genetic diagnosis and, through the proximity of the transfer and implantation dates, reduce the opportunity for embryo migration and ectopic pregnancy.[103] However, this is a new and intricate technique requiring expertise, time and expense, and with at least a theoretical risk of congenital abnormalities.[104] One group of patients that may benefit from such treatment is those with multiple IVF or ICSI failures, in whom improved clinical pregnancy rates (53%) have been shown.[105]

ENDOMETRIAL FACTORS AFFECTING IMPLANTATION

The role of the endometrium in implantation has been investigated over many years. The most common method of endometrial assessment has been endometrial biopsy but ultrasound and Doppler assessment have become more popular. Vast quantities of molecules, agents and immune mediators have been implicated in the endometrial control of implantation. Many authors have reviewed and continue to review the available data.[28,33,43,106-110] The factors that seem most likely to hold the key to endometrial control of implantation are the cytokines, adhesion molecules, growth factors, endometrial immune mechanisms and matrix proteins.

Endometrial cytokines

The term 'cytokine' was first used in 1974 to describe a soluble substance produced by T-lymphocytes and macrophages, as an immune-related response, which had a defined effect on a specific target tissue.[111] It is now recognised that cytokines have extremely diverse biological effects that may involve cell growth, differentiation and function. The interleukins and colony-stimulation factors are examples of mediators with effects on cell proliferation, while the interferons generally act as cell-growth inhibitory factors.[112] Some cytokines appear to regulate the normal functioning of the endometrium by regulation of hormone production at the level of the hypothalamo–pituitary–ovarian axis,[113] while others regulate the endometrium in an autocrine or paracrine fashion.

It appears that all the tissues involved in implantation (oocyte, embryo and endometrium) can synthesise cytokines. However, because of the complex pathways in which cytokine networks function it has proved difficult to show how cytokines play a critical role in implantation.[114] Although many cytokines may play a part in implantation, a vital role has been clarified in four, namely interleukin-1, leukaemia inhibitory factor (LIF), colony-stimulating factor and interleukin-11.

The entire interleukin-1 (IL-1) 'family' of IL-1α, IL-1β, IL receptor antagonist (IL-1ra) is expressed in human endometrium.[115] It is known that IL-1 stimulates other interleukin production, such as IL-6, in both the endometrium and developing trophoblast.[116] The most striking effect that IL-1 has on implantation is blocking of embryo implantation when mice are injected with high levels of IL-ra (i.e. antagonising the receptors for normal IL-1 action).[117] Other studies in genetically modified mice with no IL-1 showed that IL-1 is not the vital component for implantation[118] but it appears that it exerts its action by a direct effect on endometrial integrins α_4, α_v and β_3.[119]

LIF was originally identified on the basis of its ability to inhibit a mouse leukaemia cell line but has subsequently been shown to have many other actions. High concentrations of LIF appear in mouse endometrium prior to blastocyst implantation.[120] This increase in LIF is under maternal control. It appears that progesterone plays a regulatory role over LIF levels as administration of progesterone *in vivo* downregulates LIF production in the endometrium.[121] Deletion of the LIF gene in mice prevents implantation.[122] In this study, the LIF gene was targeted by homologous combination. Homozygous female mice were able to produce normal blastocysts but implantation did not occur. Notably, embryos removed from these mice implanted successfully in surrogate mothers.[123]

Colony-stimulating factor-1 (CSF-1) concentration in the endometrium increases dramatically around the time of implantation and throughout pregnancy.[124,125] Mice that totally lack CSF-1 are infertile[126] but they can have their fertility restored with administration of CSF-1 from birth.[127] Abnormal CSF expression in humans as a cause of implantation failure has not yet been established.

Interleukin-11 (IL-11) is found in the endometrium of mice and binds to a specific high affinity receptor (IL-11Rα). Expression of Il-11Rα is essential for normal decidual development.[128,129] Recent work has isolated IL-11 in human endometrium.[130] This study has also shown that IL-1 and other cytokines control IL-11 levels. It appears that IL-11 is important in decidualisation of the endometrium and may play a role in implantation.

Endometrial adhesion molecules

Adhesion molecules are cell surface receptors that include four main families: integrins, cadherins, selectins and the immunoglobulin superfamily.[131] The integrins are one of the best characterised of the immunohistochemical markers of uterine receptivity. They have many functional roles, including facilitation of cell migration and attachment to extracellular matrix and mediation of cell–cell communication.[107] There is little known about the role of cadherins or selectins in implantation.

The endometrium is rich in integrin. Notable changes occur in certain integrin expression throughout the menstrual cycle.[47,132] The role of adhesion molecules in implantation is an area of intense research that is under constant review.[46,110,133] The presence of certain integrins coincides with the period of maximum uterine receptivity.[134] The window of implantation is around day 20–24 of the cycle when three main integrins are present in the endometrium. The $\alpha_4\beta_1$ integrin first appears on endometrial glandular epithelial cells just after ovulation (day 14) and disappears on day 24. The $\alpha_v\beta_3$ is expressed from day 19 as the window of implantation opens. The $\alpha_1\beta_1$ molecule is present in the endometrium between days 15 and 28. Consequently, the only days on which these three integrins are expressed are days 20–24, coinciding with the period of uterine receptivity.

Abnormal integrin expression has been found in patients with unexplained infertility. One study found that these women had absence of α_4 from the glandular epithelium.[132] Further studies found that the patients with unexplained infertility or endometriosis had significantly reduced endometrial β_3 expression.[11,134] Lack of β_3 integrin was also noted in women with retarded endometrial development and in those with recurrent implantation failure following multiple IVF attempts.[135] These data indicate the importance of adhesion molecules in uterine receptivity and implantation.

Endometrial growth factors

Current evidence suggests that growth factors within the endometrium play a central role in implantation, decidualisation and early pregnancy maintenance.[136] The presence of growth factor receptors on early pre-implantation embryos has already been discussed.[137] The presence of epidermal and insulin growth factor receptors (EGFr and IGFr) on eight-cell embryos and platelet-derived growth factor receptors (PDGFr) on the blastocyst suggest the importance of these growth factors in the peri-implantation period.

EGF is present in the endometrium, localised in the stroma during the proliferative phase and in the glandular and luminal epithelium during the secretory phase.[138,139] The 'EGF family' comprises EGF, transforming growth factor-α (TGF-α), heparin-binding epidermal growth factor-like growth factor (HB-EGF), amphiregulin and betacellulin.[140] All of these are potent stimulators of cell proliferation capable of interacting with the EGF receptors on the developing embryo. TGF-α is found to stimulate mouse blastocyst development *in vitro*.[141] The factor that seems most important for implantation is HB-EGF, which is expressed by mouse endometrium surrounding the blastocyst just prior to implantation.[142] HB-EGF also promotes blastocyst growth, zona-hatching and trophoblast outgrowth *in vitro*. The greatest expression of HB-EGF coincides with the time of uterine receptivity.[143]

Insulin-like growth factor binding protein-1 (IGFBP-1) is a major product of the secretory endometrium and decidua.[144] This molecule inhibits the action of IGF at their target cells.[145] Concentrations of IGFBP-1 are elevated at the fetomaternal interface in pregnancies compromised by severe pre-eclampsia with poor placentation.[146] This suggests that insulin-like growth factors

17   Hertig AT, Rock J, Adams EC. A description of 34 human ova within the first 17 days of development. *Am J Anat* 1956;98:435–93.

18   Buster JE, Bustillo M, Rodi IA, Cohen SW, Hamilton M, Simon JA, *et al*. Biologic and morphologic development of donated human ova recovered by non-surgical uterine lavage. *Am J Obstet Gynecol* 1985;153:211–7.

19   Navot D, Scott RT, Droesch K, Veeck LL, Liu HC, Rosenwaks Z. The window of embryo transfer and the efficiency of human conception *in vitro*. *Fertil Steril* 1991;55:114–8.

20   Navot D, Bergh PA, Williams M, Garrisi J, Guzman I, Sandler B, *et al*. An insight into early pregnancy reproductive processes through the *in vivo* model of ovum donation. *J Clin Endocrinol Metab* 1991;72:408–14.

21   Braunstein GD, Grodin JM, Vaitukaitis J, Ross GT. Secretory rates of human chorionic gonadotrophin by normal trophoblast. *Am J Obstet Gynecol* 1973;115:447–50.

22   Lenton EA, Neal LM, Sulaiman R. Plasma concentrations of human chorionic gonadotropin from the time of implantation to the second week of pregnancy. *Fertil Steril* 1982;37:773–8.

23   Wilcox AJ, Dunson D, Baird DD. The timing of the 'fertile window' in the menstrual cycle: day specific estimates from a prospective study. *BMJ* 2000;321:1259–62

24   Thomson AJM, Drakeley AJ, Kingsland CR. Is LMP obsolete in obstetrics and gynaecology? *BMJ* 2002. In press.

25   Leader LR, Russell T, Clifford K, Stenning B. The clinical value of Clearplan home ovulation detection kits in infertility practice. *Aust N Z J Obstet Gynaecol* 1991;31:142–4.

26   Miller PB, Soules MR. The usefulness of a urinary LH kit for ovulation prediction during menstrual cycles of normal women. *Obstet Gynecol* 1996;87:13–17.

27   Ghazeeri GS, Vongprachanh P, Kutteh WH. The predictive value of five different urinary LH kits in detecting the LH surge in regularly menstruating women. *Int J Fertil Womens Med* 2000;45:321–6.

28   Horne AW, White JO, Lalani EN. The endometrium and implantation. A receptive endometrium depends on more than hormonal influences. *BMJ* 2000;321:1301–2.

29   Dickmann Z. Hormonal requirements for thaw survival of blastocysts in the uterus of a rat. *J Endocrinol* 1967;37:455–61.

30   Mead RA, Conconnon PW, McRae M. Effect of progestins in the western spotted skunk. *Biol Reprod* 1981;25:128–33.

31   Noyes RW, Hertig AT, Rock J. Dating the endometrial biopsy. *Am J Obstet Gynecol* 1975;122:262–3.

32   Martel D, Malet C, Gautray JP, Psychoyos A. Surface changes of the luminal uterine epithelium during the human menstrual cycle: a scanning electron microscope study. In: De Brux J, Mortel R, Gautray JP, editors. *The Endometrium: Hormonal Impacts*. New York: Plenum Press; 1981.

33   Ilesanmi AO, Hawkins DA, Lessey BA. Immunohistochemical markers of uterine receptivity in the human endometrium. *Microsc Res Tech* 1993;25:208–22.

34   Yoshinaga K. Receptor concept in implantation research. In: Yoshinaga K, Mori T, editors. *Development of Pre-implantation Embryos and their Environment*. New York: Liss; 1989. p. 379–87.

35   Lessey BA, Killam AP, Metzger DA, Haney AF, Greene GL, McCarty KS Jr. Immunohistochemical analysis of human uterine estrogen and progesterone receptors throughout the menstrual cycle. *J Clin Endocrinol Metab* 1988;67:334–40.

36   Lessey BA, Yeh IT, Castelbaum AJ, Fritz MA, Ilesanmi AO, Korzeniowski P, *et al*. Endometrial progesterone receptors and markers of uterine receptivity in the window of implantation. *Fertil Steril* 1996;65:477–83.

37   Tabibzadeh S. Molecular control of the implantation window. *Hum Reprod Update*

1998;4:465–71.

38   Surveyor GA, Gendler SJ, Pemberton L, Das SK, Chakraborty I, Julian J, *et al.* Expression and steroid hormonal control of MUC-1 in the mouse uterus. *Endocrinology* 1995;136:3639–47.

39   Jansen RP, Turner M, Johannisson E, Landgren, BM, Diczfalusy E. Cyclic changes in human endometrial surface glyco-proteins: a quantitative histochemical study. *Fertil Steril* 1985;44:85–91.

40   Smith RA, Seif MW, Rogers AW, Li TC, Dockery P, Cooke ID, *et al.* The endometrial cycle: the expression of a secretory component correlated with the luteinising hormone peak. *Hum Reprod* 1989;4:236–42.

41   Hey NA, Graham RA, Seif MW, Aplin JD. The polymorphic epithelial mucin MUC-1 in the human endometrium is regulated with maximal expression in the implantation phase. *J Clin Endocrinol Metab* 1994;78:337–42.

42   Aplin JD, Seif MW, Graham RA, Hey NA, Behzad F, Campbell S. The endometrial cell surface and implantation. Expression of the polymorphic mucin MUC-1 and adhesion molecules during the endometrial cycle. *Ann NY Acad Sci* 1994;734:103–21.

43   Aplin JD. The cell biology of human implantation. *Placenta* 1996;17:269–75

44   Serle E, Aplin JD, Li TC, Warren MA, Graham RA, Seif MW, *et al.* A morphological and immunohistochemical study of endometrial development in the peri-implantation phase of women with recurrent miscarriage. *Fertil Steril* 1994;62:989–96.

45   Hey NA, Li TC, Devine PL, Graham RA, Aplin JD. MUC1 in secretory phase endometrium: expression in precisely dated biopsies and flushings from normal and recurrent miscarriage patients. *Hum Reprod* 1995;10:2655–62.

46   Aplin JD. Adhesion molecules in implantation. *Rev Reprod* 1997;2:84–93.

47   Lessey BA, Ilesanmi AO, Lessey MA, Riben M, Harris JE, Chwalisz K. Luminal and glandular endometrial epithelium express integrins differentially throughout the menstrual cycle: implications for implantation, contraception and infertility. *Am J Reprod Immunol* 1996;35:195–204.

48   Nickolas JS. Development of transplanted rat eggs. *Proc Soc Exp Biol NY* 1933;30: 1111–3.

49   Mandelbaum J, Junca AM, Plachot M. The implantation window in humans after fresh or frozen-thawed embryo transfers. In: Mashiach S, Ben-Rafael Z, Laufer N, Schenker JG, editors. *Advances in Assisted Reproductive Technologies.* New York: Plenum Press; 1990. p. 729–35.

50   Davies MC, Anderson MC, Mason BA, Jacobs HS. Oocyte donation: the role of endometrial receptivity. *Hum Reprod* 1990;4:862–9.

51   Armant DR, Wang J, Liu Z. Intracellular signalling in the developing blastocyst as a consequence of the maternal-embryonic dialogue. *Semin Reprod Med* 2000;18:273–87.

52   Yoshinaga K. Uterine receptivity for blastocyst implantation. *Ann N Y Acad Sci* 1988;541:424–31.

53   McNeely MJ, Soules MR. The diagnosis of luteal phase deficiency: a critical review. *Fertil Steril* 1988;50:1–15.

54   Jones GES. Some newer aspects of the management of infertility. *JAMA* 1949;14:1123–9.

55   Asch RH, Abou-Samra M, Braunstein GD, Pauerstein CJ. Luteal function in hypophysectomized rhesus monkeys. *J Clin Endocrinol Metab* 1982;55:154–61.

56   del Pozo E, Wyss H, Tolis G, Alcaniz J, Campana A, Naftolin F. Prolactin and deficient luteal function. *Obstet Gynecol* 1979;53:282–6.

57   Kauppila A, Leinonen P, Vihko R, Ylostalo P. Metoclopramide-induced hyperprolactinaemia impairs ovarian follicle maturation and corpus luteum function in women. *J Clin Endocrinol Metab* 1982;54:955–60.

58   Li TC, Lenton EA, Dockery P, Cooke ID. A comparison of some clinical and endocrinological features between cycles with normal and defective luteal phases in women with unexplained infertility. *Hum Reprod* 1990;5:805–10.

59   Blacker CM, Ginsburg KA, Leach RE, Randolph J, Moghissi KS. Unexplained infertility: evaluation of the luteal phase; results of the national center for infertility research at Michigan. *Fertil Steril* 1997;67:437–42.

60   Garcia JE, Acosta AA, Hsiu JG, Jones HW Jr. Advanced endometrial maturation after ovulation induction with human menopausal gonadotropin/human chorionic gonadodotrophin for *in vitro* fertilization. *Fertil Steril* 1984;41:31–5.

61   Templeton A, Morris JK, Parslow W. Factors that affect outcome of *in-vitro* fertilisation treatment. *Lancet* 1996;348:1402–6.

62   Bhattacharya S, Templeton A. Factors affecting the outcome of *in-vitro* fertilization treatment. *Br J Hosp Med* 1997;58:265–7.

63   Hull MGR, Eddowes HA, Fahy U, Abuzeid MI, Mills MS, Cahill DJ, *et al.* Expectations of assisted conception for infertility. *BMJ* 1992;304:1465–9.

64   Roseboom TJ, Wermeiden JPW, Schoute E, Lens JW, Schats R. The probability of pregnancy after embryo transfer is affected by the age of the patients, cause of infertility, number of embryos transferred and the average morphology score, as revealed by multiple logistic regression analysis. *Hum Reprod* 1995;10:3035–41.

65   Taylor HS. The role of HOX genes in human implantation. *Hum Reprod Update* 2000;6:75–9.

66   McGinnis W, Krumlauf R. Homeobox genes and axial patterning. *Cell* 1992;68:283–302.

67   Krumlauf R. Hox genes in vertebrate development. *Cell* 1994;78:191–201.

68   Taylor HS, Vanden Heuvel G, Igarashi P. A conserved Hox axis in the mouse and human reproductive system: late establishment and persistent expression of the Hoxa cluster genes. *Biol Reprod* 1997;57:1338–45.

69   Satokata I, Benson G, Maas R. Sexually dimorphic sterility phenotypes in Hoxa 10-deficient mice. *Nature* 1995;374:460–3.

70   Taylor HS, Arici A, Olive D, Igarashi P. HOXA 10 is expressed in response to sex steroids at the time of implantation in the human endometrium. *J Clin Invest* 1998;101:1379–84.

71   Bagot CN, Troy PJ, Taylor HS. Alteration of maternal Hoxa 10 expression by *in vivo* gene transfection affects implantation. *Gene Ther* 2000;7:1378–84.

72   Collins JA, Burrows EA, Willan AR. The prognosis of live birth among untreated infertile couples. *Fertil Steril* 1995;64:22–8.

73   Human Fertilisation and Embryology Authority. *Seventh Annual Report.* London: HFEA; 1998.

74   Garza D, Mathur S, Dowd MM, Smith LF, Williamson HO. Antigenic differences between the endometrium of women with and without endometriosis. *J Reprod Med* 1991;36:177–82.

75   Haney AF. Endometriosis – associated infertility. *Baillieres Clin Obstet Gynaecol* 1993;7:791–812.

76   Selam B, Arici A. Implantation defect in endometriosis: endometrium or peritoneal fluid. *J Reprod Fertil Suppl* 2000;55:121–8.

77   Correa H, Jacoby J. Nutrition and fertility: some iconoclastic results. *Am J Clin Nutr* 1978;31:1431–6.

78   Frisch RE. Body weight and reproduction. *Science* 1989;246:432.

79   Lake JK, Power C, Cole TJ. Women's reproductive health: the role of body mass index in early and adult life. *Int Obes Relat Metab Disord* 1997;21:432–8.

80   Wang JX, Davies M, Norman RJ. Body mass and probability of pregnancy during assisted

reproduction treatment: retrospective study. *BMJ* 2000;321:1320–1.

81   Roussev RG, Kaider BD, Price DE, Coulam CB. Laboratory evaluation of women experiencing reproductive failure. *Am J Reprod Immunol* 1996;35:415–20.

82   Harris EN. Syndrome of the black swan. *Br J Rheumatol* 1987;26:324–6.

83   Kutteh WH, Rote NS, Silver R. Antiphospholipid antibodies and reproduction: the antiphospholipid antibody syndrome. *Am J Reprod Immunol* 1999;41:133–52.

84   Kutteh WH. Antiphospholipid antibodies and reproduction. *J Reprod Immunol* 1997;35:151–71.

85   Balasch T, Creas M, Fabregues F, Reverter JC, Carmona F, Tassies D, *et al.* Antiphospholipid antibodies and human reproductive failure. *Hum Reprod* 1996;11:2310–15.

86   Denis AL, Guido M, Adler RD, Bergh PA, Brenner C, Scott RT Jr. Antiphospholipid antibodies and pregnancy rates and outcome in *in vitro* fertilization patients. *Fertil Steril* 1997;67:1084–90.

87   Gleicher N, el-Roeiy A, Confino E, Friberg J. Reproductive failure because of autoantibodies: unexplained infertility and pregnancy wastage. *Am J Obstet Gynecol* 1989;160:1367–85.

88   Sher G, Feinman M, Zouves C, Kuttner G, Maassarani G, Salem R, *et al.* High fecundity rates following antiphospholipid antibody seropositive women treated with heparin and aspirin. *Hum Reprod* 1994;9:2278–83.

89   Stern C, Charnley L, Hale L, Kloss M, Speirs A, Baker HWG. Antibodies to β_2 glycoprotein I are associated with *in vitro* fertilization implantation failure as well as recurrent miscarriage: results of a prevalence study. *Fertil Steril* 1998;70:938–44.

90   Van Voorhis BJ, Stovall DW. Autoantibodies and infertility: a review of the literature. *J Reprod Immunol* 1997;33:239–56.

91   Birkenfeld A, Mukaida T, Minichiello L, Jackson M, Kase NG, Yemini M. Incidence of autoimmune antibodies in failed embryo transfer cycles. *Am J Reprod Immunol* 1994;31:65–8.

92   Hustin J, Jauniaux E. Morphology and mechanisms of abortion. In: Barnea ER, Hustin J, Jauniaux E, editors. *The First Twelve Weeks of Gestation.* Berlin: Springer Verlag; 1990. p. 280–96.

93   British Fertility Society. *Recommendations for Best Practice – Embryo Transfer.* Leeds: BFS Press; 1998.

94   Royal College of Obstetricians and Gynaecologists. *The Management of Infertility in Tertiary Care. RCOG Guideline No. 6.* London: RCOG Press; 2000.

95   Cohen J, Elsner C, Kort H, Malter H, Massey J, Mayer MP. Impairment of the hatching process following IVF in the human and improvement by assisted hatching using micromanipulation. *Hum Reprod* 1990;5:7–13.

96   Gordon JW, Talansky BE. Assisted fertilization by zona drilling: a mouse model for correction of oligospermia. *J Exp Zool* 1986;239:347–54.

97   Cohen J, Alikani M, Trowbridge J, Rosenwaks Z. Implantation enhancement by selective assisted hatching using zona drilling of human embryos with poor prognosis. *Hum Reprod* 1992;7:685–91.

98   Alikani M, Cohen J, Tomkin G, Garrisi GJ, Mack C, Scott RT. Human embryo fragmentation *in vitro* and its implications for pregnancy and implantation. *Fertil Steril* 1999;71:836–42.

99   Gardner DK, Schoolcraft WB, Wagley L, Schlenker T, Stevens J, Hesla J. A prospective randomized trial of blastocyst culture and transfer in in-vitro fertilization. *Hum Reprod* 1998;13:3434–40.

100   Steptoe PC, Edwards RG. Reimplantation of a human embryo with subsequent tubal pregnancy. *Lancet* 1976;24:880–2.

101   Gardner DK, Vella P, Lane M, Wagley L, Schlenker T, Schoolcraft WB. Culture and transfer of human blastocysts increases implantation rates and reduces the need for multiple embryo transfers. *Fertil Steril* 1998;69:84–8.

102   Gardner DK, Lane M, Stevens J, Schlenker T, Schoolcraft WB. Blastocyst score affects implantation and pregnancy outcome: towards a single blastocyst transfer. *Fertil Steril* 2000;73:1155–8.

103   Butterworth S. Blastocyst culture: myth or magic? *Hum Fertil* 2001;4:109–16.

104   Brison DR. Overview. Are blastocysts better? *Hum Fertil* 2000;3:227–8.

105   Sakkas D, Percival G, D'Arcy Y, Lento W, Sharif K, Afnan M. Blastocyst transfer for patients with multiple assisted reproduction treatment failures: preliminary experience. *Hum Fertil* 2001;4:104–8.

106   Best CL, Hill JA. Immunology and unexplained infertility. *Infert Reprod Clin N Am* 1997;8:545–71.

107   Klentzeris LD. The role of the endometrium in implantation. *Hum Reprod* 1997;12:170–175.

108   Johnson PM, Christmas SE, Vince GS. Immunological aspects of implantation and implantation failure. *Hum Reprod* 1999;14 Suppl 2:26–36.

109   Giudice LC. Potential biochemical markers of uterine receptivity. *Hum Reprod* 1999;14 Suppl 2:3–16.

110   Lessey BA. The role of the endometrium during embryo implantation. *Hum Reprod* 2000;15 Suppl 6:39–50.

111   Cohen S, Ward PA, Bigazzi PE. In: McClusky RT, Cohen S, editors. *Mechanisms of Cell-mediated Immunity*. New York: Wiley; 1974.

112   Rice A, Chard T. Cytokines and implantation. *Cytokine Growth Factor Rev* 1998;9:287–96.

113   Tabibzadeh S. Cytokines and the hypothalamo-pituitary-ovarian-endometrial axis. *Hum Reprod Update* 1994;9:947–67.

114   Sharkey A. Cytokines and implantation. *Rev Reprod* 1998;3:52–61.

115   Simón C, Frances A, Pellicer A. Cytokines and implantation. *Semin Reprod Endocrinol* 1995;13:142–51.

116   Laird SM, Tuckerman E, Li TC, Bolton AE. Stimulation of human endometrial epithelial cell interleukin-6 production by interleukin-1 and placental protein 14. *Hum Reprod* 1994;9:1339–43.

117   Simón C, Frances A, Piquette GN, el Dansouri I, Zurawski G, Dang W, *et al.* Embryonic implantation in mice is blocked by interleukin-1 receptor antagonist. *Endocrinology* 1994;134:521–8.

118   Abbondanzo SJ, Cullinan EB, McIntyre K, Labow MA, Stewart CL. Reproduction in mice lacking a functional Type I Il-1 receptor. *Endocrinology* 1996;137:3598–601.

119   Simón C, Valbuena D, Krussel J, Bernal A, Murphy CR, Shaw T, *et al.* Interleukin-1 receptor antagonist prevents embryonic implantation by a direct effect on the endometrial epithelium. *Fertil Steril* 1998;70:896–906.

120   Bhatt H, Brunet LJ, Stewart CL. Uterine expression of leukaemia inhibitory factor coincides with the onset of blastocyst implantation. *Proc Natl Acad Sci USA* 1991;88:11408–12.

121   Hambartsoumian E, Taupin JL, Moreau JF, Frydman R, Chaouat G. *In vivo* administration of progesterone inhibits the secretion of endometrial leukaemia inhibitory factor *in vitro*. *Mol Hum Reprod* 1998;4:1039–44.

122   Stewart CL, Kaspar P, Brunet LJ, Bhatt H, Gadi I, Köntgen F, *et al.* Blastocyst implantation depends on maternal expression of leukaemia inhibitory factor. *Nature* 1992;359:76–9.

123   Stewart CL. Leukaemia inhibitory factor and the regulation of pre-implantation development of the mammalian embryo. *Mol Reprod Dev* 1994;39:233–8.

124 Pollard JW. Regulation of polypeptide growth factor-related gene expression in the rat and mouse uterus before and after implantation. *J Reprod Fertil* 1990;88:721–31.

125 Bartocci A, Pollard JW, Stanley ER. Regulation of colony-stimulating factor 1 during pregnancy. *J Exp Med* 1986;164:956–61.

126 Pollard JW, Hunt JS, Wiktor-Jedrzejczak W, Stanley ER. A pregnancy defect in the osteopetrotic (op/op) mouse demonstrates the requirement for CSF-1 in female fertility. *Dev Biol* 1991;148:273–83.

127 Cohen PE, Zhu L, Pollard JW. Absence of colony stimulating factor-1 in osteopetrotic mice disrupts estous cycles and ovulation. *Biol Reprod* 1997;56:110–18.

128 Bilinski P, Roopenian D, Gossler A. Maternal IL-11Rα function is required for normal decidua and fetoplacental development in mice. *Genes Dev* 1998;12:2234–43.

129 Robb L, Li R, Hartley L, Nandurkar HH, Köntgen F, Begley CG. Infertility in female mice lacking the receptor for interleukin-11 is due to a defective uterine response to implantation. *Nat Med* 1998;4:303–8.

130 Cork BA, Li TC, Warren MA, Laird SM. Interleukin-11 (IL-11) in human endometrium: expression throughout the menstrual cycle and the effects of cytokines on endometrial Il-11 production *in vitro*. *J Reprod Immunol* 2001;50:3–17.

131 Springer TA. Adhesion receptors of the immune system. *Nature* 1990;346:425–34.

132 Klentzeris LD, Bulmer JN, Trejdosiewicz LK, Morrison L, Cooke ID. Beta-1 integrin cell adhesion molecules in the endometrium of fertile and infertile women. *Hum Reprod* 1993;8:1223–30.

133 Klentzeris LD. Adhesion molecules in reproduction. *Br J Obstet Gynaecol* 1997;104:401–9.

134 Lessey BA, Castelbaum AJ, Sawin SW, Buck CA, Schinnar R, Bilker W, *et al.* Aberrant integrin expression in the endometrium of women with endometriosis. *Fertil Steril* 1994;79:643–9.

135 Klentzeris LD, Moran V, Turner R. The endometrial profile of women with recurrent implantation failure in an IVF programme. *Hum Reprod* 1997;12:35.

136 Giudice LC. Growth factors and modulators in human endometrium: their potential relevance to reproductive medicine. *Fertil Steril* 1994;61:1–17.

137 Adamson ED. Activities of growth factors in preimplantation embryos. *J Cell Biochem* 1993;53:280–7.

138 Hofmann GE, Scott RTJ, Bergh PA, Deligdisch L. Immunohistochemical localization of epidermal growth factor in human endometrium, decidua and placenta. *J Clin Endocrinol Metab* 1991;73:882–7.

139 Hofmann GE, Drews MR, Scott RTJ, Mavot D, Helver D, Deligdisch L. Epidermal growth factor and its receptor in human implantation trophoblast: immunohistochemical evidence for autocrine/paracrine function. *J Clin Endocrinol Metab* 1992;74:981–8.

140 Carpenter G. Receptors for epidermal growth factor and other polypeptide mitogens. *Annu Rev Biochem* 1987;56:881–914.

141 Paria BC, Dey SK. Pre-implantation embryo development *in vitro*: cooperative interactions among embryos and role of growth factors. *Proc Natl Acad Sci USA* 1990;87:4756–60.

142 Das SK, Wang X, Paria BC, Damm D, Abraham JA, Klagsbrun M, *et al.* Heparin-binding EGF-like growth factor gene is induced in the mouse uterus temporally by the blastocyst solely at the site of its apposition: a possible ligand for interaction with blastocyst EGF-receptor in implantation. *Development* 1994;120:1071–83.

143 Leach RE, Khalifa R, Ramirez ND, Das SK, Wang J, Dey SK, *et al.* Multiple roles for heparin-binding epidermal growth factor-like growth factor are suggested by its cell-specific expression during the human endometrial cycle and early placentation. *J Clin Endocrinol*

Metab 1999;84:3355–63.

144 Zhou J, Bondy C. Insulin-like growth factor-II and its binding proteins in placental development. *Endocrinology* 1992;131:1230–40.

145 Jones JI, Clemmons DR. Insulin-like growth factors and their binding proteins. *Endocr Rev* 1995;18:1–31.

146 Giudice LC, Martina NA, Crystal RA, Tazuke S, Druzin M. Insulin-like growth factor binding protein-1 (IGFBP-1) at the maternal-fetal interface and IGF-1, IGF-II and IGFBP-1 in the circulation of women with severe pre-eclampsia. *Am J Obstet Gynecol* 1997;176:751–8.

147 Ogra PL, Ogra SS. Local antibody response to polio vaccine in the human female genital tract. *J Immunol* 1973;110:1307–11.

148 Kelly JK, Fox H. The local immunological defense system of the human endometrium. *J Reprod Immunol* 1979;1:39–45.

149 Buckley CH, Fox H. *Biopsy Pathology of the Endometrium.* London: Chapman and Hall Medical; 1989.

150 Hendricksen M, Kempson RL. The normal endometrium. In: Bennington JL, Saunders WB. *Surgical Pathology of the Uterine Corpus.* London: WB Saunders; 1980. p. 36–98.

151 Klentzeris LD, Bulmer JN, Warren A, Morrison L, Li TC, Cooke ID. Endometrial lymphoid tissue in the timed endometrial biopsy: morphometric and immunohistochemical aspects. *Am J Obstet Gynecol* 1992;167:667–74.

152 King A, Gardner L, Loke YW. Evaluation of oestrogen and progesterone receptor expression in uterine mucosal lymphocytes. *Hum Reprod* 1996;11:1079–82.

153 Stewart JA, Bulmer JN, Murdoch AP. Endometrial leucocytes: expression of steroid hormone receptors. *J Clin Pathol* 1998;51:121–6.

154 Bulmer JN, Morrison L, Longfellow M, Ritson A, Pace D. Granulated lymphocytes in human endometrium: histochemical and immunohistochemical studies. *Hum Reprod* 1991;6:791–8.

155 Loke YW, King A. Immunological aspects of human implantation. *J Reprod Fertil Steril* 2000;55:83–90.

156 Dang Y, Beckers J, Wang CR, Heyborne KD. Natural killer 1.1(+) alpha beta T cells in the periimplantation uterus. *Immunology* 2000;101:484–91.

157 Klentzeris LD, Li TC, Dockery P, Cooke ID. The endometrial biopsy as a predictive factor of pregnancy rate in women with unexplained infertility. *Eur J Obstet Gynecol Reprod Biol* 1992;45:119–24.

158 Yeaman GR, Guyre PM, Fanger MW, Collins JE, White HD, Rathbun W, *et al.* Unique CD 8+ T cell-rich lymphoid aggregates in human uterine endometrium. *J Leukoc Biol* 1997;61:427–35.

159 Klentzeris LD, Bulmer JN, Warren MA, Morrison L, Li TC, Cooke ID. Lymphoid tissue in the endometrium of women with unexplained infertility: morphometric and immunohistochemical aspects. *Hum Reprod* 1994;9:646–52.

160 Klentzeris LD, Bulmer JN, Liu DT, Morrison L. Endometrial leukocyte subpopulations in women with endometriosis. *Eur J Obstet Gynecol Reprod Biol* 1995;63:41–7.

161 Jones RS, Bulmer JN, Searle RF. Immunohistochemical characterization of stromal leukocytes in ovarian endometriosis: comparison of eutopic and ectopic endometrium with normal endometrium. *Fertil Steril* 1996;66:81–9.

162 Bulmer JN, Jones RK, Searle RF. Intra-epithelial leukocytes in endometriosis and adenomyosis: comparison of eutopic and ectopic endometrium with normal endometrium. *Hum Reprod* 1998;13:2910–15.

163 Fukui A, Fujii S, Yamaguchi E, Kimura H, Sato A, Saito Y. Natural killer cell subpopulations

and cytotoxicity for infertile patients undergoing *in vitro* fertilization. *Am J Reprod Immunol* 1999;41:413–22.

164 Aplin JD. MUC-1 glycosylation in endometrium: possible roles of the apical glycocalyx at implantation. *Hum Reprod* 1999;14 Suppl 2:17–25.

165 Bilalis DA, Klentzeris LD, Fleming S. Immunohistochemical localization of extracellular matrix proteins in luteal phase endometrium of fertile and infertile patients. *Hum Reprod* 1996;11:2713–18.

166 Zhang C, Duan E, Cao Y, Jiang G, Zeng G. Effect of 32/67 kDa laminin-binding protein antibody on mouse embryo implantation. *J Reprod Fertil* 2000;119:137–42.

167 Mueller MD, Vigne JL, Vaisse C, Taylor RN. Glycodelin: a pane in the implantation window. *Semin Reprod Med* 2000;18:289–98.

168 Edwards RG. Clinical approaches to increasing uterine receptivity during human implantation. *Hum Reprod* 1995;10 Suppl 2:60–7.

169 Purcell T, Fazleabas AT, Chwalisz K, Garfield RE, Given R. Localization of nitric oxide synthase in the endometrium during implantation in the baboon. *J Soc Gynecol Invest* 1999;6:215.

170 Chwalisz K, Garfield RE. Role of nitric oxide in implantation and menstruation. *Hum Reprod* 2000;15 Suppl 3:96–111.

171 Saxena D, Purohit SB, Kumar P, Laloraya M. Increased appearance of inducible nitric oxide synthase in the uterus and embryo at implantation. *Nitric Oxide* 2000;4:384–91.

172 Sengupta J, Ghosh D. Role of progesterone on peri-implantation stage endometrium-embryo interaction in the primate. *Steroids* 2000;65:753–62.

173 Saito S. Cytokine network at the feto-maternal interface. *J Reprod Immunol* 2000;47:87–103.

174 Bischof P, Messier A, Campana A. Mechanims of endometrial control of trophoblast invasion. *J Reprod Fertil Suppl* 2000;55:65–71.

175 Parr EL, Tung HN, Parr MB. Apoptosis as the mode of uterine epithelial cell death during embryo implantation in mice and rats. *Biol Reprod* 1987;36:211–25.

176 Galan A, O'Connor JE, Valbuena D, Herrer R, Remohi J, Pampfer S, *et al*. The human blastocyst regulates endometrial epithelial apoptosis in embryonic adhesion. *Biol Reprod* 2000;63:430–9.

Endometri:
repla

Jul

JULIA PALMER AND DAVID STURDEE

oestrogen/progestogen every day without a
oestrogen/progestogen, as well as varied ro
Oestrogen causes endometrial prolife
receptors, and also by increasing th
administration of progestogen d
and induction of 17-β oestra
thereby reducing the oest
change from a prolife
develop.

394

INTRODUCTION

In postmenopausal women, the incic
taking oestrogen therapy is relatively
recognised risk factors for endometri
replacement therapy (HRT) effectiv
surprising if HRT were an additional :

The ideal HRT will not only pi
osteoporosis and possibly reduction ..., but will also protect the
endometrium from endometrial hype...sia or carcinoma. However, despite our increasing
knowledge of the effect of hormones on the endometrium, endometrial cancer remains a
significant risk for postmenopausal women taking HRT. For over 25 years it has been recognised
that unopposed oestrogen is associated with a significant increased risk of endometrial cancer, with
relative risks ranging from 1.4[2] to 12.0,[3] and that this increases with the duration of unopposed
therapy up to a relative risk of 15.0[4] (Table 1). A cohort study in California of 5160 women
reported a relative risk of 10.0 in women who had taken unopposed oestrogen,[10] which would
mean an absolute risk of endometrial cancer of one per 100 women per year. Furthermore, it is
not widely recognised that the risk of endometrial cancer remains increased for many years after
stopping unopposed oestrogen therapy.[11] Even after 15 years or more without therapy, there is still
a significantly increased relative risk of 5.8 (95% CI 2.0–17).[10] To counteract this risk, progestogen
has been added to oestrogen replacement therapy in a sequential regimen for usually 10–14 days
in each cycle, with the intention of imitating the normal premenopausal ovarian cycle. This form
of HRT should also produce a regular bleed, which for older women in particular is unsatisfactory.
For this reason, continuous combined regimens have been developed that contain

Table 1 *Endometrial cancer risk with unopposed oestrogens: case–control studies*

Study	Year	Relative risk	
		Ever use	Long-term
Smith *et al.*[5]	1975	4.5	–
Ziel and Finkle[6]	1975	7.6	13.9
Gray *et al.*[7]	1977	3.1	11.6
Horowitz and Feinstein[3]	1978	12.0	5.2
Antunes *et al.*[4]	1979	6.0	15.0
Weiss *et al.*[1]	1979	7.5	8.2
Shapiro *et al.*[8]	1980	3.9	6.0
Kelsey *et al.*[9]	1983	1.4	3.1

cycle. There are many different combinations of
utes of administration.

ration by increasing the number of oestrogen/progesterone
mitotic rate in the glandular cells of the endometrium. The
ring oestrogen therapy causes a downregulation of the receptors,
diol dehydrogenase, which converts oestradiol to less active oestrone,
ogenic stimulus.[12] The histological evidence of a progestogenic effect is a
ative to a secretory endometrium from which hyperplasia is less likely to

LIGNANT POTENTIAL OF ENDOMETRIAL HYPERPLASIA

e is continued debate about the implications of endometrial hyperplasia and the potential for
ogressing to carcinoma. In the clinical situation, the finding of endometrial hyperplasia will
usually prompt the clinician to take some action, such as treatment with progestogen or surgery.
There are, therefore, few data on the natural history of untreated hyperplasia. In a prospective study
of 51 patients with endometrial hyperplasia who were followed for six months, Terakawa et al.[13]
found that in 69% (35 of 51) of the patients the endometrium became normal during the
observation period, but the findings persisted in 17% (6 of 35) with simple hyperplasia, in 25%
(one of four) of those with complex hyperplasia, in 14% (one of seven) with simple atypical
hyperplasia and 80% (four of the five) with complex atypical hyperplasia. In the remaining three
patients with simple hyperplasia, there was progression to complex atypical hyperplasia at the end
of six months. However, although evidence on the long-term outcome is limited, the general
consensus is that endometrial hyperplasia without atypia has a low potential for malignant
progression, but the presence of cytological atypia increases the risk considerably.[14]

In addition, there is a low background prevalence of endometrial hyperplasia and carcinoma in
postmenopausal women. In a study of 801 asymptomatic peri- and postmenopausal women,
Archer et al.[15] found a 5.2% prevalence of hyperplasia, with atypia in 0.6%. There was one case of
endometrial adenocarcinoma. A further study of endometrial biopsy specimens from 2964 women
before taking HRT found that 68.7% were atrophic, 23.5% proliferative, 0.5% secretory, 0.6% had
hyperplasia, 0.07% had adenocarcinoma and 6.6% were insufficient for classification.[16] It is on the
basis of data such as these that clinical management guidelines for HRT suggest that it is not
obligatory to perform an endometrial biopsy in every woman prior to starting HRT.

UNOPPOSED OESTROGEN

Unopposed oestrogen therapy is associated with a gradually increasing incidence of hyperplasia with
duration of therapy. A study of 596 postmenopausal women who were randomised to placebo,
unopposed oestrogen, continuous or sequential HRT over 36 months[17] found that those receiving
oestrogen alone – 0.625mg conjugated equine oestrogen (CEE) – were significantly more likely to
develop simple (27.7%), complex (22.7%) or atypical (11.7%) hyperplasia than the placebo group
(simple 0.8%, complex 0.8%, atypical 0.7%; $P > 0.001$). More recently, the Cochrane review of this
topic[18] found from all the appropriate studies that, after six months of unopposed oestrogen, the odds
ratio was 5.4 (95% CI 1.4–20.9) and after 36 months 16.0 (95% CI 9.3–27.5).

One might expect that lower-dose unopposed oestrogen therapy would be associated with less
risk of hyperplasia, and in 1997 Notelowitz reported a 1.7% rate of hyperplasia in women
receiving 0.3 mg unopposed esterified oestrogen for two years, which was similar to that in the
control women.[19] However, a further case–control study has found a five-fold higher risk of

developing endometrial cancer in women taking 0.3 mg unopposed CEE daily compared with untreated women.[20]

There is no evidence that use of the weaker oestrogen – oestriol – either vaginally or orally, will have any less effect on the risk of endometrial hyperplasia.[21]

ADDITIONAL PROGESTOGEN

The addition of progestogen in sequential regimens of HRT will reduce the incidence of hyperplasia. In 1985 Varma *et al.*[22] reported on 398 patients, and found that the addition of progestogen for seven days in each cycle did not prevent hyperplasia. Paterson *et al.*[23] found that after seven days of progestogen in each month, the incidence of hyperplasia was reduced to 3–4%, after ten days of progestogen it was 2%, and the maximum protector effect was achieved with 12 to 13 days of progestogen.[24,25] As a result, there has been some complacency about the protective effect of sequential HRT regimens. However, these early studies were of relatively short duration, with biopsies being taken after usually six to nine months of therapy. More recent studies with longer duration of HRT have raised concern about the protection of the endometrium. In the largest study of its kind to date, 1192 women who were taking standard sequential regimens of HRT for a mean of 3.29 years (median 2.56 years; 5th to 95th centile; 0.77 to 8.49 years) had endometrial aspiration biopsies taken by Pipelle® during the progestogen phase of a cycle.[21] As expected, a large proportion (47.4%) had a secretory endometrium, but complex hyperplasia was found in 5.5% and atypical hyperplasia in 0.7%.[26] There were no significant differences in the prevalence of hyperplasia between regimens containing ten or 12 days of progestogen in each cycle. A prospective cohort follow-up study of 23 244 women for a mean of 5.7 years did not, however, show an increase in the risk of endometrial carcinoma associated with sequential oestrogen and progestogen regimens.[27] However, a more recent case–control study of women aged 45–74 years[28] found that, among women who were taking sequential HRT regimens with at least ten days of progestogen in each cycle, the relative risk of endometrial cancer was not increased with up to five years' use, but with more than five years' use there was a relative risk of endometrial cancer of 2.5 (95% CI 1.1–5.5).

LONG-CYCLE THERAPY

As monthly sequential therapy results in a cyclical bleed, which is inconvenient in some patients and may prevent compliance, attempts have been made to reduce the frequency of bleeding by giving the progestogen at three-monthly intervals. Ettinger *et al.*[29] reported on 214 women using CEE and medroxyprogesterone acetate (MPA) to see whether the progestogen could be given quarterly instead of monthly without increasing the risk of endometrial hyperplasia. Hyperplasia was found in 1.5% of 199 women completing follow-up, which was similar to the 0.9% prevalence found as a baseline risk. The quarterly MPA resulted in longer bleeds (7.7 ± 2.9 versus 5.4 ± 2.0 days) and more reports of heavy bleeds (31.1% versus 8.0%) and unscheduled bleeding (15.5% versus 16.8%). Nevertheless, the women reported a preference for the quarterly regimen compared with a monthly sequential regimen of four to one. A randomised prospective or blind controlled trial with a quarterly sequential HRT regimen[30] found that simple hyperplasia without cytological atypia developed at the end of the oestrogen phase, which was independent of the oestrogen dose, and was already corrected to an inactive or atrophic endometrium by the addition of gestodene for 12 days. The study claimed that this combination offered good cycle control, but no statistical analysis of the results was offered and only 30 women were studied.

More recently, the Scandinavian Long-Cycle Study Group[31] reported a four-year study of 240 early postmenopausal women. They found that the incidence of endometrial pathology (simple, complex or atypical hyperplasia or carcinoma) was significantly higher in the 12-week cycle group ($P = 0.0003$) with an annual incidence of 5.6%, compared with 1% in the monthly cycle group. They further confirm that long-cycle therapy resulted in more irregular bleeding but reported no improved compliance. Another study from Finland[32] found that long-cycle HRT was associated with a higher relative risk of endometrial pathology than monthly cycle HRT, with a standardised incidence ratio (SIR) for the quarterly cycle of 2.0 (95% CI 1.6–2.6), compared with an SIR for the monthly cycle of 1.3 (1.1–1.6), which gives further support to the previous studies.

All these data indicate that progestogens will reduce the risk of endometrial hyperplasia and carcinoma, but the duration of progestogen in each cycle is important and should be for at least ten days, but that there may still be a risk with long-term use.

CONTINUOUS COMBINED THERAPY

The biochemical and morphological changes in the endometrium that are induced by progestogen[33] are maintained as long as progestogen is administered. If this is continuous, the proliferative effect of oestrogen will be prevented, and the endometrium should become atrophic. This was the rationale for the introduction of continuous combined therapy (CCT), since without any cycle or a progestogen phase, and with no tissue to be shed, there should not be any bleeding,[34] whereas the benefits should be the same as for sequential therapy (see Hillard[35] for review).

Although the main aim of CCT is to avoid cyclical bleeding, all studies of CCT have found a high incidence of bleeds, particularly in the first three months, varying from 50–80%. This occurs more often in women who are within one year of the menopause, rather than in postmenopausal women, probably as a result of some residual ovarian activity.

Several studies have confirmed that an atrophic endometrium is achieved with CCT in 90–100% of women, even after only three months of treatment, with daily doses of progestogen as low as 0.25 mg norethisterone acetate or 2.5 mg MPA. After one year of treatment with CEE 0.625 mg and MPA 2.5 or 5.0 mg daily, Woodruff and Pickar[36] found endometrial hyperplasia without atypia in less than 1% of women, which is lower than the background rate in postmenopausal women. The Cochrane review[18] reported that endometrial hyperplasia may be less likely with CCT than a sequential regimen, in particular with long duration of therapy; OR 0.3 (95% CI 0.1–0.97). Endometrial cancer has also only rarely been reported in women taking continuous combined regimens, and most of these cases had other risk factors.[37–40]

Hill et al.[41] assessed the risk of endometrial cancer in 969 women taking CCT. They found a relative risk of 0.6 (95% CI 0.3–1.3) and concluded that there was no increased risk for endometrial cancer over the baseline, and that there may even be a decreased risk. Archer et al.[42] reported a randomised trial of 625 women using a transdermal CCT regimen of oestradiol and norethisterone acetate, which also prevented endometrial hyperplasia. Both of these studies, however, were of relatively short duration (72 months and 12 months), so the long-term effects are not known.

In the PEPI trial,[17] conducted over three years, there were no recorded cases of complex hyperplasia in women on CCT, compared with 1.7% of 118 women treated with sequential HRT and 0.8% of women taking a placebo. Another study of CCT using oestrone sulphate and MPA over a two-year period also reported no cases of endometrial hyperplasia.[43]

From the UK,[26] a multicentre study of 751 women who had previously been taking sequential HRT and 445 untreated postmenopausal women (total 1196) completed nine months of CCT with oestradiol 2 mg and norethisterone acetate 1 mg daily. There were no cases of endometrial hyperplasia, and the endometrium was atrophic in more than two-thirds of women. Furthermore,

39   Ulrich LG. Accumulated knowledge of Kliogest safety aspects. *Br J Obstet Gynaecol* 1996;103:99–103.

40   Comerci JT, Fields AL, Runowicz CD, Goldberg GL. Continuous low-dose combined hormone replacement therapy and the risk of endometrial cancer. *Gynecol Oncol* 1997;64:425–30.

41   Hill DA, Weiss NS, Beresford SA, Voigt LF, Daling JR, Stanford JL, *et al.* Continuous combined hormone replacement therapy and risk of endometrial cancer. *Am J Obstet Gynecol* 2000;183:1456–61.

42   Archer DF, Furst K, Tipping D, Daine MP, Vandepool C. (Combipatch Study Group). A randomised comparison of continuous combined transdermal delivery of estradiol –norethindrone acetate and estradiol alone for menopause. *Obstet Gynecol* 1999;94:498–503.

43   Nand SL, Webster MA, Baber R, O'Connor V, for the Ogen/Provera Study Group. Bleeding pattern and endometrial changes on continuous combined hormone replacement therapy for 2 years. *Obstet Gynecol* 1998;91:678–84.

44   Wells M, Sturdee DW, Barlow DH, Ulrich LG, O'Brien K, Campbell MJ, *et al.* The endometrial response to continuous combined HRT. *BMJ* 2002;325:239–42.

45   Moore RA. Livial: a review of clinical studies. *Br J Obstet Gynaecol* 1999;106:1–21.

46   Ginsburg J, Prelevic GM. Cause of vaginal bleeding in postmenopausal women taking tibolone. *Maturitas* 1996;24:107–10.

47   Cummings SR, Morton S, Eckert D, *et al.* Raloxifene reduces the risk of breast cancer and may reduce the risk of endometrial cancer in post-menopausal women, two year findings from the Multiple Outcomes of Raloxifene Evaluation (MORE) Trial. American Society of Clinical Oncology 1998 Program/Proceedings of ASCO annual meeting, Los Angeles, 16–19 May 2002. Abstract 3.

48   Fugene P, Scheele WH, Shah A, Strack TR, Glant MD, Jolly E. Uterine effects of raloxifene in comparison with continuous-combined HRT in post-menopausal women. *Am J Obstet Gynecol* 2000;182:568–74.

49   Wren BG. Hormonal therapy following female genital tract cancer. *Int J Gynecol Cancer* 1994;4:217–24.

50   Creasman WT, Henderson D, Hinshaw W, Clarke-Pearson DL. Estrogen replacement therapy in the patient treated for endometrial cancer. *Obstet Gynecol* 1986;67:326–30.

51   Woolas RP, Hammond IG, MacCarthy AJ. Endometrial cancer before age 35 and subsequent use of HRT. *J Obstet Gynaecol* 1993;13:468–70.

52   Lee RB, Burke TW, Park RC. Oestrogen replacement therapy following treatment for Stage I endometrial cancer. *Gynecol Oncol* 1990;36:189–91.

Index